Women, Families, and Communities

Readings in American History

Volume Two: From 1865

Nancy A. Hewitt
University of South Florida

SCOTT, FORESMAN/LITTLE, BROWN HIGHER EDUCATION
A Division of Scott, Foresman and Company
Glenview, Illinois   London, England

To my brother Will and in memory of Tom.

Credits

Appendix, "A Statistical Portrait" by Ruth Milkman. Copyright © 1989 by Ruth Milkman. Reprinted by permission of the author.

Photographs: Unless otherwise acknowledged, all photos are the property of Scott, Foresman and Company.

Cover: *City Street*, 1939 by Kenneth Hayes Miller, Collection of the Bayly Art Museum of the University of Virginia, Charlottesville. Photograph of painting by Christopher Bunn.

x Cook Collection/Valentine Museum, Richmond, Virginia **2** June 4, 1870/ *Harper's Weekly* **8** *Folks All Home* © 1875, Lightfoot Collection, Photo by O. Pierre Havens. **24** Southern Pacific **29** The Kansas State Historical Society, Topeka **38** *Harper's Weekly*, December 16, 1876/Culver Pictures **45** Library of Congress **55** North Carolina Department of Cultural Resources, Department of Archives & History **70** Cook Collection/Valentine Museum, Richmond, Virginia **76** Hull House Association Papers, Special Collections, The University of Chicago Library **90** Photo by Byron, the Byron Collection, The Museum of the City of New York. **101** Gumby Collection, Columbia University **116** From the Collection of the Henry Ford Museum & Greenfield Village, Dearborn, MI. **130** Colorado Historical Society **139** Culver Pictures **154** *Child Life*, November, 1927 **168** Photo by Dorothea Lange for F.S.A., Library of Congress **178** *The San Antonio Light* Collection/Institute of Texan Cultures, University of Texas **179** Gebhardt Mexican Foods, Institute of Texan Cultures, University of Texas **191** Walter P. Reuther/The Archives of Labor and Urban Affairs, Wayne State University **193** Library of Congress **206** AP/Wide World **212** Nina Leen © Time Inc./Life Magazine **232** UPI/Bettmann Newsphotos **237** AP/Wide World

Library of Congress Cataloging-in-Publication Data

Women, families, and communities: readings in American history /
  [edited by] Nancy A. Hewitt.
      p.   cm.
  Includes bibliographies.
  Contents: v. 1 To 1877--v. 2. Since 1865.
  ISBN 0-673-18859-0 (v. 1) -- ISBN 0-673-18860-4 (v. 2)
  1. Women--United States--History. 2. United States--Social conditions. I. Hewitt, Nancy A.
  HQ1410.W646 1990b
  305.4'0973--dc20
                                    89-36113
                                        CIP

93 94 95 RRD 10 9 8 7 6 5 4 3

PREFACE

Good research and good teaching go hand in hand. *Women, Families, and Communities: Readings in American History* grows directly out of the connection between these two activities in my own work. As a student of women's history—and more specifically of women's activism and women's work in Rochester, New York, and Tampa, Florida—I have traced the ways that ordinary mothers, wives, and daughters contributed to the development of their families and communities. At the same time, as a teacher of introductory American history, I have focused on the ways that the major events in our nation's past—wars, elections, depressions, and technological revolutions—shaped and were shaped by the lives and actions of common women and men.

The articles collected here provide an introduction for students and instructors to the rich historical literature on women, families, and communities as well as a means for integrating the insights of this research into the story of North America's past. Traditionally focused on political, economic, and intellectual developments, U.S. history survey texts now include material on social relationships and popular culture and on the lives of women, workers, minorities, and immigrants. Still, it is difficult in a textbook or in lectures to cover both the broad sweep of American history and the particular experiences and actions of a wide array of historical actors. By combining the readings from this anthology with texts, lectures, and other monographs, students will learn how ordinary individuals, like themselves, participated in the shaping of America's past.

What is clear in looking at the table of contents to this volume and to works on social history in general is the diversity of American experiences. Though it is impossible to capture this diversity in a single collection, it is possible to encourage students to think about the range and richness of the American past. How did Native Americans respond to European colonization? How did Africans respond to slavery? How did the experience and meaning of industrialization, World War I, or the Great Depression differ by region, race, class, ethnic background, and gender? How and when did groups generally viewed as oppressed—Native Americans, African Americans, workers, women, immigrants—find the means to organize and protest on their own behalf? Each of these questions and the many others raised by the authors of the articles included here challenge us to see how everyday life and the "great events" of history intersect.

It is precisely at such intersections that women's historians most often are struck by the impossibility of separating women's experiences from those of men. In teaching American history, many of us have now integrated research on female activists and female workers into the larger stories of social reform and industrial development. Even if we focus on seemingly more masculine historical endeavors such as war, we quickly see how the activities and experiences of women and men are intertwined. We cannot fully understand the causes of wars, their short-term consequences or long-term significance, the means by which one side wins and the other loses, or even the particular strategies and tactics employed, without examining women's as well as men's participation.

In the earliest wars studied in an American history survey course—the French and Indian War, the Revolutionary War, the Civil War—the boundaries between the battlefield and the home front were blurred and always changing. During such conflicts, though women and men were expected to carry out different tasks, either sex might find itself called upon to nurse, cook, sew, spy, or fight. In later periods, when North Americans fought their wars overseas— in Cuba, the Philippines, Europe, and Asia—women's and men's roles were more distinct. Still, as men left for training camp and foreign combat, women expanded their activities on the home front to encompass many traditionally male jobs within the family, community, industries, government, and professions. Moreover, whatever the location or duration of battles, family and community members found their normal relations disrupted and transformed—sometimes temporarily, sometimes forever.

Developing links between women's history and history that has traditionally emphasized men and masculine activities is one of the goals of this work. Thus, the readings included here, most of which were written by women's historians, were selected because they chronicle local as well as national history, social as well as political and economic development, and women's as well as men's experiences and actions.

These articles provide case studies of individuals, families, and communities which illustrate broader historical themes. The introductions to each of the chronological parts, the headnotes to each of the articles, and the Suggested Readings and Questions for Study and Review at the end of each article place the individual essays in a wider context. At the same time, this material suggests how larger historical developments were themselves shaped by the events that occurred in particular families and communities. For each article, the first three study and review questions require students to relate the material presented to major issues of the time period and to other articles in the reader. The last question asks students to think about how the particular reading relates to other historical events and eras, thus pushing them to consider long-term continuities and changes in the American experience.

As researchers, scholars generally approach history as a complex process in which a wide range of individuals, experiences, and institutions come into play. As teachers, we often find it difficult to convey such complexities to our students. This volume is an attempt to introduce into the survey course more of the process of studying history. By asking students to connect political events with social forces, great affairs of state with common occurrences such an birth, marriage, housework, childrearing, and sharecropping, washing clothes, and watching television, we can help them understand what was involved in forming, sustaining, and transforming the people, families, and communities that built our nation.

Accompanying this collection is an Instructor's Resource Manual which provides detailed outlines for syllabi, coordinates the readings included here with chapters in a number of leading survey textbooks, and offers suggestions for in-class projects, library assignments, and further readings. In addition, the Instructor's Resource Manual includes sample questions for multiple choice, essay, and take-home exams.

ACKNOWLEDGMENTS

Good books owe much to good editors. I am deeply indebted to Larry Malley of Duke University Press who introduced me to the editors at Scott, Foresman/Little, Brown, and to Charlotte Iglarsh, Bruce Borland, and especially Barbara Muller and Betty Slack, who guided this project from conception to completion. I would also like to thank Julie Howell, Julie Hotchkiss, and Catherine Skintik. My colleagues and friends in the Department of History at the University of South Florida have contributed more than they know through their constant reminders of the intimate connection between excellence in teaching and research. I owe a special thanks to my newest coworkers, Giovanna Benadusi and Fraser Ottanelli, who at a critical moment provided me with a safe haven as well as strong coffee and encouraging comments. I also greatly appreciate the support of my department and university along with that of the College of Social and Behavioral Sciences and the United Faculty of Florida for providing me with the sabbatical that allowed me to complete this work.

For the contributors to this volume, my warmest regards for your generosity and assistance, especially Sarah Deutsch, Lori Ginzberg, Jacquelyn Hall, Joanne Meyerowitz, and Ruth Milkman, whose efforts went well beyond the call of sisterhood. To those whose research on women, families, and communities inspired my own, and especially to William Chafe who reinvigorated my commitment to local studies, my deepest thanks.

I am grateful also to the following, who read this volume before publication and offered many insightful, helpful, and encouraging suggestions: Robert Abzug, University of Texas at Austin; Jim Cobb, University of Alabama; Sarah J. Deutsch, Massachusetts Institute of Technology; Margaret Goodart, California State University at Sacramento; George C. Rable, Anderson College; Marilyn Rhinehart, North Harris Community College; Ingrid W. Scobie, Texas Women's University; and Kathryn Kish Sklar, State University of New York at Binghamton.

My most long-standing debt is owed to those special teachers whose eloquence and encouragement inspired me to pursue this career—Mendel Dick, Robert Smith, Susan Stuard, and Drew Faust—and to my fellow teaching assistants at Penn—Steven Zdatny, Marcus Rediker, and Andrew Feffer—with whom I shared my first forays into the classroom. My students in American history and women's history courses at the University of South Florida also deserve acknowledgment for keeping me informed, in ways both subtle and direct, of the effectiveness of my approach to teaching.

Steven Lawson has sustained me in this project from the beginning. His trenchant comments, timely infusions of humor, and masterful editing, along with his willingness to supervise an amazing array of household crises as I finished the manuscript, were only the most visible expressions of his support. These pages are dedicated to my brothers, Will and Tom, who gave me my first sense of how intertwined family and community could be. To them, to my parents, and to all those women, families, and communities who have shaped my own history, my deepest appreciation and affection.

Nancy A. Hewitt
University of South Florida

CONTENTS

Introduction

History has a dual meaning: It refers both to the events of the past and to interpretations of those events. The events that make up American history involved all kinds of people and took place in every type of setting. Rich, middling, and poor; white, brown, and black; native-born and immigrant; young and old; female and male; in cities and on farms; in metropolitan centers and in small villages; in long-settled communities and on the move; North and South; East and West; all Americans shaped the nation's history. Indians, blacks, and Hispanics as well as Europeans populated the North American continent; immigrant and farm families as well as "first families" produced its citizens; workers and grass roots activists as well as entrepreneurs and political leaders shaped its development.

Yet for a long time, scholars' interpretations of the past concentrated on Western Europeans and their American-born descendants, especially the men who served as business, political, or military leaders. These figures received far more attention than any other group, often more than all other groups combined. Such interpretations directed our eyes to a narrow segment of the continent's rich history. Like viewfinders at the Grand Canyon, they focused our gaze on the most spectacular peaks and valleys but failed to reveal the more mundane materials and processes that helped forge these vistas.

Historians are less like viewfinders than photographers. They actively select the angle of vision and the subject that they think will best reflect or illuminate a particular moment. A photographer covering a presidential campaign rally may stand in the crowd, but he or she will use a telephoto lens to zoom in on the candidate. In the morning paper, then, one will see only blurred, background images of the women and men who will vote in the election but a detailed, larger-than-life portrait of the man or woman who seeks to represent them. If we think of history textbooks as providing snapshots of significant moments in America's past, then this volume is an attempt to bring the blurred backgrounds into focus; indeed, to bring those background figures momentarily to the forefront.

To do so, we can draw on the voluminous work produced in the last two decades by social historians. Social history emphasizes the experiences of common women and men, allowing us to hear the voices of those rendered "inarticulate" by traditional interpretations. Viewing the past as a dynamic process in which all Americans participated, these scholars have revealed the ways that native Americans, African-Americans, immigrants, workers, and women shaped their worlds and our history.

Social historians have been especially concerned to discover the ways that those with only limited resources influenced the course of economic, social, and political development. By focusing on individual forms of resistance to exploitation (such as a slave feigning illness or purposely setting a slow pace of work) as well as collective acts of protest (such as boycotts, demonstrations, and organized social movements), social historians have illuminated an entirely new historical terrain. This terrain is one on which ordinary women and men, regardless of their wealth, status, or formal political power, become active agents of change, affecting critical historical developments.

To uncover the activities and ideas of less powerful groups, social historians often search out evidence on individual families and communities as a means of exploring the occurrences of everyday life. These events are then placed beside those we conventionally think of as important in America's past to illuminate the relations between ordinary people and extraordinary events. The present volume will draw on this rich body of research to bring these background figures into focus.

The purpose of focusing on more common people and their daily routines, of moving apparently peripheral figures to center stage, is not simply to replace one angle of vision with another. While we are examining seemingly unremarkable women and men in their families and communities, we will often discover their remarkable qualities—courage, persistence, strength, ingenuity. We will find that common folk performed uncommon feats when social upheaval, economic crisis, wartime mobilization, or personal necessity demanded that they do so. Yet at the same time, we will find women and men prevented from acting in their own interests or those of their neighbors by poverty, prejudice, and other disabling factors.

This volume, then, will examine how ordinary people both shaped and were shaped by the persons and events traditionally considered central to the nation's development. Ultimately, a new vision of our history will appear, one that brings into simultaneous focus national events and leaders and ordinary people in local communities. In this way, relationships between common folk in their everyday lives (people like most of you reading this book) and individual leaders of states, armies, corporations, and social movements will be made clearer.

Photographs are not only selective images of persons and events. They are also often idealized versions, simple images that reflect complex realities. The portrait of a former slave holding a white child (facing page) can carry many captions, none of which will fully capture the intimate and ambiguous relations between black women and their white charges. The look in this unnamed woman's eyes may be resignation or defiance. Her employment as a nanny after the Civil War may be a sign of new opportunities or renewed bondage. The baby may grow up to be a member of the Ku Klux Klan or a founder of the National Association for the Advancement of Colored People.

We all develop images of the kinds of people who make up the population—of women and men, blacks and whites, workers and bosses, rural Southerners and cosmopolitan Northerners. Our perceptions range from accurate to stereotypical to fanciful. These images emerge from newspapers, television, schoolrooms, novels, films, advertising, community and family attitudes, and a host of other sources. In past centuries, sermons, paintings, magazines, lectures, traveling museums, cartoons, folktales, and songs were even more important in shaping Americans' views of the world around them and, perhaps more markedly, of people and places far distant. Such images, regardless of their accuracy, affected the ways that any one group of Americans responded to others—Europeans to native Americans, whites to blacks, country folk to city dwellers, Southerners to Northerners, women to men.

Depictions of women, family, and community have changed dramatically over the years, but in each era dominant images have provided ideals to be either emulated or defied. Indian princesses, Salem witches, hardy pioneers, black nannies, Victorian ladies, flamboyant flappers, wartime riveters, happy homemakers, women's libbers—each presented a portrait with which or against which women were measured and measured themselves. Since most such figures were based on a single class or race of women, it is only by examining a variety of individuals from a range of families and communities that we can begin to understand how such ideal types arose and what their effects were on women and men of particular times and places.

Family and community are also idealized notions. Leading commentators from every generation of American citizens have lamented the decline of the "traditional" family and the loss of the "close-knit" community. Puritan clergy and born-again Christians, female moral reformers of the mid-nineteenth century and political candidates of the late twentieth, eighteenth-century diarists and contemporary documentarians have all bemoaned the failure of real-life families and communities to live up to the models we carry in our minds. We should not let the similarity of these laments obscure real differences in the changing forms of family and community life over time and across region, race, ethnicity, and class.

Yet commonalities in these laments can tell us something important about people's shared desire for a sense of place and of belonging, regardless of how big or developed or powerful the nation as a whole becomes. Again, only by examining a variety of settings and situations over the course of American history can we begin to understand the multiple forms family and community have taken and their effects on regional, racial, ethnic, and class relations and on national development.

Among social historians, women's historians have devoted particular attention to these dimensions of our American heritage: common folk, daily life, dominant cultural symbols and images, definitions of family and community, popular forms of protest, and differences in each of these rooted in race, class, ethnicity, and region. Women's historians, focusing initially on the differences in women's and men's experiences in the past, have asked new questions, have introduced new sources, have offered new interpretations of the roles that women played in America, and have suggested new ways of marking major transitions and turning points in our nation's history.

Emerging from the women's movement of the 1960s and 1970s, these scholars have applied the feminist rubric—"the personal is political"—to examinations of history. Thus, they focus on the relations between public and private spheres, home and work, domesticity and politics. They consider whether changes in household technology and birth control methods might be as important as presidential elections and wars in determining how to divide American history into meaningful units of study. To probe these and other issues, researchers examine diaries and letters, census data and wills, sermons and novels, clothing and advertisements, and other artifacts left by those whose words and actions were not purposely recorded for posterity.

This research provides portraits of women as mothers, daughters, and wives; as servants, slaves, and free women; as wage earners, housewives, and volunteers; as immigrants, migrants, and settlers; and the whole range of roles that formed the female half of society. Some scholars focus on notable women—Abigail Adams, Elizabeth Cady Stanton, Ida B. Wells, Eleanor Roosevelt, Rosa Parks—demonstrating their right to be set alongside their male counterparts in the pantheon of American heroes. Others study all-female organizations and institutions—women's colleges and prisons, suffrage associations, literary societies, or single-sex reform groups—arguing for women's vital contributions to every phase of the nation's development. Some examine women's work, in and outside the family, and analyze its contributions to farming, commerce, slavery, industry, and the ever expanding service sector. Many follow the lives of ordinary women, as individuals and in groups, from birth to death, seeking to understand the parameters of female lives and how they have changed over time and place.

Yet researchers are not interested only in looking at women in relation to other women, as important as that dimension of our history is. Rather, they also want to study women in relation to men, to communities, and to the larger society. From this dual perspective—women's own experiences as women and their relationships with men—women's historians have begun rewriting American history to reflect the contributions and activities of the whole population. In doing so, they introduce gender—the cultural prescriptions and social roles assigned to individuals on the basis of their sex—as a critical category of analysis.

This volume highlights the work of those who analyze women in the context of their families and communities. In such studies, the new scholarship on women is integrated with that on men, and the lives of native-born white women and men are set beside those of native Americans, African-Americans, and immigrants. The particular communities examined here cover various regions of the country and include members of a wide range of races, classes, and ethnic groups. Using gender as a key category of analysis, each study illuminates some important aspect of our nation's development. Collectively, these readings reveal the changing nature of women's and men's roles and of family and community across the course of American history and analyze how these changes shaped and were shaped by larger social, economic, and political forces.

The articles in this book will provide evidence that can be used in combination with information from other readings, lectures, and discussions to draw a new portrait of our national past. Imagine for a moment what American history would look like if viewed for the first time through the lens of a video camera held by a woman standing in her local community. Imagine the Pocahontas legend if it had been recorded and embellished by Indian women rather than English men. Think for a moment of the way Sherman's March to the Sea during the Civil War would have been portrayed by a house slave in Atlanta. How might the the breaking waves of the Atlantic Ocean or the overland trail to the west have been seen by a young wife with a child in tow and another on the way? Consider what a document listing the advantages of technological progress might contain if it were compiled by a Lowell mill worker in the 1840s or the owner of a new wringer washer in the 1920s. Contemplate what Pearl Harbor meant to a black domestic servant in Texas or a Japanese-American girl completing her senior year of high school. Speculate on the way organized black women in Montgomery, Alabama, would remember Martin Luther King, Jr., whom they had to persuade to lead the city's bus boycott in 1955.

How might these portraits of the past vary if in each situation the woman recording or recalling the moment was replaced by her brother? How would they differ if history were recorded not from the perspective of their family and community, but from yours? By combining the rich documentation of ordinary women's and men's lives collected by social historians with traditional interpretations of significant events and with our own understanding of how change occurs, we can begin to focus on a more complete picture of the past. This picture brings into view diverse groups of Americans and a wide range of issues, individuals, and events. If we could make it move, we would have something like a videotape of the past, perhaps the closest we could come to making the events of history and our interpretations of them converge. Even then, however, we might not agree with another person's idea of American history, for each person's view of historical events is unique. That uniqueness reflects in part America's heritage of diversity.

From the moment when native Americans, Europeans, and Africans first encountered one another in the New World, diversity characterized the continents development. In the present, diversity—and the creativity and conflict it nurtures—continues to define our nation. Differences in race and region, ethnicity and class, wealth and power, sex and social status shaped our nation's history as they shape our lives, our culture, our economy, and our government. By capturing that half of history which occurred in local communities, among ordinary families, composed of common women and men, we reveal this diversity and thus more fully illuminate both the past and the present. The readings in this book will remined us that everyone— presidents, generals, corporate leaders, students, wage earners, and housewives—is a creator of history.

Suggested Readings

Nancy F. Cott and Elizabeth H. Pleck, eds., *A Heritage of Her Own: Toward a New Social History of American Women* (1979).

Sara Evans, *"Born for Liberty": Women in American History* (1989).

Jean E. Friedman, William G. Shade, and Mary Jane Cappazzoli, eds., *Our American Sisters: Women in American Life and Thought* (4th ed., 1987).

Michael Gordon, ed., *The American Family in Social-Historical Perspective* (3rd ed., 1983).

Carol Groneman and Mary Beth Norton, eds., *"To Toil the Livelong Day": America's Women at Work, 1780-1980* (1987).

Carol Hymowitz and Michaele Weisman, *A History of Women in America* (1978).

Jacqueline Jones, *Labor of Love, Labor of Sorrow: Black Women, Work and the Family, from Slavery to the Present* (1986).

Linda K. Kerber and Jane DeHart-Mathews, eds., *Women's America: Refocusing the Past* (2nd ed., 1987).

Mary Beth Norton, ed., *Major Problems in American Women's History* (1989).

Mary P. Ryan, *Womanhood in America: From Colonial Times to the Present* (3rd ed., 1983).

Susan Ware, ed., *Modern American Women: A Documentary History* (1989).

Nancy Woloch, *Women and the American Experience* (1984).

PART ONE

Reconstructing the Nation

Civil War and the Reconstruction that followed were turning points in American history. Much blood and much ink have been spilled on each. As the nation was ripped apart and then partially repaired, not only were the political, economic, and social systems of the nation transformed but so, too, were the lives of ordinary women and men. The war drew individuals from all regions, races, and classes into a world of battle, injury, death and constant labor. For women, the war opened up new jobs in nursing or civil service, expanded the efforts of local voluntary associations, and provided some brief respite for slaves from the constant surveillance of owners and overseers.

The United States Sanitary Commission, which employed thousands of women—a few in paid positions—was one of the most important organizations in reshaping the scope of women's public work and setting key precedents for female activism in the postwar period. At the same time, it reflected the general trend toward centralization and bureaucratization in government, a trend that would affect all citizens by the late nineteenth century, some for better and some for worse.

Black and white, North and South, rich and poor, women labored on behalf of the Union or Confederate cause. Few gained fortune, some gained fame, most simply got along as best they could, sustaining losses and maintaining what was left of their former lives. Many recorded their thoughts in letters and diaries, perhaps fearing they would not survive the cataclysm or hoping to pass on some memento of these convulsive times to children and grandchildren. One such chronicler, Mary Ann Gay, wrote this description of her trip to an Atlanta battlefield, where she gathered munitions in hopes of bartering them for food:

> In a marshy place, encrusted with ice, innumerable bullets, minie balls, and pieces of lead seemed to have been left by the irony of fate to supply sustenance to the hungry ones. . . . It was so cold! Our feet were almost frozen, and our hands commenced to bleed . . . .

FIRST MUNICIPAL ELECTION IN RICHMOND SINCE THE END OF THE WAR—REGISTRATION OF COLORED VOTERS.—[DRAWN BY W. L. SHEPPARD.]

Following the Civil War, constitutional amendments granted African-Americans freedom, citizenship, and men the right to vote. Many female abolitionists were dismayed when voting rights were extended only to black men and wording of the Fifteenth Amendment seemed to restrict suffrage to men.

> Lead! Blood! Tears! Oh how suggestive! Lead, blood, and tears, mingled and commingled! . . . I cried like a baby, long and loud.

Many women throughout the country experienced such pain. Though most northern women came into less immediate contact with the ravages of war, they, too, must have cried long and loud at times. Irish women watched as their husbands and sons were drafted into Union ranks instead of building the new life they had migrated to find. Native American women saw their male relatives march off to fight for a nation that had spurned them. Frontier women, many isolated from family and friends, found themselves left behind to manage farms and children. The wives of the South's small farmers worried over the heavy casualties, knowing they would profit little even if the rebels won. Female slaves were helpless to keep husbands and sons from being forced into Confederate service but were helpful in sending them on their way north, hoping the freedom they sought there would eventually find its way south. Widows and orphans on all sides waited for peace to come, not knowing what it would bring.

When peace came, it did not wash away the hardships and doubts nor did it crush the spirit and pride of those who survived the ordeal of war. Once again, the experiences of women and men differed, by race, region, and class as well as by sex. Southern blacks had freedom but not the resources to enjoy it. Northern whites had victory, but the price in dead, wounded, maimed, imprisoned, and missing was high. Most southern whites had neither victory nor resources and harbored wounds that neither time nor medicine healed.

Americans shared the enormous consequences of the war—more rapid industrialization and an increasingly more powerful centralized national government, the encouragement of further western migration, and the tensions of incorporating blacks, at least black men, into the country's ranks of voters. These changes and the national policies that spawned them comprise the formal history of Reconstruction, but it was their impact on and implementation in local communities that shaped the lives of ordinary women and men.

Of the one million men who served in the Confederate Army, more than one-fourth died. Another 360,000 perished in Union ranks, including 38,000 African-Americans. The South lost $2 billion in property, raising immense economic and social barriers for defeated whites and freed black women and men trying to build new lives. Though Northern missionaries and teachers, many of them women, traveled south to educate freed blacks, and though the Freedmen's Bureau sent agents to assist needy families of both races, most Americans reconstructed their lives without outside help. Jacqueline Jones traces this process among southern blacks, offering a moving portrait of the limits and opportunities of freedom.

One of the most fundamental transformations resulting from Reconstruction was the incorporation of African-Americans into political citizenship. Former slaves were granted their freedom by the Thirteenth Amendment and citizenship by the Fourteenth. Black men were given voting rights by the Fifteenth, or, more precisely, could not be denied the vote "on account of race, color, or previous condition of servitude." For southern blacks of both sexes, attempts to claim these "rights" often led to retribution, including physical violence.

The rise of the Ku Klux Klan and other white supremacist organizations occurred in direct response to blacks' success in making their freedom count. A federal investigation of such terrorist activity in 1871 revealed a horrible catalog of beatings, burnings, rapes, and lynchings throughout the South. Ellen Parton from Meridian, Mississippi, testified that on

> Wednesday night last they came to my house; by "they," I mean bodies or companies of men; they came on Monday, Tuesday, and Wednesday; on Monday night they said they came to do us no harm; on Tuesday night they said they came for the arms; I told them there was none, and they said they would take my word for it; on Wednesday night they came and broke open the wardrobe and trunks and committed rape upon me; there were eight of them in the house; I do not know how many there were outside.

Her testimony was repeated hundreds of times over by other voices, leading to the legal suppression of the Klan but failing to end the physical and legal intimidation of black women and men.

In the North, meanwhile, the old abolitionist coalition had broken down. Many women formerly sympathetic to the slaves' plight were distressed by the ratification of the Fourteenth and Fifteenth amendments, which for the first time used the term "male inhabitants" to define voters and then extended suffrage to black men only. Of those women who recognized the severity of the setback to their own hopes for full citizenship, some gave up working for racial equality and focused their efforts instead on women's advancement alone. As new generations of female activists emerged after the war, without a grounding in abolitionism, the woman's movement took on an increasingly white cast and voiced a more exclusive agenda. Black and white women still made efforts to reach across the racial divide, but the gap seemed somehow greater and more forbidding after Reconstruction than before.

By the late nineteenth century, the Western territories provided fruitful terrain for both blacks seeking economic independence and women seeking political influence. By then, Jim Crow laws in the South had deprived African-Americans of much they had been promised or had hoped for in the first glow of Union victory. In the North, industrial development and increased immigration shaped most women's and men's lives more forcefully than did the vote. On the frontier, native Americans found their societies once again restructured as the federal government settled the remaining members of once-powerful tribes on small reservations scattered across the Far West. The economic hopes of native-born Americans in the same region brightened as the Homestead Act (1862), the Morrill Land Grant Act (1862), the completion of the transcontinental railroad (1869), and the passage of ever more generous land allotment legislation in the 1870s testified to Congress's commitment to continued expansion.

In each region, reconstructing families and communities in the postwar period required the labor of ordinary women and men, some of whom gained distinct advantages in the midst of upheaval. Others, however, suffered serious setbacks or found themselves caught in a new web of constraints and conflict.

Suggested Readings

Gerda Lerner, ed., *Black Women in White America: A Documentary History* (1973).

C. Vann Woodward, ed., *Mary Chestnut's Civil War* (1981).

Dorothy Sterling, ed., *We Are Your Sisters: Black Women in the Nineteenth Century* (1984).

Jacqueline Jones, *Soldiers of Light and Love: Northern Teachers and Georgia Blacks, 1865–1973* (1980).

Ellen Carol DuBois, *Feminism and Suffrage: The Emergence of an Independent Women's Movement in America, 1848–1869* (1978).

ONE

Freed Women? The Civil War and Reconstruction

Jacqueline Jones

"Devastated, demoralized, and destitute" is how one historian described the post-Civil War South. As the primary battlefield during both the war and the peace that followed, this region experienced more dramatic and traumatic changes than any other section of the country. In the decade and a half of upheaval, plantation mistresses sought to maintain their families' estates, often as sole managers in the absence of male kin, while slave women and men struggled to expand their freedom and to sustain or re-create black family and community life. While northern women joined local soldier's aid societies, the products of which were channeled into the massive United States Sanitary Commission, southern women labored individually or through informal associations, and without the assistance of the Confederate government in dispensing their relief.

Black women found the war years especially difficult. Black men were hauled off to war alongside planters and their sons or forced into munitions factories, or became convinced that flight across Union lines was the best hope for freedom. Black women were often left behind on plantations to fend for themselves and their children. The end of the war and the guarantee of freedom relieved blacks of both sexes of the burdens of slavery, yet caused new problems of unemployment, homelessness, and racial violence. As the federal government struggled to erect a legal framework for reconstructing the nation, black families struggled simply to survive.

African-Americans traveled across the South to reconnect with long-lost kin, to find a better piece of land or a higher wage, and to track down those government agents who they heard would supply them with forty acres and a mule. As they attempted to throw off the psychological and physical legacies of bondage, black women and men also redefined their relations with each other and with white society.

Jones examines the contradictory meanings of emancipation, tracing the struggle of black women and men to give substance to their new-found freedom. Not unexpectedly, "southern planters could not reconcile themselves" to the new order. Yet even northern whites "feared that black people's desire for family autonomy" and "the preference among wives and mothers to eschew wage work in favor of attending to their own households" represented the failure of ex-slaves to adopt proper attitudes and behaviors. Documenting the variety of ways black women adapted to freedom and its limits, Jones demonstrates how they gained respect and authority in their communities even as they continued to be viewed as "a despised caste" by the larger white society.

In the Reconstruction South, white farm wives often were accorded less respect and authority within their family and community than were their black counterparts, though later in the century many poor whites moved toward a similar concern with elevating women's status. Yet white farm families rarely had to contend with the kinds of physical violence and emotional tension under which newly freed men and women suffered in the post-war South. Nor could blacks, even with the joint efforts of women and men, overcome the political repression, economic exploitation, and social ostracism heaped upon them when Reconstruction ended without significantly redistributing power or resources between the races.

Soon after he assumed the position of assistant commissioner of the Louisiana Freedmen's Bureau in 1865, Thomas W. Conway had an opportunity to state his policy regarding families of southern black Union soldiers. The northern federal agent found distressing the reports that former slaveowners near Port Hudson had, "at their pleasure," turned freedwomen and children off plantations "and [kept] their pigs chickens and cooking utensils and [left] them on the levee a week in a starving condition. . . ." Still, he remained firmly convinced that the government should not extend aid to soldiers' dependents; Conway wanted the "colored Soldiers and their families . . . to be treated like and expected to take care of themselves as white Soldiers and their families in the north." Moreover, the commissioner observed, the bureau "could not compel the planters to retain those women if their husbands were not on the place, unless contracts had been made with them." He appreciated the sacrifices that black men had made for the "Noble Republic," but with their wages from military service (no matter how meager or unpredictable) "and the amount which can be earned by an industrious woman," he saw no reason why their families could not "be maintained in at least a comfortable manner." The freed people needed only to demonstrate "a little economy and industry" and they would become self-supporting.

The postbellum debate over the fate of the emancipated slaves cast the major white participants into new roles which they embraced with varying degrees of enthusiasm. Neoaboli-

tionists now sought to implement their notions about the moral significance of honest toil, and standard bearers of the northern Republican "free labor" ideology—Union military officials, carpetbagging planters, and Freedmen's Bureau agents—intended to provide the former slaves with the opportunity to exchange their labor in a new competitive marketplace that would replace the slavemarkets of old. These whites feared that black people's desire for family autonomy, as exemplified by the "evil of female loaferism"—the preference among wives and mothers to eschew wage work in favor of attending to their own households—threatened to subvert the free labor experiment. Like the Irish and French-Canadian immigrant women who labored in New England textile mills to help support their families, freedwomen were considered exempt from the middle-class ideal of full-time domesticity. Still, the irony did not escape the notice of one Yankee journalist: Of a newly arrived northern planter in the South, he wrote in 1866, "An abolitionist making women work in the fields, like beasts of burden—or men!"

For their part, southern planters could not reconcile themselves to the fact of emancipation; they believed that "free black labor" was a contradiction in terms, that blacks would never work of their own free will. An unpredictable labor situation therefore required any and all measures that would bind the freed people body and soul to the southern soil. Black women—who had reportedly all "retired from the fields" in the mid-1860s—represented a significant part of the region's potential work force in a period when cotton planters' fears about low agricultural productivity reached almost hysterical proportions. Ultimately, southern whites embarked on a "Prussian road" of authoritarian labor arrangements, but not without stopping along the way to alternately accommodate, cajole, and brutalize the people

In African-American families after emancipation, domestic chores were perceived to be the major responsibility of women, but when necessary women joined men in the field. Children, too, had tasks to perform—washing, cutting and carrying wood, and supervising younger children.

whom they had once claimed to care for and know so well. Thus by the end of the Civil War, it was clear that the victorious Yankees and the vanquished Confederates agreed on very little when it came to rebuilding the war-torn South; but one assumption they did share was that black wives and mothers should continue to engage in productive labor outside their homes.

Throughout this era of bloodshed and turmoil, freed blacks resisted both the northern work ethic and the southern system of neoslavery: "Those appear most thriving and happy who are at work for themselves," noted one perceptive observer. The full import of their preference for family sharecropping over gang labor becomes apparent when viewed in a national context. The industrial North was

increasingly coming to rely on workers who had yielded to employers all authority over their working conditions. In contrast, sharecropping husbands and wives retained a minimal amount of control over their own productive energies and those of their children on both a daily and seasonal basis. Furthermore, the sharecropping system enabled mothers to divide their time between field and housework in a way that reflected a family's needs. The system also removed wives and daughters from the menacing reach of white supervisors. Here were tangible benefits of freedom that could not be reckoned in financial terms.

Emancipation was not a gift bestowed upon passive slaves by Union soldiers or presidential proclamation; rather, it was a process by which black people ceased to labor for their masters and sought instead to provide directly for one another. Control over one's labor and one's family life represented a dual gauge by which true freedom could be measured. Blacks struggled to weld kin and work relations into a single unit of economic and social welfare so that women could be wives and mothers first and laundresses and cotton pickers second. The experiences of black women during these years revealed both the strength of old imperatives and the significance of new ones; in this regard their story mirrors on a personal level the larger drama of the Civil War and Reconstruction.

＊

The institution of slavery disintegrated gradually. It cracked under the weight of Confederate preparations for war soon after cannons fired on Fort Sumter in April 1861 and finally crumbled (in some parts of the South many years after the Confederate surrender) when the last slaves were free to decide whether to leave or remain on their master's plantation. The specific ways in which southern defense strategy affected blacks varied according to time and place; before the war's end a combination of factors based on circumstance and personal initiative opened the way to freedom for many, but often slowly, and only by degrees. For women, the welfare of their children was often the primary consideration in determining an appropriate course of action once they confronted—or created—a moment ripe with possibilities.

Three individual cases suggest the varying states of awareness and choice that could shape the decisions of slave women during this period of upheaval. In 1862 a seventy-year old Georgia bondswoman engineered a dramatic escape for herself and twenty-two children and grandchildren. The group floated forty miles down the Savannah River on a flatboat and finally found refuge on a federal vessel. In contrast, Hannah Davidson recalled many years later that she and the other slaves on a Kentucky plantation lived in such rural isolation—and under such tyranny—that they remained in servitude until the mid-1880s: "We didn't even know we were free," she said. Yet Rosaline Rogers, thirty-eight years old at the war's end and mother of fourteen children, kept her family together on her master's Tennessee plantation, even after she was free to leave: "I was given my choice of staying on the same plantation, working on shares, or taking my family away, letting them out [to work in return] for their food and clothes. I decided to stay on that way; I could have my children with me." But, she added, the arrangement was far from satisfactory, for her children "were not allowed to go to school, they were taught only to work."

The logic of resistance proceeded apace on plantations all over the South as slaveholders became increasingly preoccupied with the Confederacy's declining military fortunes. On a Mississippi plantation, Dora Franks overheard her master and mistress discuss the horror of an impending Yankee victory. The very thought of it made the white woman "feel lak jumpin' in de well," but, Dora Franks declared, "from dat minute I started prayin' for freedom. All de res' of de women done de same." Slaves did not have to keep apprised of rebel maneuvers on the battleground to take advantage of novel situations produced by an absent master, a greenhorn overseer, or a nervous mistress uncertain how to maintain the upper hand. Under these conditions black women, men, and children slowed their workpace to a crawl. "Awkward," "inefficient," "lazy," "erratic," "ungovernable," and "slack" (according to exasperated whites), they left weeds in the cotton fields, burned the evening's supper to a crisp, and let the cows trample the corn.

Their chains loosened by the distractions of war, many slaves challenged the physical and emotional resolve of whites in authority. For the vast majority, however, the war itself only intensified their hardships. As the Confederacy directed more of its resources and manpower toward the defense effort, food supplies became scarce throughout the region. Planters and local government officials, anxious in the midst of black (and even white) rebels on their own soil and uncertain about the future of their new nation, reacted violently to isolated cases of real and imagined insubordination. The owner of a Georgia coastal plantation was so infuriated by the number of his slaves who had fled to Union lines that he took special precautions to hold onto his prized cook; he bound her feet in iron stocks so that "she had to drag herself around her kitchen all day, and at night she was locked into the corn-house."

During wartime the responsibility for the care of the children, the ill, and the elderly devolved upon slave women to an even greater extent than had been the case during the antebellum period. Military mobilizations wreaked havoc on the already fragile ties that held slave families together. Efforts to restrict slave mobility prevented husbands from visiting their "broad" wives on a regular basis and discouraged cross-plantation marriages in general. Confederate slave impressment policies primarily affected men, who were put to work on military construction projects and in armies, factories, and hospitals. The practice of "refugeeing" highly valued slaves to the interior or to another state also meant that the strongest, healthiest men were taken away from plantation wives and children.

During the conflict, at different times in different parts of the South, the approaching Union army provided slaves with both an opportunity and an incentive to flee from their masters. Soon after the Union forces took control of the South Carolina Sea Islands, Elizabeth Botume, a newly arrived northern teacher, observed a refugee mother and her three children hurrying toward a government steamer:

A huge negress was seen striding along with her hominy pot, in which was a live chicken, poised on her head. One child was on her back with its arms tightly clasped around her neck, and its feet about her waist, and under each arm was a smaller child. Her apron was tucked up in front, evidently filled with articles of clothing. Her feet were bare, and in her mouth was a short clay pipe. A poor little yellow dog ran by her side, and a half-grown pig trotted on before.

To women like the Louisiana mother who brought her dead child ("shot by her pursuing master") into a Yankee army camp, "to be buried, as she said, *free*," Union territory symbolized the end of an old life and the beginning of a new one. But it was an inauspicious beginning. Crowded together, often lacking food, shelter, and medicine, these human "contraband of war" lived a wretched existence. Moreover, in 1863 the refugee settlements—and virtually any areas under federal control—became targets for military officials seeking black male conscripts. Black men wanted to defend their families and fight for freedom, and almost a quarter of a million served the Union war effort in some formal capacity—half as soldiers, the rest as laborers, teamsters, craftsmen, and servants. However, the violent wrenching of draftees from their wives and children caused great resentment among the refugees. The women of one camp, wrote Elizabeth Botume, "were proud of volunteers, but a draft was like an ignominious seizure."

Whether southern black men volunteered for or were pressed into Union military service, the well-being of their families remained a constant source of anxiety for them. Wives and children who remained behind in Confederate territory on their master's plantation, and even some of those who belonged to owners sympathetic to the northern cause, bore the brunt of white men's anger as a way of life quickly began to slip away. Frances Johnson, a Kentucky slave woman whose husband was a Union soldier, reported that in 1864 her master had told her, "all the 'niggers' did mighty wrong in joining the Army." One day the following spring, she recalled, "my masters son . . . whipped me severely on my refusing to do some work for him which I was not in a condition to perform. He beat me in the presence of his father who told him [the son] to 'buck me and give me a thousand' meaning thereby a thousand lashes."

In an effort to stay together and escape the vengeance of southern whites, some families followed their menfolk to the front lines. But soldiers' wives, denounced as prostitutes and "idle, lazy vagrants" by military officials, found that the army camps offered little in the way of refuge from callousness and abuse. The payment of soldiers' wages was a notoriously slow and unpredictable process, leaving mothers with responsibility for the full support of their children. The elaborate application procedures discouraged even qualified women from seeking aid from the Army Quartermaster Department. A few wives found jobs as laundresses and cooks in and around the camps, but gainful employment was not easy to come by during such chaotic times. Meanwhile, not only did many families lack basic creature comforts in the form of adequate clothing and shelter, they were at times deprived of what little they did have by Union officers who felt that the presence of black wives impaired the military efficiency of their husbands. At Camp Nelson, Kentucky, in late 1864, white soldiers leveled the makeshift shantytown erected by black women to house their children and left four hundred persons homeless in bitterly cold weather.

Although many women had no choice but to seek food and safety from northern troops, often with bitterly disappointing results, others managed to attain relative freedom from white interference and remain on or near their old homesites. In areas where whites had fled and large numbers of black men had marched—or been marched off—with the Union army, wives, mothers, daughters, and sisters often grew crops and cared for each other. For example, several hundred women from the Combahee River region of South Carolina made up a small colony unto themselves in a Sea Island settlement. They prided themselves on their special handicrafts sent to their men "wid Mon'gomery's boys in de regiment": gloves and stockings made from "coarse yarn spun in a tin basin and knitted on reed, cut in the swamps." Together with men and women from other areas, the "Combees" cultivated cotton and potato patches, gathered ground nuts, minded the children, and nursed the ill.

The end of the war signaled the first chance for large numbers of blacks to leave their slave quarters as a demonstration of liberty. Asked why she wanted to move off her master's South Carolina plantation, the former slave Patience responded in a manner that belied her name: "I must go, if I stay here I'll never know I'm free."

During the first fearful months of freedom, many black women and men traveled to nearby towns to escape the masters who had extracted so much pain and suffering from them. But before long a reverse migration occurred among those people who had to return to the countryside in order to search for work. The degree to which the antebellum elite persisted (in both a social and economic sense) varied throughout the South. Nevertheless, the failure of the federal government to institute a comprehensive land confiscation and redistribution program, combined with southern whites' systematic refusal to sell property or extend credit to the former slaves, meant that the majority of blacks would remain economically dependent upon the group of people (if not the individuals) whom they had served as slaves. The extent of black migration out of the South during this period was negligible—and understandable, considering the lack of viable job opportunities for blacks elsewhere in the country. Most freed people remained concentrated in the Cotton Belt, in the vicinity of their enslavement; the proximity of kin groupings helped to determine precisely where they would settle.

Indeed, whites felt that blacks as a race would

gradually die out as a result of their inability to care for themselves and work independent of the slaveholder's whip. The eagerness with which blacks initially fled the plantations convinced these white men that only "Black Laws" limiting their freedom of movement would insure a stable labor force. The Yankees' vision of a free labor market, in which individual blacks used their wits to strike a favorable bargain with a prospective employer, struck the former Confederates as a ludicrous idea and an impossible objective.

When it came to reconstructing southern society, northerners were not all of the same stripe. But those in positions of political authority tended to equate freedom with the opportunity to toil on one's own behalf. Yankees conceived of the contract labor system as an innovation that would ensure the production of cotton (necessary for the New England textile industry) and protect blacks against unbridled exploitation at the hands of their former masters. If a person did not like the terms or treatment accorded by an employer, he or she should look for work elsewhere, thereby encouraging diehard rebels to conform to enlightened labor practices. In time, after a thrifty household had accumulated a little cash, it could buy its own land and become part of the independent yeomanry. To this end northern Republicans established the Freedmen's Bureau, which oversaw contract negotiations between the former slaves and their new masters.

The contract system was premised on the assumption that freed people would embrace gainful employment out of both economic necessity and natural inclination. Still, the baneful effects of slavery on the moral character of blacks caused whites like Bureau Commissioner Oliver O. Howard to express the pious hope that, initially, "wholesome compulsion" would lead to "larger independence" for the masses. "Compulsion" came in a variety of shapes and sizes. For the Yankee general stationed in Richmond and determined to get the families

of black soldiers off federal rations, it amounted to "hiring out" unemployed women or creating jobs for them in the form of "a grand *general* washing establishment for the city, where clothing of any one will be washed gratis." Indeed, even many northern teachers commissioned to minister to the freed blacks believed that hard manual labor would refresh the souls of individual black women and men even as it restored the postwar southern economy.

If few slave women ever had the luxury of choosing between different kinds of work, freedwomen with children found that economic necessity bred its own kind of slavery. Their only choice was to take whatever work was available—and that was not much. Field hands and domestic servants who decided to stay on or return to their master's plantation and work for wages needed the children's help to make ends meet; at times it seemed as if only seasoned cotton pickers would be able to eat.

All women had to contend with the problem of finding and keeping a job and then depending upon white employers for payment. The largest single category of grievances initiated by black women under the Freedmen's Bureau "complaint" procedures concerned nonpayment of wages, indicating that many workers were routinely—and ruthlessly—defrauded of the small amounts they had earned and then "run off the place." Few southern planters had reserves of cash on hand after the war, and so they "fulfilled" commitments to their employees by charging prices for supplies so exorbitant that workers were lucky if they ended the year even, rather than indebted to their employer.

The bureau recommended that blacks receive a monthly wage ($10–12 per month for adult men, $8 for women) and that employers refrain from using physical force as a means of discipline. However, thousands of freed blacks contracted for rations, clothing, and shelter only, especially during the period 1865–1867. Employers retained unlimited authority in using various forms of punishment and felt free to disregard the agreements at the first sign of recalcitrance on the part of their laborers. Prohibitions against movement on and off the plantation were routine; blacks had to promise to "have no stragling about their houses and not to be strowling about at night," and they needed written permission to go into town or visit relatives nearby. The bureau tolerated and even, in most cases, approved these harsh terms. As the teacher Laura Towne noted, "enforcement" of the contracts usually meant ensuring that "the blacks don't break contract and [then] compelling them to submit cheerfully if the whites do."

Most northerners in positions of formal authority during the Reconstruction period detested southern planters as Confederate rebels but empathized with them as fledgling capitalists attempting to chain their workers to a "free labor" contract system. Moreover, few Union officials were inclined to believe that freedwomen as a group should contribute anything less than their full muscle power to the rebuilding of the region's economic system.

High rates of geographical mobility (as blacks moved about the southern countryside, in and out of towns, and to a lesser extent, to new homes in the southwestern part of the region) make it difficult to pinpoint with any precision the number of black women in specific kinds of jobs immediately after the war. Charlie Moses's mother moved the family from one Louisiana farm to another in search of work; "We jus' travelled all over from one place to another," he recalled. Freedwomen accepted any work they could find; in Columbia, South Carolina, they took the places of mules and turned screws to press cotton. The seasonal nature of agricultural labor meant that families often had to locate new sources of employment. When the cotton-picking season ended, for instance, Mingo White and his mother cut and hauled wood on an Alabama plantation. However, the overwhelming majority of women continued to work as field hands cultivating cotton for white landowners.

Other freedwomen relied on their cooking, gardening, dairying, and poultry-raising experience in an effort to make money as petty tradeswomen. In Aiken, South Carolina, a roving Yankee newspaper correspondent noted with approval that a black woman given 50 cents one day had appeared the next selling cakes and fresh fruit purchased with the money. Some women peddled berries, chickens, eggs, and vegetables along the road and in towns.

Other women tried to turn special talents and skills into a secure means of making a living. Nevertheless, former slaves were too poor to pay much for the services of midwives and seamstresses, and whites proved unreliable customers, to say the least. Even the small number of literate women who aspired to teaching had to rely on the fortunes of local black communities, most of which were unable to support a school on a regular basis. Susie King Taylor taught pupils in Savannah soon after the war; she and other independent instructors could hardly compete with a free school operated by a northern freedmen's aid society, the American Missionary Association (AMA). As a result, she was eventually forced from teaching into domestic service. A tiny number of teachers did qualify for aid from the Freedmen's Bureau or a private group like the AMA. In Georgia between 1865 and 1870, for example, perhaps seventy-five freedwomen received a modest salary for at least a few months from a northern source. However, New Englanders eager to help the cause of freedmen's education preferred to commission white teachers from the northern and midwestern states.

Although the freed people remained largely dependent upon whites for employment and supplies, strikes and other forms of group labor resistance began to surface soon after the Yankee invasion of the south. During the busy harvest season in the fall of 1862, for instance, female field hands on a Louisiana sugar plantation in Union-occupied territory engaged in a slowdown and then refused to work at all until the white landowner met their demand for wages. Then men on the plantation also struck within a week. The planter, fearful that his entire crop would be lost if it were not cut and processed immediately, finally agreed to pay them. And in 1866, the "colored washerwomen" of Jackson, Mississippi, organized themselves and established a price code for their services. Though the strike in June of that year was unsuccessful, according to Philip Foner it marked the "first known collective action of free black working-women in American history, as well as the first labor organization of black workers in Mississippi."

Slowly and grudgingly some whites began to learn a basic lesson of Reconstruction: Blacks' attitudes toward work depended on the extent of their freedom from white supervision. Edward S. Philbrick, a shrewd Yankee planter masquerading as a missionary on the South Carolina Sea Islands, marveled in March 1862 over the ability of former slaves to organize themselves and prepare hundreds of acres for planting cotton "without a white man near them." Frances B. Leigh, daughter of the renowned actress and abolitionist Fanny Kemble but more similar in temperament to her slaveholding father, returned to the family's Georgia estate in 1866 and soon discovered that the elderly freed people were "far too old and infirm to work for me, but once let them get a bit of ground of their own given to them, and they became quite young and strong again." One day she discovered that the aged Charity—"who represented herself as unable to move"—walked six miles almost every day to sell eggs (from her own chickens) on a neighboring plantation.

In their desire for household determination and economic self-sufficiency, blacks challenged the intentions of bureau agents and northern and southern planters alike. Northerners underestimated the extent to which black people would be prevented from accumulating cash and acquiring property. On the other hand,

southerners had not counted on the leverage wielded by workers determined to pry concessions out of them in the form of days off and garden privileges, and to press their own advantage during times of labor shortages. Some of this leverage assumed the form of meaningful political power at the local and state levels; for example, South Carolina rice workers (as members of the Republican party) played a vital role in that state's political process until Reconstruction ended in 1877. Ultimately, in making certain decisions about how family labor was to be organized, black people not only broke with the past in defiance of the white South, they also rejected a future of materialistic individualism in opposition to the white, middle-class North.

*

The northerner's hope that black workers would be able to pursue their interests as individuals did not take into account the strong family ties that bound black households tightly together. More specifically, although black women constituted a sizable proportion of the region's labor force, their obligations to their husbands and children and kin took priority over any form of personal self-seeking. For most black women, then, freedom had very little to do with individual opportunity or independence in the modern sense. Rather, freedom had meaning primarily in a family context. Freedwomen derived emotional fulfillment and a newfound sense of pride from their roles as wives and mothers. Only at home could they exercise considerable control over their own lives and those of their husbands and children and impose a semblance of order on the physical world.

The withdrawal of black females from wage-labor—a main theme in both contemporary and secondary accounts of Reconstruction—occurred primarily among the wives and daughters of able bodied men. (Women who served as the sole support for their children or other family members had to take work wherever they could find it.) According to a South Carolina newspaper writer in 1871, this development necessitated a "radical change in the management of [white] households as well as plantations" and proved to be a source of "absolute torment" for former masters and mistresses. The female field hand who plowed, hoed, and picked cotton under the ever-watchful eye of an overseer came to symbolize the old order.

Employers made little effort to hide their contempt for freedwomen who "played the lady" and refused to join workers in the fields. To apply the term ladylike to a black woman was apparently the height of sarcasm; by socially prescribed definition, black women could never become "ladies," though they might display pretensions in that direction. The term itself had predictable racial and class connotations. White ladies remained cloistered at home, fulfilling their marriage vows of motherhood and genteel domesticity. But black housewives appeared "most lazy"; they stayed "out of the fields, doing nothing," demanding that their husbands "support them in idleness."

In their haste to declare "free labor" a success, even northerners and foreign visitors to the South ridiculed "lazy" freedwomen working within the confines of their own homes. Hypocritically—almost perversely—these whites questioned the "manhood" of husbands whom they charged were cowed by domineering female relatives. South Carolina Freedmen's Bureau agent John De Forest, for example, wrote that "myriads of women who once earned their own living now have aspirations to be like white ladies and, instead of using the hoe, pass the days in dawdling over their trivial housework, or gossiping among their neighbors." He disdained the "hopeless" look given him by men told "they must make their wives and daughters work."

Most southern and northern whites assumed that the freed people were engaged in a misguided attempt to imitate middle-class white norms as they applied to women's roles. In fact, however, the situation was a good deal more complicated. First, the reorganization of female labor resulted from choices made by *both* men and women. Second, it is inaccurate to speak of the "removal" of women from the agricultural work force. Many were no longer working for a white overseer, but they continued to pick cotton, laboring according to the needs and priorities established by their own families.

An Alabama planter suggested in 1868 that it was "a matter of pride with the men, to allow all exemption from labor to their wives." He told only part of the story. There is good reason to suspect that wives willingly devoted more time to childcare and other domestic matters, rather than merely acquiescing in their husbands' demands. A married freedwoman, the mother of eleven children, reminded a northern journalist that she had had "to nus' my chil'n four times a day and pick two hundred pounds cotton besides" under slavery. She expressed at least relative satisfaction with her current situation: "I've a heap better time now'n I had when I was in bondage."

The humiliations of slavery remained fresh in the minds of black women who continued to suffer physical abuse at the hands of white employers and in the minds of freedmen who witnessed or heard about such acts. At this point it is important to note only that freedmen attempted to protect their womenfolk from rape and other forms of assault; as individuals, some intervened directly, while others went to local Freedmen's Bureau agents with accounts of beatings inflicted on their wives, sisters, and daughters. Bureau records include the case of a Tennessee planter who "made several base attempts" upon the daughter of the freedman Sam Neal (his entire family had been hired by the white man for the 1865 season). When Neal protested the situation, he was deprived of his wages, threatened with death, and then beaten badly by the white man and an accomplice. As a group, men sought to minimize chances for white male–black female contact by removing their female kin from work environments supervised closely by whites.

In the late 1860s this tug of economic and psychological warfare between planters determined to grow more cotton and blacks determined to resist the old slave ways culminated in what historians have called a "compromise"— the sharecropping system. It met the minimal standards of each party—a relatively reliable source of labor for white landowners, and, for freed people (more specifically, for families), a measure of independence in terms of agricultural decision making. Sharecroppers moved out of the old cabins and into small houses scattered about the plantation. Contracts were renegotiated around the end of each calendar year; families not in debt to their employers for equipment and fertilizer often seized the opportunity to move in search of a better situation. By 1870 the "fifty-fifty" share arrangement under which planters parceled out to tenants small plots of land and provided rations and supplies in return for one-half the crop predominated throughout the Cotton South.

Although 1870 data present only a static profile of black rural households in the Cotton South, it is possible to make some generalizations (based on additional forms of evidence) about the status of freedwomen five years after the war. The vast majority (91 percent) lived in rural areas. Illiterate and very poor (even compared to their poor white neighbors), they nonetheless were not alone, and shared the mixed joys of work and family life with their husbands, children, and nearby kin. Fertility rates declined very slowly from 1830 to 1880; the average mother in 1870 had about six or seven children. The lives of these women were severely

circumscribed, as were those of other family members. Most of the children never had an opportunity to attend school—or at least not with any regularity—and began to work in the fields or in the home of a white employer around the age of ten or twelve. Young women found it possible to leave their parents' home earlier than did the men they married. As a group, black women were distinguished from their white neighbors primarily by their lower socioeconomic status and by the greater reliance of their families on the work they did outside the realm of traditional domestic responsibilities.

Within the limited public arena open to blacks, the husband represented the entire family, a cultural preference reinforced by demographic and economic factors. In 1870, 80 percent of black households in the Cotton Belt included a male head and his wife (a proportion identical to that in the neighboring white population).

Landowners, merchants, and Freedmen's Bureau agents acknowledged the role of the black husband as the head of his family at the same time they encouraged his wife to work outside the home. He took "more or less land according to the number of his family" and placed "his X mark" on a labor agreement with a landowner. Kin relationships were often recognized in the text of the contract itself. Indeed, just as slaveholders had opportunistically dealt with the slave family—encouraging or ignoring it according to their own perceived interests—so postbellum planters seemed to have had little difficulty adjusting to the fact that freedmen's families were structured "traditionally" with the husband serving as the major source of authority. Patrick Broggan, an employer in Greenville, Alabama, agreed to supply food and other provisions for wives and children—"those who do not work on the farm"—"at the expense of their husbands and Fathers," men who promised "to work from Monday morning until Saturday night, faithfully and lose no time. . . ."

The Freedmen's Bureau's wage guidelines mandated that black women and men receive unequal compensation based on their sex rather than their productive abilities or efficiency. Agents also at times doled out less land to families with female (as opposed to male) household heads. Moreover, the bureau tried to hold men responsible for their wives' unwillingness to labor according to a contractual agreement. For example, the Cuthbert, Georgia, bureau official made one black man promise "to work faithfully and keep his wife in subjection" after the woman refused to work and "damned the Bureau" saying that "all the Bureaus out cant make her work."

A black husband usually purchased the bulk of the family's supplies (either in town or from a rural local merchant) and arranged to borrow or lease any stock animals that might be needed in plowing. He received direct payment in return for the labor of a son or daughter who had been "hired out." Finally, complaints and criminal charges lodged by black men against whites often expressed the grievances of an entire household.

Thus the sexual division of labor that had existed within the black family under slavery became more sharply focused after emancipation. Wives and mothers and husbands and fathers perceived domestic duties to be a woman's major obligation, in contrast to the slave master's view that a female was first and foremost a field or house worker and only incidentally the member of a family. Women also worked in the fields when their labor was needed. At planting and especially harvest time they joined their husbands and children outside. During the late summer and early fall some would hire out to white planters in the vicinity to pick cotton for a daily wage. In areas where black men could find additional work during the year—on rice plantations or in phosphate mines or sugar mills, for example—they left their "women and children to hoe and look after the crops. . . ." Thus women's agricultural labor partook of a more seasonal character than that of their husbands.

The rural *paterfamilias* tradition exemplified by the structure of black family relationships after the Civil War did not challenge the value and competence of freedwomen as fieldworkers. Rather, a distinct set of priorities determined how wives and mothers used their time in terms of housework, field labor, and tasks that produced supplements to the family income. Thus it is difficult to separate a freedwoman's "work" from her family-based obligations; productive labor had no meaning outside the family context. These aspects of a woman's life blended together in the seamless fabric of rural life.

Since husbands and wives had different sets of duties, they needed each other to form a complete economic unit. As one Georgia black man explained to George Campbell in the late 1870s, "The able-bodied men cultivate, the women raise chickens and take in washing; and one way and another they manage to get along." When both partners were engaged in the same kind of work, it was usually the wife who had stepped over into her husband's "sphere." For instance, Fanny Hodges and her husband wed the year after they were freed. She remembered, "We had to work mighty hard. Sometimes I plowed in de fiel' all day; sometimes I washed an' den I cooked. . . ." A family's ability to obtain financial credit from one year to the next depended upon the size of past harvests and the promise of future ones. Consequently the crop sometimes took precedence over other chores in terms of the allocation of a woman's energies.

The status of black women after the war cannot be separated from their roles as wives and mothers within a wider setting of kinship obligations. More than one-third of all black households in the Cotton Belt lived in the immediate vicinity of people with the identical (paternal) surname, providing a rather crude—

and conservative—index of local kinship clusters. As the persons responsible for child nurture and social welfare, freedwomen cared not only for members of their nuclear families, but also for dependent relatives and others in need. This postemancipation cooperative impulse constituted but one example of a historical "ethos of mutuality" developed under slavery.

The former slaves' attempts to provide for each other's needs appear to be a logical and humane response to widespread hardship during the 1860s and 1870s. But whites spared from physical suffering, including southern elites and representatives of the northern professional class, often expressed misgivings about this form of benevolence. They believed that any able-bodied black person deserved a "living" only to the extent that he or she contributed to the southern commercial economy. Blacks should reap according to the cottonseed they sowed.

Too many blacks, according to bureau agent John De Forest, felt obliged to look after "a horde of lazy relatives" and neighbors, thus losing a precious opportunity to get ahead on their own. This tendency posed a serious threat to the South's new economic order, founded as it was, in De Forest's view, on individual effort and ambition. He pointed to the case of Aunt Judy, a black laundress who barely eked out a living for herself and her small children. Yet she had "benevolently taken in, and was nursing, a sick woman of her own race. . . . The thoughtless charity of this penniless Negress in receiving another poverty-stricken creature under her roof was characteristic of the freedmen. However selfish, and even dishonest, they might be, they were extravagant in giving." By calling the willingness to share a "thoughtless" act, De Forest implied that a "rational" economic being would labor only to enhance her own material welfare.

The racial self-consciousness demonstrated by black women and men within their own kin networks found formal, explicit expression in the political arena during Reconstruction. As Vincent Harding and others have shown, freedmen actively participated in postwar Republican politics, and leaders of their own race came to constitute a new and influential class within black communities. Class relationships that had prevailed before the war shifted, opening up possibilities of cooperation between the former slaves and nonelite whites. The two groups met at a historical point characterized by landlessness and economic dependence, but they were on two different trajectories—the freed people on their way up (no matter how slightly) from slavery, the poor whites on their way down from self-sufficiency. Nevertheless, the vitality of the political process, tainted though it was by virulent racial prejudice and violence, provided black men with a public forum distinct from the private sphere inhabited by their womenfolk.

Black men predominated in this arena because, like other groups in nineteenth-century America, they believed that males alone were responsible for—and capable of—the serious business of politicking. This notion was reinforced by laws that barred female suffrage. However, black husbands and fathers, unlike their white counterparts, perceived the preservation and physical welfare of their families (including protection from terrorists) to be distinct political issues, along with predictable measures like land reform and debt relief. In political activity, freedmen extended their role as family protector outside the boundaries of the household. One searches in vain for any mention of women delegates in accounts of formal black political conventions held during this period—local and state gatherings during which men formulated and articulated their vision of a just postwar society. Freedwomen sometimes spoke up forcefully at meetings devoted to specific community issues, but they remained outside the formal political process.

It is true that freedmen monopolized formal positions of power within their own communities during Reconstruction. But that did not necessarily mean that women quietly deferred to them in all matters outside the home. For example, in some rural areas two sources of religious authority—one dominated by men, the other by women—coexisted uneasily. At times formal role designations only partially reflected the "influence" wielded by individuals outside their own households. In the process of institutionalizing clandestine religious practices formed during slavery and separating them from white congregations, freed people reserved church leadership positions for men. In other ways, individual congregations fashioned a distinctly inferior role for women; some even turned women out of the sanctuary "before the men began to talk" about matters of church policy.

These examples must be contrasted with equally dramatic cases of women who exercised considerable influence over their neighbors' spiritual lives, but outside of formal religious bodies and, indeed, of Protestant denominationalism altogether. Elderly women in the long line of African and Afro-American conjurers and herb doctors were often eagerly consulted by persons of both sexes. They included the African-born Maum Katie, "a great 'spiritual mother,' a fortune-teller, or rather prophetess, and a woman of tremendous influence over her children," as well as other women whose pronouncements and incantations were believed to be divinely inspired.

✳

[Freedwomen's assertion of authority within and outside the black community threatened whites' views of proper sex roles.] In their descriptions of southern society during the fifteen years after the war, northern and foreign observers conveyed the distinct impression that black women were particularly outspoken and aggressive (by implication relative to black men) in their willingness to confront white authority figures, "Freedmen's Bureau officers not ex-cluded," noted one shocked Georgia agent. First, large numbers of freedwomen might have in fact found a release for their anger by publicly denouncing their white tormentors, taking their grievances to a local bureau agent, or goading into action other blacks more reticent or fatalistic than themselves. In his study of northern planters in the postbellum South, Lawrence Powell suggests that "the freedwomen did not give in easily to pressures from the planters. Women hands seem to have been among the most militant fighters for their rights among the ex-slaves."

However, a somewhat different approach to the problem would suggest that Yankee journalists, officials, travelers, and planters were intrigued by exceptionally strong-willed freedwomen and so tended to highlight individual cases and exaggerate their importance. Defenders of the notion of early Victorian (white) womanhood could not help but be struck by black women who openly challenged conventional standards of female submissiveness. Freedwomen were described as "growling," "impertinent," "impudent," "vulgar" persons who "spoke up bold as brass" and, with their "loud and boisterous talking," demanded fair treatment for "we people [left] way back."

As a group and as individuals, black women paid dearly for their own assertiveness and for that of their sisters who dressed, spoke up, shouted, and acted like free women. One night in April 1867, Harriett Murray, a servant in the home of Dick Porter near Panola, Mississippi, was dragged from the house into the nearby woods by her employer and another white man. There "her hands were tied to the fork of a limb" and she was whipped "until the two men were tired out; two candles were burnt out in the time." Porter then took her down from the tree, stripped her of her clothing, and held her while the other man continued to beat her. The cause of the assault is unknown, although the advice given to the victim by a local magistrate—that she should accept $38 in pay from

Porter and forget about the whipping—indicates that a wage dispute was involved. Neither assailant was arrested.

Lacking any alternatives, some freedwomen continued to toil as they had under slavery and thus remained susceptible to "punishment" for any number of "offenses." The amount and quality of work performed by a woman, and disagreements over the compensation due her, provoked the rage of white men who were slave masters in all but name. In Athens, Georgia, Margaret Martin left her place of work to visit a niece one day in the spring of 1868 and was "badly beaten and choked" by her employer when she returned. The defiant freedwoman Caroline appeared before a Greensboro, North Carolina, Freedmen's Bureau official and reported that Thomas Price had failed to pay for her services; and when she next appeared on Price's plantation, the white man "knocked her down and Beat her with his fist" and ordered his overseer to bring him "the strap"; "then he whipped her with it holding her head between his knees on the bare flesh by turning her clothes up. . . ." The overseer also administered "a hundred lashes or more" after Price told him to "ware her out." Lucretia Adams of Yorkville, South Carolina, endured a night of terror initiated by eight drunken white men (she recognized all her assailants, including Oliver and Charles Boehmgart and Bill and Newman Thomas). They "just talked as anybody would" and told her, "We heard you wouldn't work. We were sent for . . . to come here and whip you, to make the damned niggers work."

The incidents just described were exceptional only in that they were reported to northern officials. Like Harriett Murray, most women heeded the warnings issued by their attackers to remain silent or leave the area if they did not want to be killed. Local officials often refused to make arrests despite overwhelming evidence against a man or group of men; most shared the view—expressed candidly by a Mississippi deputy—that "there was neither money nor glory" in making such arrests.

Even if a man were held to await trial, post-emancipation southern justice was less than forthright, rivaling in fact mythical Wild West lawlessness for sheer outrageousness. In specific cases concerning freedwomen, a town mayor assisted in helping an accused rapist to make his escape; and a judge charged with beating a women presided over his own trial, declared himself innocent, jailed his victim, and then forced her husband to pay for her release. Cases for black women plaintiffs were argued by drunken lawyers, and jury members stood up in the midst of proceedings to expound on behalf of the defendant. In June of 1868 an Upperville, Virginia, white man accused of assaulting a black woman leaped up during the trial and began beating her ferociously; he was acquitted.

The social consequences of freedom—the coming together of families to work and live—were accompanied by changes in the way women worked, dressed, and thought about themselves. But if liberation from bondage brought tangible, immediate benefits to some women, for others it represented but a fervent hope that their children would some day live as truly free people. A mother's belief that the future might be better for her offspring gave proof of the passing of slavery. The cook who "said she should die very happy, feeling that her children can spend 'the balance of their days in freedom, though she had been in bonds'" thought of freedom in terms of her family's future welfare and not her own current material condition. Black women throughout the South joined with men to form local education committees, build schoolhouses, and hire teachers at a time when their neighborhoods' material resources were slim indeed.

These mothers tried to prepare their children for a new kind of life. Poor but proud women refused to let their sons and daughters accept clothing (donated by whites) they considered ill-fitting or immodest; it was considered "highly indecorous to have the feet and ankles show below the dress," for example. Northern teachers and Freedmen's Bureau officials often showed a lack of sensitivity toward these women who chose self-respect over convenience. Mary Ames, a Yankee teacher, recorded a revealing incident in her diary: "One girl brought back a dress she had taken home for 'Ma says it don't fit, and she don't want it.' It was rather large and short, but she was very dirty and ragged, and we told her she must keep it." In other instances, parents disciplined their children with the liberal use of the rod, but they reserved the right to decide how and whether it should be used. Two years after the war, a Georgia bureau agent sustained charges brought against Eliza James because she had "impudently" refused to punish her son at the behest of a white man "and said she would not whip her child for no poor white folks etc." For a white person to demand the punishment of a child smacked of slavery, and this freedwoman would not tolerate it.

The elderly Sea Island evening-school pupil "who was much bent with rheumatism" but said she was "mighty anxious to know something"; the Savannah laundress who fastened her textbook to the fence so she could read "while at work over the wash tub"; and the Greenville, South Carolina, dressmaker who attended classes in the morning and worked at her trade in the afternoon were three of the few freedwomen to receive some formal education soon after emancipation. (In 1870 more than eight out of ten southern blacks were illiterate.) For most women, the rigors of childbearing and rearing, household chores and outside employment, represented a continuum from slavery to freedom, unbroken by schooling or other opportunities to expand their horizons beyond the cabin in the cotton field.

The Alabama Freedmen's Bureau agents assigned to conduct a "Negro Census" for 1865 in the Athens-Huntsville area probably resented spending so much time and energy on what they considered bureaucratic nonsense. Before too long they became careless in recording the ages and previous occupations of people they interviewed. However, for a while initially, they dutifully noted the required information: each person's name, age, sex, address, former owner, slave occupation, and "present employment." The first few pages of the census include these bits of data on about three hundred people. More than the gory details of an "outrage" report, or the tedious wording of a labor contract, this remarkable document chronicles the quiet revolution wrought in the lives of black women after emancipation.

Consider the Jones family: Caroline, formerly a house servant, and her daughter, Savannah, both of whom had been owned by John Haws, were now reunited with husband William (previously owned by a white man named Crawford). Caroline reported no occupation but instead said she was "caring for her family." William continued to work in a railroad shop. Two months before the census interview they had celebrated their new life together with the birth of a son, James, who was listed as "Free born." Nearby, Nelson and Phoebe Humphrey and their five children came together from two plantations (Nelson from one and Phoebe and the children from another). Both former field hands, Nelson was doing "Miscellaneous: for other people" and Phoebe took in laundry. Joanna (aged fourteen), who used to work as a house servant, was now attending school, and her thirteen-year-old sister Elizabeth no longer worked in the fields; she probably helped her mother with the washing.

Not too far away two young women in the Hammond clan took up employment as laundresses so that Easter (sixty), a former domestic, would no longer have to work; she was listed as ill. The women, Nettie (thirty-three) and Ata (twenty-nine), had six children between them, but no husband was listed for either. In the same neighborhood resided a second Jones family, consisting of Gilbert (fifty) and Julia (forty-eight) and the children they had retrieved from two different slave masters. The father had found work as a blacksmith and son William (twenty-one) continued to labor as a field hand. Gilbert, Jr. (fourteen), stayed at home rather than working in the fields as he had before, and Amanda (eighteen), also a former hand but "subject to fits" was now able to "help her mother."

Freedwomen like Phoebe Humphrey and Julia Jones would have had no difficulty listing the blessings of freedom: a reunion at long last with their families, the opportunity to devote more time to household affairs, and children attending school. Although it would be difficult to argue that their work was any less arduous than that of their slave mothers, these women were now in a position to decide, together with their husbands, how and when various family members should contribute to the welfare of the household. Nettie and Ata Hammond probably had fewer alternatives when it came to supporting their children, but at least they were able to relieve the elderly Easter of her duties as a house servant.

Still, all black women continued to occupy two distinct statuses that shaped their daily lives. In their neighborhoods they commanded respect as wives, mothers and upholders of cultural tradition. In the eyes of whites busy laying the foundations for the "New South"—planters and federal officials—they were still workers who belonged to a despised caste, considered apart from white women no matter how downtrodden. Yet freedwomen perceived freedom to mean not a release from backbreaking labor, but rather the opportunity to labor on behalf of their own families and kin within the protected spheres of household and community.

Questions for Study and Review

1. In what ways were black and white southern women's experiences of the Civil War similar? In what ways were they different?

2. From where did the belief that every freedman would get forty acres and a mule emerge, and in what ways did the lack of such support shape postwar race relations?

3. To what extent did black women and men continue to share familial and communal authority as black men gained the franchise, as marriage was legalized, and as contracts signed by husbands and fathers verified labor relations for the entire family?

4. Some historians have called the Civil Rights movement of the 1960s the Second Reconstruction. Why was a Second Reconstruction needed, and how did black women's roles change between the two periods?

Suggested Readings

Herbert Gutman, *The Black Family in Slavery and Freedom, 1750–1925* (1976).

Ira Berlin, Joseph P. Reidy, and Leslie Rowland, eds., *Freedom: A Documentary History of Emancipation, 1861–1867, Series II: The Black Military Experience* (1982).

Darlene Clark Hine, "Lifting the Veil, Shattering the Silence: Black Women's History in Slavery and Freedom," in *The State of Afro-American History, Past, Present and Future* (1986).

Suzanne Lebsock, "Radical Reconstruction and the Property Rights of Southern Women," *Journal of Southern History* (May 1977).

PART TWO

The

New Order

With Reconstruction put to rest in 1877, Americans once again harnessed themselves to an expansive vision. For political, military, and business leaders, this meant the conquest of new lands and new markets. For ordinary women and men, it meant the decision to move west (or further west), to take up a new occupation, to make a new start in life. Western migration surged forward, culminating in the "closing" of the frontier by 1890. Railroads came to dominate the nation's transportation system as telephones and the telegraph sped communications across the country. Industrial tycoons and technology together reshaped large-scale manufacturing. Markets expanded in burgeoning urban centers and overseas. The commercialization of agriculture blossomed in response to the needs and demands for food in the fast-growing cities.

Yet this new order also created new problems. Native Americans suffered a series of military defeats, ending with the battle at Wounded Knee Creek in 1890. Three years earlier, the Dawes Severalty Act had disrupted tribal life once again by encouraging Indians to accept individual plots of land, land on which buffaloes no longer roamed, in exchange for the promise of citizenship. The railroads, which hastened the extinction of the bison, transformed labor relations along with Indians' lives. The transcontinental railroad was completed in 1869, the same year that the Knights of Labor was founded. In 1877, a spontaneous strike by tens of thousands of railroad workers alerted the nation to the dislocations, tensions, and violence underlying industrial change. In the next decade, the Knights built on the forces let loose by the 1877 protest and later worker uprisings.

Many women and men needed no strikes to warn them about the problems of too rapid expansion. Such disruptions were already obvious to those barely able to sustain themselves and their families during the extended recession of the mid-1870s. This economic slump only temporarily slowed western settlement, however. Not until the next decade did farmers on the

The completion of the transcontinental railway made it possible for large numbers of immigrants to travel west in search of new lives on the frontier. Travel by train was less arduous—and less expensive—than by wagon, which meant that greater numbers of women and children could undertake the long journey.

Plains and across the South face the devastating effects of drought and debt, falling agricultural prices and rising railroad rates. Then, farmers enthusiastically infused existing organizations with a new militancy and created new associations to achieve specifically political ends. Among all groups—Indians, industrial workers, pioneers, and farmers—women and men joined hands to sustain family and community life. Yet in each case, differences in the resources and rights accorded the two sexes created distinct opportunities for and limits on collective action.

During the Civil War, women North and South took over traditionally male jobs. So, too, in the new wave of western migration did many women find themselves performing unconventional tasks and accepting unusual responsibilities. Less burdened by the cultural conventions of eastern society and more pressured by the challenges of frontier life, pioneer women of the 1870s and 1880s found their chances for education, professional careers, and formal political participation enhanced. Female doctors, lawyers, ranchers, entrepreneurs, and publishers dotted the West. Coeducational colleges and female seminaries sprang up almost overnight. Suffrage campaigns originating in the East before the Civil War now found their most fertile fields across the Mississippi. There the power of the Women's Christian Temperance Union (WCTU), founded at Cleveland, Ohio, in 1874, combined religious and moral zeal with demands for the "Home Ballot" by which women could protect their families through the vote.

In 1884, the recently established National Equal Rights Party met in San Francisco, California, to nominate Belva A. Lockwood, a lawyer, and Marietta L. Stowe, a newspaper publisher, for president and vice-president of the United States. Four years later, the organization convened in Des Moines, Iowa, to renominate Lockwood. This time, however, they named a male running mate, Alfred H. Love, to put in practice their own demand for "equality of the sexes." Still, women's real electoral strength lay not in national campaigns, but in local communities where school or municipal suffrage gave them a measure of influence, even power. Rosalind Urbach Moss examines one such community—Syracuse, Kansas—where women gained control of the town council in 1887. By exploring developments there, she reveals the possibilities and limits of women's electoral participation.

Female activism was not confined to the formal political arena. In the WCTU and other voluntary organizations, in labor unions, and in farmers' organizations, women responded to the changing economic, social, and political order. Mechanization, for example, transformed the face of agriculture and industry in the late nineteenth century and called forth a variety of responses from employers and workers. Yet it affected these groups unevenly. Textile operatives, for example, were faced with far more serious disruptions of their traditional work roles in this period than were cigar workers. Technological advances created previously unheard of jobs for women, as telephone operators and "typewriters," for instance; while other forms of traditional female employment, such as hand sewing and shoebinding, almost disappeared.

Many women, like men, sought individual solutions to these changes. They sent sons or daughters to replace mothers whose skills were now outdated; they retrained in order to learn how to use new machines; they moved to areas not yet touched by mechanization; or they left the work force and lived on less. Other workers, pressured not only by mechanization but by speed-ups, wage cuts, and poor working conditions, organized collective protests. Some did so spontaneously, reacting to a particularly inflammatory local incident; a smaller number joined regional or national associations, the most powerful of which was the Knights of Labor. Susan Levine captures the intersection of these local and national developments by focusing on the carpet weavers of Philadelphia, Pennsylvania. Here, women and men confronted different problems and options as a result of mechanization, yet joined together—first in neighborhood associations and then in the Knights— to combat the new forms of exploitation that accompanied industrial expansion.

So, too, in the agrarian south, as Julie Roy Jeffrey demonstrates, women and men found common cause in protesting the ravages of deflation, drought, and commercialization. Women in the Southern Farmers' Alliance, like those in the Knights of Labor, attempted to walk a fine line between feminine propriety and effective protest. Drawing on the words of WCTU president Frances E. Willard, one Alliance spokeswoman assured her Carolina sisters, "Drudgery, fashion and gossip are no longer the bounds of woman's Sphere." Yet Southern Alliance leaders found it hard to determine what were the bounds. Certainly Southerners were less supportive than their western counterparts of women's direct political participation. The specter of black political power, crushed in the late nineteenth century through disfranchisement and Jim Crow laws, may account for much of this regional variation. On issues concerning both blacks and women, Southerners seeking to promote collective action found they had to carefully balance agrarian protest with the maintenance of traditional sexual and racial boundaries.

Neither the Alliance nor the Knights survived long enough to reshape social or economic relations in the nation at large. Similarly, despite early victories for female suffrage in the West, the movement for women's political equality stalled by 1890, far short of achieving its goals. Still, for workers and farmers, politicians and protesters across the country, local participation in electoral politics, unionization, or farmers' associations gave ordinary women and men a sense of control over their own destiny. And in making their own history, they also helped shape the new order.

Suggested Readings

Nell Painter, *Standing at Armageddon: The United States, 1877–1919* (1987).

Alice Kessler-Harris, *Out to Work: A History of Wage-Earning Women in America* (1982).

Ruth Bordin, *Women and Temperance: The Quest for Power and Liberty, 1873–1900* (1980).

TWO

The "Girls" from Syracuse: Kansas Women in Politics, 1887-1890

Rosalind Urbach Moss

The Homestead Act, the railroads, and the defeat of hostile Indians occupying rich western lands moved the frontier quickly toward the Pacific in the decades following the Civil War. For some women, this westward move meant drudgery, isolation, and depression; for others, it spelled opportunity, emancipation, and the promise of equality. It is this latter experience that Moss traces for the women of Syracuse, Kansas.

The debates over the Fifteenth Amendment ended with black men receiving guarantees of suffrage and with women, black and white, being further removed from enfranchisement. From the 1870s on, disappointed women's rights advocates across the nation focused increasing attention on the battle for the vote. However, most did not have to wait until the passage of the nineteenth Amendment in 1920 to cast their first ballot. Municipal and school suffrage was approved in numerous communities in the nineteenth century and state suffrage existed in a number of western states and territories.

A variety of arguments have emerged to explain female suffragists' greater success in the West: territorial politics, the battle over polygamy in Utah; the expansive and democratic spirit of the frontier; the good humor of a few random legis-lators, and the necessity of mollifying women whose labor was essential to survival. Whatever the answers, by the time the frontier "closed" in 1890, Wyoming and Utah along with numerous towns in Kansas, Nebraska, and other western states had granted women the vote in one form or another. More surprisingly, women were elected to a number of positions, including some for which they could not yet vote.

Through a detailed study of elections in Syracuse, Moss illuminates the meaning of suffrage and officeholding for an understanding of western development and of the transformation of relations between women and men. Here we find not the underappreciated farm wives of mid-century, but rather the high-spirited and efficient female activists of the Civil War era. Here, too, we see the debate over the rationale for women's public activism—female moral superiority versus natural equality—played out on a new stage. Whatever their rationale, women would increasingly find their way into the public and political domain over the next century, with the women of Kansas serving as a model and a challenge.

On April 4, 1887, the town of Syracuse, Kansas, became one of two communities in that state and in the nation to elect women to their municipal governments. Syracuse elected an all-female town council; Argonia in south-central Kansas elected a male council and the first female mayor in the country. (A year later, Oskaloosa near Lawrence elected women to both the mayor's office and the council.) Then in November 1887, Hamilton County (of which Syracuse became the seat) elected its first female county school superintendent, an office for which women had been permitted to run since 1872 but for which they could still not vote. Another woman succeeded her in 1890. Because of this burst of female political activity, Kansas provided the nation a testing ground for women's entry into politics; feminists, suffragists, and antisuffragists watched the Kansas towns eagerly for signs of support for their causes.

As women entered politics in Hamilton County in the late 1880s, something else was occurring—the county's women and men were negotiating the place and proper activities of women in the West. The long-standing myth of the westerner's being freer than other Americans was put to a severe test when women entered local politics: Was the myth for men only? In her book *Frontier Women,* Julie Roy Jeffrey demonstrates the pull of nineteenth-century domestic ideology on most female immigrants to the West; however, Sheryll Patterson-Black shows that some women *did* go west seeking different lives than they knew in the East. These two impulses met in Syracuse,

Kansas, in the 1880s and sought mutual accommodation.

Hamilton County lies in the far southwestern corner of Kansas, bordering Colorado. In the late 1880s this area consisted of rangelands, boomtowns, and dusty frontier homesteads. The county's major settlements, Coolidge, Syracuse, and Kendall, stretched between the Arkansas River and the Atchison, Topeka & Santa Fe Railroad tracks, along the old Sante Fe Trail. Although Syracuse and Coolidge had been settled since about 1873, the boom period began around 1885. By 1887 the towns were busily distancing themselves from the "wild West." Schools and churches were organized as more people, particularly more women, moved into the county. In 1885 there had been "not half a dozen women" in Syracuse; two years later there were enough "good" women to have organized Baptist, Methodist, and Presbyterian ladies' aid societies, even though separate churches had not yet been built. By the end of 1887 their influence was being felt: at least one "bad" woman ("Kate Evans, a courtesan") had been brought before the town judge.

The years 1887 and 1888 are best remembered locally, however, for the drought and for the "county seat war." These disasters brought the county and its three warring towns close to financial collapse. At the same time the tax base was diminishing because of the drought, all three towns erected massive limestone schoolhouses to bolster their claims for becoming the county seat. Worse, though, was the period of bitter and corrupt politics that competition for county seat initiated. At least once, this little "war" nearly became a shooting match.

In the midst of this local uproar the Kansas Supreme Court ruled that the female municipal suffrage law passed by the legislature in January 1887, was valid. Notice of this ruling appeared in county newspapers in mid-March,

Women could not vote in national elections, but many states, territories, and communities allowed women to vote in municipal elections. In the freer political climate of the western states, women began to participate actively in political contests, both as voters and as candidates. The town of Syracuse, Kansas, elected an all-female city council in 1887. A year later, the voters of Oskaloosa, Kansas, chose the women in this photograph to sit on their City Council. They also elected a woman to be mayor.

giving barely three weeks' warning before the next town elections. Suddenly women as voters became participants in an ongoing political struggle within the Syracuse town council, the exact nature of which is unclear at this distance of time. Whatever the circumstances, on March 25, H. N. Lester, editor of the *Syracuse Journal,* published an announcement of a political meeting "for the purpose of nominating a law-abiding ticket for the city election. All voters, male and female, are expected to be present." Lester, one of the few remaining members of the original 1873 Syracuse colony, had plans to head up that "law-abiding" ticket, but he miscalculated his support. The *Sentinel,* a rival paper, soon published a veiled accusation against Lester, calling for the election of officials "who will live up to the laws they make and enforce; . . . who will use their office for the public benefit and not to further their own personal designs." The *Sentinnel's* editor ex-pressed confidence that "now that women can vote, there is no reason why men of known morality and upright character cannot be elected." He urged all women to vote, "but don't vote the way your husband, your best fellow, or any one else tells you without it suits."

A week before the election, opposing political factions saw the women as votes to be won, but the women soon discovered their voting rights could produce something tangible. The *Sentinnel's* Will C. Higgins had joined forces with others to oppose Lester's candidacy and to elect as mayor N. E. Wheeler, a current council member. Wheeler's allies were the women of the church ladies' aid societies and their husbands, people interested in protecting their homes through municipal reforms. At some point (probably during a women's political meeting not quite a week before the election), this group decided to nominate an all-woman council slate. One of the candidates was Caroline E. Barber, like Lester an original settler, and the wife of the town's leading merchant, who was then a council member. The other council candidates were Sarah M. Coe and Mary E. Riggles; Hannah D. Nott, president of the Baptist Ladies' Aid, later elected president of the town council; and Lizzie M. Swartwood, active in the Methodist Ladies Aid.

Lester lost the mayoral race decisively (114 to 46) to the women's "City Ticket," largely because he failed to corral enough of the sixty-two women's votes, a fact he acknowledged, however condescendingly, in the *Journal's* headlines: "Syracuse Leads! The Ladies (God Bless Them) Rally to the Polls and Rustle the Voters." Lester's official reaction in his article about the election was restrained, but he was careful to print the names of all those who had "planned the campaign" against him. He acknowledged, however, that the "ladies voted without hesitation and as if they had done so for the last twenty-one years." He even conceded that the election was "a great victory for the advocates of female suffrage." Lester reassured Syracuse citizens, and himself as well, that the "ladies elected are intelligent and worthy. Many of them have had extensive experience in business, are quick of perception, and more than ordinarily self-reliant. . . . At all events we are in favor of giving them a chance."

Despite his official magnanimity, Lester could not resist getting in an oblique, ambiguous editorial comment elsewhere in the issue:

> The ancient and eminent order of the Knights of the Garter has been reinstated in Syracuse, and at the next meeting of our city council the degrees will be conferred and a number of our prominent citizens decorated with the distinctive features of the order for valiant service rendered in the "battle of the ballot."

Sentinnel editor Higgins published his own dig from another, more relevant perspective: "Don't you wish you had been a little mouse in the corner at the ladies' political meeting last week Wednesday?"

Lester's world had changed even more dramatically than he thought. The election of an all-female town council had focused national attention on his frontier community. Not only did Laura Johns, president of the Kansas Equal Suffrage Association, decide to come to see for herself what was going on, but Syracuse faced less friendly and more facile scrutiny. On May 6, 1887, before he had had time to "give the ladies a chance," Lester was forced by his earlier magnanimity into defending the councilwomen from attack by (among others) his old hometown paper in Syracuse, New York. He reprinted the offending editorial and then accused its author of being "one of the original 'moss-backs' who cannot imagine a woman to be anything but a Victoria Woodhull or a Dr. Mary Walker, whenever she endeavors to take a position higher than a cook, washerwoman or handmaid." But Lester was not at home in his support of the women, and he allayed fears of "masculine women" and "petticoat rule" with the rather astounding assurance that

> these women are ladies of refinement, culture and ability. None of them so far as we are informed, with one exception, is a woman suffragist in the common acceptation of the term . . . , but rather believe that by their example, moving in their own sphere, working by their own methods, they can transact public business and accomplish desired results without steeping themselves in corruption.

Lester's paradigm of "the way things are" was under severe stress, particularly if he could see five women sitting on the town council as "moving in their own sphere." He defended the councilwomen as best he could, however, leaving it to the more sympathetic Higgins of the *Sentinnel* to report that the "ladies" of

Syracuse had indeed organized their own equal suffrage society. Two of its officers, Nott and Barber, were council members; the third officer was Mrs. Wheeler, wife of the new mayor. There was more suffrage activity and support in town than Lester, and no doubt others, wanted to acknowledge, and they were going to have to live with it for the coming year.

After the women had completed their year in office, however, even Lester acknowledged that Syracuse had become "renowned as a city of good government, good morals, fine streets." Nothing catastrophic had occurred. The women had begun their administration by having the streets graded and ordering property owners to build sidewalks; later they voted on municipal bonds and split on an issue of business licensing. The women appear to have established a pattern of good government operated for the benefit of the community as a whole. But none of Syracuse's "city mothers" ran for reelection in 1888. The councilwomen evidently felt they had done their part to make the town better. They modestly retired in favor of male successors who would continue their course of municipal improvements geared toward making the place a "home" town.

With no women at work in City Hall, it would have been easy for citizens to forget the questions about women's proper role raised by the presence of women in public office. By this time, however, another woman was keeping the issues alive by venturing into more turbulent county politics in the midst of the county-seat war. Elizabeth (Lizzie) Culver ran for the office of Superintendent of Public Instruction in the fall of 1887. Even though *Journal* editor Lester believed that the school superintendency was more "appropriate" for a woman than was serving on the city council, and although Culver's father was one of the county treasurers, her election was not an easy one. Owing to issues related to the county-seat war, as well as those raised by her gender, she had to fight to get and then to keep her post.

Her father, Martin S. Culver, was a Texas cattleman who lobbied for the National Cattle Trail after the Kansas legislature quarantined Texas cattle in 1885. He was a founder of Trail City, two miles west of Coolidge, which was known as "the wickedest city in Colorado" during its brief life in the late 1880s. Culver had moved his family from Corpus Christi, Texas, to Coolidge and had become involved in county politics during the county-seat fight as treasurer for the Kendall-Coolidge faction. In the fall of 1887, though ill, Martin Culver stood for reelection, while daughter Lizzie ran for the superintendency. She did not run on her father's Coolidge ticket, however: her "Independent County" ticket was nominated by Syracuse delegates disgruntled by two previous county conventions. Apparently her father's cronies did not agree with Lester that the superintendency was "a public position which . . . women were adapted to fill with credit to themselves and benefit to education."

It is likely that, despite the politicization of the office of school superintendent by its being elective rather than appointive, many people in the county saw no problem with voting for a woman because they had come, like Lester, to see education as "woman's work." The factionalization of county politics at that time no doubt played a role in Culver's election, too. The county newspapers characteristically provided few details of this campaign at the height of Kansas's longest county-seat war. Lizzie Culver won, however, against two opponents and by a nine-vote margin.

Journal editor Lester again provides us with our only insight into this woman's experience in politics. Although Lester won the post of state legislator on the same ticket, he—and probably much of the rest of the county—knew little about Culver until after the election, when he announced in the *Journal* that she was "a Catholic and [had] received a convent education." Another of Lester's revelations provides an indication of what Culver's first campaign must have been like. Immediately afterward she hired a lawyer to sue the "colorful" Syracuse Methodist minister Sprague Davis for $5,000 in damages, charging him with slander. The basis of her slander charge was not reported in any county newspaper, but we can surmise what might have upset a Protestant preacher, whether or not he was aware of her Catholicism. Although she had left her father's political faction, Culver probably could not leave her association with Trail City wickedness. Her youth and her gender no doubt made her more vulnerable to attack when she entered public life. She was, after all, no matron as were the Syracuse councilwomen, whose status was at least a partial defense. During the campaign even one of her supporters, the *Syracuse Democratic Principle,* had made a thinly veiled reference to the beauty of one of the candidates. Not only had she entered the public arena very quickly after her father's death, but she probably had campaigned alone, both serious mistakes in the nineteenth century. If these surmises are correct, the reactions they evoked undoubtedly led many county residents to question further the propriety of permitting women to become involved in politics.

After her election Culver moved to Syracuse and, staying with the Barbers, tried to carry out her official duties under difficult circumstances. The county records were being held at Kendall, whose citizens were contesting her election and where J. R. Campbell was acting as superintendent, though he had not run for the office. Culver kept a makeshift office in Syracuse when she could not get offices in Kendall, legally the temporary county seat. In the summer she organized and conducted the third normal institute held in the county. That fall she ran for reelection in a court-ordered contest after Syracuse had been declared the permanent seat. Culver was renominated, though not without challenges, and ran against Campbell, this time the official nominee of the Kendall-Coolidge faction.

From all indications this election was also a nasty one, and Culver's earlier defection to Syracuse may have been a central issue. Lester encouraged his town to "be as true to [Culver] as she has been to us" because "petty jealousies in some localities may help Mr. Campbell." The other Syracuse papers, while more enthusiastic in her support, did not add other points in her favor; they repeated only that the election was "owed" her by Syracuse. This time Culver won by more than 100 votes, a good margin, though smaller than the margins of her male colleagues. When the Kansas dust settled, Culver married H. Clay Price, a rancher who had worked on her campaign committee. Their marriage, however, was not announced by the Syracuse papers, but rather by the *Kendall Boomer,* recently a bitter rival.

Clearly she had made another mistake, though there is no way to know what people actually thought of Culver's marriage. The lack of any comment by her friends in Syracuse indicates ambivalence if not disapproval. The female city council members were already married when they won office, so being married in itself probably was not seen as a disqualification for office. But Lizzie Culver Price was a newlywed, a delicate condition for a nineteenth-century woman. She did not let this condition or people's opinions interfere with her duties as superintendent, however, as she energetically went about building and rebuilding the county school system. And she was not even slowed down at first by her pregnancy in 1890.

Unlike the Syracuse councilwomen, Culver apparently did not realize that she should "retire" after she had made her point. Despite her convent education, she was after all a cattleman's daughter and perhaps not as observant of social niceties as she might have been. She had already crossed two boundaries—the geopolitical and the moral ones between the cattle interests associated with Coolidge and Trail City and the settlement interests of many in Syracuse. Perhaps she was not aware that in failing to retire from public life and public view when her newlywed condition became even more "delicate" she was crossing another, more sensitive social border. Lizzie Culver Price had been a good superintendent, but the newspaper editors, and no doubt many others, did not—perhaps could not—acknowledge that fact until she had left office. Even the formerly enthusiastic *Democratic Principle* in the summer of 1890 referred to her snidely as "the present incumbent who will not be a candidate again, she having tired of office life." Lizzie Price's fine record as an officeholder had been obscured by her far from exemplary behavior as a conventional woman. Consequently, the question of women's suitability for public office became foremost in people's minds.

Even the woman who next ran for the superintendency felt her election had been jeopardized precisely because Price had not quit and had continued to "drive over the country in a very pregnant state, turning public opinion against her sex." It is unclear what bothered people most about Price's behavior: their assumption that pregnancy was incapacitating and therefore interfered with her public duties, or their objection to someone in such a "private" condition continuing to perform public duties. Whatever the reason, the next female candidate, Kate Warthen, found herself waging two campaigns—one for office and the other for the right of women to run for and serve in public office. She was eminently well equipped to do both and mounted a hard-nosed and quite modern "media" campaign for county superintendent in 1890.

Sarah Catharine Warthen was born in 1866 and spent her early life in Indiana, the only daughter (with four brothers) of a Union Army veteran. From the time she was fifteen, her family had homesteaded, first in Texas, then in southeastern Kansas. She had taught in country schools since she was seventeen, but in April 1887, she quit teaching and following her family to southwestern Kansas, determined to

homestead land of her own. Her claim lay in the southeastern part of Hamilton County, while her parents' lay near Lakin, farther northeast in adjacent Kearny County. The Warthens moved to the area at what proved to be a very bad time. Owing to a drought and a hard winter, in 1887, Kate Warthen earned only $37.08 from her farm. She returned to teaching in a country school in Kearny County in March 1888.

Warthen was ambitious, however, and by September 1889 she had been elected principal teacher of the big new limestone schoolhouse in Kendall. In April 1890 she decided to run for the superintendency. Warthen successfully negotiated political boundaries in the county, but it was harder to deal successfully with the problem of her gender, which had become more directly an issue because of Lizzie Culver's legacy. Indeed, Warthen had to worry a good deal more about being defeated by her sex than by her Democratic opponent, who clearly had neither the administrative nor the political qualifications she possessed.

Typically, the issue of her being a woman was never raised directly in any of the county papers, but the *Syracuse Journal* approached the problem of "allowing women to hold office" obliquely when it published without comment an essay, "Women as Public Officers," signed only "Observer." Kate Warthen was the author. Although she offered primarily egalitarian feminist arguments, she buttressed these with assertions of women's special suitability for public office similar to those used by the Home Protectionists associated with the Women's Christian Temperance Union and other "social purity" groups. Significantly though, Lester and the other county newspaper editors stressed Warthen's competency in their endorsements, something they had not done—perhaps could not have conceived of doing—for Culver. Warthen managed to gain the support of all the county papers, even the *Democratic Principle,* which had to support her opponent perfunctorily because of its party affiliation.

Once she had won the Republican nomination, Warthen campaigned actively over the entire county—careful always to be accompanied by one of her brothers. She won the election, 236 votes to 179. It was a smaller margin than Culver's in 1888, but considerably larger than those of the men elected with her to other county offices—a significant indication that her political acumen and competence won out over considerations of both partisan politics and women's proper place.

Warthen's self-made feminism and open ambition pushed her to try herself further. Even while she served two terms as county superintendent from 1891 to 1894 and fulfilled her campaign promise to be a full-time professional administrator, she wrote as a small-time journalist, was commissioned a notary public (also an unusual job for a woman), and, after reading law with the county judge, became the first woman admitted to the county bar in March 1894. Indeed, Warthen's pursuit of traditionally male positions, from homesteader to politician and lawyer, was so determined that the community was quite surprised when, in late November 1894, she married. Warthen had learned from Culver's unfortunate experience to keep her private life to herself, and the people of the county had apparently written her off as a spinster, under the assumption that education and ambition were a double handicap in a woman's search for a man.

The article in the *Syracuse Journal* about Warthen's wedding reads strangely like an obituary and indicates how much she had resolved for the people of the county by providing an acceptable model for a woman in public life. The editor drew a lesson for the community from her exemplary life: as she left public office, and the county, Warthen stood as a "shining example of the bright, versatile western girl who, while possessing all the fine womanly instincts of her eastern and southern sister[s], has besides the pluck and indomitable [sic] energy peculiar to western progress and independence." The western woman, it seems, did not rise fully formed from the prairie. She had to be cultivated arduously through the trial and error of collective experience. Local boundaries for eastern womanhood had been negotiated by the "girls" from Syracuse, Hamilton County, Kansas, in the 1880s and 1890s. The ideal respectable western woman was not, as it turns out, a larger-than-life "Marlboro woman" but a hybrid like Kate Warthen, who was able to combine competence with awareness and observance of the social limits of her conduct of public life. The limits Warthen observed remained unwritten barriers to middle-class women's participation in politics and, to a large extent, work until quite recently (i.e., if women must participate in either area, they should be unmarried professionals or experienced matrons).

Today the Syracuse councilwomen are remembered in Hamilton County as a list of names constituting a noteworthy but anomalous "first." Lizzie Culver is described only as a daughter of M. S. Culver, founder of Trail City, Colorado, and wife of H. C. Price, Hamilton County rancher. Kate Warthen, who left the state after her marriage in 1894, is recorded not at all in the county history. The negotiations of the 1880s about women's role in public life have likewise been forgotten. Lessons must become traditions to be truly learned; traditions depend on stable populations for transmission. Unfortunately, by the early 1890s, Hamilton County had reached the bottom of its population curve: many of those who had witnessed the negotiations left, to be replaced years later by others who were ignorant of that experience. More important, the newcomers were not presented with a living tradition. No women held public office in Hamilton County after 1894 until well into this century; the pioneers retired and were not replaced. The new tradition of women in public life faded uncontested into rumor and then into dusty, documentary (as opposed to living, oral) history.

Questions for Study and Review

1. In both the West and the South agriculture predominated, and many residents continued to confront frontier conditions. How and why did women's position differ so dramatically in the two regions?

2. What factors do you think best explain women's greater electoral opportunities in the West?

3. In many western communities, there was a shortage of women relative to men. In what ways did this create opportunity or hardship for women and men?

4. Compare the mid-century farm wives described by John Mack Faragher (selection 12)—who included women from Kansas—with the female residents of Syracuse.

Suggested Readings

Susan Armitage and Elizabeth Jameson, eds., *The Women's West* (1987).

Anne M. Butler, *Daughters of Joy, Sisters of Mercy: Prostitutes in the American West, 1865-1890* (1987).

Jane Underwood, "Civilizing Kansas: Women's Organizations, 1880-1920," *Kansas History* (Winter 1984/85).

Lawrence B. deGraf, "Race, Sex, and Region: Black Women in the American West, 1850-1920," *Pacific Historical Review* (May 1980).

Ellen DuBois, "Working Women, Class Relations, and Suffrage Militance: Harriet Stanton Blatch and the New York Woman Suffrage Movement, 1894-1909," *Journal of American History* (June 1987).

THREE

The Transformation of a Laboring Community: Mechanization and the Mobilization of Women Weavers

Susan Levine

If western towns offered new opportunities for women in politics, eastern cities offered the same in industry as technological development transformed women's and men's work. At the 1876 Centennial Exposition in Philadelphia, female textile operatives staffed rows of machines in testimony to industrial progress. Only two years later, 400 of the city's female carpet weavers walked away from their machines and staged a massive strike against wage cuts. These two events capture much of the conflict surrounding industrial development in the late nineteenth century, particularly as it affected relations between workers and employers, women and men, family and community.

As new forms of transportation and communication knit the nation together, the introduction of technology tore apart local communities. Allowing for the replacement of skilled male workers with less skilled women or children, automation threatened the balance of power between husbands and wives, parents and children. Yet the lower wages paid female operatives assured their continued dependence on a family economy. Working-class women and men did not have to turn against each other, however. They might instead join forces in the Knights of Labor, the premier labor organization of the Gilded Age.

By examining one occupation in a single city—carpet weaving in Philadelphia—Levine traces the changing relationships between employers and employees, workers and unions, male weavers and female machine tenders. She demonstrates the ways that both manufacturers and laborers consolidated their organizations and reveals the critical role of the Knights of Labor in recruiting women as well as men into the late nineteenth-century labor movement.

Still, the Knights were less the instigators than the beneficiaries of worker militancy among Kensington carpet weavers. The intricate kinship and neighborhood networks in that section of Philadelphia encouraged and sustained female operatives in the Long Strike of 1878–79 and led them into the Knights two years later. Once in the Knights, Kensington carpet weavers and other women workers found themselves caught between ideals of labor solidarity and assumptions of gender difference. During the relatively short history of the Knights, the most active women sought to shape a "labor feminism" that combined elements of worker militancy and female sensibility.

This article, along with those by Moss and Julie Roy Jeffrey, illustrate the variety of ways that women, in conjunction with men of their particular class and region, helped to shape and were shaped by, the new economic and political order.

On 11 November 1878, four hundred Philadelphia women weavers left their workplaces and gathered in the streets of Kensington, the city's textile neighborhood. Soon, a crowd of over fifteen hundred people joined the young power loom carpet operatives outside the mills. Some were skilled carpet weavers, others local townspeople, but all, it appeared, wished the women well. Two days later the city's entire power loom establishment was shut down as the strike spread, and the owners locked the carpet workers out of the factories. On the strike's first day the women formed shop committees in every mill. Each committee held daily meetings assessing the progress of the strike. They established relief committees throughout the neighborhood and sent delegates to a city-wide strike association.

The strike's precipitating issue was a 10 percent wage cut instituted by the industry's newly formed manufacturers' association. According to James Dobson, one of Philadelphia's leading carpet manufacturers, "the greatest hardship will doubtless fall on the workmen," but, he added, the wage cut would "bring prices up to a profitable level." John Bromley, the city's second largest carpet manufacturer, expected the strike to last only a short time, long enough, he said, "to make necessary improvements and alterations." The manufacturers believed that as soon as they chose to re-open their mills the women would happily return to work. Instead the women surprised the manufacturers as well as other carpet workers by effectively halting Philadelphia's carpet production for six months.

The Long Strike finally ended in defeat for the women, but their experience during those months became a crucial base for subsequent industry-wide organizing among both skilled men and unskilled women. A successful strike by hand loom weavers, following the women's effort, was the first repercussion from their revolt. The weavers' trade organization only hastened a systematic managerial response to both labor- and market-related problems. Mechanization and consolidation together with a search for industrial stability characterized the years following the Long Strike. The women's strike and subsequent developments in the carpet industry point to the strategic role of women in the industrial revolution.

Carpet weaving occupies a special place in the history of American textile manufacturing. Centered in Philadelphia, carpet production, unlike wool and cotton manufacture, remained characterized by hand loom production well into the 1880's. Every other branch of the American textile industry had mechanized by midcentury. Indeed, during the 1870's New England's textile factories ranked among the nation's largest industrial plants, often employing hundreds of operators. By contrast, an 1876 industrial census estimated that the majority of Philadelphia carpet mills employed fewer than twenty hands. As late as 1890, one quarter of Philadelphia's carpet looms were still hand powered.

In 1880 Philadelphia stood as the nation's premier textile center and was second only to New York City in general manufacturing. Light manufacturing and especially textiles provided the city's economic base. A variety of cotton and woolen mills, knit-goods shops, and carpet mills characterized Philadelphia's industrial neighborhoods. The combined needle and textile trades employed over 40 percent of the city's working population, far more than any

Women made up almost three-quarters of the work force in Philadelphia's booming textile industry in the latter part of the nineteenth century. Women weavers formed a strong labor community that challenged factory owners' attempts to cut their wages. Even though they were not successful in their action, their strike strengthened the union sympathies that would eventually bring the women into the Knights of Labor.

other industry. The boot and shoe industry, building trades, and metal industry employed from 5 to 11 percent of the work force, and miscellaneous light industries, including hat making and printing, employed between 2 and 4 percent each.

The carpet trade was a crucial prop to Philadelphia's economy. In 1880 carpet production represented the city's fifth largest industry in value of output and amount of capital invested. In 1880, 88 percent of the nation's carpet mills could be found within Philadelphia, almost all in the city's Nineteenth Ward neighborhood of Kensington. These shops accounted for over half the nation's annual carpet yardage and almost half the industry's value of production.

As a center of textiles and other light manufacturing industries, Philadelphia drew large numbers of working women into its shops. In 1880 women made up 26 percent of the city's work force, almost twice the national average. Within the city's textile industry women constituted almost three quarters of the work force. Knit goods shops and cotton mills in particular were generally dominated by young female operatives. Philadelphia's carpet shops were, however, an exception. Because hand craft shops still characterized the trade, Philadelphia's carpet mills employed many fewer women. In 1879 women made up only about 27 percent of the city's carpet work force, while in the east [New York and Massachusetts] they constituted 60 percent.

Kensington was one of those late nineteenth-century American neighborhoods where the variety and nature of women's work defied popular assumptions. Because women's work was often hidden or not reported, it is difficult to estimate just how many Kensington women were wage workers. It is clear, however, that in addition to women employed in shops and factories, many workers' wives did laundry or sewing or kept boarders in their homes. Because the neighborhood held so many industrial opportunities, most women shunned the traditional female occupations. Only 13 percent of Kensington's wage-earning women worked as servants; by contrast, in Philadelphia generally over a third of all employed women were servants, and nationally over half of all female nonagricultural workers were servants.

As one of Philadelphia's most densely populated industrial areas, Kensington had the aura of an immigrant city. In 1880, more than 31 percent of Philadelphia's labor force were immigrants or the children of immigrants. In Kensington, the figure must have been even higher. Among the wage-earning women, over three quarters were immigrants or the daughters of immigrants. The Germans and the Irish dominated the neighborhood. Nineteenth Ward German women generally worked as servants or seamstresses. Textile workers were more often Irish in background.

Kensington's "factory girls" provided a crucial link in the area's network of kin relations and family economies. Like Gilded Age working women generally, Kensington's wage-earning women were young and single. Only 6 percent of the ward's working women were married while half were under twenty years

old and three quarters were under twenty-five. Twenty percent of the ward's working women lived as boarders; the rest lived with their families or with widowed mothers.

For Kensington's working women, family economy and neighborhood ties encompassed both home and workplace. In 1880 most of the area's employed women came from families of skilled workers. Weavers, tailors, and loom bosses as well as bakers, tanners, shoemakers, and carpenters sent their daughters to work. Two thirds of Kensington's power loom weavers were daughters of skilled workers, and many of these were weavers' daughters. "Among carpet weavers," noted one observer, "many of the women give wages to their families or pay board." Family ties continued at the workplace. In 1880, Philadelphia's power carpet mills all housed hand looms as well. In the shops, therefore, the young women frequently encountered skilled workers who might have been their own fathers, brothers, or neighbors.

Neighborhood ties reinforced workplace contacts between power loom weavers and other workers. Kensington's "long rows of neat two and three story dwelling houses" housed a mixture of residents from skilled loom bosses to general laborers. On one block of Hope Street, for example, in the heart of the carpet district, lived a German shoemaker whose eighteen-year-old daughter worked in the carpet mills. Next door lived a house painter whose wife kept a young woman carpet weaver as a boarder. Down the block lived an Irish tanner whose fourteen-year-old daughter worked in the carpet mills. Nearby was a morocco finisher whose son also worked carpets. In addition, a score of hand loom weavers and their families made Hope Street their home.

Kensington's working women lived in a lively world of immigrant institutions and labor traditions. The neighborhood hosted numerous churches, building associations, and benevolent clubs. The area's past, however, had not always been peaceful. During the 1840's Kensington witnessed violent riots between Orangemen, many of whom were hand loom weavers, and newer Irish Catholic immigrants. According to many reports, neighborhood women figured prominently in these affairs. Many Scots-Irish weavers who later became small manufacturers in fact were Orangemen.

Kensington also hosted a long and no less unsettled trade union tradition. Carpet weavers joined printers, shoemakers, molders, and others in maintaining trade organizations from the antebellum period through the post-war era. Philadelphia artisans were prominent among the tradesmen who formed the National Labor Union during the 1860's. Several years later a group of local craftsmen formed what would became the era's largest labor organization, the Knights of Labor. Among the Knights' charter assemblies were two groups of hand loom carpet weavers.

Hand loom carpet weavers traditionally were a proud trade. Skilled weavers knew the fine details of their craft and generally spent years in apprenticeship before becoming master weavers. During the antebellum period, carpet weavers often selected their own materials and, according to early trade agreements, might refuse to work on inferior goods. The work was hard, as the heavy wooden beams "generally taxed muscles of the back and arms," but the weavers enjoyed high wages and considerable respect in the industry.

During the 1840's carpet weavers first began to experience the pressures of the factory system. Enterprising weaver-entrepreneurs began to buy several looms and combine operations under one roof. The newer factories for the first time centralized operations under one roof and made supervision of the weavers' work routines possible.

Along with the new factory arrangements came increased pressure on weavers' wages. Competition from the newly formed eastern power mills began to threaten Philadelphia's old industry. During the 1840's and 1850's Kensington hand loom weavers often staged short strikes in an effort to protect their wage rates. By the end of the 1840's weavers from both New York and Philadelphia formed a national association aimed at protecting their trade.

Until the Civil War hand loom weavers were able to keep their rates relatively high. According to one old weaver, "Time was when a guid weaver could make a substantial livin with a hand loom, a body cud raise uns family cumfertable, cud send the children to skule, pay his rent regular and live content." By 1880, he commented, "that's all changed. We that's left are jest peggin away like." Indeed, after the Civil War, increased demand combined with intensified competition from eastern power mills began to drive hand loom wages down. The trade's hand loom force declined from over three thousand workers during the early part of the century to fewer than one thousand in 1876. By 1880 not many men were left "to swing the beam."

While hand loom weavers suffered after the Civil War, carpet manufacturers in general prospered. The trade press boasted in 1886 that "not a few of the opulent carpet manufacturers of today are descendants of hard working weavers who laid the foundations of the industry and wrested substantial fortunes from the struggles of their craft." And indeed quite a few of Kensington's carpet manufacturers in 1880 could trace their roots to the artisan shop. As late as 1880 many of Kensington's smaller manufacturers might have still considered themselves artisans. Thomas Spence, for example, a forty-nine-year-old Irish weaver, ran a small shop of ten hand looms. Spence shared his Hancock Street shop with John Wilson, who owned four hand looms. Spence's two daughters worked in a nearby cotton mill and his wife took in three boarders.

Even Kensington's most prosperous power manufacturers could claim affinity with artisan experience. John Bromley, for example, patriarch of one of the city's wealthiest carpet families, began his career in his father's Lancashire worsted mill. At the age of twenty-eight Bromley went into business for himself and sought his fortune in America. Two years later he began carpet production with one hand loom but quickly increased his stock to thirty-seven and moved to a large Philadelphia shop. In 1860 Bromley's oldest sons, George and James, became partners with their father while the youngest son, Thomas, began work as a bobbin winder. After the Civil War the three brothers formed their own carpet firm. By 1881, the Bromley clan ran over 200 hand looms and 138 power looms and employed 450 operatives.

Although small manufacturers numerically dominated Philadelphia's carpet industry, the larger companies controlled the trade by the late 1870's, [when] depression threw Philadelphia's carpet industry into crisis. The crisis drove some manufacturers out of business, but it afforded grand opportunities to those who managed to hold on and expand. Within four short years between 1876 and 1880 the Philadelphia carpet industry was transformed. Where only one firm, James Dobson's giant Falls of Schuylkill mills, ran power machinery in 1876, forty-five firms operated mechanized looms in 1880.

Power production transformed the ambiance of the old carpet neighborhood. The "rapid click of the shuttle" that visitors had once described was replaced by the loud roar of machinery. Both the size and the nature of the mills changed. George Bromley's new mill, completed in 1880, covered an entire city block. His five-story brick building loomed over Front and Howard streets and included a dye house, stable, and engine shed. Henry Horner also built a new mill in 1880. His operation filled seven buildings, all carefully arranged so that the operator's entrance was in "full view of those in the office." The buildings included a two-story office complex, a six-story weaving mill with fireproof stairs, and a large elevator.

The growth of power mills signalled new rifts within Philadelphia's carpet community. The trade was now divided between hand and power manufacturers. A chaotic market and intensified competition forced the larger proprietors to seek ways of controlling the trade. In early 1878, Philadelphia's major manufacturers, led by James Dobson and Thomas Leedom, allied with their eastern competitors and formed a manufacturers' association. According to Dobson, their purpose was clear: "To give the manufacturers the needed control of the market." The carpet men knew that controlling the market meant not only bringing their smaller competitors into line but their work force as well.

When the employers announced their wage cut on 11 November 1878, the weavers responded immediately with their own version of marketplace logic. The wage question for them implied not only living standards but respectability. "Even if the employers have to compete with the east," the strikers announced, "we do not consider the cases parallel." They continued. "We are forced to do more work on inferior looms and hence lose considerable time in waiting for warps or fillings." In addition, the women argued, slack times in Philadelphia were greater than in the East and the cost of living in Kensington far exceeded that in eastern mill towns. According to one weaver, women in Lowell paid only $2.10 for board while the cheapest female boarding house in Kensington charged $3.00 per week.

The issue of power loom weaving rates affected hand loom weavers as well. If the women proved unsuccessful in countering the manufacturers' association, hand loom wages would drop also. During the early days of the power loom weavers' strike the skilled craftsmen made a decision of lasting importance. Rather than view the women as competitors in the trade the men chose to support the power loom weavers' organization and encourage their strike. Knowing that industry-wide wage rates ultimately depended on the outcome of the strike, the hand loom weavers "supplied most of the money to support the strike." As one newspaper reporter noted, "If the strike should prove unsuccessful, all their hopes would be blighted."

At the end of December 1878, the manufacturers' association announced it would end the power loom lockout and re-open all shops the day after Christmas. The lockout's end signalled the beginning of the real test between weavers and manufacturers. Saying they expected little trouble from the women "so long as the men do not join the strike," the manufacturers nonetheless asked Philadelphia's mayor for extra police guards in the mill district. When Bromley Brothers opened their doors, a guard of sixty policemen was present.

The young strikers seemed to require few lessons in the ways of worker solidarity. Each evening the strikers appeared in the streets to bring "strong influences to bear upon those who returned to work." On 30 December, shortly after the manufacturers' threat to replace the work force, five hundred women paraded through Kensington's streets carrying large banners that called for "Six Cents or Nothing" and announced "NO SURRENDER!" As the strikers marched from mill to mill, over two hundred men joined the procession. The women met with derision only from the local newspaper, which chided the hand loom weavers for "sending women to the front to do the fighting" and warned the women that the police captain "is no respector of persons and he scatters Amazons with the same impartial vigor with which he charges any other mob that happens to come his way."

The manufacturers fully expected all their old workers to come back once the lockout ended. James Kitchenman told his weavers he

had received "applications from those anxious to learn the business," but, he said, he preferred his former employees, for whom the doors would be kept open. John Dornan promised the same, saying he had had applications but saw "no necessity of considering them as yet." "It will not be long," commented one employer, "before all the old hands will want to come back."

The weavers' solid refusal to accept the wage cut and return to work surprised and then embittered the manufacturers. Some employers, like John Gay, were unable to re-open at all. The manufacturers' association vowed to train a new work force. John Dornan announced that he had "instructed many of the strikers in the knowledge of the business," and, he said, "what was done before can be done again." Another employer claimed he would seek workers from as far away as England in order to keep his looms running. By 18 January the manufacturers formally announced that if the strikers would not yield within the week they would "all be discharged and new hands taken on to run their looms."

The women's militance slowed production, but they could not entirely close down the looms. By mid-January the manufacturers successfully brought in close to one hundred new recruits and nearly a quarter of the strikers faced the loss of their jobs. Once the manufacturers directly bypassed their old hands and sought workers from outside the carpet community, the weavers were forced to admit defeat. On 22 January, after three months, the weavers reluctantly agreed to accept their employers' terms.

In calling off the strike, the women assumed that they could reclaim their positions. The manufacturers, however, had learned their own lessons from the strike. The employers refused to "turn out the girls whom they took in to learn the business." The message to the strikers was clear. One manufacturer told the strikers he hoped this action would "have a tendency to the repression of future strikes." Having trained new hands whose loyalty they now trusted, the manufacturers no longer felt any obligation to their old work force.

From the Long Strike the contending parties drew different but equally important lessons. For the women, the strike became a crucible of trade union organization. The women continued to bear allegiance to the weavers' union even after their defeat. Meetings as late as February distributed strike funds and vocalized community support. The weavers' shop committees continued to function, representing the women at the trade's semiannual rate negotiations. Within two years these committees led the weavers into the rapidly expanding Knights of Labor movement.

For manufacturers, the Long Strike held a different meaning. Although the strike lasted far beyond the expected two weeks, the employers felt they had successfully weathered the confrontation. The strike confirmed their commitment to a docile work force. It also confirmed the desire of the larger manufacturers for control over the market. According to one manufacturer, "We are more than ever impressed with the importance the enforced stoppage of machinery should have upon the demand for goods." Unbridled competition in the industry, they knew, would mean disaster for all.

The general question of control in the industry was by no means settled with the demise of the power loom weaver's strike. In March 1879, just two months after the women's defeat, the manufacturers attempted to reduce hand loom weavers' wages as well. The weavers added a new element of their own to the rapidly changing carpet industry. Led by a "secret organization" (the Knights of Labor) the weavers immediately demanded not only restoration of their old rate but an advance as well.

Demonstrating a sophisticated understanding of the structure of Philadelphia's hand loom industry, the weavers retaliated with an ingenious series of selective strikes. By targeting "only those firms we know to have outstanding orders," the weavers received continual support from their fellows still at work while placing maximum pressure on the most vulnerable small employers. Since the spring season was well upon the industry and orders had already been promised, even a few idle days could prove disastrous. Within a few days the two firms agreed to the weavers' terms. The trade's official journal marveled, "No more successful strike was ever inaugurated in our city." By May the weavers had forced most of the city's hand loom shops to adopt the higher rates. "Oddly enough," observed one manufacturer, "while the power loom weavers, after a stubborn resistance of three months against a reduction had to finally submit, the hand loom weavers have in most instances been able to carry their points against the employers notwithstanding that hand loom work was thought to be doomed to early extinction."

The weavers' strike provided larger manufacturers an opportunity to initiate plans for industrial order and stability. The trade's journal recommended what it called "a cooperative league between weavers and manufacturers." Asserting the weavers' own trade union motto, "In union there is strength," the journal declared, "The evils resulting from a mis-understanding or lack of sympathy between employers and employed are obviously detrimental to both." In late May weavers' representatives met with employers from half the city's carpet shops and formed a committee of ten weavers and ten employers. This committee was to set the weaving scale and "see that the plan is carried out." By 9 June a scale was agreed upon that represented an overall increase for weavers and was to be re-negotiated by the same body every six months. Greeting the agreement with obvious relief, the trade journal commented, "The manufacturers would now have a definite base upon which to treat with customers." In return for the wage increase the weavers agreed not to strike in shops paying the scale.

The new alliance signaled war within the industry. Many of the smaller owners claimed they could not afford the new rates. A few larger firms opposed the alliance simply out of a stubborn anti-union sentiment. Thomas Leedom declared he wanted to "run the business [my] own way." Boggs & White refused to join the combination, claiming they could not afford the rate, and Robert Huston refused to join any organization with his employees. He favored, instead, "separate organizations of weavers and manufacturers."

Those firms committed to the alliance were ruthless in their pursuit of order in the trade. James Judge immediately contributed five hundred dollars to the weavers' strike fund and vowed to give as much more "to force this thing through." John Shegog called upon his fellows to pay their hands "the same as his neighbor" and counseled the weavers to "strike against those not cooperating." The combination proved highly successful. By July only a few small firms operated outside the scale. After eight months of strife stability appeared to have been achieved.

For hand loom weavers, however, the new equilibrium proved a pyrrhic victory. In the short run, many of the city's smaller firms were forced out of business, thus increasing the crisis of unemployment. In the long run, the larger firms used the period of labor stability to consolidate their resources and ultimately eliminate the more inefficient hand looms entirely. After 1879 the number of power looms in Philadelphia rose dramatically. One manufacturer observed, "If there had been no strikes there would have been no power looms in Kensington." John Dornan announced that he planned to sell all his hand looms and replace them with power. John Bromley also declared he would employ no more men on his looms and the carpet trade journal announced that "hand looms are for sale throughout Kensington."

The crisis in Kensington's carpet shops during 1878–1879 consolidated both weavers' and manufacturers' organizations. Indirectly, it also assured women power loom weavers a central place in the industry for at least the next decade. Although the women failed to achieve their demands during the Long Strike, they were more successful the following year when they won a wage increase. As a result of the Long Strike, labor organizer Henry Skeffington claimed to have brought the power loom carpet weavers into the Knights of Labor. The visible record indicates that when the Knights officially admitted women in 1881, the Kensington carpet weavers were among the first recruits. With the shoe stitchers' Pioneer Garfield Assembly, the weavers became charter lady Knights. Other Kensington carpet workers followed suit as setters, winders, and loom fixers organized their own locals. The spirit of collective organization, it seemed, informed the power mill work force much as it had the old craftsmen's shops.

✳

Through their contact with the Knights of Labor, the carpet weavers entered the larger world of labor reform at a most decisive period in the history of American workers' movements. For the decade of the 1880's the Knights of Labor captured the national imagination as the representatives of a vast field of skilled trade unionists and unskilled factory workers, immigrant and native-born workers, and intellectual and radical republican reformers. Equally forceful was its critique of corporate industrial power and articulation of a counter-vision of cooperation, equality, and social responsibility.

At its height, during the Great Upheaval of mid-decade, the Knights' movement attracted almost one million members and countless other sympathizers. Founded in 1869 by a small group of skilled craftsmen, the Knights determined to spread the "benefits of organization" to all productive citizens "irrespective of party, race or social standing" and "irrespective of sex" as well. Schooled in an egalitarian republican

With a long-standing tradition of collective organization and labor action, the women carpet weavers of Kensington were among the first female workers admitted to the Knights of Labor. Although women made up about 10 percent of the Knights's membership and held positions of responsibility in the organization, their activism often earned them criticism from their male colleagues, other women, and the popular press of the day

tradition, the Knights believed in equal rights for women. Terence V. Powderly, the Order's grand master workman for thirteen years, told his followers, "The rights of the sexes are co-equal. . . . The working women of America ask for the cooperation of men . . . as a right to which they are entitled by reason of the nobility of toil no matter by whom performed."

The congruence of trade unionism and broad-based social reform in the Knights of Labor was particularly important for Gilded Age working-class women. For the first time women had access to a national labor movement, committed in principle to equal rights and pledged to support their workplace struggles. The nature of women's activities within the Knights shaped

a world outside the traditional domestic sphere. Workplace actions combined with educational and cultural activities to encompass a visible public role for women.

In Richmond, Virginia's late summer heat of 1886, sixteen women caucused together at the Knights of Labor General Assembly. Amidst the smoke and noise of the Order's annual national meeting, the women developed a plan that they hoped would encourage the organization of women into the Knights' rapidly expanding movement. "As this is certainly work that can only be done by women," Philadelphia saleswoman Mary Hanifin announced, "we think we should be accorded the privilege of forming an association inside the Knights of

Labor." The purpose of the women's department, Hanifin told the delegates, would be "to investigate the abuses to which our sex is subjected by unscrupulous employers, to agitate the principles which our Order teaches of equal pay for equal work and the abolition of child labor." With little debate or opposition the assembled Knights approved the women's committee and appointed Amsterdam knit-goods worker Leonora M. Barry general investigator of women's work. As a member of the Order's general executive board, Barry was to receive a salary and "devote all her time to the work."

The women's committee in Richmond united for the first time the expanding numbers of working-class women within the Knights. Beginning during the early 1880's in the urban centers of Philadelphia, New York, and Chicago, women's assemblies quickly spread to other parts of the country, forming a small but significant force within the labor movement. In 1887, Leonora Barry estimated that about 65,000 women belonged to the Order. This figure represented about 10 percent of the Knights' total membership, just under the percentage of women in the work force generally. During the 1880's the Knights chartered over four hundred local assemblies that included women. Of these, two thirds were "ladies' locals," while the others were mixed assemblies of men and women.

Women came to the Knights from widely varying occupational backgrounds as well as from every geographic region of the country. Textile workers comprised about a quarter of all women's local assemblies. These locals, mainly in eastern industrial towns, were among the Order's largest assemblies. The Yonkers carpet weavers, for example, claimed fifteen hundred members in 1884 and the Haverhill shoe stitchers numbered over one thousand. Most women's assemblies were of a more moderate size. Indianapolis' Martha Washington Local, for example, numbered only forty members. Other midwestern assemblies included textile and clothing workers, tobacco workers, and housekeepers and domestic servants. Al-

though the bulk of Knights' female membership centered in the East and Midwest, women joined assemblies in the West and South as well. Locals of school teachers, miners' wives, and waitresses dotted western states like Colorado, Montana, and California. Southern locals, while generally small in size, were widespread. Virginia women, for example, chartered more local assemblies than any state except New York. Southern locals included farm hands, servants, tobacco workers, and housewives. Many southern assemblies included black as well as white members. Although the locals were usually racially distinct, the Knights became the first labor organization to include black women under its banner.

The Knights' appeal rested in part on their broad definition of the "producing class." Unlike the craft unions, the Knights invited all productive citizens to join their organization. Only liquor dealers, lawyers, bankers, and professional politicians were excluded from membership. The Knights thus reached beyond wage-earning women and industrial workers to organize domestic servants and housewives as well. Ladies' locals encompassed both housewives and employed women sometimes together and sometimes in distinct assemblies. For the first time the labor movement recognized women's major arena of employment. Domestic workers, housewives, servants and housekeepers represented a quarter of all women's local assemblies. Cooks in Georgia, black parlor maids in Arkansas, and housekeepers in Illinois all became lady Knights.

By addressing housewives as well as wage earners, the Knights opened important options for working-class women. Defining productive toil by a moral rather than a strictly economic yardstick, the Order offered women a role in the movement not directly dependent upon their status in the labor market. One female correspondent to *John Swinton's Paper* referred to "the housekeeping wives of laboring men" as a "class of people" whose conditions—long hours, a subsistence standard of living—were no better than that of female wage earners. Another woman informed Chicago's Knights, "The wives of nine out of ten laboring men work more hours per day than you do."

As a self-conscious microcosm of the society it was trying to build, the Order extended its claims to the entire family. Married or single, wage earner or housewife, women were encouraged to join the "noble endeavor." Married women were encouraged to attend local assembly meetings and even to bring their children. A Michigan Knight commented that in his area "the sisters have enough sense to take their babies along with them and thereby not be detained from the meeting."

Like other Victorian thinkers, the Knights celebrated the family unit and sought to use their organization to strengthen familial bonds in a variety of ways. The *Journal of United Labor* approvingly quoted Republican orator and free thinker Robert Ingersoll, who observed: "The family is the heart of all society. If we have no family we can have no community, no township, no state, no nation. The greatest patriots are those who seek to preserve the family intact; the most unpatriotic are those who disintegrate the family by compelling women and children to toil for scanty subsistence." During the mid-1880's a number of labor newspapers that had been carrying women's columns initiated children's pages as well. The columns included games and stories as well as practical advice. The Detroit *Labor Leaf* advised all boys and girls, "Recollect when you hear of a strike that somebody's father is trying to make things easier for you and always remember to be honorable to union men and women." The Knights' moral code strongly condemned any abuse of home or family. Along with embezzlement and slander, the Knights counted desertion, drunkenness, or wife beating as grounds for expulsion.

While it is unlikely that any contemporary would have faulted the Knights' emphasis on private morality in a family setting, the Knights' emphasis on women's public role did encoun-

ter opposition within as well as outside the workers' movement. Although the Knights' official rhetoric unambiguously encouraged women to join the Order, many men did not accept their sister Knights willingly. According to Leonora Barry, "There are some who reject a woman simply because she is a woman." To those working men who feared women's competition in the labor market, Barry warned, "Unless the wages of women are raised to those of men, men must sink to the level of the wages of women." Only through organization would the movement be assured a respectable level of wages for women and hence for the class in general.

Other Knights worried about the moral implications of women in their organization. George Bennie, a loyal Knight from Erie, Pennsylvania, confided his hesitations to Powderly. "I submit, sir," he wrote, "that it was never meant that men and women should sit in each other's company from half past seven at night until eleven o'clock p.m. in an assembly of the Knights of Labor. . . . Before I would allow my wife to rise up amongst a lot of men I would leave the Knights a thousand times over and bear the brand of scab or anything else they chose to put upon me." Powderly tried to reassure Bennie and urged him to include his wife in the labor movement. "I regret that you entertain so poor an opinion of your wife," the grand master workman wrote, "as to say of her that you would not allow her to mix among a lot of men who are sworn to defend her life interest and reputation, . . . who are pledged to aid and sustain her. . . . She does not unsex herself by going where her father, brother or lover goes in the evening. If the assembly is a bad place for a woman to go it is a bad place for the man to go."

An equally serious obstacle facing the women's committee came from women themselves. Too many women, Barry wrote, "are entirely ignorant of the economic and industrial question." Although women often accepted minor leadership roles as secretaries, treasurers, and judges in their local assemblies, few became visible leaders within the movement. Grand Master Workman Powderly frequently received letters from women's assemblies requesting permission to appoint a man as their master workman. Despite the rhetorical support for women's role in the movement, many women were reluctant to assume leadership.

Women who stepped actively into the labor movement often faced abuse and condescension from the popular press of the day. Unsympathetic local newspapers, for example, commonly referred to trade union women as "amazons."

Employers' general distrust of the Knights also made women's organizing all the more difficult. In 1888, Barry reported that her organizing tour had met with poor response because so many women feared "being fired." Indeed, the previous year Barry's visit to a silk mill resulted in the dismissal of Annie Conby, the woman who had shown her around. After that episode Barry concluded, "I was obliged to refrain from going through establishments where owners were opposed to our Order lest some of our members be victimized."

The difficulty of organizing women combined with the Order's belief in education and cooperation led Barry and the women's committee to concentrate on education and cooperative activities. Putting principle into action, many women experimented with cooperative production.

Women's cooperatives were widespread although generally short-lived. In Indianapolis the Martha Washington Assembly initiated a cooperative underwear factory to "give employment to unemployed women and also to give the laborers the profit of their labor." Lady Knights in Danville, Massachusetts, formed a cooperative underwear factory and urged men in the order to "help the noble women on to success." Massachusetts shoe stitchers formed a cooperative stitching room, as did their sisters in Philadelphia and in Binghamton, New York. In addition, Knights in many neighborhoods and towns formed consumer cooperatives designed to help members keep down the cost of living.

Lady Knights extended their notion of cooperation to housework as well as wage labor. Picking up the arguments of contemporary domestic reformers like Melissina Fay Pierce, some Knights recommended cooperative housekeeping. "Only cooperation," wrote one woman, "offers escape for the overtired housekeeper." She assured her readers that "there are many ways in which housemothers can help one another that will serve to lighten daily toil and increase happiness." One cooperative scheme called simply for "neighborly neighbors to work together: Let their bread making all be done one day and let them take turns at baking it, even including the making of it. One doing it one week, the other the next. It entails upon the one extra work for that week, but she finds compensation in being exempt from this duty the succeeding two, three or four weeks." Following this suggestion, Toledo's Joan of Arc Assembly formed a home-baked-goods cooperative, and New York tenement women reported a saving of nearly 50 percent in their weekly budgets.

Taking the Order's constitution literally, women shaped their local assemblies into social reform clubs as well as trade union centers. The Order commonly asserted that "the local assembly is not a mere trade union, it is more and higher." Ladies' locals sponsored entertainments, educational sessions, and fund-raising events, all geared toward uniting the producers' community and promoting the values of the labor movement.

Ladies' assemblies often resembled women's reform clubs in their atmosphere and activities. Like the temperance movement, the Knights of Labor brought women together in friendly parlor meetings to discuss the issues of the day and to plan strategy. The Knights promised women a respectable forum for their public interests.

Lady Knights greeted new members in a warm, familiar atmosphere and introduced them to labor's cultural and literary world as well as to the business of labor organizing. Local Assembly No. 481, for example, initiated new members with singing and general handshaking. Then the local conducted its business. Afterward the members were treated to various educational and cultural activities. One sister read essays, and a fellow Knight and painter, C. W. Hoffman, exhibited his works. The meeting ended with a labor lesson from the Bible.

The local assembly gave working-class women a forum in which they could debate the major political issues of the day. Through their range of activity in the Knights' movement, women were encouraged to become informed and active citizens. Women could listen to lectures on the labor question or the land problem in Ireland as well as on spiritualism, temperance, or the woman question. Women's columns in the labor press combined news of women's strikes and industrial conditions with lessons in cooperation, suggestions for self-education, and advice on domestic concerns. The "Labor Book News Agency" printed in every local labor newspaper recommended reading for local assemblies and offered books at discount rates, particularly to locals desiring to establish libraries or book exchanges. For women, the lists and libraries represented a crucial link to the Knights' movement, which expected them to be as educated in the "questions of the day" as their brothers.

The Knights' list included books on the woman question, such as August Bebel's *Women and Socialism,* Margaret Fuller's *Woman in the Nineteenth Century,* and the feminist lectures of Lillie Devereux Blake. The lists also suggested readings in political economy, science, and literature. Among the recommended authors were Karl Marx, Ferdinand LaSalle, Charles Darwin, George Eliot, and Samuel Taylor Coleridge. One woman encouraged the read-

ers of *John Swinton's Paper* to take their education seriously. "Human misery must be cured and not diminished," she wrote, "but in order to cure, one must know the cause of the malady. Think then, think hard, working girl! To find out the *cause,* and when you have done so, new duties, new obligations toward yourself and society are in store for you."

The Order's literary overtures lessened the isolation of women in the home and brought them into contact with contemporary political and cultural trends. Domestic advice in the columns of the labor press served a similar end. Suggestions on "Food for Hard Workers" were interspersed with reminders that "to organize is justly one of women's rights." Another note informed women: "Fourteen states now grant the right to women to vote in school board elections. Demand this in your state." Lists of famous women appeared side by side with articles on painless childbirth, comments on food adulteration, and advice on child-rearing.

The Knights of Labor supported women's rights in a broad sense and forged what might be termed a labor feminism. Women in the Knights insisted upon full equality with men, including equal pay, equal rights within the organization, and equal respect for their productive work whether in the home or in the factory. The lady Knights did not challenge the notion of a domestic sphere for women. Rather, like many nineteenth-century feminists, they believed in a particularly feminine sensibility, one that upheld the values of hearth and home and that could at the same time infuse the public world with a more moral, humane, and cooperative character. The broad reform vision of the Knights provided women with a link between their industrial concerns and the issues addressed by the contemporary women's movements, most notably suffrage and temperance.

The Knights vocally supported women's suffrage and frequently welcomed suffrage speakers to their local assemblies and lecture platforms. One woman told John Swinton's readers, "If women have the right of suffrage it will double the number of voices in the hands of the working people."

Despite their support for the principle of suffrage, the lady Knights differed from the suffrage movement in important ways. Women in the Order, like many trade union activists later, tended to see industrial problems as their major concerns, while the suffrage movement increasingly focused on the vote as the key to women's equality. In 1886 the Knights' committee on women's work said there was "more important work for women to do before they are prepared to vote in the affairs of the nation." The *Journal of United Labor* focused on the central problem for working women when it observed, "In the matter of the individual relation of woman to her employer, while the ballot would doubtless make her an important factor in social and political economies, it does not touch the more important business relations."

The issue that most clearly united lady Knights with the Gilded Age women's movement was temperance. The notions of sobriety and respectability easily complemented their vision of domesticity and the critique of competitive industrial America. "The cause of intemperance," wrote one lady Knight, "is the industrial condition. The cure—social and industrial reform." Another woman noted, "The piece work system does more to drive men to liquor, insanity and suicide than anything else. . . . Doing away with the piece work system will in a great measure aid temperance." Leading women from the temperance movement, most notably Frances Willard from the Women's Christian Temperance Union (WCTU), often spoke at Knights' events, drawing the links between industrial reform and the issue of drink. Willard praised the Order's stand on equal pay and temperance and observed: "I see that the Knights of Labor are also the Knights of the new chivalry. Who knows but these men shall bring in the new republic?" For Gilded Age women the temperance movement represented the most inclusive critique of social and domestic arrangements. The organization of the WCTU, in particular, afforded women of varying class and ethnic backgrounds an opportunity for independent political action. Infused with the energy and vision of Willard's "do everything" strategy, the WCTU became perhaps the most significant women's movement of the century.

For working-class women the issue of temperance held special importance. In many working-class communities the saloon was the traditional meeting place for trade unions as well as for political organizations. Lady Knights, and a significant number of men, argued that using the saloon as a meeting place not only gave support to the monopolistic brewing interests but also encouraged division within the family by separating the husband from his wife and children. The Knights proposed their own local assemblies as alternatives to saloon culture and posed their movement as the alternative focus for working-class community life. Willard noted the success of this effort, saying, "The Local Assembly in every town and village draws young men away from the saloon, its debates help to make them better citizens, and thus the mighty Labor movement has, by outlawing the saloon socially, done more for temperance than we who devote our lives to its propaganda have been able to achieve in the same period."

The Knights touched deeply held concerns of Gilded Age working-class women. The organization they forged legitimated women's participation in the world of labor reform and politics. The significance of the Knights' experience for women can be seen in the next generation of labor and reform activists. Many early twentieth-century labor organizers and social reformers testified to the importance of the Knights in their early education. Mary Harris Jones ("Mother Jones"), the "Miner's Angel," who remained active until her death in the

1930's, recalled her experience in the Order's early days. "The Knights of Labor was the labor organization of those days," she wrote. "I used to spend my evenings at their meetings, listening to splendid speakers." Mary Elizabeth Lease, the well-known populist organizer, began her career as a Knights' lecturer and in 1887 became master workman of one of Kansas' largest local assemblies. Leonora O'Reilly, who served on the board of the Women's Trade Union League, turned to the Knights in 1886, after having accompanied her mother to "labor and radical meetings." Agnes Nestor, also active in the Women's Trade Union League, was too young to join the Order, but her father, a staunch Knight of Labor, taught her trade union principles. Alzina P. Stevens, a "bright and brainy little woman" who taught herself the printing trade and became the first woman member of Toledo's Typographical Union No. 63, also used her experience in the Knights to become an active labor reformer and trade union advocate throughout the populist era and into the twentieth century. During the 1890's Stevens became assistant factory inspector for the State of Illinois. She later joined Jane Addams at Hull House and became active in social work and juvenile reform. Although scant records of lady Knights survive, those that we have attest to the impact of the Order among working-class women of the Gilded Age and to the important part the Knights played in contributing to a wide range of reform concerns.

The Knights' movement opened unique opportunities for Gilded Age working-class women. An ideology of equal rights within the movement legitimated women's role in workplace politics as well as in broad-based labor reform. Women's locals functioned not simply as ladies' auxiliaries but as integral parts of the movement's cultural world. Reaching out simultaneously to wage-earning women and to working men's wives, the Knights extended their jurisdiction to include all members of the working-class community. The labor movement defined its mission broadly to encompass issues outside the strict realm of trade unionism. For women this proved critical. Within the context of the labor movement women could address issues ranging from child-rearing philosophy through suffrage and industrial reform. Women's role in the movement—and their interest in the Knights—was tied to their role as productive citizens in their communities, not exclusively to their often short-lived careers in the labor market.

Questions for Study and Review

1. In many communities and occupations, male and female workers remained isolated from each other or actively competed against each other. What conditions in Kensington allowed for their cooperation?

2. In what ways did the Knights of Labor encourage and in what ways inhibit working women's organization?

3. How effective were late nineteenth-century strikes in changing working women's and men's relations with employers? With unions? With each other?

4. In the 1830s and 1840s, automation in factories and on farms had differential effects on women's status in the economy and the family. Compare these circumstances with those of the Kensington weavers.

Suggested Readings

Margery W. Davies, *Woman's Place is at the Typewriter: Office Work and Office Workers, 1870–1930* (1984).

Alice Kessler-Harris, "Where Are the Organized Women Workers?" *Feminist Studies* (Fall 1975).

Daniel Walkowitz, *Worker City, Company Town: Iron and Cotton Worker Protest in Troy and Cohoes, New York, 1855–1884* (1978).

Mary Blewett, *Men, Women and Work Culture: Class, Gender and Protest in the New England Shoe Industry, 1780–1910* (1988).

Patricia Cooper, *Once a Cigarmaker: Men, Women and Work Culture in American Cigar Factories, 1900–1919* (1987).

FOUR

Farmers' Wives and the New South: Women in the Southern Farmers' Alliance

Julie Roy Jeffrey

Kansas and Kensington women entered the public domain through officeholding and union organizing; Carolina women did so through the Farmers' Alliance. Prior to the Civil War, southern women were less likely than their northern counterparts to engage in public activism. In the war's aftermath, black and white women, rural and urban, poor and affluent, became increasingly involved in efforts both inside and outside the home to rebuild the South.

Despite the influx of industry into former Confederate states, agriculture continued to be the mainstay of the region's economy. At the same time, farmers in the South and the West felt increasingly pinched by indebtedness, depleted soil, and sharecropping contracts. They also felt pushed out of the national mainstream by urban and industrial growth, the benefits of which seemed concentrated in the Northeast. Through newspapers, pamphlets, lecturers, and, most important, local and state clubs, the Farmers' Alliance sought to organize the agrarian masses for social, economic, and political empowerment and protest. Urging the participation of blacks (though in separate associations) and of white women alongside white men, the Southern Alliance offered one of the most democratic programs of any organization in the post-Civil War era.

Jeffrey's study of the North Carolina Alliance reveals the new opportunities for farm wives in the areas of education, economic self-sufficiency, and even politics. Yet Jeffrey notes as well the ambivalence, on the part of both women and men, surrounding assertions of female partnership. As earlier women activists had discovered, appeals to female moral and spiritual superiority often sat uncomfortably beside demands for full equality and proclamations of natural inferiority.

Recognizing that women's cooperation was essential to agricultural modernization in the South, Alliance leaders emphasized the practical benefits of men's and women's joint efforts. At the same time, some Alliance spokesmen encouraged women to enter new industries in order to support faltering farms with wages, while spokeswomen focused on female education and moral training.

Like the Knights of Labor and Kansas civic leaders, Alliance leaders offered new opportunities for women in the late nineteenth century, opportunities eagerly grasped in part because they were framed within acceptable if expanded parameters of womanly behavior.

In the spring of 1891, Mrs. Brown, secretary of the Menola Sub-Alliance in North Carolina, welcomed an audience of delegates to the quarterly meeting of the Hertford County Farmer's Alliance. After introductory remarks to both the women and men in the audience, Brown addressed her female listeners directly.

> Words would fail me to express to you, my Alliance sisters, my appreciation of woman's opportunity of being co-workers with the brethren in the movement which is stirring this great nation. Oh, what womanly women we ought to be, for we find on every hand, fields of usefulness opening before us. Our brothers . . . are giving us grand opportunities to show them, as Frances E. Willard says, that "Drudgery, fashion and gossip are no longer the bounds of woman's Sphere."

So enthusiastically was Brown's speech received, that the County Alliance unanimously requested its publication in the official paper of the Farmers' Alliance, the *Progressive Farmer*. In a similar fashion, the Failing Creek Alliance asked the *Progressive Farmer* later that year to reprint a speech Katie Moore had delivered to them. Moore had also spoken before an audience of women and men, and she too had had some special words for the women. "'Tis not enough that we should be what our mothers were," she told them. "We should be more, since our advantages are superior. . . . This is the only order that allows us equal privileges to the men; we certainly should appreciate the privi-

"Women in the Southern Farmers' Alliance: A Reconsideration of the Roles and Status of Women in the Late 19th-Century South" by Julie Roy Jeffrey, *Feminist Studies,* Volume 3, #1/2 (1975): 72–91, by permission of the publisher *Feminist Studies,* Inc., c/o Women's Studies Program, University of Maryland, College Park, MD 20742.

lege and prove to the world that we are worthy to be considered on equal footing with them."

That the two audiences had approved of these speeches to the point of urging their wider circulation was not surprising. For the slogan of the Southern Farmers' Alliance itself was, "Equal rights to all, special privileges to none." As one Alliance publication explained, "The Alliance has come to redeem woman from her enslaved condition, and place her in her proper sphere. She is admitted into the organization as the equal of her brother . . . the prejudice against woman's progress is being removed."

Such statements about the condition of Alliance women were important, for they came from an organization which had millions of members and which was a significant force at the regional and national level in the 1880s and 1890s. In part, the Alliance was a rural protest against the inferior social, economic and political position its members felt farmers occupied in the emerging urban-industrial society. But, like civil service reformers and other protest groups in the Gilded Age, the Farmers' Alliance argued that the finely balanced two-party system responded only to the demands of special interest groups and political machines rather than to the needs of the people. Alliance members first tried to change this situation by pressing at the state level for control of monopolies and other unfriendly interests and for favorable legislation. Better public schools for rural children, state agricultural colleges, colleges for women, laws controlling the railroads, better prices for farm products were some of the goals the Alliance sought to enable rural classes to survive within a new world. As this strategy proved frustrating, about half of the Alliance membership moved into the Populist party which ran its first presidential candidate in 1892. Although the Populist party ultimately failed, it offered the most serious challenge to

The Farmers' Alliance gave southern women an opportunity to voice their concerns on economic, political, and social issues, both at public meetings and especially through letters to the *Progressive Farmer,* the official newspaper of the Alliance. The major goals of the Alliance to improve the status of agriculture and through cooperative action to help farmers achieve economic self-sufficiency are reflected in this advertisement from the *Progressive Farmer* touting "the only genuine Alliance tobacco in the world."

the two-party system in the late nineteenth century and contributed to the reshaping of the American political system.

These exhortations and demands emphasizing female equality and opportunity were important, then, because the Alliance was important, but they have an unfamiliar ring in the context of what has generally been known about sex roles and relationships in the post-Civil War South. The accepted interpretation of late nineteenth-century southern society has

argued that the model of the southern lady, submissive and virtuous, "the most fascinating being in creation . . . the delight and charm of every circle she moves in," still marked the parameters of appropriate behavior for middle-class women, though the model had been predictably weakened by the traumatic experience of civil war. As for lower-class women, this interpretation suggests, they were "not much affected by role expectations," although "farmers' wives and daughters and illiterate black women . . . in some inarticulate way doubtless helped to shape [society]" and its standards.

Yet an investigation of the Farmers' Alliance in North Carolina, where the Alliance had great success, indicates this explanation does not hold true for that state. If the North Carolina experience is at all typical of other southern Alliance states, and there is little reason to think it is not, the reality of southern attitudes toward women was more complex than recent analyses have allowed. The Civil War had been the initial catalyst for women entering new areas of activities; after the war, poverty and loss of fathers, brothers, husbands, and other male relatives forced many women to run farms, boarding houses, to become seamstresses, postmistresses, and teachers. As the traditional view of woman's sphere crumbled under the impact of the post-war conditions, at least one alternative to the older view emerged in the South—one exemplified by the case of North Carolina. Responsive to social changes stemming from war and defeat, the Alliance in the 1880s and 1890s urged women to adopt a new self-image, one that included education, economic self-sufficiency, one that made a mockery of all false ideas of gentility. The activities and behavior that the Alliance sanctioned were not only considered appropriate for middle-class women but for women on all social levels. Although evidence on the social class composition of the Alliance is limited, recent work suggests that approximately 55 percent of the North Carolina membership owned their land, about 31 percent were tenants, and 14 percent rural professionals. Since many wives and daughters joined the Alliance, it seems reasonable to assume that female membership, like male membership, crossed class lines. Certainly, the new female role was applicable to all of them. Finally, although it was not actually created by Alliance women, the new cultural model was consciously elaborated by some of them, thus offering one way of understanding how middle-class farming women, later deemed

"inarticulate" because they left so few written records, perceived and shaped their social role.

Furthermore, a case study of the North Carolina Farmers' Alliance shows that the Alliance also offered numerous rural women the rare privilege of discussing important economic and political issues with men and of functioning as their organizational equals. Few southern institutions offered women similar opportunities. The political party barred them altogether. The Methodist and Baptist churches, which with the Presbyterian claimed a majority of church members, still supported the traditional view that women ought to remain at home although they had allowed women a new area of activity in establishing female missionary societies. This expansion of their sphere was considered to be "no compromise . . . [to] female modesty and refinement," although, in reality, women could and did acquire political experience and skills in them. After 1883, North Carolina women also gained valuable organizational knowledge through their involvement in the Women's Christian Temperance Union. But the W.C.T.U., the church missionary societies and women's clubs of the 1880s were all-female organizations and thus did not offer women the chance to establish a pragmatic working relationship with men as the Alliance would do.

One other rural organization in the South, the Grange, which reached its height of popularity in North Carolina between 1873 and 1875, admitted both sexes before the Alliance did so. Unlike the Alliance, however, the Grange made clear distinctions between most of the offices and ranks women and men could hold. Nevertheless, the Grange clearly provided women with some practical organizational experience with men and, presumably, offered some kind of rough equality. Still, partly because of its Northern origins, the impact of the Grange was limited in the South. In North Carolina, the Grange's total membership never surpassed the 15,000 mark, and by the 1880s, numbers had dwindled. Moreover, since the Grange was primarily an educational body, it failed to provide the same kind of experience for southern women as the Alliance would in the 1880s and 1890s. Ostensibly apolitical, the Alliance was actually devoted to a discussion of the "science of economical government" and was deeply involved in political questions. Within the North Carolina Alliance, the spheres of women and men drew closer as both sexes voted, held office, and discussed together the stirring issues of the day as they had rarely done before.

Within the framework of the Alliance, then, southern women had the opportunity to discuss pressing economic, political, and social questions, to try out ways of behaving in mixed groups and to gain confidence in newly acquired skills. One might expect [to see] a group of women, and perhaps men, eventually emerge whose Alliance experience would lead them ultimately to demand or sympathize with the greater expansion of woman's role that the organization officially supported. Yet this never happened. At the same time that the Alliance offered new roles and organizational possibilities for women, the meaning of equality for women was constricted by the organization's main goal of reviving southern agriculture. Political rights within the Alliance were not seen as the first step toward political rights outside of the Alliance.

The evidence for this study comes from many sources. Most useful is the State Alliance paper, the *Progressive Farmer,* whose policy it was to publish the views of the Alliance membership. Few of these rural correspondents provided the leading articles for the paper, but rather they contributed letters to the correspondence page. Since these long forgotten farm women and men left virtually no other personal records, their letters, some literary, most artless, provide a crucial insight into the grassroots level of the Alliance and an important view of their responses to the opportunities the Alliance held out to them.

Initial interest in a farmers' organization in North Carolina resulted from the depressed state of southern agriculture in the 1880s. By 1886, Colonel Leonidas Polk, editor of the new agricultural weekly, the *Progressive Farmer,* was vigorously urging the paper's readers to organize local farmers' clubs as the basis for a future state wide organization. From the beginning he visualized at least some women in the clubs, for he advised they could be "elected as honorary members." Yet farmers' clubs were not to have a long life in North Carolina. By May 1887 Alliance organizers from Texas, where the agricultural order had originated, had begun to establish local Alliances in North Carolina, while a Carolinian, J. B. Barry, also began recruiting. Polk, aware of the growth potential of the Alliance, joined one of Barry's Alliances in July 1887, and was soon meeting with Texas Alliance leaders to discuss a merger between the Alliance and his farmers' clubs. After the merger was made the North Carolina Alliance grew by leaps and bounds. In the summer of 1888 the membership stood at 42,000. By 1891 the Alliance claimed 100,000 members in over 2,000 local chapters.

Requirements for membership in the Alliance, formalized in the state constitution adopted in October 1887, were far more positive to female members than Polk's farmers' clubs had been. Membership was open to rural white women and men over sixteen years of age who had "good moral character," believed in "the existence of a Supreme Being," and showed "industrious habits." While men were to pay fifty cents as an initiation fee in addition to quarterly dues of twenty-five cents, women had no required fee or dues, no doubt a recognition of their marginal economic status and their desirability as members. Membership of both sexes was essential to Alliance goals as state Alliance president, Captain Sydenham B. Alexander, indicated. The purpose of the Alliance, Alexander wrote in 1887 was "to encourage education among the agricultural and laboring classes, and *elevate to higher manhood and womanhood* those who bear the burdens of productive industry."

Alliance leaders did not leave the issue of female participation in the organization to chance but stressed it forcefully. Harry Tracy, a National Lecturer of the order, urged *"the ladies to come out and hear him,"* and warned Alliance members: "The ladies eligible must join the order before we can succeed." Despite emphatic support from the top, however, letters from local Alliances to the *Progressive Farmer,* now the official organ of the North Carolina Alliance, indicate some male resistance to the idea of female members. As the Secretary of the Davidson College Alliance explained: "I think that the ladies are best suited to home affairs." Verbal opposition to female members led one woman to comment, "They don't want us to join, and think it no place for us." Other, more subtle techniques of discouraging female membership seem to have existed. Holding meetings in places where women would be uncomfortable or feel out of place kept the number of female members down. As the correspondent from Lenoir Alliance noted, his Alliance had fifty men and one woman because meetings were held in the court house. As one frequent contributor to the *Progressive Farmer* who favored female members pointed out: "Each Sub-Alliance needs a hall. . . . We cannot urge the ladies to attend until we can seat them comfortably."

Numerous questions addressed to Polk, now secretary of the state Alliance as well as editor of the *Progressive Farmer,* indicated that even if not opposed to female membership, men were often hesitant and confused about the membership of women. A variety of questions focused on what women were eligible for membership and, if elected, what their rights should be. Were women, in fact, to have the same "rights and privileges of the male members"? Over and over again Polk replied that

women were to have equal rights and privileges; they were to vote on new members, participate in all Alliance business and to know "all the secret words and signs" of the order.

If some men were unenthusiastic about female members, so too were some of the women. As one Allianceman explained: "Our female friends seem to repose great confidence in our ability to conduct affairs of the Alliance without their direct union and assistance. Indeed, our wives, mothers and sisters have as much as they can do to attend their own business." Other letters from men more enthusiastic about female members agreed that women refused to join because they were "too modest, or think it out of their line." There was even some outright female opposition to Alliance membership as one "bright and energetic young lady," the first woman to join the Alliance in Vance County, discovered when her friends ridiculed "the idea of young ladies joining." The traditional view of woman's sphere, then, constituted a barrier to active female participation in the Alliance, and it was one which female members consciously tried to undermine. When Alliancewomen wrote to the *Progressive Farmer* they frequently urged the other women to overcome feelings of timidity. "Dear Sisters, go to work; don't stay home and die, then say I have something else to do; that will never do," wrote Addie Pigford. "Sisters, what are you doing?" asked Mrs. Carver. "There is work for us to do, and we shall not be found wanting. We can help in many ways, and we must do it."

Opposition and hesitation on the subject of female members obviously existed as the reports of local and county Alliances and male and female correspondents to the *Progressive Farmer* show. But evidence suggests that the message that women were to be encouraged as vigorous participants of the Alliance eventually came through clearly to most local groups. By 1889, for example, the State Line Alliance reported it was planning to discuss the desirability of female members. Rather ruefully, the writer commented: "That indicates *how far we are behind,* but we do not intend to remain there." Questions about membership requirements and privileges, membership breakdowns sent into the *Progressive Farmer,* and local minute books, indicate that women were presenting themselves for membership. Not only did the wives and daughters of male members join but so too did unattached women. As the Alliance grew so did the number of women in the organization. In some cases, women comprised one-third to one-half of local groups. "We can work just as well as the brethren," pointed out one Alliance woman. "If we want to derive good from the Alliance, we must work in love and harmony with our fellow-man."

As thousands of women responded to the Alliance's invitation to join "the great army of reform," there were hints that women felt increasingly at ease in their new organizational role. Although it is difficult to recover the perceptions of these rural women, their letters to the *Progressive Farmer* from 1887 through 1891 can serve as an imperfect measure for their thoughts and feelings about their participation in the Alliance.

One of the most striking aspects of the women's correspondence is the initial hesitation about writing to a newspaper at all. Only one woman communicated to the editor in 1887. Gradually, however, women began to send letters, many of them conscious of departing from past patterns of behavior. "Being a farmer's wife, I am not in the habit of writing for the public prints," wrote the first female correspondent of 1888, a certain Mrs. Hogan who was concerned about stray dogs. Replied the second, "Mr. Editor:—I have never written anything for the public to read, but I feel just now, after reading Mrs. Hogan's trouble . . . that I want to tell her I truly sympathize with her." Other correspondents in 1888 and 1889 often began their letters with the polite request for a

"small space" for a few words from a farm woman or with the phrase, "I am but a female." "I suppose your many subscribers will not expect much from a female correspondent," wrote one corresponding secretary, "and if so, they will not be disappointed when they read this article, but if I can be of any service to the Alliance by putting in my little mite, I am willing to do what I can." By 1890 such protestations and expressions of humility had disappeared. A series of letters from Evangeline Usher exemplifies the growing confidence on the part of women that their letters and reports on Alliance activities were appropriate and acceptable. In an early letter, Usher urged other women to write to the paper, with the typical hope that Polk would "give us a little space somewhere." Describing herself as fearful that her letter would go into the wastebasket, she further explained that her feelings of delicacy would prevent her from contributing her Alliance's news regularly. "I already imagine I see Brother 'R' smiling ludicrously at the idea." Within a few months, however, Usher wrote again, confessing "a kind of literary pride in seeing my name in print." By 1889, she could begin her letter, "I feel like I must intrude again, and as I am quite independent of all disfavor, I do not care whether you like the intrusion or not." Though Usher was unusually outspoken, her growing boldness correlates with the straightforward and secure tone women gradually adopted in writing to the paper and suggests their greater feelings of confidence within the organization.

Local reports, letters, and records also give information on another crucial consideration concerning women's involvement in the Alliance. If women only sat on the back benches during Alliance meetings, listening silently while men discussed the great economic and political issues of the day, their membership would have been insignificant. If, on the other hand, women actually helped to run the organization and helped contribute to its success, even if they were not equal in every respect to men, then the Alliance was an important departure from the typical southern organization.

Although there is no indication that women were ever elected to the office of president of local Alliances, they were occasionally, at least, voted into important positions. The Jamestown Alliance Minute Book, for example, records that a year after the subject of female members was first discussed, a woman was elected as assistant secretary; she declined, but two months later was elected as treasurer. Other women held the office of secretary, with the responsibility not only for making "a fair record of all things necessary to be written," but also for "receiving all moneys due" and for communicating with Secretary Polk. Still others became lecturers or assistant lecturers, both crucial positions since they were to give addresses, lead discussions, and furnish "the material of thought for the future consideration of the members." Women as well as men read papers "on subjects of importance for the benefit of the order." In one Alliance, records show that women conducted the business on an Alliance meeting day. At the county level where meetings were held quarterly, women were included in the membership count on which representation was based, were delegates, and at least one was elected vice-president. Others gave key addresses to large audiences. Women could also be found at the annual meetings of the state Alliance. As the *Progressive Farmer* warmly replied to two women who had written to ask if they could go to the meeting, "You are not only *allowed,* but you will be most cordially welcomed to a seat." Though such evidence is fragmentary, it does imply that many women took an active part in running Alliance affairs.

Women participated in the Alliance in a variety of other areas too. Several letters to the *Progressive Farmer* noted that women subscribed to the State Business Agency Fund, an important Alliance effort aimed at eliminating middlemen in purchasing fertilizers, groceries, and agricultural goods. Alliance leaders urged local groups to donate at least fifty cents a member to the fund. A few reports show women carrying their financial share. Women also sent in news to the paper, wrote articles, and worked to increase the subscription list, a job which Polk and other leaders saw as vital to Alliance success since they argued that earlier efforts to arouse farmers had foundered on ignorance and lack of proper information.

If not all women were active members in the Alliance, enough were to be reported and praised in the *Progressive Farmer.* Clearly, many women welcomed the chance to work in the organization. Moreover, as their letters indicate, they shared men's interest in the compelling subjects of the day: agricultural cooperation, the role of combines and trusts in creating the farming crisis, the need to diversify southern agriculture, all standard themes for discussion and instruction in Alliance meetings and reading material. But as much as women were involved with such topics, as much as they enjoyed the social conviviality of the Alliance, many must have agreed with the woman who reminded her Alliance, "This is the only order that allows us equal privileges to the man; we certainly should appreciate the privilege."

North Carolina Alliance's support of "equal rights" for women within the organization and of the new role described for them outside it may seem startling, yet it corresponded to the reality of life for southern women in the late 1880s and early 1890s. It would have been surprising if the changes in southern society following the Civil War had failed to result in some ideological reconsideration of women's status. Yet the Alliance's stance was not merely a response to social change in the South. The National Alliance upheld the concept of equal rights. State leaders recognized that the farmer and his wife worked as an agricultural unit. It made sense to involve both in the Alliance for as one farmer pointed out, "We know we can scarcely dispense with the labor of our wives and children on the farm." Furthermore, leaders reasoned that the Alliance could not count on continued enthusiasm and good attendance unless women as well as men came to meetings. "Meetings must be interesting" to spur membership and attendance, one pamphlet pointed out, "and the first step in this direction is to get more women and young people into the Order." At least one member agreed. The presence of women, he wrote, "cheers us on." Clearly, if the Alliance and its work were to prosper, both sexes would have to be involved.

The social composition of the leadership suggests another important reason for the Alliance support for women. Although men like Colonel Polk and Sydenham Alexander, president of the State Alliance, had been or were farmers genuinely concerned with agricultural problems, they were also members of the rural upper-class. Polk had had a long career as a planter, army officer, legislator, commissioner of agriculture, and editor. Alexander had headed the state Grange in the 1870s. Other leaders were teachers, doctors, and clergymen. As members of North Carolina's elite, these men partially accepted the traditional view of woman as the beacon of social morality. "If our organization means anything," one prominent supporter of female members wrote, "it means a moral reformation, morality must be our guide. The ladies are and always have been the great moral element in society; therefore *it is impossible to succeed without calling to our aid the greatest moral element in the country.*"

This was how Alliance leaders conceived of the role and importance of women within their organization. But women themselves had their own ideas about their role, as an examination of their letters to the *Progressive Farmer* reveals. The writers stressed their pride in farm life, the need to throw off female passivity, the vital importance of women to the Alliance effort. "While it has been remarked that women are necessary evil," wrote Fannie Pentecost, "let us by our untiring energy, and zeal show them

that it is a mistake. . . . We should devise plans and means by which we can assist those who have to bear the burdens of life." In the Alliance, another woman pointed out, women had the unique opportunity of helping men "in the thickest of the fight" by encouragement, prayers, self-denial, and endurance. Some correspondents clearly saw their role as one of moral support, but others visualized a more active role, using words like helpmate or companion to describe how they saw themselves.

That women perceived themselves occasionally as the major support for men corresponds with the way in which Alliance leaders visualized them. But there was a sharp edge to the role of moral guide as some correspondence revealed. Again, Evangeline Usher provides an insight into this kind of thinking. In a letter of September 1890, Usher wrote that someone had recently sent her a compliment, "saying they were just as strong an Alliance boy as I was an Alliance girl." Evangeline's rather surprising comment was "Brother . . . I only hope you are, for I am one that believes in working and not talking." Other letters and articles convey a similar skepticism of men. "Why," asked assistant lecturer Lizzie Marshburn, "is it that the farmer and laboring class generally, have got no self-will or resolution of their own? . . . as a general rule they have been ever ready to link their destinies with any political aspirant who can get up and deliver a flowery address of misrepresentation." Allie Marsh told her audience at a Randolph County meeting, "We come to these meetings with an unwritten agreement to take things as they are." Women, she said, were "perfectly content" that men exercise political rights "as long as you are vigilant in making [the ballot box] as efficient as possible." Yet the remainder of her speech suggested that she had found the men "wanting." A letter from still another woman acidly observed, "Some men can't see beyond their nose."

Although most women and men probably agreed upon the function of women's participation within the Alliance, it appears that some Alliance women saw the matter differently and that they suspected that the commonly accepted view of women as the quiet impetus behind male reformers was inadequate. Their letters convey misgivings about the ability of men to persist in their support of reform and implicitly suggest that these women perceived themselves as steadier leaders than the men. As one Alliance woman explained: "My sisters, this is something we should know, that our names are on this list [of reformers] and [we should] regret we could not be allowed this opportunity years ago, for no doubt our country would be in a much better condition to-day had we taken this step." Added another, apparently filled with misgivings about men: "I would earnestly *beg the brethren* when they put their hands to the plow *not to look back . . . if they do,* they will not reap the harvest we all desire. *We must work* and *wait,* and not grow discouraged." Yet, despite these indications that women suspected that they rather than men were possibly the most steadfast and reliable leaders of reform, they were hardly ready to challenge openly the Alliance's basic assumptions because of the positive support the Alliance was already providing for southern women in many areas of life.

Indeed, women's rights within the organization was only part of the Alliance's reformulation of women's status. A woman's role in the Alliance was understood to parallel the more significant role the Alliance suggested women could enjoy in society at large. The *Progressive Farmer's* policy of reporting on the achievements of women who were doctors, surgeons, journalists, lawyers, government workers, even pastors, indicated the wide range of possibilities beyond the conventional one of marriage and motherhood. These career options, of course, depended on educating women, a goal that the Alliance and its official newspaper consistently supported as part of the general attempt to improve all educational facilities for "farmers and laborers."

"The ability of girls," the *Progressive Farmer* stated flatly, "has been found equal to that of boys." As the resolutions of the 1890 State Alliance meeting show, the Alliance went on record that year not only in favor of public schools for boys and girls but also in support of "ample [state] appropriations [for] the training and higher education of females." The paper explained, "The lopsided system of education in North Carolina . . . provides for the education of men and neglects that of women. Gentlemanly instinct, to say nothing of justice and mercy, requires that women should be given as good a chance for education as men possess. . . . Give the noble girls of the State—those who are not able to go to our expensive colleges a chance to get an education," the paper urged. Responding to pressure from the Alliance and other interested groups, the legislature of 1891 appropriated $10,000 a year to establish a normal and industrial training school for girls.

The reason for the Alliance's concern with women's education becomes obvious in the *Progressive Farmer's* discussions of private girls' schools. Traditionally, these schools had stressed teaching female accomplishments to the would-be southern lady of means. But now the *Progressive Farmer* enthusiastically reported, Salem Female Academy had expanded its offering by establishing a business course featuring music, telegraphy, phonography (shorthand), typing and bookkeeping. Such a course, the *Progressive Farmer* pointed out, was most desirable with its "studies of a practical character, fitting the learners for active avocations when required to depend upon their own efforts in the battle of life." Other schools, the paper urged, ought to follow Salem Academy's example. The fundamental point, the paper emphasized, was that *all* young women of *all* social classes should be prepared for jobs. It was true, of course, that education would help poor girls by enabling them "to make an honest living," but all women ought to learn to be self-sufficient and self-supporting.

Women themselves stressed the importance of economic self-sufficiency. They did not want to "be entirely dependent upon the bounties of others" if they lost their protectors. And, as an additional point in favor of education, one Alliance woman brought up the important question of marriage. Self-sufficiency would allow women to marry because they wanted to, not because they needed financial support. Thus education of a certain kind would help women avoid the "fatal blunder," incompatibility in marriage.

Alliance support for practical education for women was based on a rejection of the concept of gentility which had been such a fundamental component of the idea of the southern lady. The search for a "pale and delicate" complexion, the interest in elaborate clothing and accomplishments were all denounced in the pages of the *Progressive Farmer*. These traditional female concerns were misguided since they undermined the importance of hard work and, thus, the opportunities for female independence. The idea that labor was degrading, the *Progressive Farmer* reminded its readers, was just another unfortunate remnant of slavery, and, in fact, contributed in an important way to poverty itself. True Alliance men and women wanted young people "to see that it is no disgrace, but a high honor, to know how to work and to be able to do it." The feminine ideal was the woman who was independent and practical, educated either to support herself or to marry wisely.

Better education for both sexes was an issue with which many Alliance members sympathized, hoping their children's future would be more promising than their own. Yet the Alliance could not concern itself exclusively with the new options for young women who still had their lives ahead of them. With so many

adult female members, the Alliance also considered how to reshape life styles for those women who would never leave the farm for school or a job. "Is the life of the Farmer's wife under present systems, calculated to give her virtue and intelligence full play," asked the Southern Alliance paper, the *National Economist*. "Is she not a slave and a drudge in many cases?" The *Progressive Farmer* gave the answer: there were "thousands and tens of thousands" of farmers' wives "worked to their graves." Improving this dreary situation necessitated a multipronged approach. First, the paper's scientific articles on housekeeping and cooking could show the farm wife how to lighten her work load. Then, too, her husband was to be prodded into helping her out. As one correspondent to the *Progressive Farmer* explained, men needed tough words. "Our Lecturer, in trying to discuss the social feature [of the Alliance], handles husbands quite roughly, but it is received in the proper spirit. If country life is ever made more attractive, there must be more congeniality in spirit and aggressiveness between the one that follows the plow handles and the one of all beings earthly that acts as a helpmeet to man." What were "the conveniences for the good and faithful wife?" asked Colonel Polk. How far did she have to walk to the woodpile or the spring? Had the bloom on her cheeks faded prematurely? These were the subjects, he urged, that ought to be discussed in Alliance circles so that "new life, new energy, new action . . . and new views of life and living" might emerge for both sexes.

The Alliance's concern with helping hard working farmwomen fused with the order's major objective, the overall improvement of agricultural life. To this end, the Alliance sought to discover "a remedy for every evil known to exist and afflict farmers and other producers." The remedy of improved farming methods was especially important as a number of articles in the *Progressive Farmer* attest. The paper argued that the one-crop system was the obvious and basic cause of the state's agricultural depression. Over and over again, the paper and Alliance meetings focused on the need to farm properly and to stay out of debt. Consider the two kinds of farmers, the *Progressive Farmer* urged. One raised cotton on his land, bought milk, bread, hay and fertilizers on credit. The other chose the Alliance route and would prosper. And "his wife, dear devoted woman, instead of wearing out her life in cooking for a lot of negroes to work cotton, has time to look after the adornment and the beautifying of her home, to attend to her milk and butter, eggs, garden, bees, chicken and other poultry, and with all this they have a little time to spare socially with their neighbors and to go to church."

The *Progressive Farmer* might describe the tasks of the wise farmer's wife enthusiastically, but the list of her activities highlights a crucial problem in the Alliance's approach to women. Although the Alliance supported expanding women's rights and privileges, its over-all objective was to put farmers on an economic, social, and political parity with other occupations. To do so, or to try to do so, had definite implications for women's lives and shaped the Alliance's conception of equality. If the home was to be made attractive enough to discourage children from abandoning farm life, if it was to be "a place of rest, of comfort, of social refinement and domestic pleasure," then women would have to make it so. If the farm was to stay out of debt, if the farmer was to remain free of the supply merchant by raising as many of his necessities as he could, his wife must help. Woman's "judgment and skill in management may be essential to the success of her husband," one article reminded Alliance readers. "And this responsibility . . . continues to the close of her life."

The Alliance proposed a position for women that embodied an equality of sorts, the economic equality of a diligent coworker. In its recognition of the importance and difficulty of woman's work, the role model differed from that of the southern lady. Nor did the model merely update the characters of the yeoman farmer's family. The Alliance's concern with diversifying southern agriculture, with eliminating the disastrous dependency on the one-crop system, was not an attempt to recreate the small farm and agricultural myth of an idealized past but to create a new kind of farm and a new cast of characters. Agricultural reform, in fact, was seen as part of a modernizing process, and it was favored not only by the Alliance but also by leaders of the New South movement. Spokesmen for each group agreed that the South had to end its colonial status both through substantial industrial growth and through agricultural diversification.

But what were the implications of such a view for women? "The housewife, who, by her industry, transforms the milk from her dairy into butter . . . is as truly a manufacturer as the most purse-proud mill-owner of Britain," explained the *National Economist*. Labeled manufacturers or helpmates, women were to carry a heavy burden in creating the new order. The truth was that even though the Alliance talked of a variety of opportunities available for women, most women in North Carolina would continue to live on the farm, and Alliance leaders thought this right in terms of the world they wished to create. Farm women were important for they would share in the task of restoring agriculture to its rightful position in the economy. Even the Alliance's interest in women's education was partially tied to this goal. If women were to become efficient, modern coworkers in the task of agricultural reconstruction, they needed an education. As Polk explained: "The great and imperative need of our people and our time, is the practical education of the masses. . . . It will be a glorious day for the South when her young ladies, educated in all the higher and refined arts of life, shall boast and without blushing of equal proficiency in the management of the household and flower-garden."

Moreover, women needed to be educated so that, in turn, they could teach Alliance children, first at home and then at school. Rural children, many Alliance members were convinced, needed a special kind of education, one that embraced "the moral, physical and industrial, as well as the mental training of our children." By providing such an education, women could offer an "invaluable service." For "this system will strengthen the attachment of these classes [to agricultural life] instead of alienating [them] from it . . . it will better qualify them for success and happiness in life . . . increase the opportunity and inclination to adorn the home and practice the social virtues."

Other pragmatic considerations led to the support of women's education. Education could provide poor girls with the opportunity "to make an honest living." Most, but not all, women would marry. To prepare for the possibility of spinsterhood, every careful mother must see not only that daughters were trained in their domestic and spiritual responsibilities, but would also "have them taught a trade or profession and thus equip them fully to 'face the world' if this need shall come to them." No one, not even a woman, ought to be an economic drain on others. Teaching provided one means of support. So too would factory work, which the Alliance leaders, like spokesmen of the New South movement, hoped would be a growing field of employment. North Carolina's Piedmont region, the *Progressive Farmer* enthusiastically suggested, should be covered with factories. "Then we could have money because our boys and girls and women who are now consumers would find constant, honorable and remunerative employment and would thus become self-supporting." Women not only had the option but, indeed, the duty of being self-

supporting and of adding "to the general wealth of the place." The more educated and useful women became, "the better for them and for our State."

The part that the Alliance encouraged women to play in southern life was more expansive than the traditional role of the southern lady at the same time that it had definite limitations. Women need no longer cultivate the appearance of genteel passivity; they required education as the preparation for a useful life. But the Alliance defined utility in terms of the organization's over-all objectives, the profitability of agriculture, the prosperity of the state. Thus, it was vital that women learn to be skilled managers or teachers. Whether spinsters or widows, women must never be parasites on their families or on their state. Beneath the rhetoric, the lifestyle the Alliance supported for women was one of constant hard work and low wages, if women were to be paid for their labor at all. These limitations, harsh though they seem, were realistic both in terms of the Alliance's major goals and in terms of available options in the South. As one northern observer testified, "There is yet no rapid development of opportunity for profitable labor for young white women in the South."

There may be yet another reason for the contradictory meaning of equality that the Alliance proposed for women. Despite the support the Alliance gave to an expanded life style for women, Alliance leaders were affected by the circumstances of time, place, and class. Like other well-born Southerners, they had not rejected the traditional view of women as the source of morality and goodness. Because of their moral qualities, women had to participate in the Alliance, but it is doubtful whether North Carolina Alliance leaders would have supported enlarging women's sphere in any way that might threaten their own social or political position. As the *Progressive Farmer* firmly acknowledged, it had no sympathy with "that spirit which could encourage class feeling or class prejudice. . . . It is . . . *subversive of the social order.*" Leaders wanted changes, but not at the expense of social stability. Thus women might share in a kind of social and economic equality with men but they would hardly be offered political rights.

There are few indications that this strategy was unacceptable to the majority of Alliance women. Most letters from women indicate that the new parameters for female behavior were thankfully welcomed. Only occasionally can one discern an undercurrent of unrest, when women remarked on men's failure to be vigorous Alliance fighters or when they pointed out how much better a place the world would be had women, long ago, taken a more active part in shaping it. Then, too, a few women dared to write on political matters, giving their own opinions and urging men to take notice. At least one woman realized how far she had stepped out of her place. After mocking Alliance men who were "willing to wave Alliance principles and swallow the whole Democratic party," she observed, "I could say a good deal more on this line, but will stop, for fear some fool will ask: 'Are you a woman?'"

The *Progressive Farmer* not surprisingly steered away from the explosive issue of women's participation in politics. In two unusual references to the question of women's political rights, however, it is clear that the issue had come up in local meetings. At one county rally, the lecturer told the women, "He did not invite them to suffrage, though it was gaining rapidly in public favor and if they had the ballot they would drive out the liquor traffic of this country and other evils." In Almance County, the Alliance lecturer warned his female listeners, "Do not spend your time in longing for opportunities that will never come, but be contented in the sphere the Lord hath placed you in. If the Lord had intended you for a preacher or lawyer he would have given you a pair of pantaloons."

But the desire to maintain the *status quo* did not automatically succeed. Though Alliance leaders delineated definite boundaries to the theoretical and actual position women might occupy in the world, the fact that suffrage was mentioned at all may indicate a turbid undercurrent of half conscious challenge to the leadership. The way the two Alliance speakers spoke of the suffrage issue suggests that some Alliance circles had discussed it. A few letters to the *Progressive Farmer* and other fragmentary evidence point to the same conclusion. On a visit to North Carolina in 1893, for example, a Mrs. Virginia Durant who had established a suffrage organization in South Carolina, reported she found "suffrage sentiment" of an unfocused kind in the state. Perhaps she sensed incipient interest among those women exposed to the Alliance.

Yet there is not enough evidence to resolve the issue. If there were some support for the further expansion of women's activities through the Alliance, however, it never had the time to grow strong and vocal. For although the Alliance lingered on into the twentieth century, by the mid-1890s it had ceased to be an institution of importance. The failure of the Alliance cooperative economic ventures, continued hard times, and a split within the organization over the support of the Populist party all contributed to a decline in membership. A changing political climate brought new issues, new questions to the fore; many of them would have conservative implications. By the end of the decade, the shape of southern life would be set. After the Populist challenge, franchise for both poor whites and blacks would be limited and the question of political participation closed. Voting was a privilege, not a right. "Equal rights for all, special privileges for none" was a slogan best forgotten.

Though the Alliance did not survive long enough to dislodge the traditional ideas of woman's sphere, its spirited attempt to work out a new place for her both in theory and practice shows greater complexity in late nineteenth-century attitudes and behavior with respect to sex roles than previously recognized, and suggests that there may have been other attempts to create new roles for women in the South.

Questions for Study and Review

1. Why did southern leaders of the Alliance shy away from support for women's suffrage while western civic leaders supported women's electoral activities?

2. In what ways were the Alliance's positions on black and female participation similar or different?

3. To what extent did southern women and men perceive similar advantages in agricultural modernization?

4. In the mid-nineteenth century, midwestern farm wives seem to have lost status as new technology limited their role in agricultural production. What were the differences and similarities in their situation and that of their post-Civil War counterparts in the South?

Suggested Readings

Marilyn Dell Brady, "Populism and Feminism in a Newspaper by and for Women of the Kansas Farmers' Alliance, 1891–1894," *Kansas History* (Winter 1984/84).

Pamela Tyler, "The Ideal Rural Southern Woman as Seen by *Progressive Farmer* in the 1930s," *Southern Studies* (Fall 1981).

Donald B. Marti, "Sisters of the Grange: Rural Feminism in the Late Nineteenth Century," *Agricultural History* (July 1984).

Minnie Miller Brown, "Black Women in American Agriculture," *Agricultural History* (January 1976).

Dolores Janiewski, *Sisterhood Denied: Race, Gender and Class in a New South Community* (1985).

PART THREE

Progress and Its Discontents

During the 1890s, the pace of change accelerated. The wave of immigrants became a flood; mass production and mechanization revolutionized industry; corporate mergers and consolidations swept the country; women entered the work force in unprecedented numbers; farm prices, which had been falling, now plummeted and the prices of other commodities dropped even faster; de facto segregation received constitutional sanction; and designs for imperialism became blueprints for empire building. In response to these developments, union membership soared above the million mark. Third parties, backed by farmers, laborers, and socialists surged in popularity at the polls. Female activists revamped strategies and headed toward victory in campaigns for suffrage and prohibition. Organizations to promote the interests of blacks, workers, and immigrants flourished. New forms of activism channeled a younger generation's energy into movements for social change. Economic depression, urban and industrial development, immigration, segregation, and imperialism vied for national attention in the decades surrounding 1900, changing the face of America and transforming the lives of ordinary women and men in every section of the country.

Progress was the watchword of corporate capitalists and financiers, of diplomatic leaders and party officials. Yet progress had its price. The problems it spawned produced a wave of social movements that, ironically at times, took their name from the very source of the ills they sought to cure—progressivism. Adopting different definitions of progress or rejecting its very tenets, Progressive reformers formulated a range of strategies, some contradictory, for improving society. Alternately advocating and opposing state intervention, protective legislation, racial and sexual equality, American imperialism, socialism or anarchism, prohibition, women's suffrage, and many other approaches to change, Progressive organizations formed no unified front. Instead, clusters of associations competed to advance their own social vision and political agenda. One common feature of these multiple movements, however, was the significant involvement of women.

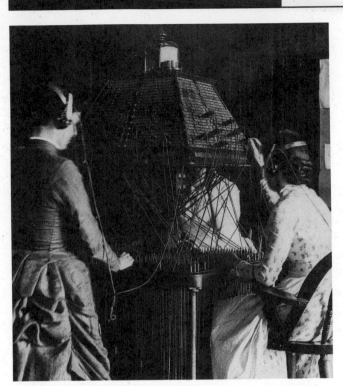

One noticeable trend of the nineteenth century was women's increasing participation in the paid labor force. By the end of the century, 20 percent of women in the United States were working outside the home. Most women workers were young and single, although a large proportion of black married women worked, most often in low-paying jobs in domestic or laundry service. New technologies like the telephone broadened opportunities for young, single, white, native-born women, who learned new clerical skills and moved into formerly "male" occupations as telephone operators, stenographers, typists, and salesclerks in the new department stores.

Between 1890 and 1900, the number of women in the work force climbed from 4 to 5.3 million, with black women, then immigrants, leading the way proportionally. Though domestic service and the sewing trades remained the largest employers of women, clerical, sales, telegraph and telephone work, and waitressing provided new job opportunities, especially for native-born white women. Educational opportunities also expanded for both black and white women, though far more for the latter, as more coeducational and women's colleges opened their doors to female students. At the beginning of the twentieth century, 85,000 women comprised 37 percent of the college and university population; in 1920, the numbers rose to 283,000 and 47 percent. More of these college graduates went on to receive professional degrees than ever before, gaining entry to such male bastions as law and medicine or entering newly feminized fields such as social work and library science. At the same time, the rate of both marriages and births declined.

With more women in the workplace, more in colleges and universities, and fewer fully absorbed with marriage and childrearing, female activism, and specifically an era of female self-organization, blossomed. The largest women's organizations—the General Federation of Women's Clubs, the Women's Christian Temperance Union, the National American Women's Suffrage Association, the National Association of Colored Women—had national boards, annual meetings, and sophisticated legislative agendas. Yet in each of these groups the thousands of local societies scattered across the country carried out most of the work. Moreover, many other women's or mixed associations existed only on the local or regional level, including such groups as black neighborhood unions, immigrant mutual aid societies, and ethnic political organizations. Among the last of these, women were particularly active in black Republican circles and in Cuban revolutionary clubs during the late nineteenth century.

The forms and styles of women's activism—like men's—varied by race, class, region, ethnicity, education, and issue. Despite hymns of praise to the "melting pot," a term popularized by Israel Zangwell's play by the same name, American society at the turn of the century more closely resembled vegetable soup. Common experience and identity resulting from the mingling of peoples and cultures in America represented the broth. Yet each group retained much of its distinctive flavor, like that of the vegetables. Thus, both in society at large and in Progressive movements, a shared concern for the nation's future was counterbalanced by the particular programs and policies favored by any one group.

The common broth for female activists was the assumption that women's public efforts were directly linked to their family roles. Even those who remained single throughout their lives, such as Jane Addams and Susan B. Anthony, employed domestic analogies to promote and justify women's involvement in the political arena. As suffragist and journalist Rheta Childe Dorr proclaimed in the early 1900s:

> Woman's place is Home, but Home is not contained within the four walls of the individual house. Home is the community. The city full of people is the Family. The public school is the real Nursery. And badly do Home and Family need their "mother."

Dorr captured the sentiments of a broad spectrum of female Progressives. Her peers in urban settlement houses—mostly white, middle-class, and college-educated—certainly shared her vision. Kathryn Kish Sklar examines the specifically female milieu of Chicago's Hull House where such women created an alternative form of family life, using names like "Sister Kelley" to emphasize their kindred spirit. Though many of these women, including Florence Kelley, were attracted to socialist and other radical doctrines, they nonetheless rooted their political agenda in protection of the domestic arena. Jane Addams noted, for instance, that "as society grows more complicated, it is necessary that woman shall extend her sense of responsibility to many things outside her own home if she would continue to preserve the home in its entirety."

So, too, did immigrant women on New York's Lower East Side and elsewhere justify their participation in public activism on the basis of domestic responsibilities. Paula Hyman traces the organization of kosher meat boycotts by Jewish housewives in 1902, demonstrating how women were mobilized to militant action through neighborhood networks. Mothers of small children with little experience in public protest became boycott leaders and explained their actions in familial terms:

> Our husbands work hard. . . . They try their best to bring a few cents into the house. We must manage to spend as little as possible. We will not give away our last few cents to the butcher and let our children go barefoot.

Some of those children entered garment factories at young ages to contribute to the family income and became part of the massive women's garment strike of 1909–10. Lessons learned at home may have been one source of inspiration for these militant immigrant daughters.

A world away in southern cities, women leaders in black communities came together "for the purpose of encouraging habits of cleanliness and industry, promoting child welfare, and bringing about culture and efficiency in general homemaking." Ida B. Wells, Lugenia Burns Hope, Charlotte Hawkins Brown, Margaret Murray (Mrs. Booker T.) Washington, and others who advocated self-help programs among African Americans voiced a generation's concern that until and unless racist violence was controlled neither their families nor communities could hope to achieve a decent, secure life. In the 1890s—a decade of widespread racial violence—such women viewed collective protest as "the painful, patient, and silent toil of mothers to gain title to the bodies of their daughters." They called on southern white women for assistance in this crusade: "what a mighty foe to mob violence" they might be "if they would arise in the purity and power of their womanhood to implore their fathers, husbands, and sons no longer to stain their hands with the black man's blood!"

Perhaps this shared concern with the protection of home and family allowed a few women to cross the racial divide, however hesitantly, and form interracial organizations. Jacquelyn Dowd Hall uncovers this common bond of womanhood and its specifically religious roots in the South as she traces the development of the Women's Committee of the Commission on Interracial Cooperation in the early twentieth century. Yet her study also reveals the continued barriers of racial prejudice and suspicion that shaped black and white women's interactions in that endeavor.

Despite a shared rhetoric and a common commitment to domestic values, female Progressives found themselves arguing for different, sometimes opposing, solutions to social problems. Whereas Hull House residents successfully sought state legislation to relieve the horrors of sweatshops, Jewish women as housewives and workers preferred to employ the collective economic power of neighborhood and factory networks to achieve their goals. Black women, especially in the South, simultaneously sought and feared government intervention, preferring federal action to the involvement of racist state legislatures.

Some advocated protective legislation; others promoted union organization. Many sought government intervention, but a smaller number preferred community-based protest. A few favored cross-class, interethnic, and biracial organization; the majority formed sex, class, ethnic, or race-specific associations. Progressive reformers, then, followed different paths to social improvement and social justice, and in the process set the framework for debates among social activists for decades to follow. Among women as among men, those discontented with the direction of the nation's development or inspired to action by the evils spawned in the name of progress held different visions of the proper social order and chose different paths to social change. Nonetheless, collectively, they redefined the meaning of progress and, here and there, alleviated its discontents.

Suggested Readings

Elizabeth Ewen, *Immigrant Women in the Land of Dollars: Life and Culture on the Lower East Side* (1985).

Aileen Kraditor, *The Ideas of the Woman Suffrage Movement, 1890–1920* (1965).

Nancy F. Cott, *The Grounding of Modern Feminism* (1987).

Paula Giddings, *When and Where I Enter: The Impact of Black Women on Race and Sex in America* (1984).

Anne Scott, *The Southern Lady: From Pedestal to Politics, 1830–1930* (1970).

Mari Jo Buhle, *Women and American Socialism, 1870–1920* (1983).

FIVE

Hull House in the 1890s: A Community of Women Reformers

Kathryn Kish Sklar

As female pioneers, farm wives, and women weavers worked to sustain their families and communities in the face of urban-industrial and technological development, more privileged women sought new ways to involve themselves in shaping the forces of social change. In the 1890s—a decade of economic crisis and partisan political realignments—a generation of female college graduates forged a new institutional base from which to launch their reform programs. Young idealists established settlement houses in New York, Boston, Philadelphia, Chicago, and dozens of other cities, in the hope that their efforts could lessen the ills produced by inner-city life and massive immigration.

Both women and men joined the settlement house movement, though most houses were sex-segregated in accommodating their full-time residents. Men, however, had numerous other vehicles for pursuing social change and did so while leading independent lives. Women had few alternatives if they wished to maintain their respectability while living outside the traditional family circle and dedicating themselves to public activism. Also, in the decades before the vote was won nationally, women relied more heavily than men on scientific studies and collective lobbying efforts to make their influence felt.

For Jane Addams, Florence Kelley, Lillian Wald, and hundreds of women like them, the all-female communities created in the settlement houses provided emotional and economic support, afforded contacts with other women's organizations and with male allies, and increased female activists' social and political clout. Sklar's examination of one of the most influential settlement communities—Chicago's Hull House—reveals how sisterly bonds were forged from common family backgrounds and then mobilized in the service of a shared social vision. At the same time, Hull House functioned as part of the complex network of alliances and organizations that rendered the settlement so effective in the political arena.

Using the example of antisweatshop legislation, Sklar demonstrates the capacity of settlement women to affect practical change and recognizes the complex implications of that single piece of legislation for the lives of Chicago's working-class and immigrant women and families. As settlement women and other mostly middle-class females gained access to the formal political arena, they began to determine what types of legislation were most beneficial not only for themselves but for women of all ethnic, race, and class backgrounds. The efforts of Hull House leaders illustrates both the benefits and the dangers of that situation.

What were the sources of women's political power in the United States in the decades before they could vote? How did women use the political power they were able to muster? This essay attempts to answer these questions by examining one of the most politically effective groups of women reformers in U.S. history—those who assembled in Chicago in the early 1890s at Hull House, one of the nation's first social settlements, founded in 1889 by Jane Addams and Ellen Gates Starr. Within that group, this study focuses on the reformer Florence Kelley (1859–1932). Kelley joined Hull House in 1891 and remained until 1899, when she moved to Lillian Wald's Henry Street Settlement on the Lower East Side of New York, where she lived for the next twenty-seven years. According to Felix Frankfurter, Kelley "had probably the largest single share in shaping the social history of the United States during the first thirty years of this century," for she played "a powerful if not decisive role in securing legislation for the removal of the most glaring abuses of our hectic industrialization following the Civil War." It was in the 1890s that Kelley and her colleagues at Hull House developed the patterns of living and thinking that guided them throughout their lives of reform, leaving an indelible imprint on U.S. politics. This essay attempts to determine the extent to which their political power and activities flowed from their collective life as coresidents and friends and the degree to which this power was attributable to their close affiliation with male reformers and male institutions.

From "Hull House in the 1890s: A Community of Women Reformers" by Kathryn Kish Sklar, *Signs: Journal of Women in Culture and Society 1985,* vol. 10, no. 4. Copyright © 1985 by The University of Chicago. Reprinted by permission of The University of Chicago Press and the author.

The effects of both factors can be seen in one of the first political campaigns conducted by Hull House residents—the 1893 passage and subsequent enforcement of pathbreaking antisweatshop legislation mandating an eight-hour day for women and children employed in Illinois manufacturing. This important episode reveals a great deal about the sources of this group's political power, including their own collective initiative, the support of other women's groups, and the support of men and men's groups. Finally, it shows how women reformers and the gender-specific issues they championed helped advance class-specific issues during a time of fundamental social, economic, and political transition.

✳

The community of women at Hull House made it possible for Florence Kelley to step from the apprenticeship to the journeyman stage in her reform career. A study of the 1893 antisweatshop campaign shows that the community provided four fundamental sources of support for her growth as a reformer. First, it supplied an emotional and economic substitute for traditional family life, linking her with other talented women of her own class and educational and political background and thereby greatly increasing her political and social power. Second, the community at Hull House provided Kelley with effective ties to other women's organizations. Third, it enabled cooperation with men reformers and their organizations, allowing her to draw on their support without submitting to their control. Finally, it provided a creative setting for her to pursue and develop a reform strategy she had already initiated in New York—the advancement of the rights and interests of working people in general by strengthening the rights and interests of working women and children.

At a time when women were denied access to most legal, political, and academic professions, the settlement house movement gave them a means for translating the Progressive doctrine of reform into action. The community of women reformers at Hull House, founded in Chicago in 1889 by Jane Addams and Ellen Gates Starr, played an essential role in the drafting and passage of legislation to protect women and child laborers. Settlement houses also offered classes, ran day nurseries, and provided emergency relief for the inner-city poor.

As a community of women, Hull House provided its members with a lifelong substitute for family life. In that sense it resembled a religious order, supplying women with a radical degree of independence from the claims of family life and inviting them to commit their energies elsewhere. When she first crossed the snowy threshold of Hull House "sometime between Christmas and New Year's," 1891, Florence Kelley Wischnewetzky was fleeing from her husband and seeking refuge for herself and her three children, ages six, five, and four. "We were welcomed as though we had been invited," she wrote thirty-five years later

in her memoirs. The way in which Kelley's family dilemma was solved reveals a great deal about the sources of support for the political activity of women reformers in the progressive era: help came first and foremost from women's institutions but also from the recruited support of powerful men reformers. Jane Addams supplied Kelley with room, board, and employment and soon after she arrived introduced her to Henry Demarest Lloyd, a leading critic of American labor policies who lived with his wife Jessie and their young children in nearby Winnetka. The Lloyds readily agreed to add Kelley's children to their large nursery, an arrangement that began a lifelong relationship between the two families. A sign of the extent to which responsibility for Kelley's children was later assumed by members of the Hull House community, even after her departure, was the fact that Jane Addams's closest personal friend, Mary Rozet Smith, regularly and quietly helped Kelley pay for their school and college tuition.

A bit stunned by her good fortune, the young mother wrote her own mother a summary of her circumstances a few weeks after reaching Hull House: "We are all well, and the chicks are happy. I have fifty dollars a month and my board and shall have more soon as I can collect my wits enough to write. I have charge of the Bureau of Labor of Hull House here and am working in the lines which I have always loved. I do not know what more to tell you except this, that in the few weeks of my stay here I have won for the children and myself many and dear friends whose generous hospitality astonishes me." This combination of loving friendship and economic support served as a substitute for the family life from which she had just departed. "It is understood that I am to resume the maiden name," she continued to her mother, "and that the children are to have it." It did not take Kelley long to decide to join this supportive community of women. As she wrote Friedrich Engels in April 1892, "I have cast in my lot with Misses Addams and Starr for as long as they will have me." To her mother she emphasized the personal gains Hull House brought her, writing, "I am better off than I have been since I landed in New York since I am now responsible *myself* for what I do." Gained at great personal cost, Kelley's independence was her most basic measure of well-being. Somewhat paradoxically, perhaps, her autonomy was the product of her affiliation with a community.

One significant feature of Hull House life was the respect that residents expressed for one another's autonomy. Although each had a "room of her own," in Kelley's case this room was sometimes shared with other residents, and the collective space was far more important than their small private chambers. Nevertheless, this intimate proximity was accompanied by a strong expression of personal individuation, reflected in the formality of address used at Hull House. By the world at large Kelley was called Mrs. Kelley, but to her close colleagues she was "Sister Kelley," or "Dearest F. K.," never Florence. Miss Addams and Miss Lathrop were never called Jane or Julia, even by their close friends, although Kelley occasionally took the liberty of calling Addams "gentle Jane." It was not that Hull House was bleak and business-like, as one resident once described male settlements in New York, but rather that the colleagues recognized and appreciated one another's individuality. These were superb conditions for social innovation since the residents could draw on mutual support at the same time that they were encouraged to pursue their own distinct goals.

This respect for individuality did not prevent early Hull House residents from expressing their love for one another. Kelley's letters to Jane Addams often began "Beloved Lady," and she frequently addressed Mary Rozet Smith as "Dearly Beloved," referring perhaps to Smith's special status in Addams's life. Kelley's regard for Addams and Addams's for her were revealed in their correspondence after Kelley left in 1899. Addams wrote her, "I have had blows before in connection with Hull House but nothing like this"; and Mary Rozet Smith added, "I have had many pangs for the dear presiding lady." Later that year Addams wrote, "Hull House sometimes seems a howling wilderness without you." Kelley seems to have found the separation difficult since she protested when her name was removed from the list of residents in the *Hull House Bulletin*. Addams replied, "You overestimate the importance of the humble Bulletin," but she promised to restore Kelley's name, explaining that it was only removed to "stop people asking for her." Fourteen years later in 1913 Addams wrote "Sister Kelley," "It is curious that I have never gotten used to you being away from [Hull House], even after all these years!"

One source of the basic trust established among the three major reformers at Hull House in the 1890s—Jane Addams, Julia Lathrop, and Florence Kelley—was similarity of family background. Not only were they all of the upper middle class, but their fathers were politically active men who helped Abraham Lincoln found and develop the Republican Party in the 1860s. John Addams served eight terms as a state senator in Illinois, William Lathrop served in Congress as well as in the Illinois legislature, and William Kelley served fifteen consecutive terms in Congress. All were vigorous abolitionists, and all encouraged their daughters' interests in public affairs. As Judge Alexander Bruce remarked at the joint memorial services held for Julia Lathrop and Florence Kelley after their deaths in 1932, "Both of them had the inspiration of great and cultured mothers and both had great souled fathers who, to use the beautiful language of Jane Addams in speaking of her own lineage, 'Wrapped their little daughters in the large men's doublets, careless did they fit or no.'"

These three remarkable women were participating in a political tradition that their fathers had helped create. While they were growing up in the 1860s and 1870s, they gained awareness through their fathers' experience of the mainstream of American political processes, thereby learning a great deal about its currents—particularly that its power could be harnessed to fulfill the purposes of well-organized interest groups.

Although Hull House residents have generally been interpreted as reformers with a religious motivation, it now seems clear that they were instead motivated by political goals. In that regard they resembled a large proportion of other women social settlement leaders, including those associated with Hull House

after 1900, such as Grace and Edith Abbot, whose father was Nebraska's first lieutenant governor, or Sophonisba Breckinridge, daughter of a Kentucky congressman. Women leaders in the social settlement movement seem to have differed in this respect from their male counterparts, who were seeking alternatives to more orthodox religious, rather than political, careers. In, but not of, the Social Gospel movement, the women at Hull House were a political boat on a religious stream, advancing political solutions to social problems that were fundamentally ethical or moral, such as the right of workers to a fair return for their labor or the right of children to schooling.

Another source of the immediate solidarity among Addams, Lathrop, and Kelley was their shared experience of higher education. Among the first generation of American college women, they graduated from Rockford College, Vassar College, and Cornell University, respectively, in the early 1880s and then spent the rest of the decade searching for work and for a social identity commensurate with their talents. Addams tried medical school; Lathrop worked in her father's law office; Kelley, after being denied admission to graduate study at the University of Pennsylvania, studied law and government at the University of Zurich, where she received a much more radical education than she would have had she remained in Philadelphia. In the late 1880s and early 1890s, the social settlement movement was the right movement at the right time for this first generation of college-educated women, who were able to gain only limited entry to the male-dominated professions of law, politics, or academics.

While talented college women of religious backgrounds and inclinations were energetically recruited into the missionary empires of American churches, those seeking secular outlets for their talents chose a path that could be as daunting as that of a missionary outpost. Except for the field of medicine, where women's institutions served the needs of women physicians and students, talented women were blocked from entering legal, political, and academic professions by male-dominated institutions and networks. In the 1890s the social settlement movement supplied a perfect structure for women seeking secular means of influencing society because it collectivized their talents, it placed and protected them among the working-class immigrants whose lives demanded amelioration, and it provided them with access to the male political arena while preserving their independence from male dominated institutions.

Since Hull House drew on local sources of funding, often family funds supplied by wealthy women, Jane Addams found it possible to finance the settlement's activities without the assistance or control of established religious or educational institutions. In 1895 she wrote that Hull House was modeled after Toynbee Hall in London, where "a group of University men . . . reside in the poorer quarter of London for the sake of influencing the people there toward better local government and wider social and intellectual life." Substituting "college-trained women" for "University men," Hull House also placed a greater emphasis on economic factors. As Addams continued, "The original residents came to Hull House with a conviction that social intercourse could best express the growing sense of the economic unity of society." She also emphasized their political autonomy, writing that the first residents "wished the social spirit to be the undercurrent of the life of Hull-House, whatever direction the stream might take." Under Kelley's influence in 1892, the social spirit at Hull House turned decisively toward social reform, bringing the community's formidable energy and talents to bear on a historic campaign on behalf of labor legislation for women and children.

The settlement did play a critical leadership role in this venture, but it was never alone. Indeed it was part of a complex network of women's associations in Chicago in the 1890s.

About thirty women's organizations combined forces and entered into local politics in 1888 through the Illinois Women's Alliance, organized that year by Elizabeth Morgan and other members of the Ladies Federal Union no. 2073 in response to a crusading woman journalist's stories in the *Chicago Times* about "City Slave Girls" in the garment industry. The alliance's political goals were clearly stated in their constitution: "The objects of the Alliance are to agitate for the enforcement of all existing laws and ordinances that have been enacted for the protection of women and children—as the factory ordinances and the compulsory education law. To secure the enactment of such laws as shall be found necessary. To investigate all business establishments and factories where women and children are employed and public institutions where women and children are maintained. To procure the appointment of women, as inspectors and as members of boards of education, and to serve on boards of management of public institutions." Adopting the motto "Justice to Children, Loyalty to Women," the alliance acted as a vanguard for the entrance of women's interests into municipal and state politics, focusing chiefly on the passage and enforcement of compulsory education laws. One of its main accomplishments was the agreement of the city council in 1889 "to appoint five lady inspectors" to enforce city health codes.

The diversity of politically active women's associations in Chicago in the late 1880s was reflected in a list of organizations associated with the alliance. Eight bore names indicating a religious or ethical affiliation, such as the Woodlawn branch of the Women's Christian Temperance Union and the Ladies Union of the Ethical Society. Five were affiliated with working women or were trade unions, such as the Working Women's Protective Association, the Ladies Federal Union no. 2703, and (the only predominantly male organization on the list) the Chicago Trades and Labor Assembly.

Another five had an intellectual or cultural focus, such as the Hopkins Metaphysical Association or the Vincent Chatauqua Association. Three were women's professional groups, including the Women's Press Association and the Women's Homeopathic Medical Society. Another three were female auxiliaries of male social organizations, such as the Lady Washington Masonic Chapter and the Ladies of the Grand Army of the Republic. Two were suffrage associations, including the Cook County Suffrage Association; another two were clubs interested in general economic reform, the Single Tax Club and the Land Labor Club no. 1; and one was educational, the Drexel Kindergarten Association.

Florence Kelley's 1892 entrance into this lively political scene was eased by her previous knowledge of and appreciation for the work of the alliance. Soon after its founding she had written the leaders a letter that was quoted extensively in a newspaper account of an alliance meeting, declaring, "The child labor question can be solved by legislation, backed by solid organization, and by women cooperating with the labor organizations, which have done all that has thus far been done for the protection of working children." In Chicago Kelley was perceived as a friend of the alliance because in 1889 and 1890 she had helped to organize the New York Working Women's Society's campaign "to add women as officials in the office for factory inspection." According to Kelley, the Society, "a small group of women from both the wealthy and influential class and the working class, . . . circulated petitions, composed resolutions, and was supported finally in the years 1889 and 1890 in bringing their proposal concerning the naming of women to factory inspectorships to the legislature, philanthropic groups and unions." As a result in 1890 the New York legislature passed laws creating eight new positions for women as state factory inspectors. This was quite an innovation since no woman factory inspector had yet been appointed in Great Britain or Germany, where factory inspection began, and the only four previously appointed in the United States had been named within the last two years in Pennsylvania. Writing in 1897 about this event, Kelley emphasized the political autonomy of the New York Working Women's Society: "Their proposal to add women as officials in the office for factory inspection was made for humanitarian reasons; in no way did it belong to the goals of the general workers' movement, although it found support among the unions." Thus when Kelley arrived at Hull House, she had already been affiliated with women's associations that were independent of trade unions even though cooperating with them.

For Kelley on that chilly December morning the question was not whether she would pursue a career in social reform but how, not whether she would champion what she saw as the rights and interests of working women and children but how she would do that. The question of means was critical in 1891 since her husband was unable to establish a stable medical practice, even though she had spent the small legacy inherited on her father's death the year before on new equipment for his practice. Indeed so acute were Kelley's financial worries that, when she decided to flee with her children to Chicago, she borrowed train fare from an English governess, Mary Forster, whom she had probably befriended at a neighborhood park. Chicago was a natural choice for Kelley since Illinois divorce laws were more equitable, and within its large population of reform-minded and politically active women she doubtlessly hoped to find employment that would allow her to support herself and her children. Although the historical record is incomplete, it seems likely that she headed first to a different community of women—that at the national headquarters of the Women's Christian Temperance Union (WCTU). She had been well paid for articles written for their national newspaper, the *Union Signal*—the largest women's newspaper in the world, with a circulation in 1890 of almost 100,000—and the WCTU was at the height of its institutional development in Chicago at that time, sponsoring "two day nurseries, two Sunday schools, an industrial school, a mission that sheltered four thousand homeless or destitute women in a twelve-month period, a free medical dispensary that treated over sixteen hundred patients a year, a lodging house for men that had . . . provided temporary housing for over fifty thousand men, and a low-cost restaurant." Just after Kelley arrived, the WCTU opened its Women's Temple, a twelve-story office building and hotel. Very likely it was someone there who told Kelley about Hull House.

The close relationship between Hull House and other groups of women in Chicago was exemplified in Kelley's interaction with the Chicago Women's Club. The minutes of the club's first meeting after Kelley's arrival in Chicago show that on January 25, 1892, she spoke under the sponsorship of Jane Addams on the sweating system and urged that a committee be created on the problem. Although a Reform Department was not created until 1894, minutes of March 23, 1892, show that the club's Home Department "decided upon cooperating with Mrs. Kelly [sic] of Hull House in establishing a Bureau of Women's Labor." Thus the club took over part of the funding and the responsibility for the counseling service Kelley had been providing at Hull House since February. (Initially Kelley's salary for this service was funded by the settlement, possibly with emergency monies given by Mary Rozet Smith.) In this way middle- and upper-middle-class clubwomen were drawn into the settlement's activities. In 1893 Jane Addams successfully solicited the support of wealthy clubwomen to lobby for the antisweatshop legislation: "We insisted that well-known Chicago women should accompany this first little group of Settlement folk who with trade-unionists moved upon the state capitol in behalf of factory legislation." Addams also described the lobbying Hull House

residents conducted with other voluntary associations: "Before the passage of the law could be secured, it was necessary to appeal to all elements of the community, and a little group of us addressed the open meetings of trades-unions and of benefit societies, church organizations, and social clubs literally every evening for three months." Thus Hull House was part of a larger social universe of voluntary organizations, and one important feature of its political effectiveness was its ability to gain the support of middle-class and working-class women.

In 1893 the cross-class coalition of the Illinois Women's Alliance began to dissolve under the pressure of the economic depression of that year, and in 1894 its leaders disbanded the group. Hull House reformers inherited the fruits of the alliance's five years of agitation, and they continued its example of combining working-class and middle-class forces. In 1891 Mary Kenney, a self-supporting typesetter who later became the first woman organizer to be employed by the American Federation of Labor, established the Jane Club adjacent to the settlement, a cooperative boardinghouse for young working women. In the early 1890s Kenney was a key figure in the settlement's efforts to promote union organizing among working women, especially bookbinders. Thus the combination of middle-class and working-class women at Hull House in 1892–93 was an elite version of the type of cross-class association represented by the Illinois Women's Alliance of the late 1880s—elite because it was smaller and because its middle-class members had greater social resources, familiarity with American political processes, and exposure to higher than average levels of education, while its working-class members (Mary Kenney and Alzina Stevens) were members of occupational and organizational elites.

By collectivizing talents and energies, this community made possible the exercise of greater and more effective political power by its members. A comparison of Florence Kelley's antisweatshop legislation, submitted to the Illinois investigative committee in February 1893, with that presented by Elizabeth Morgan dramatically illustrates this political advantage. The obvious differences in approach indicate that the chief energy for campaigning on behalf of working women and children had passed from working-class to middle-class social reformers. Both legislative drafts prohibited work in tenement dwellings, Morgan's prohibiting all manufacturing, Kelley's all garment making. Both prohibited the labor of children under fourteen and regulated the labor of children aged fourteen to sixteen. Kelley's went beyond Morgan's in two essential respects, however. Hers mandated an eight-hour day for women in manufacturing, and it provided for enforcement by calling for a state factory inspector with a staff of twelve, five of whom were to be women. The reasons for Kelley's greater success as an innovator are far from clear, but one important advantage in addition to her greater education and familiarity with the American political system was the larger community on which she could rely for the law's passage and enforcement.

Although Elizabeth Morgan could draw on her experience as her husband's assistant in his work as an attorney and on the support of women unionists, both resources were problematic. Thomas Morgan was erratic and self-centered, and Elizabeth Morgan's relationship with organized women workers was marred by sectarian disputes originating within the male power structure of the Chicago Trades and Labor Assembly. For example, in January 1892, when she accused members of the Shirtwaist Union of being controlled by her husband's opposition within the assembly, "a half dozen women surrounded [her] seat in the meeting and demanded an explanation. She refused to give any and notice was served that charges would be preferred against her at the next meeting of the Ladies' Federation of Labor." Perhaps Morgan's inability to count on a supportive community explains her failure to provide for adequate enforcement and to include measures for workers over the age of sixteen in her legislative draft. Compared to Kelley's, Morgan's bill was politically impotent. It could not enforce what it endorsed, and it did not affect adults.

Kelley's draft was passed by the Illinois legislature in June 1893, providing for a new office of enforcement and for an eight-hour day for women workers of all ages. After Henry Demarest Lloyd declined an invitation to serve as the state's first factory inspector, reform governor John Peter Altgeld followed Lloyd's recommendations and appointed Kelley. Thus eighteen months after her arrival in Chicago, she found herself in charge of a dedicated and well-paid staff of twelve mandated to see that prohibitions against tenement workshops and child labor were observed and to enforce a pathbreaking article restricting the working hours of women and children.

Hull House provided Kelley and other women reformers with a social vehicle for independent political action and a means of bypassing the control of male associations and institutions, such as labor unions and political parties; at the same time they had a strong institutional framework in which they could meet with other reformers, both men and women. The drafting of the antisweatshop legislation revealed how this process worked. In his autobiography, Abraham Bisno, pioneer organizer in the garment industry in Chicago and New York, described how he became a regular participant in public discussions of contemporary social issues at Hull House. He joined "a group . . . composed of Henry D. Lloyd, a prominent physician named Bayard Holmes, Florence Kelley, and Ellen G. [Starr] to engage in a campaign for legislation to abolish sweatshops, and to have a law passed prohibiting the employment of women more than eight hours a day." Answering a question about the author of the bill he endorsed at the 1893 hearings,

Bisno said, "Mrs. Florence Kelly [sic] wrote that up with the legal advice of myself, Henry Lloyd, and a number of prominent attorneys in Chicago." Thus as the chief author of the legislation, Florence Kelley drew on the expertise of Bisno, one of the most dedicated and talented union organizers; of Lloyd, one of the most able elite reformers in the United States; and, surely among the "prominent attorneys," of Clarence Darrow, one of the country's most able reform lawyers. It is difficult to imagine this cooperative effort between Bisno, Kelley, and Lloyd without the existence of the larger Hull House group of which they were a part. Their effective collaboration exemplified the process by which members of this remarkable community of women reformers moved into the vanguard of contemporary reform activity, for they did so in alliance with other groups and individuals.

What part did the Hull House community, essential to the drafting and passage of the act, have in the statute's enforcement? Who benefited and who lost from the law's enforcement? Answers to these questions help us view the community more completely in the context of its time.

During the four years that Kelley served as chief factory inspector of Illinois, her office and Hull House were institutionally so close as to be almost indistinguishable. Kelley rented rooms for her office across the street from the settlement, with which she and her three most able deputies were closely affiliated. Alzina Stevens moved into Hull House soon after Altgeld appointed her as Kelley's chief assistant. Mary Kenney lived at the Jane Club, and Abraham Bisno was a familiar figure at Hull House evening gatherings. Jane Addams described the protection that the settlement gave to the first factory inspection office in Illinois, the only such office headed by a woman in her lifetime: "The inception of the law had already become associated with Hull House, and when its ministration was also centered there, we inevi-

tably received all the odium which these first efforts entailed. . . . Both Mrs. Kelley and her assistant, Mrs. Stevens, lived at Hull House; . . . and one of the most vigorous deputies was the President of the Jane Club. In addition, one of the early men residents, since dean of a state law school, acted as prosecutor in the cases brought against the violators of the law." Thus the law's enforcement was just as collective an undertaking as was its drafting and passage. Florence Kelley and Alzina Stevens were usually the first customers at the Hull House Coffee Shop, arriving at 7:30 for a breakfast conference to plan their strategy for the day ahead. Doubtlessly these discussions continued at the end of the day in the settlement's dining hall.

One important aspect of the collective strength of Kelley's staff was the socialist beliefs shared by its most dedicated members. As Kelley wrote to Engels in November 1893, "I find my work as inspector most interesting; and as Governor Altgeld places no restrictions whatever upon our freedom of speech, and the English etiquette of silence while in the civil service is unknown here, we are not hampered by our position and three of my deputies and my assistant are outspoken Socialists and active in agitation." In his autobiography Bisno described the "fanatical" commitment that he, Florence Kelley, and most of the "radical group" brought to their work as factory inspectors. For him it was the perfect job since his salary allowed him for the first time to support his wife and children and his work involved direct action against unfair competition within his trade. "In those years labor legislation was looked on as a joke; few took it seriously," he later wrote. "Inspectors normally . . . were appointed from the viewpoint of political interest. . . . There were very few, almost no, court cases heard of, and it was left to our department to set the example of rigid enforcement of labor laws." Although they were replaced with "political interests" after the election of 1896, this group of inspectors showed what could be accomplished by the enactment of reform legislation and its vigorous enforcement. They demonstrated that women could use the power of the state to achieve social and economic goals.

Kelley and her staff began to take violators of the law to court in October 1893. She wrote Lloyd, "I have engaged counsel and am gathering testimony and hope to begin a series of justice court cases this week." She soon completed a law degree at Northwestern University and began to prosecute her own cases. Kelley found her work enormously creative. She saw potential innovations in social reform all around her. For example, she thought that the medical chapter of her annual report would "start a new line of activity for medical men and factory inspectors both." True to her prediction, the field of industrial medicine later was launched at Hull House by Alice Hamilton, who arrived at the settlement in 1897. Thus the effects of this small band of inspectors continued long after their dispersal. The community of women at Hull House gave them their start, but their impact extended far beyond that fellowship, thanks in part to the settlement's effective alliance with other groups of women and men.

✳

Historians of women have tended to assume that protective labor legislation was imposed on women workers by hostile forces beyond their control—especially by men seeking to eliminate job competition. To some degree this was true of the 1893 legislation since, by closing tenement dwellings to garment manufacture and by depriving sweatshop contractors of the labor of children under fourteen, the law reduced the number of sweatshops, where women and children predominated, and increased the number of garment workers in factories, where men prevailed. Abraham Bisno was well aware of the widespread opposition to the law and took time to talk with offenders, "to educate the parents who sent their children to work,

and the employers of these children, the women who were employed longer than eight hours a day, and their employers." Jane Addams also tried to help those who were deprived of work by the new law: "The sense that the passage of the child labor law would in many cases work hardship, was never absent from my mind during the earliest years of its operation. I addressed as many mother's meetings and clubs among working women as I could, in order to make clear the objective of the law and the ultimate benefit to themselves as well as to their children."

Did the children benefit? While further research is needed on this question, recent scholarship pointing to the importance of working-class support for the schooling of working-class children has revised earlier estimates that children and their families did not benefit. At best the law was a halfway measure that encouraged but could not force parents to place their children in school. Nevertheless, Florence Kelley was pleased with the compliance of parents and school officials. As she wrote Henry Demarest Lloyd, "Out of sixty-five names of children sent to the Board of Education in our first month of notifying it when we turned children under 14 yrs. of age out of factories, twenty-one were immediately returned to school and several others are known to be employed as nursegirls and cashgirls i.e. in non-prohibited occupations. This is good co-operation." While schools were inadequate and their teachers frequently prejudiced against immigrants, education was also an important route out of the grinding poverty that characterized immigrant neighborhoods. Thus it is not surprising that a large minority of parents complied with the law by enrolling their children in school.

The chief beneficiaries of the law, apart from those children who gained from schooling, were garment workers employed in factories. Most of these were men, but about one in four were women. The 1893 law was designed to prevent the erosion of this factory labor force and its replacement by sweatshop labor. Bisno described that erosion in his testimony before the state investigating committee early in 1893, stating, "Joseph Beifeld & Company have had three hundred and fifty employees some eleven or twelve years ago inside, and they have only eighty now to my knowledge, and they have increased their business about six times as much as it was eleven years ago." This decline of the factory population inevitably caused a decline of union membership since it was much more difficult to organize sweatshop workers. Thus as a union official Bisno was defending his own interests, but these were not inimical to all women workers.

Demonstrating the support of women unionists for the law's enforcement, members of the Women's Shoemakers Union chastised the Chicago Trades and Labor Assembly in February 1894 for their lukewarm support of the by-then-beleaguered eight-hour restriction. They "introduced resolutions, strongly condemning the manufacturers of this City for combining to nullify the state laws. . . . The resolutions further set forth that the members of the Women's Shoemakers Union effected as they were by the operation of the Eight hour Law unanimously approved the Law and for the benefit of themselves, for their sister wage workers and the little children, they pleaded for its maintenance and Enforcement." Although some women workers—particularly those who headed households with small children—must have opposed the law's enforcement, others, especially single women and mothers able to arrange child care, stood to gain from the benefits of factory employment. In a study completed for the Illinois Bureau of Labor Statistics in 1892, Florence Kelley found that 48 percent of Chicago working women lacked the "natural protectors" of fathers or husbands. Viewing them as a permanent feature of the paid labor force, she pointed to the importance of their wages to their families, thereby refuting the notion that all working women were supported by male wage earners. Although the historical evidence does not reveal how many, some young women who had formerly worked in sweatshops and whose families relied heavily on their wages doubtlessly benefited from the legislation by moving into larger factories with better working conditions.

The 1893 statute made it possible for women as well as men to move from exploitative, low-paying sweatshops into larger shops and factories with power machinery, unions, and higher wages. While the law's prohibition of tenement manufacturing obviously enabled such mobility, its eight-hour clause was no less instrumental since it attacked the basic principles of the sweating system—long hours and low wages. The average working day in the garment industry was about ten hours, but in some sweatshops it could be as long as twelve, thirteen, or fourteen hours. Reducing the working day from ten to eight hours did not significantly decrease production in factories with electric or steam-powered machinery since productivity could be raised by increasing a machine's speed or a worker's skill level. However, the eight-hour law drove many subcontractors or "sweaters" out of business since it eliminated the margin of profit created by workers' long hours at foot-powered sewing machines. From the sweatshop workers' perspective, it reduced wages even further since they were paid by the piece and could finish a much smaller amount of goods in eight hours. The wages of factory workers, by contrast, were likely to remain the same since negotiations between employers and employees customarily included a consideration of what it cost to sustain life, a factor absent from the sweaters' calculations.

Another group who benefited indirectly from this "antisweating" legislation were the men who worked in industries employing large numbers of women workers. Historians of protective labor legislation in England and the United States have noticed the tendency of male co-workers to benefit from legislation passed to protect women. This was true as early as the 1870s in Massachusetts and as late as the 1930s, when many states had laws limiting the hours of women but not the hours of men. The strategy of extending the legislation de facto to men seems to have been a deliberate intent of Kelley and her staff in the mid-1890s. At a high point in her experience as a factory inspector, Kelley wrote Engels on New Year's Eve, 1894: "We have at last won a victory for our 8 hours law. The Supreme Court has handed down no decision sustaining it, but the Stockyards magnates having been arrested until they are tired of it, have instituted the 8 hours day for 10,000 employees, men, women and children. We have 18 suits pending to enforce the 8 hours law and we think we shall establish it permanently before Easter. It has been a painful struggle of eighteen months and the Supreme Court may annul the law. But I have great hopes that the popular interest may prove too strong." When the eight-hour clause of the law was declared unconstitutional in 1895, therefore, it was beginning to affect industry-wide changes in Chicago's largest employers, extending far beyond the garment district.

The biggest losers from the enforcement of the 1893 legislation, as measured by the volume of their protest, were Chicago's manufacturers. Formed for the explicit purpose of obtaining a court ruling against the constitutionality of the eight-hour law, the Illinois Manufacturer's Association (IMA) became a model for other state associations and for the National Association of Manufacturers, formed in 1895. After 1899, when Kelley embarked on a thirty year campaign for state laws protecting women and children, the National Association of Manufacturers was her constant nemesis and the chief rallying point of her opposition. Given the radical ideas and values behind the passage and enforcement of the 1893 legislation, it is no surprise that, at this stage of her career, Kelley's success inspired an opposition that remained her lifelong foe.

After the court decision the *Chicago Tribune* reported, "In far reaching results the decision is most important. It is the first decision in the United States against the eight-hour law and presents a new obstacle in the path of the movement for shorter hours." An editorial the next day declared: "Labor is property and an interference with the sale of it by contract or otherwise is an infringement of a constitutional right to dispose of property. . . . The property rights of women, says the court, are the same as those of men." For the first but not the last time in her reform career Florence Kelley encountered opponents who claimed the banner of "women's rights." In 1921 with the introduction of the Equal Rights Amendment by Alice Paul and the National Women's Party, the potential conflict between women's rights and the protection of women workers became actual. Nearly a generation earlier in 1895 the opposition was clearly a facade for the economic interests of the manufacturers.

What conclusions can be drawn about the Hull House community from this review of their activities on behalf of antisweatshop legislation? First, and foremost, it attests to the capacity of women to sustain their own institutions. Second, it shows that this community's internal dynamics promoted a creative mixture of mutual support and individual expression. Third, these talented women reformers used their institution as a means of allying with male reformers and entering the mainstream of the American political process. In the tradition of earlier women's associations in the United States, they focused on the concerns of women and children, but these concerns were never divorced from those of men and of the society as a whole. Under the leadership of Florence Kelley, they pursued gender-specific reforms that served class-specific goals.

In these respects the Hull House community serves as a paradigm for women's participation in Progressive reform. Strengthened by the support of women's separate institutions, women reformers were able to develop their capacity for political leadership free from many if not all of the constraints that otherwise might have been imposed on their power by the male-dominated parties or groups with which they cooperated. Building on one of the strengths of the nineteenth-century notion of "women's sphere"—its social activism on behalf of the rights and interests of women and children—they represented those rights and interests innovatively and effectively. Ultimately, however, their power encountered limits imposed by the male-dominated political system, limits created more in response to their class-specific than to their gender-specific reform efforts.

Questions for Study and Review

1. How would the "girls" from Syracuse and the carpet weavers of Kensington have responded to the activities at Hull House?

2. What does settlement life tell us of the changing relations of educated, middle-class women to their families and communities at the turn of the century?

3. To what extent did Hull House residents represent the wishes and concerns of working-class and immigrant women and families?

4. Why did the settlement house movement attract so many women at the turn of the century, and how did this movement differ from earlier forms of female activism?

Suggested Readings

Allen F. Davis, *American Heroine: The Life and Legend of Jane Addams* (1973).

Barbara Solomon, *In the Company of Educated Women: A History of Women in Higher Education in America* (1985).

Estelle Freedman, "Separatism as Strategy: Female Institution Building and American Feminism, 1870–1930," *Feminist Studies* (Fall 1979).

Blanche Weisen Cook, "Female Support Networks and Female Activism," *Chrysalis* (#3, 1977).

Kathleen Berkeley, "'Colored Ladies Also Contributed'. Black Women's Activities from Benevolence to Social Welfare, 1866–1896," in Walter J. Fraser, Jr., et al., eds , *The Web of Southern Social Relations. Women, Family and Education* (1985).

SIX

Immigrant Women, Community Networks, and Consumer Protest: The New York City Kosher Meat Boycott of 1902

Paula E. Hyman

Settlement house residents focused much of their attention on the millions of immigrants, most from southern and eastern Europe, who entered the United States in the thirty years after 1890. Italian and Slavic, Catholic and Jewish families dominated this wave of migration, pouring into seaboard cities and then spreading out into industrial centers across the Northeast and Midwest. They provided not only a challenge for youthful reformers but also a labor force to fuel industrial growth. They also created whole new communities in the heart of America's cities, communities with distinctive sounds, foods, rituals, dress, and values. New York City's Little Italy, Chinatown, and Lower East Side were among the most vital of these ethnic enclaves. However, the newcomers were not unreservedly welcomed, and their ethnic diversity frightened many native-born Americans, including some second-generation immigrants.

In many fictional accounts of life on the Lower East Side, we read of hard-working fathers—eager to find success in the New World—rebellious sons and daughters—many seeking Americanization with a vengeance—and home-bound mothers—struggling to sustain Old World values. The Jewish women and men—especially the daughters and fathers—who populate the pages of these stories and those of the numerous historical studies of their communities are often portrayed as radicals who gained their political ideals through Old World confrontations with virulent anti-Semitism and vibrant labor militancy.

Paula Hyman reveals another dimension to life on the Lower East Side. She traces the translation of Jewish housewives' traditional roles and Old World values into political mobilization and streetwise militancy. Seeking to provide for their families by assuring a fair price for meat and vegetables, middle-aged immigrant women combined their power as consumers with "the traditional communal tactic of interrupting the Torah reading when a matter of justice was at stake." Politicizing the neighborhood networks that were central to housewives' daily existence and arousing editors, civic and religious leaders, trade unionists, and their own husbands and sons, the women quickly formed an association to coordinate their boycott of unscrupulous merchants.

The development of the kosher meat boycott reveals tensions among the women and between militant housewives and male socialist organizers. Yet it also demonstrates how vital to the community's survival were women's domestic skills and resources. Food riots are one of the oldest and most specifically female forms of protest, having occurred throughout Europe, sporadically in the colonies, in Richmond, Virginia, during the Civil War, and elsewhere. Immigrant, especially Jewish, women would continue to employ food boycotts as a vehicle for economic protest at least into World War I.

Women have always participated in politics. Despite their eclipse in the conventional seats of political power, women in preindustrial societies frequently engaged in popular protest, particularly when the price, or availability, of basic foodstuffs was at issue. As the English historian E. P. Thompson has pointed out, women were "those most involved in face-to-face marketing [and hence] most sensitive to price significancies . . ." In fact, "it is probable that the women most frequently precipitated the spontaneous actions." In the popular ferment of the early days of the French Revolution, women were also conspicuous by their presence. The image of grim-faced market women on the march to Versailles to bring the royal family back to Paris has been sharply etched in the mind of every student of history or enthusiast of historical dramas. Even before the emergence of modern political movements committed to the recruitment of women into the political process, the "crowd" was an important means of expression for women's economic and political interests.

Immigrant Jewish women, too, took to the streets in spontaneous food riots on several occasions. Like their British and French forerunners more than a century before, they were reacting to the sharp rise in the price of food. Most noted and flamboyant of these incidents were the 1902 kosher meat riots in New York City. Erupting in mid-May, they precipitated political activity which continued for almost a month, attracting considerable attention both within the Jewish community and the larger

urban society. Indeed, in a fierce and vitriolic editorial of May 24, 1902, the *New York Times* called for a speedy and determined police repression of this "dangerous class . . . especially the women [who] are very ignorant [and] . . . mostly speak a foreign language. . . . It will not do," the editorial continued, "to have a swarm of ignorant and infuriated women going about any part of this city with petroleum destroying goods and trying to set fire to shops of those against whom they are angry."

What impelled immigrant Jewish housewives to take to the streets (of Williamsburg, in this case) with bottles of kerosene in their hands? Was this simply an act of spontaneous rage, a corroboration of the English writer Robert Southey's comment that "women are more disposed to be mutinous [than men.]" Are the kosher meat riots a late manifestation of preindustrial sensibility that focused upon the illegitimacy of violating a fair price for food? Finally, and most importantly, what can we learn of the self-perceptions, political consciousness, and sense of community of immigrant Jewish women by examining their role in this incident?

Despite their superficial similarity to earlier food riots, the kosher meat riots of 1902 give evidence of a modern and sophisticated political mentality emerging in a rapidly changing community. With this issue of the high price of food, immigrant housewives found a vehicle for political organization. They articulated a rudimentary grasp of their power as consumers and domestic managers. And, combining both traditional and modern tactics, they temporarily turned their status as housewives to good advantage, and used the neighborhood network to stage a successful three-week boycott of kosher meat shops throughout the Lower East Side, parts of Upper Manhattan and the Bronx, and Brooklyn. The dynamics of the kosher meat boycott suggest that by focusing

From "Immigrant Women and Consumer Protest: The New York City Kosher Meat Boycott of 1902," *American Jewish History,* Vol. 70, September 1980. Copyright © 1980 by American Jewish Historical Society. Reprinted by permission of the American Jewish Historical Society and the author.

Food boycotts have a long history as a means of economic protest. In 1902 the rise in kosher meat prices provoked outrage among the housewives of the Jewish community in New York City's Lower East Side. Although these women had played no role in organized politics or labor movements, they combined their familiarity with traditional political rhetoric, their understanding of the market economy, and their sense of their power as consumers into an effective neighborhood organization that succeeded in forcing the meat merchants to lower their prices.

almost exclusively upon organized political activity in the labor movement and the socialist parties, historians have overlooked the role of women. Although for a great part of their life absent from the wage-earning market, immigrant Jewish women were not apolitical. They simply expressed their political concerns in a different, less historically accessible arena—the neighborhood—where they pioneered in local community organizing.

In early May, 1902, the retail price of kosher meat had soared from twelve cents to eighteen cents a pound. Small retail butchers, concerned that their customers would not be able to afford their produce, refused to sell meat for a

week to pressure the wholesalers (commonly referred to as the Meat Trust) to lower their prices. When their May 14th settlement with the wholesalers brought no reduction in the retail price of meat, Lower East Side housewives, milling in the street, began to call for a strike against the butchers. As one activist, Mrs. Levy, the wife of a cloakmaker, shouted, "This is their strike? Look at the good it has brought! Now, if *we women* make a strike, then it will be a strike." Gathering support on the block—Monroe Street and Pike Street—Mrs. Levy and Sarah Edelson, owner of a small restaurant, called a mass meeting to spread the word of the planned boycott.

The next day, after a neighborhood canvas staged by the organizing committee, thousands of women streamed through the streets of the Lower East Side, breaking into butcher shops, flinging meat into the streets, and declaring a boycott. "Women were the ringleaders at all hours," noted the *New York Herald*. Customers who tried to carry their purchased meat from the butcher shop were forced to drop it. One woman emerging from a butcher store with meat for her sick husband was vociferously chided by an elderly woman wearing the traditional sheitel that "a sick man can eat tref meat." Within half an hour, the *Forward* reported, the strike had spread from one block through the entire area. Twenty thousand people were reported to have massed in front of New Irving Hall. "Women were pushed and hustled about [by the police], thrown to the pavement . . . and trampled upon," wrote the *Herald*. One policeman, trying to rescue those buying meat, had "an unpleasant moist piece of liver slapped in his face." Patrol wagons filled the streets, hauling women, some bleeding from their encounters with the police, into court. About seventy women and fifteen men were arrested on charges of disorderly conduct.

After the first day of street rioting, a mass meeting to rally support and map strategy was held at the initiative of the women activists, who had formed a committee. Two of their number addressed the crowd, as did the popular figure Joseph Barondess and the Zionist leader Rabbi Zeft. The next day, May 16, Lower East Side women again went from house to house to strengthen the boycott. Individuals were urged not to enter butcher shops or purchase meat. Pickets were appointed to stand in front of each butcher shop. On each block funds were collected to pay the fines of those arrested and reimburse those customers whose meat had been confiscated in the first day of rioting. The *Tribune* reported that "an excitable and aroused crowd roamed the streets . . . As was the case on the previous day, the main

disturbance was caused by the women. Armed with sticks, vocabularies and well sharpened nails, they made life miserable for the policemen." On the second day of rioting another hundred people were arrested. The boycott also spread, under local leadership, to the Bronx and to Harlem, where a mass meeting was held at Central Hall.

On Saturday, May 17th, the women leaders of the boycott continued their efforts, going from synagogue to synagogue to agitate on behalf of the boycott. Using the traditional communal tactic of interrupting the Torah reading when a matter of justice was at stake, they called on the men in each congregation to encourage their wives not to buy meat and sought rabbinic endorsement of their efforts. For once, urged a boycott leader, citing a Biblical passage, let the men use the power of "And he shall rule over her" to the good—by seeing to it that their wives refrain from purchasing meat.

By Sunday, May 18th, most butcher shops on the Lower East Side bowed to reality and closed their doors. And the boycott had spread to Brooklyn, where the store windows of open butcher shops had been broken and meat burned. That night, the women held another meeting, attended by more than five hundred persons, to consolidate their organization, now named the Ladies' Anti-Beef Trust Association. Under the presidency of Mrs. Caroline Schatzburg, it proposed to continue house-to-house patrols, keep watch over butcher stores, and begin agitating for similar action among Christian women. Circulars bearing a skull and crossbones and the slogan "Eat no meat while the Trust is taking meat from the bones of your women and children" were distributed throughout the Jewish quarters of the city. The Association established six similar committees to consolidate the boycott in Brownsville, East New York, and the Bronx. Other committees were set up to visit the labor and benevolent societies, labor union meetings, and lodges and to plan the establishment of cooperative stores.

The Association also sent a delegation to the mayor's office to seek permission for an open air rally. Local groups of women continued to enforce the boycott in their neighborhoods. In Brooklyn four hundred women signed up to patrol neighborhood butcher stores. Buyers of meat continued to be assaulted and butcher shop windows smashed. In Harlem two women were arrested when they lay down on the elevated tracks to prevent a local butcher from heading downtown with meat for sale. Throughout the city's Jewish neighborhoods restaurants had ceased serving meat.

However, competition between Sarah Edelson, one of the founders of the boycott, and Caroline Schatzburg, the president of the Ladies' Anti-Beef Trust Association, erupted by May 18th into open quarrels between their followers at meetings. Taking advantage of this rivalry and winning the support of Edelson and her backers, on May 21st male communal leaders, with David Blaustein of the Educational Alliance presiding, held a conference of three hundred representatives of synagogues, *hevras*, landsmanshaften, and unions "to bring order to the great struggle for cheap meat." In his remarks at the conference meeting, Joseph Barondess made explicit that a new leadership was asserting itself. Urging the women to be quiet and leave the fighting to the men, he noted that otherwise the women would be held responsible in the event of the boycott's defeat. Calling themselves the Allied Conference for Cheap Kosher Meat, the male conference leaders appointed a ten person steering committee, among whom were only three women. (Women continued, however, to engage in propaganda activities and sporadic rioting in their neighborhoods.) The Allied Conference published a circular in both Yiddish and English, noting that "brave and honest men [were] now aiding the women" and declaring that the conference had "decided to help those butchers who [would] sell cheap kosher meat under the supervision of the rabbis and the confer-

ence." "The people feel very justly," continued the statement, "that they are being ground down, not only by the Beef Trust of the country, but also by the Jewish Beef Trust of the City."

On May 22, the Retail Butchers Association succumbed and affiliated itself with the boycott against the Trust. On May 27, Orthodox leaders, who had hesitated to express formal endorsement of the boycott, joined the fray. By June 5 the strike was concluded. The wholesale price of kosher meat was rolled back to nine cents a pound so that the retail price would be pegged at fourteen cents a pound. Kosher meat cooperatives, which were established during the strike in both Brooklyn and Harlem, continued in existence. While meat prices began to rise inexorably again in the period following the conclusion of the boycott, the movement can still be considered a qualified success.

The leaders of the boycott were not typical of other women political activists of the period. Unlike the majority of women organized in the nascent garment unions, they were not young. Unlike the female union leaders, they were housewives with children. The mean age of those boycott leaders who could be traced in the 1905 New York state manuscript census was 39. They ranged from Mamie Ghilman, the thirty-two year old Russian-born wife of a tailor to Mrs. L. Finkelstein, a fifty-four year old member of the Women's Committee. All but two were more than thirty-five years of age at the time of the boycott. These women were mothers of large families, averaging 4.3 children apiece living at home. Fannie Levy, who initiated the call for the strike, was the mother of six children, all below the age of thirteen. None had fewer than three children. While only two women were United States citizens, the strike leaders were not, for the most part, recent arrivals to America. They had been living in New York City from three to twenty-seven years, with a median residence of eleven years. Having had sufficient time to accommodate themselves to the American scene, they were not simply expressing traditional forms of cultural resistance to industrial society imported from the Old Country.

In socioeconomic terms, the women initiators of the boycott appear representative of the larger immigrant Jewish community of the Lower East Side. Their husbands were, by and large, employed as artisans in the garment industry, though three were self-employed small businessmen. The husband of Annie Block, a member of the Women's Committee, was a tailor, as were three other husbands. Fannie Levy's husband was a cloakmaker and Bessie Norkin's a carpenter, while J. Jaffe's husband, Meyer, and Annie Levine's husband, Morris, topped the occupational scale as a real estate agent and storekeeper respectively. With one exception, all of their children above the age of sixteen were working—two-thirds of them in artisan trades and the remainder as clerks or low level business employees (e.g. salesladies). Only the eighteen year old son of the real estate agent was still in school (though his older brothers were employed as garment industry operators). Thus, the women formed not an elite in their community, but a true grass roots leadership.

It is clear from their statements and their activity that the women who led the boycott had a distinct economic objective in mind and a clear political strategy for achieving their goal. Unlike traditional food rioters, the Lower East Side housewives were not demanding the imposition of a just and popular price on retailers. Nor were they forcibly appropriating meat for purchase at a popularly determined price, though they did retain a traditional sense of a moral economy in which food should be available at prices which the working classes could afford. Rather, recognizing that prices were set by the operation of the laws of supply and demand, as modified, in this case, by the concentration of the wholesale meat industry, they hit upon a boycott of meat as the most effective way to dramatically curtail demand.

They referred to themselves as strikers; those who did not comply with the boycott were called "scabs." When they were harassed in the street by police, they complained that denial by police of their right to assemble was an attack on their freedom of speech. Thus, Lower East Side women were familiar with the political rhetoric of their day, with the workings of the market economy, and with the potential of consumers to affect the market.

While the impulse for the boycott originated in spontaneous outrage of women consumers at the price of kosher meat and their sense that they had been manipulated (or swindled, as they put it) by the retail butchers, who had sold out their customers in their agreement with wholesalers, this incident was not simply an explosion of rage. It was a sustained, though limited, movement, whose success lay in its careful organization. As the *New York Herald* rightly commented, "These women were in earnest. For days they had been considering the situation, and when they decided on action, they perfected an organization, elected officers, . . . and even went so far as to take coins from their slender purses until there was an expense fund of eighty dollars with which to carry on the fight."

In fact, the neighborhood focus of the boycott organization proved to be its source of strength. The initial boycott committee, composed of nineteen women, numbered nine neighbors from Monroe Street, four from Cherry Street, and six from adjacent blocks. This was not the anonymous city so often portrayed by antiurban polemicists and historians but a neighborhood community whose residents maintained close ties. The first show of strength on May 15th was preceded by an early morning house-to-house canvas of housewives in the heart of the boycott area. A similar canvas occurred the next day in Harlem under the aegis of local women. Rooted in the neighborhood, where many activities were quasi-public rather than strictly private, housewives were able to exert moral (as well as physical) suasion upon the women whom they saw on a daily basis. They assumed the existence of collective goals and the right to demand shared sacrifices. Individual desires for the consumption of meat were to be subordinated to the larger public good. As one boycott enthusiast stated while grabbing meat from a girl leaving a butcher store, "If we can't eat meat, the customers can't eat meat." Shouting similar sentiments in another incident, striking women attempted to remove the meat from cholent pots which their neighbors had brought to a local bakery on a Friday afternoon. Participants in the boycott picketed local butchers and also resolved not to speak to the "scabs" in their midst. The constant presence in the neighborhood of the housewife leaders of the boycott made it difficult for individuals to evade their surveillance. The neighborhood, a form of female network, thus provided the locus of community for the boycott: all were giving up meat together, celebrating dairy shabbosim together, and contributing together to the boycott fund.

The women who organized and led the boycott considered themselves the natural leaders of such an enterprise. As consumers and housewives, they saw their task as complementary to that of their wage-earning spouses: "Our husbands work hard," stated one of the leaders at the initial planning meeting. "They try their best to bring a few cents into the house. We must manage to spend as little as possible. We will not give away our last few cents to the butcher and let our children go barefoot." In response, the women shouted, "We will not be silent; we will overturn the world." Describing themselves as soldiers, they determined to circulate leaflets calling upon all women to "join the great women's war." An appeal to their "worthy sisters," published by the Ladies Anti-Beef Trust in the *Forward,* expressed similar sentiments, calling for "help . . . in the name of humanity in this great struggle which we have undertaken out of need."

Sharper formulations of class resentment mingled with pride in their own talents in some of the women's shouts in the street demonstrations. One woman was heard lamenting to another, "Your children must go to work, and the millionaires snatch the last bit from our mouths." Another called out, "My husband brings me eight dollars a week. Should I give it away to the butcher? What would the landlord say?" Still another screamed, "They think women aren't people, that they can bluff us; we'll show them that we are more people than the fat millionaires who suck our blood." When the son of the Chief Rabbi, who supervised the kashrut of the meat, passed through the area, he was met with shouts of "Trust—Kosher *Korobke,*" a reference to the kosher meat tax, much despised by the poor in Czarist Russia.

The ringleaders who were arrested and charged with disorderly conduct defined their behavior in political terms and considered it both just and appropriate to their status as housewives. "Did you throw meat on the street?" Rosa Peskin was asked. "Certainly," she replied. "I should have looked it in the teeth?" When the judge condescendingly commented, "What do you know of a trust? It's no business of yours," she responded, "Whose business is it, then, that our pockets are empty . . . ?" "What do you have against a woman who has bought meat," the judge persisted. "I have nothing against her," retorted Peskin. "It doesn't matter to me what others want to do. But it's because of others that we must suffer." Rebecca Ablowitz also presented the boycotters' rationale to the judge: "We're not rioting. Only see how thin our children are, our husbands have no more strength to work harder . . . If we stay home and cry, what good will that do us?"

Of similar conviction and eloquence was Mrs. Silver, one of the most articulate spokeswomen of the boycott, who headed the campaign to interrupt services in the synagogues. When one irate opponent roared that her speaking thus from the bima was an effrontery (*chutzpah*) and a desecration of God's name (chillul ha-Shem), Mrs. Silver coolly responded that the Torah would pardon her.

The climate of the immigrant Jewish community facilitated the resolute behavior of the women. While a few rabbis, particularly those with close ties to the meat industry, were hostile to the boycott enterprise, they were the exception. Support for the boycott was widespread within the community. Friendly crowds packed the courtroom to cheer the arrested women. In every one of the synagogues on the Lower East Side, it was reported, "the uprising of the Hebrew women was referred to by the rabbis." Most synagogue members warmly greeted the women who brought their cause to the congregation. When police were brought in to arrest Mrs. Silver after a disturbance erupted in one synagogue, a congregant rose to compare the women to the prophet Zachariah, "who preached truly and whose blood demanded vengeance." So persuasive was he that Mrs. Silver was released. Feeling that they could count upon the support of the traditionally observant community, the Ladies' Anti-Beef Trust Association, in an appeal printed by the *Forward,* called for communal ostracism of the one prominent rabbi, Dr. Adolph N. Radin of the People's Synagogue, who had not only refused to approve the boycott but had treated representatives of the Association rudely in his synagogue. He should be removed from his position as chaplain to Jewish prisoners, urged the women, for if this "half-German" could refer publicly to the boycotting women as "beasts" and receive them so coarsely in front of his congregation, how must he treat the unfortunate Jewish inmates he sees within the confines of the prison?

Both the socialist *Forward* and the Orthodox *Yiddishes Tageblat* portrayed the initial disturbances as well as the later movement in a sympathetic manner and were offended by the rough treatment meted out to the women and their families by the police as well as by the unsympathetic attitude of much of the English language press. Jewish socialists, in particular, stood squarely behind the protest. The *Forward* heralded the boycott with the banner headline, "Bravo, bravo, bravo, Jewish women!" To the *Forward,* the boycott provided an opportunity not only to support a grass roots protest action but also to level an attack upon the collusion of the rabbis with the German Jewish meat trust. There was little reason for the differential between kosher and non-kosher meat to stand at five to six cents a pound, proclaimed the newspaper's editorial. Those who raised the prices "are Yahudim with gilded beards, who never eat kosher. Why are they suddenly so *frum* (pious)? Since when is there a partnership between those who give rabbinic endorsements in the Chief Rabbi's name and those Yahudi meat handlers . . . The chief Rabbi's son is merely a salesman for the Trust," continued the editorial. "He goes about in carriages collecting money in the name of his unfortunate father's endorsement . . . Whether the strike of the good Jewish women brings down the prices or not," concluded the *Forward,* "one thing remains certain, the bond between the Trust and the rabbis must end. If they are truly pious, let them serve their religion and not the Trust in whose pay they are in." In Russian Poland, noted the paper the next day, the meat tax was seven cents a pound, but at least there the *korobke* supported all kehilla (communal) activities. Here, on the other hand, it went only to the Trust.

While the *Forward* conducted its pro-boycott campaign, the labor movement as a whole extended monetary donations and aid to the boycott; two men active in the Ladies' Garment Workers' Union were appointed as vice-president and secretary of the Ladies' Anti-Beef Trust Association, while the posts of president and treasurer remained in women's hands. In Harlem it was the Women's Branch No. Two of the Workmen's Circle, with the support of the parent organization, that coordinated local boycott activity.

Communal support was not, however, without its limits. Jewish communal leaders were clearly upset by the initiative assumed by the women activists. The sight of Jewish women engaged in picketing and in the physical coercion of butcher shop customers as well as of their arrest at the hands of a none too gentle police force aroused concern. "Don't give the Trust and the police an opportunity to break heads," cautioned the *Forward*. "More can be accomplished lawfully than not . . . Agitate quietly in your homes." Moreover, when the boycott was recognized as a force to be reckoned with, men tried to wrest control of the movement from its female leaders. However, the women were never entirely displaced, and Yiddish language media continued, if somewhat ambivalently, to view the success of the boycott as a legitimate example of the "power of women."

In a larger sense, the immigrant Jewish community was quite supportive of women's political activity. East European Jewish immigrants were highly politicized; just how highly can be seen in the meat boycott, whose participants were sufficiently traditional to buy kosher meat and to use the synagogues and *hevras* as areas for potential recruitment. Indeed, the development of the boycott suggests that the compartmentalization of the immigrant community by historians into Orthodox, socialist and anarchist, and Zionist sectors does not do justice to the interplay among the groups. Boundary lines were fluid, and socialist rhetoric tripped easily from the tongues of women who still cared about kosher meat, could cite Biblical passages in Hebrew, and felt at ease in the synagogue. Moreover, the boycotters consciously addressed themselves to several different constituencies—synagogues, landsmanshaften, the labor movement, and socialist groups.

Even within the traditional community, women had never been banned from the *secular* public sphere. In developing cadres of female activists, both the Jewish labor and Zionist movements in Russia built upon the relative freedom of public activity accorded women within the Jewish community. As Mary Van Kleeck of the Russell Sage Foundation commented in her study of one Lower East Side trade which employed Jewish women, "The Jewish girl . . . has a distinct sense of her social responsibility and often displays an eager zest for discussion of labor problems . . . Her attitude is likely to be that of an agitator. Nevertheless, she has the foundation of that admirable trait, 'public spirit,' and a sense of relationship to a community larger than the family or the personal group of which she happens to be a member." Sufficient toleration existed within the family circle to enable Jewish women to express their "public spirit," to permit wives and mothers to attend evening meetings and to demonstrate in the streets. As the *Yiddishes Tageblat* put it, somewhat condescendingly, at the beginning of the boycott, "The women this time let the men play at home with the children while they went to attend the meeting." While this was clearly a situation worthy of comment, it was not a violation of communal values.

If the immigrant Jewish community helped to sustain the meat boycott, the English-language socialist press was far more ambivalent in its attitude to this form of political activity. Indeed, it saw the only appropriate weapon for workers in the struggle against capitalism in the organization of producers rather than consumers. As *The Worker* commented:

The Meat Trust does not care two-cents for such opposition as this, no matter how sincere the boycotters may be . . . [A boycott] is so orderly and law abiding, so free from all taint of socialism or confiscation or class hatred, so truly individualistic, and above all, so perfectly harmless—to all except the poor workingmen . . . We cannot oppose the aggression of twentieth century capitalism with weapons fitted to the petty conflicts of eighteenth century small producers.

Added the *Daily People,* organ of the Socialist Labor Party, "It does not make the capitalist hungry if the workingman goes without food. . . ." Such an attitude overlooked the potential of community organization outside the workplace. It precluded reaching out to the neighborhood as a possible secondary locus of political activism, and incidentally resulted in an inability on the part of the socialists to tap the ranks of the politically conscious housewife.

The difference in attitudes between the Yiddish-speaking and English-language socialists is also of broader interest. While the Jewish socialists were often seen as assimilationist, they remained closer to the shared values of their own immigrant community than to the perhaps ideologically purer stance of the American radicals.

The boycott movement enables us to look at the potential for political organization among Lower East Side women, the majority of whom were housewives unaffiliated in any formal sense with the trade union movement. But it also raises questions for which there are no readily available answers.

Was there any precedent for this type of direct action among married women in Eastern Europe? One can find a tenuous connection to the Eastern European scene in a reference to the *korobke,* the meat tax, which in the nineteenth century constituted as much as one-third of the budget of some Jewish communities and was passionately resented. Same Hasidic rebbes in the first half of the last century urged passive resistance against the tax, even including a boycott on the purchase of meat. Clearly, the ability to draw an analogy, as both the women activists and the *Forward* editorials did, between the *korobke* and the high price of kosher meat caused by collusion between the meat trust and rabbis selling their hechsher (certification of kashrut) was an appealing propaganda device. It linked the 1902 boycott to the longstanding disaffection of the poor with the authorities of the Eastern European kehilla. However, the boycott's leaders do not refer to earlier Eastern European examples of reaction against the *korobke,* nor is there any other evidence of direct influence from the Eastern European to the American scene.

As interesting as the boycott is as a vehicle for examining the political sensibilities and assessing the political potential of Jewish housewives on the Lower East Side, the fading away of the Ladies' Anti-Beef Trust Association is as significant as its sudden appearance. If the neighborhood network was so effective a means to reach women and mobilize them, why was it not sustained to deal with other social problems? True, the 1904 and 1907–08 rent strikes on the Lower Side espoused similar tactics and hailed the meat boycott as their model. Beginning with a house-to-house canvas initiated by women, strike leaders promoted neighborhood solidarity by collecting written pledges of refusal to pay rent. In 1908 women also lent their support to retail butchers protesting the rising cost in wholesale meat prices. These further incidents of local activism confirm the growing consumer consciousness of Lower East Side women. However, there appears to be no overlap in leadership between these several expressions of female popular protest. Were women coopted into already established fraternal and political organizations, or did the politics of crisis bring with it inertia once the crisis had passed?

Because its leaders faded into obscurity with the conclusion of the boycott, because of the very nature of a short-lived grass roots movement, it is impossible to assess the impact of the movement upon its participants. However, it is likely that the political awareness expressed by the boycotters was no isolated phenomenon but was communicated effectively, if quietly and informally, to their younger sisters and daughters. The boycott alerted the immigrant community as a whole and the labor movement in particular to the political potential of women. Moreover, the communal support of the boycott could only have encouraged women themselves to further activity. As Alice Kessler-Harris notes of Jewish women in the garment trades, whose numbers in the unions exceeded their proportion in the industry as a whole, they "unionized at their own initiative" and were "responsible for at least one quarter of the increased number of unionized women [in America] in the second decade of the twentieth century." In that sense the kosher meat boycott should be seen not as an isolated incident but as a prelude to the explosion of women activists in the great garment industry strikes at the end of the decade.

Questions for Study and Review

1. What does the kosher meat boycott reveal about conditions of life in new immigrant communities?

2. What were the connections between housewives' traditional domestic roles, their new public militancy, and Jewish support for socialist and other radical political programs?

3. How might female leaders of the kosher meat boycott have responded to programs offered by settlement house residents?

4. In the late 1700s, colonial housewives employed domestic resources and skills in support of the American Revolution. How would you compare their actions to those of Jewish women in the early twentieth century?

Suggested Readings

Dana Frank, "Housewives, Socialists, and the Politics of Food: The 1917 New York City Cost of Living Protests," *Feminist Studies* (Summer 1985).

Ruth Milkman, ed., *Women, Work and Protest: A Century of U.S. Women's Labor History* (1985).

Judith E. Smith, *Family Connections: A History of Italian and Jewish Immigrant Lives in Providence, Rhode Island, 1900–1940* (1985).

Meredith Tax, *The Rising of the Women: Feminist Solidarity and Class Conflict, 1880–1917* (1980).

Maxine Schwartz Seller, ed., *Immigrant Women* (1981).

SEVEN

A Bond of Common Womanhood: Building a Women's Interracial Coalition in the Jim Crow South

Jacquelyn Dowd Hall

As immigration changed the face of northern society, so too did the institution of Jim Crow laws affect race relations in the South. The opportunities and hopes of blacks in the immediate post-Civil War period and the promises offered to poor whites and some blacks by the Alliance campaign withered under the reassertion of white supremacy in the 1890s. Contacts between the races, which had been in a state of flux during Reconstruction, now became tightly regulated and restricted. The Supreme Court's ruling in *Plessy* v. *Ferguson* (1896) gave constitutional sanction to segregationist laws in the South as well as to racist practices in the North.

In response to these events, concerned voices were raised in both black and white communities, though those in the latter were fewer and less urgent. The urgency among blacks resulted not only from the economic and political disabilities heaped upon them, nor solely from the social ostracism institutionalized through legal segregation, but also from the fear and the fact of physical violence. The return of the Ku Klux Klan—North and South—after World War I was only the most lurid example of racism run rampant.

Lynching was perhaps the worst manifestation of the deteriorating racial climate. One of the most widely cited justifications for lynching black men was the molestation or rape of white women. Beginning in the 1890s, Ida B. Wells, a black journalist and teacher from Memphis, focused the black community's attention on the need to protest such episodes with "earnest, united action." About the same time, white women in the Methodist Church were forging their first autonomous organization through the establishment of a Home Mission Society. This association would ultimately provide white women with a forum for joining the antilynching campaign and for pursuing interracial cooperation more generally.

In 1906, black women in Atlanta formed a Neighborhood Union that became a model for other self-help projects throughout the South. At the same time, white women in the North founded the national Young Women's Christian Association, a linchpin in the developing interracial women's movement against racial violence. These efforts were part of a larger interracial movement, the most well-known manifestation of which was the National Association for the Advancement of Colored People. Founded in 1910, the NAACP brought together Ida B. Wells, Mary Church Terrell, W. E.B. DuBois, and other black activists with Jane Addams and other white progressives. In the South, however, few if any whites joined the NAACP. Instead, the Commission on Interracial Cooperation, which was formed a decade later and took a more cautious approach to reshaping race relations, was the first association to try to bring black and white Southerners together.

Hall traces the development of southern black and white women's organizations concerned with racial justice in this period and depicts the intricate, often strained, interactions among these advocates of racial harmony. She illuminates as well the vital contribution of Protestant evangelicalism to the decades of grass roots activism that spanned World War I in black and white communities across the South. Finally, by demonstrating the continuities between turn-of-the-century missionary and mutual aid efforts and the interracial movement of the 1920s, Hall reminds us that World War I and its aftermath could spur as well as stifle social activism.

In the 1830s, the feminist-abolitionist Sarah Grimké began closing her letters with the phrase, "Thine in the bonds of womanhood." Implicit in her choice of words were the premises of nineteenth-century feminism: women's oppression combined with their common experience to create a bond of sisterhood across class and racial lines. From the outset, however, such assertions of collective identity obscured profound differences in women's lives. By the turn of the century, the historic association between women's rights and abolitionism had faded from memory and the organized women's movement spoke primarily for the white middle class. Suffragists adopted nativist and racist arguments in behalf of their cause; clubwomen barred blacks from their national federation. Black women were ignored or excluded by every major women's group in the country.

Meanwhile, black women created parallel organizational networks. Inspired by a distinctive feminist ideology that saw the fight for women's rights as part of a larger struggle against the patriarchal manipulation of race and sex, black women fought for equal rights within the church and formed mutual aid societies, temperance groups, and settlement houses. By the

1890s they were coordinating local efforts through national women's organizations and producing their own theories of race and sex oppression.

Black women were quite aware of developments within the white organizational world, and after 1910 they became increasingly active in the suffrage campaign. But black feminism was largely ignored by whites. This was especially so in the South, where the late nineteenth-century emergence of a black middle class produced strong women leaders at a time when white elites had distanced themselves from the black community more sharply than ever before.

The first organized, regionwide attempt to bridge this gap appeared in the South after World War I. The Women's Committee of the Commission on Interracial Cooperation, founded in Memphis, Tennessee, in 1920, blended Victorian ideals of moral motherhood with a long tradition of southern white patronage of selected black leaders. But it also looked forward to a new development: a native white liberalism in which women would play a prominent role. For the black women involved, it represented a victory over the racial stereotypes that mocked their claims to respectable middle-class womanhood and served as a benchmark in a long campaign to enlist white women in the struggle for the advancement of the race.

✳

From "A Bond of Common Womanhood" from *Revolt Against Chivalry: Jessie Daniel Ames and the Women's Campaign Against Lynching* by Jacquelyn Dowd Hall. Copyright © 1974, 1979 Columbia University Press. All rights reserved. Used by permission.

Author's note: This essay is a compressed and revised version of chapter 3 of *Revolt Against Chivalry: Jessie Daniel Ames and the Women's Campaign Against Lynching* (New York: Columbia University Press, 1979). Much significant work has appeared since 1979, especially in the blossoming field of black women's history, but I have not attempted a thorough rewriting to take all those contributions into account. I owe special thanks to Glenda Gilmore, who read that earlier chapter with a fine critical eye and generously shared her current research on black women in North Carolina with me.

In 1919, a war to make the world safe for democracy ended and a "red summer" of racial violence began. Although the police power of the state was arrayed on the side of white vigilantes, blacks managed to inflict considerable damage on their attackers. Most white southerners, alarmed by what they saw as a resurgence of the militancy defused by turn-of-the-century disfranchisement campaigns, de-

THE SHAME OF AMERICA

Do you know that the United States is the Only Land on Earth where human beings are BURNED AT THE STAKE?

In Four Years 1918-1921, Twenty-Eight People were publicly BURNED BY AMERICAN MOBS

3436 People Lynched, 1889-1921

Is Rape the "Cause" of Lynching?

83 WOMEN HAVE BEEN LYNCHED IN THE UNITED STATES

AND THE LYNCHERS GO UNPUNISHED

THE REMEDY

The Dyer Anti-Lynching Bill Is Now Before the United States Senate

In the years following World War I, racial tensions, spurred in part by competition over housing and jobs, erupted into race riots and other forms of violence, including lynching. Activist reformers united to protest the violence and promote racial harmony. Black and white southern women, excluded from the biracial Commission on Interracial Cooperation (CIC), the South's major reform organization, met in Memphis in 1920 to form a separate Women's Committee of the CIC. By the end of the decade it had become clear that the committee's efforts toward interracial cooperation were generally ineffective. A more successful organization was the all-white Association of Southern Women for the Prevention of Lynching (ASWPL), founded in 1930 by Jessie Daniel Ames and devoted to the single goal of abolishing lynching. Yet its establishment also reflected the inability of white women to cooperate fully with their black "sisters" in pursuit of a common goal.

manded repression. But a small group of moderates advocated a more positive response to black grievances. Meeting in Atlanta in January 1919, these men inaugurated an "After the War Program" designed to "substitute reason for force" by bringing local black and white leaders together. By the beginning of 1920, they had transformed the "After the War Program" into a permanent institution, the Commission on Interracial Cooperation (CIC), and had chosen as its director a young Methodist minister named Will W. Alexander. By the mid-twenties the CIC had grown into the major interracial reform organization in the region.

There were no women among the blacks who were invited to join the group. Nor did any female names appear on an initial list of white southerners "known to be sympathetic and intelligent regarding the race situation." Indeed, even the suggestion that white women should be admitted met spirited resistance. Bringing "white women and colored men into interrelationships that symbolize equality" would open a Pandora's box of sexual fears and taboos. CIC leaders feared being accused of fostering "social intermingling," miscegenation, and intermarriage. They argued that the attitudes of white women were unpredictable. Some believed that women constituted "the Hindenburg line" in race relations; more timid and conservative than men, they would remain the last holdouts for the status quo. Others maintained that women were emotional and sentimental and would become "wild-eyed fanatics" in behalf of reform.

In fact, white southern women had already provided abundant evidence of their approach to social problems. Most studies of the interracial movement have ignored its origins in prewar women's activities, viewing the CIC Woman's Committee as an afterthought of Will Alexander and its successor, the Association of Southern Women for the Prevention of Lynching (ASWPL), as an organization that sprang full blown from the mind of its director, Jessie Daniel Ames. A different angle of vision reveals that neither development is explicable apart from the laity rights and social gospel movements within the Southern Methodist Church and the struggle for racial equality within the Young Women's Christian Association. From the Protestant, and especially Methodist, missionary societies that appeared throughout the South in the 1870s and the YWCAs that spread slowly into the region after the turn of the century, came the rhetoric and the constituency for interracial cooperation among southern women.

The women's missionary movement drew its inspiration from an evangelical experience that had potentially liberating implications for female converts. Sweeping across the South in the opening decades of the nineteenth century, evangelicalism offered women a conversion experience, a new birth, that initiated them into membership in an intimate community of believers. The rise of family religion and the decline of clerical power invested women with responsibility for Christian nurture. The ideal evangelical woman was set apart from the idle lady by her domesticity, piety, seriousness, and commitment to benevolent action. By the 1830s, however, the churches had made their peace with slavery. In doing so, they may also have

ceased to offer an alternative vision of womanhood. Moreover, for white women as for the slaves, evangelical Christianity cut two ways: it could promote resignation even as it offered an implicit critique of a man-made world.

Developments that undermined traditional sex roles in the late nineteenth century heightened the contradictions in the ideal of the evangelical woman and set in motion a struggle to transform women's place in the institutional church. Women had become the mainstay of church life, yet they continued to be excluded from formal positions of authority. The opportunity to work outside the home changed the ideal of domesticity into a boundary to be maintained rather than an elevation of women's separate culture. Expanding educational opportunities like evangelicalism emphasized seriousness and benevolence over frivolity and idleness, encouraging middle-class women with increased leisure to demand a wider expression for piety.

Among white women, the first organizational response to these developments came from the Methodist Episcopal Church, South. In 1878, Southern Methodists formed a regionwide Woman's Foreign Mission Society. In the name of evangelical expansion, church women administered funds, made policy decisions, and managed complex overseas operations. Twenty years later, missionary leaders parlayed this opening wedge into an autonomous Woman's Home Mission Society. Under the presidency of Belle Harris Bennett, the Home Mission Society grafted onto the evangelical idiom the language of the social gospel and used both to expand women's role in the church and the social order.

Institutional autonomy, together with cultural assumptions that encouraged women to channel aggression and achievement into benevolent action, eventually enabled female leaders to challenge the church hierarchy on a number of social issues. When the Home Mission Society began to transform city missions into settlement houses, opponents ridiculed their experiments as "playhouses for women" or condemned them as centers of secular radicalism. Nevertheless, by 1920 Methodist women had created a network of more than twenty-five social settlements in mill towns, coal fields, and industrial centers. They advocated equal pay for women workers, protective legislation, and the elimination of child labor. Although, like other Progressives, they deplored class conflict and hoped for amelioration of working conditions from the top down, they raised a wavering voice in behalf of labor's right to organize.

At first Methodist leaders simply ignored the black community. Their blindness reflected the post-Civil War retreat to segregated churches and the disengagement and alienation that marked the attitudes of moderate whites in the period. But as they took on ever-widening responsibilities, Home Mission Society leaders inevitably confronted the question of race. When they did so, they turned naturally to Booker T. Washington's industrial education ideal.

Bennett's first move was to lay before the Home Mission Board a request for funds to build a women's annex at the Colored Methodist Episcopal Church's Paine College in Augusta, Georgia. The rationales presented for this "new and, as some felt, objectional work" reveal not only the master-servant model that characterized the Methodist women's approach to racial issues, but also a hint of identification with black women across racial lines. The time has come, Bennett admonished, for Methodist women to redefine "our relation to our colored sisters who live among us." Through setting individual examples for their servants and providing industrial training for girls, white women could lead the way toward the resolution of racial conflict and the gradual elevation of a "child race."

Within a decade after these maternalistic beginnings, Methodist women's work in the black community entered a new phase. In 1911, Mary De Bardeleben became the first southern white woman to present herself for mission service among blacks. In 1912, Southern Methodist women assumed financial responsibility for a settlement run by the women of the Colored Methodist Episcopal Church in Nashville, Tennessee. Two years later, they entered a pioneering joint program with the Urban League and Fisk University (a black institution in Nashville) to provide professional training for black social workers.

The biracial staffs, governing boards, and welfare leagues associated with such institutions provided models for postwar efforts at interracial cooperation. Indeed, Will Alexander, then a Vanderbilt University divinity student, gained his first experience in interracial work as a member of the board of the Nashville Bethlehem House. "On that board I grew accustomed to accepting the Negroes as human beings," he recalled. "The women had that attitude, and I learned something from them. I have felt for several years," he concluded, that the Woman's Home Mission Society "was the most progressive and constructive religious group in the South."

Through all these experiences, Methodist women developed a visible and articulate leadership, able to speak to and for women as a group, and an increasingly complex understanding of social problems. Yet the steady expansion of women's roles did not translate into positions of formal authority or an official voice in church affairs. Mission society leaders chafed under the condescension of "the reluctant brethren," but their goal remained control over their own institutions rather than equal rights within the church. That changed in 1906 when a show of force awakened them to the dangers of exclusion. The General Conference, partly in reaction to the emergence of a southern suffrage movement and partly out of a desire to appropriate women's enormously effective fundraising abilities, moved to curb the autonomy of the women's societies by placing them under the control of the male-dominated Board of

Missions. In response, the women launched a struggle for laity rights. Twelve years later, in 1918, they gained the overwhelming endorsement of the General Assembly and the church's district conferences. For the first time, Southern Methodist women could participate in the governance of the church they had done so much to create.

On the eve of the creation of the Commission on Interracial Cooperation, then, Methodist women stood at a critical juncture. Fresh from victory in the laity rights campaign, they were confident, optimistic, at the peak of their group identity. Yet the distance they had traveled could be seen in terms of declension as well as of progress. The autonomy and vigor of the women's societies had been eroded. By 1920, Methodist women leaders implicitly saw themselves as a sisterhood within an alien institution. A paradoxical mixture of triumph and defeat, estrangement and bondedness prepared them to combine the evangelical mode with the concerns of twentieth-century racial liberalism and to join with other women in pursuing their social goals outside the structures of the Methodist church.

✳

A second historical strand leading to the creation of the Interracial Woman's Committee emerged from the struggle of black women for equality and autonomy within the predominantly white Young Women's Christian Association (YWCA). The women who spearheaded the YWCA effort were the children or grandchildren of slaves, the first generations of southern blacks born in freedom. They were also members of a small black elite that, after the turn of the century, grew increasingly class conscious without abandoning an ethic of racial solidarity and mutual self-help. Because daughters were often sent to school while their brothers pursued farming and skilled trades, women played a major role in the fight for education.

Many were teachers and school founders, but they defined that role broadly, assuming community responsibilities that went far beyond the schoolhouse door. Despite their relative privilege, they suffered from the double jeopardy of race and sex discrimination. Taking as their special mission the defense of black women's morality, they adhered to an ideal of womanhood that mixed gentility with forceful public expression. And they played a pivotal role in the building of black institutions and of a resistant, and ultimately insurgent, black community.

In the 1870s, southern black women joined the nationwide impetus toward female self-organization. From the outset, the stimulus for their voluntary activities was political. They banded together as a means of meeting urgent social welfare needs, protesting against lynching, and counteracting the stereotyped image of black sexuality in the white mind.

The most well-known southern pioneer in this effort was a Memphis teacher and journalist named Ida B. Wells. In 1892, she denounced the lynchings of three black store owners. In retaliation, a mob destroyed the offices of her newspaper and forced her to leave the city. What had enraged whites most was Wells' attack on the myth of the black rapist. In the beginning, even she believed "that although lynching was irregular and contrary to law and order, unreasoning anger over the terrible crime of rape led to the lynching." But the Memphis incident convinced her that the rape charge was often a cover-up for economic competition. After a three-month investigation, she began to argue that interracial love affairs rather than forcible rape lay behind many lynchings. "Nobody in this section of the country," she announced, "believes the old thread-bare lie that Negro men rape white women." Fleeing Memphis for New York, Wells took a position on the New York *Age* and launched a one-woman anti-lynching crusade. Later, she moved to Chicago, organized one of the first black women's suffrage clubs, and helped to create the National Association of Colored Women (NACW).

Other southern black women were also active in the national club movement from the start, and by 1920 they had established their own regionwide organizational network. In Atlanta, this group was led by Lugenia Burns Hope, wife of John Hope, the president of Atlanta University. Educated in Chicago, where she had worked at Hull House, Hope had moved to Atlanta with her husband in 1897. From their apartment, she looked out not upon the green serenity of a college campus, but upon an urban slum of the New South. Unpaved roads in Atlanta's West Side black community made travel difficult. The city refused to supply water mains or street lights. Garbage was dumped and burned on the road. As Hope came "face to face with one aspect of injustice and oppression after another," she "rolled up her delicate muslin sleeves" and began to organize her neighbors into a core of volunteer social workers.

By 1906, she had created the Neighborhood Union, a settlement house and community organizing project financed, administered, and controlled by black women. Unique in the South for its scope and continuity, the Neighborhood Union furnished a wide range of social services to the black community. The local white press saw the organization as a harmless attempt to elevate black moral standards. Indeed, the group's activities did reflect the class interests of its members, as they sought to stabilize and improve the neighborhood surrounding the university by driving out the forces of crime, gambling, and prostitution. But these women also addressed themselves to issues of vital importance to the poor; and their efforts brought them into conflict with local merchants, the Sanitation Department, the Board of Education, and, in the 1930s, with the discriminatory administrators of New Deal relief agencies.

In other parts of the South, black women undertook similar projects of education and self-help. Lucy Craft Laney, born in 1854, was the daughter of a carpenter who had paid for

his own and his wife's manumission from slavery. In 1886, she opened Haines Normal and Industrial Institute in Augusta, Georgia. At a time when custom limited black education to vocational training and when Georgia provided no public high schools for blacks, Haines Institute maintained a liberal arts curriculum that prepared students for college and careers in teaching.

The most famous of Lucy Laney's many protégées was Mary McLeod Bethune. One of seventeen children born to slave parents in Mayesville, South Carolina, Bethune established Bethune-Cookman School in Daytona Beach, Florida, in 1904. Founder and president of the National Council of Negro Women and of the Southeastern Federation of Colored Women's Clubs, Bethune went on to become director of the National Youth Administration's Division of Negro Affairs, the only woman member of Franklin Delano Roosevelt's "Black Cabinet."

Janie Porter Barrett and Charlotte Hawkins Brown, also protégées of Lucy Laney, were tireless and resourceful institution builders. In 1890, Barrett organized the Locust Street Social Settlement, the first settlement house in Virginia and among the first for blacks in the country. Fourteen years later, she created the Virginia Industrial School for Colored Girls in Peaks Turnout, supported by the fundraising efforts of the Virginia State Federation of Colored Women's Clubs. Charlotte Hawkins Brown opened Palmer Memorial Institute in Sedalia, North Carolina, in 1902 and maintained it by a mighty effort of will until her death in 1961.

Many of the institutions run by these clubwomen, educators, and social workers grew out of a concern for the special plight of black girls, and in the years before World War I, they began to look toward the YWCA, a national organization devoted to the spiritual and physical welfare of young working women, as a means of coordinating and broadening their efforts. Under the leadership of Lugenia Hope, they pressed for the inclusion of black women in the YWCA on a basis of equality. When their efforts failed, they became a moving force in the creation of the women's interracial movement.

The YWCA, like the women's missionary societies, was rooted in Protestant evangelicalism. It spread to college campuses and urban centers in response to the entry of women into higher education and wage labor. In the decade before World War I, the "Y" developed vigorous industrial and student departments and moved from its early emphasis on moral protection to a concern for social justice.

Like the Methodist missionary societies, however, the YWCA found it easier to address the problems of white women than to offer a critique of racism either within its own ranks or in the larger society. The first black branch was established in 1893, and segregated locals appeared here and there in northern and western cities. After 1906, when a group of southern white women met in Asheville, North Carolina, to consider extending the YWCA's work into the black community, the National Board accepted *de facto* segregation as official policy and began chartering black YWCAs as subordinate branches of central white associations in southern cities.

World War I hastened the spread of black "Ys" in the region. Through its War Work Council, the YWCA supplied recreational facilities to soldiers and aid to young women entering war industries. In belated recognition of the needs of black soldiers and the fact that black as well as white women were coming to the city to work, the "Y" appropriated $200,000 for a "Colored Department" of the War Work Council one year before the armistice.

The YWCA placed Eva Bowles, its first black field secretary, in charge of this work and furnished her with a small staff. Plunging into public service with the same sense of "joyful release" felt by many white women during the war, Bowles and her staff established recreational and industrial centers in forty-five com-

munities by the end of 1919, and twelve thousand young women enrolled in YWCA branches. In Atlanta, Lugenia Hope's Neighborhood Union formed the core of an Atlanta Colored Women's War Council that led public protests against the mistreatment of black soldiers on streetcars and the harassment of black civilians and soldiers by police officers.

Black YWCA workers were determined to build on their accomplishments when peace came. "The war," wrote Eva Bowles at the end of 1919, "has given opportunity to the colored woman to prove her ability for leadership. She had her chance and she made good." But such euphoria quickly evaporated as black women were forced to abandon their precarious foothold in industry and race riots shattered the hopes raised by the democratic rhetoric that had justified the war.

Lugenia Hope, attempting to form a black YWCA group in Atlanta, found herself thwarted by two problems that would continue to beset the interracial movement: divisions among southern white women over issues of racial hierarchy and disagreements among black women over the proper balance between aggressiveness and circumspection. The president of the Atlanta central "Y," Susan L. Davis (who would later become a founder and chairman of the CIC Woman's Committee), encouraged Hope's plan. But Adelle Ruffin, a northern black sent south to serve as field supervisor of colored work in the region, objected to the site chosen for the branch. She also accused Hope of using the organization not to aid respectable young women but to "save" immoral "Alley Girls." Other southern black women joined Hope in raising objections to Ruffin's leadership. Ruffin, however, had gained the confidence of the white field staff headquartered in Richmond.

In response to these encroachments from regional YWCA officers, Hope and her coworkers demanded the right to manage their own affairs. An interracial conference held in

Louisville, Kentucky, in 1915, had tried to hammer out the principles that would define the relationship of black branches to white central associations and to the National Board. Hope had attended that gathering, and on April 6, 1920, she called a group of southern black leaders to a meeting at her home in Atlanta to clarify its findings. "Northern women," Hope explained, "thought they knew more about it than Southern women—Colored women believed they knew more than both and that's why they wanted to represent themselves." Black women, she reported, never agreed to the principle that work in the field should advance only as fast as "the Southern whites will permit," nor that young women who needed the "Y" most (Adelle Ruffin's "Alley Girls") should be excluded, nor that black national secretaries could be prohibited from working in the South. Claiming to represent over 300,000 organized southern black women, the group drew up a petition asking that Ruffin be removed on the grounds that she "does not know her own people," that "in all work affecting our people full recognition of leadership be given Negro women," and that blacks be allowed to form branch organizations without waiting for permission of central associations.

Hope, Lucy Craft Lancy, and Lancy's co-worker and Baptist church leader, Mary J. McCrorey presented this petition to the YWCA national convention in Cleveland in May. But the convention avoided taking action by deferring to the authority of the southern field staff to handle all problems in its jurisdiction. Disappointed by the evasiveness of the National Board, Mary McCrorey concluded that "the whole policy is to keep us strictly subordinated" and urged the caucus to "keep wide awake and remain fearless." A follow-up meeting in the Richmond headquarters of the southern field staff proved equally fruitless. Not only were the demands of the black committee rejected, but in the official account of the meeting sent to the National Board, they were ignored altogether.

Frustrated by the failure of their efforts to work within established channels, the black caucus brought public pressure to bear on the "Y." In response, a Louisville "Conference on Colored Work" appointed Charlotte Hawkins Brown to a post as member-at-large of the southern field staff. But even this victory proved illusory, for the southern field staff appropriated no travel funds to bring the "non-resident" member to Richmond, nor did they inform Brown of scheduled meetings or encourage her to attend.

Firing off one final protest, Hope expressed her indignation and disappointment: "I have no regrets for the stand that I took . . . even if I had to be misrepresented and rather cruelly treated because of it." She had grown increasingly disillusioned with the emphasis of YWCA officials on "technique" and compromise. But she had not given up her belief that black women "could stand side by side with women of the white race and work for full emancipation of all women."

The black women's caucus that met in Lugenia Hope's home in April 1920 had discussed not only "some vital interracial work of the YWCA," but also the possibility that "the time was ripe [to] go beyond the YWCA and any other organization and reach a few outstanding white and Negro women, Christian and with well-balanced judgment and not afraid." By cutting across the boundaries of existing organizations, they hoped to bring the strongest black women leaders together with the most progressive whites in an organization specifically devoted to improving race relations.

This desire meshed fortuitously with events taking place at the same time within the Methodist Woman's Missionary Council. At the annual meeting of April 1920 in Kansas City, Missouri, Belle Bennett delivered a presidential address calling upon newly enfranchised southern women to join the movement for interracial cooperation. Her plea was emphasized by a special guest speaker, Will Alexander. Together they urged upon the council a new departure.

Missions to the poor should be replaced by cooperative ventures with black women on the local and regional level. In response, the council created a commission empowered to "study the whole question of race relationship, the needs of Negro women and children, and methods of cooperation by which better conditions can be brought about." Carrie Parks Johnson, who had demonstrated her unusual "powers of initiative" by securing petitions from throughout the church in behalf of the laity rights memorial, assumed the chairmanship of the group.

Lugenia Hope, informed by Will Alexander of the creation of the Methodist commission, seized this opportunity to carry forward "the spirit and purpose" of the YWCA struggle. She invited Johnson and Sara Estelle Haskin, director of the Nashville Bethlehem House, to attend the biennial conference of the National Association of Colored Women at Tuskegee Institute in July. Afterward she arranged a meeting in Booker T. Washington's home between the two white women and her southern co-workers.

Tuskegee Normal and Industrial Institute, founded by Washington in 1881, provided an appropriate location for such a unique and unconventional venture: an encounter of white and black women on a black college campus. The white women did not expect to find any surprises at Tuskegee; its beautifully landscaped grounds, industrial courses, and genteel atmosphere made it an ideal showcase for visiting philanthropists interested in black education. When they arrived, Johnson and Haskin were offered segregated housing and dining facilities. But when they appeared at the first session of the NACW conference, they were startled to find themselves treated simply as members of the group rather than as honored white guests.

Black women, for their part, viewed the Tuskegee meeting with mixed emotions. As they sat down together at a teakwood table in Booker T. Washington's library, these black and white southern women faced each other across "a gulf of distance, of mistrust and suspicion." The black women suspected that the concern of their white visitors for "Negro betterment" was related to their desire for more efficient domestic servants. The hostility of black women toward whites, the inability of white women to comprehend the meaning of that hostility, and the confusion of etiquette and expectations threw the group into paralyzing discomfort.

The shared language of evangelicalism made it possible for the women to regain their bearings and overcome their uneasiness. "Only after an hour spent in the reading of God's word and in prayer, face to face on the platform of Christ Jesus," reported Johnson, "did these white women and black women come to the liberty and frankness that made possible a discussion." Lugenia Hope broke the ice: "We have just emerged from a world war that cost the lives of thousands of our boys fighting to make the world safe for democracy—for whom? . . . Women, we can achieve nothing today unless you . . . who have met us are willing to help us find a place in American life where we can be unashamed and unafraid." Black participants waited tensely to see how Johnson and Haskin would respond and then followed Hope's lead with statements of their own grievances and concerns. Looking back thirteen years later, McCrorey felt that "the spirit of that meeting will last me the remainder of my life." I saw in "the hearts of those Negro women . . . all the aspirations for their homes and their children that I have for mine," Johnson remembered. "My heart broke and I have been trying to pass the story on to the women of my race."

Johnson and Haskin returned to Will Alexander's office in Atlanta convinced that "the men might as well hang their harps on a willow tree, as to try to settle the race problems in the South without the aid of Southern white women." They had discovered a network of educated black women engaged in self-help and institution-building quite apart from the activities of their white counterparts. "While we have thought we were doing the best we could, a race has grown up in our very midst that we do not know," Johnson explained. "We know the cook in the kitchen, we know the maid in the house, we know the man in the yard[,] we know the criminal in the daily papers, we know the worst there is to know—but the masses of the best people of my race do not know the best of the Negro race." If only the Tuskegee experience could be duplicated for larger numbers of women, Johnson and Haskin argued, the indifference of white middle-class women and the assumption of black inferiority could be effectively challenged.

Overcoming the skepticism of his co-workers, Alexander persuaded the CIC to sponsor a region-wide women's conference in Memphis on October 6-7, 1920. Ninety-one women representing the major Protestant denominations, the women's clubs, and the YWCA accepted a vaguely worded invitation to a gathering for the consideration of "important problems." Four black women agreed to address the meetings. Determined to avoid publicity of any sort because "the whole situation was too strange and delicate," Alexander arranged for the conference to be held in a secluded room in a Memphis YMCA where it would be possible to "control the press."

Johnson and Haskin opened the meeting with an account of their sojourn at Tuskegee and "informed the rest of the group that they had been invited to hear the stories these Negro women had to tell." Anyone who objected could withdraw before the afternoon session when the black women would appear. First on the agenda was Tuskegee's Margaret Murray Washington. Like her more famous husband, Margaret Washington was a proponent of accommodation, combining an assertion of black cultural achievements and racial pride with a conciliatory stance toward whites. "I belong to the South and I love it," Washington assured her audience. Referring obliquely to "the system" which, through no fault of the ladies present, had destroyed the black home, she recounted her own efforts at Tuskegee to impress

upon black field workers the necessity of "legally solemnized marriage, and legal children." She described the inequities of black education and portrayed the difficulties faced by black mothers working long hours in a white woman's home. "Give us a chance," she ended, "and you won't find a more law-abiding people in the world."

Jennie Dee Moton, Washington's successor at Tuskegee, and Elizabeth Ross Haynes, a YWCA worker, followed Washington to the podium. But it was Charlotte Hawkins Brown who brought the meeting to a dramatic and surprising culmination. Brown was born in Henderson, North Carolina, but when she was six years old her mother had led her clan of twenty children north to Cambridge, Massachusetts. Through the patronage of Alice Freeman Palmer, president of Wellesley, Brown secured an education. She returned to North Carolina in 1901 and opened Palmer Memorial Institute a year later. She was president of the North Carolina Federation of Colored Women's Clubs and a strong advocate of women's suffrage. Six months earlier, she had been invited to address the annual meeting of the North Carolina Federation of [White] Women's Clubs, where she delivered a stirring plea for cross-class female cooperation and, by some reports, defended "the right of the Negro woman to share equally in the franchise which would soon be granted to the womanhood of the state." When the Nineteenth Amendment passed in September, a month before the Memphis conference, she began mobilizing black women to register and vote.

Brown opened her address with the story of her trip from North Carolina to Tennessee. A menacing crowd of white men had forced her out of a Pullman berth into a Jim Crow day coach. "And the shame of the whole affair was that southern white women passing for Christians were on that very car" bound for the Memphis meeting. She arrived at her destination, shaken with anger, and Johnson and Haskin gingerly kept her off the first day's program. By the last morning of the conference she had translated her rage into an electrifying piece of oratory, perfectly tailored to her audience. "I came to Memphis crushed and humiliated," she told the gathered women. But I am now prepared to deliver "the message which God had given me."

She began by challenging southern white women to accept responsibility for the evil done in their names.

> The Negro women of the south lay everything that happens to the members of her race at the door of the Southern white woman. . . . We all feel that you can control your men . . . that so far as lynching is concerned . . . if the white women would take hold of the situation that lynching would be stopped.

Brown then pursued a theme that she and other black women on the Interracial Commission would bring up repeatedly, the refusal of whites to recognize social distinctions among blacks or to grant educated and virtuous women the respect they deserved. One symbol of those attitudes was the unwillingness of whites to address a married black woman as "Mrs.— whether she be cook, criminal or principal of a school." Terrible assumptions, rooted in slavery, lurked beneath this discourtesy: the belief that black women were promiscuous, that they could not lay claim to the protection that marriage was supposed to afford, that they were fair game for sexual assault. Brown closed her address with a statement that was both an appeal and a warning. "I know that if you are Christian women, that in the final analysis you are going to have to reach out for the same hand that I am reaching out for but I know that the dear Lord will not receive it if you are crushing me beneath your feet."

The white delegates rose to their feet in the ritual response of the evangelical church: heads bowed, spontaneously singing a familiar hymn of Christian fellowship and solidarity. Years later participants

still recalled the fervor of the Memphis conference. Confronted by proud and articulate black women, exhorted passionately, yet in acceptable generalities and in the language of common religious tradition, to accept responsibility for the plight of women whose aspirations were so much like their own, the white women present responded with an outpouring of emotion that would become the paradigm for—and often the only accomplishment of—interracial meetings for a decade.

The conference concluded by asking the Interracial Commission to create a Committee on Woman's Work funded jointly by the CIC and the Woman's Missionary Council and headed by Carrie Parks Johnson. Charlotte Hawkins Brown described the Memphis meeting as "the greatest step forward . . . taken since emancipation." But the vision of a bond of common womanhood that made the Tuskegee and Memphis conferences so memorable faded as the new organization attempted to develop an analysis of concrete social problems and a program for change. Spontaneity gave way to a reassertion of traditional hierarchies and assumptions, and black participants found themselves in a struggle for "self-determination and self-expression" not unlike the YWCA battle from which they had just emerged.

During the months before the Memphis Conference, the black women's caucus had hammered out a position paper meant to serve as the basis for CIC women's work. It dealt with a wide range of issues: the working conditions of domestic servants, child welfare, transportation, education, lynching, the treatment of blacks in the white press, and the right to vote. Without consulting the authors, however, Johnson read a version of the statement that added to its straightforward condemnation of lynching a preface to deploring "any act on the part of Negro men which excites the mob spirit." She omitted the resolution on suffrage altogether. Most significantly, she left out the preamble demanding for black women "all the privileges and rights granted to American womanhood."

Although angered by these changes, the black delegates at first accepted Margaret Washington's counsel of silence: "Let us stand shoulder to shoulder with the two white women and their followers," she admonished. "This Mrs. Johnson, in my mind, is a sincere southern white woman and certainly will need our cooperation and sympathy. . . . We are expected to mark time." But when Johnson decided to publish the black women's statement in this altered form, Lugenia Hope led a protest against the plan. "Mrs. Johnson's crowd," she wrote, "refuses to . . . believe that we are ready for suffrage and . . . are trained in all activities of American life." Convincing Johnson to delay the printing of the pamphlet, Hope called a meeting of the Tuskegee participants to reaffirm their commitment to the original platform.

After months of negotiation, the group drew up a compromise statement. But before it could be submitted for approval to other black CIC members, Johnson decided to drop the matter and notified the black women that there would be no printed pamphlet at all. Hope's response expressed the frustration of being forced to spend inordinate amounts of time and energy trying to influence white moderates who were, in any case, largely outside the mainstream of political and economic power. While racist demagogues controlled public discussion and the Ku Klux Klan surged to power, Interracial Commission leaders quibbled over wording. "In the meantime," Hope concluded, "the forces of darkness manage to agree about what is 'best for Negroes.'"

Four days after this letter was written, on June 28, 1921, the Southeastern Federation of Colored Women's Clubs, meeting in Atlanta, adopted the black women's statement as the platform of the Federation. Published in pamphlet form under the title *Southern Negro Women and Race Co-operation,* the statement omitted the controversial preamble, retained the suffrage plank, and adopted a conciliatory tone in its discussion of lynching. The publication of this pamphlet may have represented a strategic retreat, a willingness on the part of Hope and her supporters to compromise rather than "retard progress." But it may also have reflected divisions among black women themselves, as evidenced by the fact that the version of the statement published by Tuskegee's journal, *The Southern Workman,* dropped the demand for suffrage, as Margaret Washington had, from the outset, urged her compatriots to do.

Agreeing on a statement of purpose had been difficult enough, putting principles into practice would be harder still. CIC Woman's Committee leaders assumed that white women would take the lead in organizing state women's groups, then locate black women to form a "parallel committee"—a procedure not unlike that followed by the YWCA. Lugenia Hope's experience in Georgia, however, indicated both the problem with relying on white initiatives and the importance to blacks of an urban base. Responses to Hope's invitation to "outstanding, forward thinking, level-headed women" from rural southwest Georgia expressed fear of white retaliation as well as suspicion of the motives of white women. When Hope did manage to organize a local black committee, no white group materialized with which to "cooperate." In Atlanta, on the other hand, the Neighborhood Union and other black institutions provided a base for the development of self-confident and experienced black women leaders, and an active and successful local women's committee flourished.

Both black and white members assumed that the "point of contact" across the color line lay in women's mutual experience of motherhood; "women's work" would naturally take as its central concern the integrity and well-being of "the Negro home." In the view of the Woman's Committee, the chief threat to that well-being lay in the double standard and the exploitation of black women by white men. Interracial sex had been a chief cause of antebellum white women's discontents. But plantation mistresses had been as likely to translate their resentment into cruelty toward their female slaves as into condemnation of white men. The CIC Woman's Committee came down firmly on the side of black women, expressing sympathy for their vulnerability and blaming interracial liaisons on men.

The demand for a single standard of sexual morality had been a staple of the nineteenth-century women's movement. Like their predecessors, CIC leaders hoped to hold men to middle-class women's standards of sexual decorum. But their critique had a double-edged racial content as well. A black man who slept with a white woman might be "burned at the stake," while a white man could cross the race line with impunity. Their solution was not free choice but repression: they aimed to eliminate not only rape and seduction but all forms of miscegenation.

Black women viewed the situation differently. Opposition to lynching and a desire to defend black women against the charge of immorality had stimulated the formation of black women's organizations from the beginning. Black women shared with whites a concern for "racial integrity." But they were motivated more by outrage at sexual abuse than by opposition to legitimate human relationships.

The Woman's Committee's attack on the double standard was largely symbolic. It sought to register disapproval of sexual relations across the color line and to provide, in formal meetings between "the best type of white women and the best type of colored women," a recognition of the dignity of the black middle class. Yet even symbolic purposes were by no means easy to accomplish. Little open conflict between black and white members erupted after the issue of the black women's statement was settled, but a number of incidents illustrate the subtle and not-so-subtle racism under which black participants labored. One black participant described an incident in which a group of Baptist women invited her to address them "about the work of the 'niggers'" and instructed her to enter by the back door. "When we colored people come to your assemblies and churches and you send us to the galleries or put us in a corner," admonished Janie Porter Barrett, "it is as humiliating as if you hung a banner over us with the flaming words 'UNCLEAN' written across it."

At the same time, black and white women did occasionally form lasting alliances based on mutual respect. In South Carolina, for instance, Alice Spearman Wright, the daughter of a wealthy planting and business family, returned home from a year at the YWCA's National Training School and a YWCA-sponsored trip around the world to become a mainstay of the state branch of the Interracial Commission. The most militant black member of the group was Modjeska Simkins, a young teacher and social worker from Columbia. Over the years, the two women found themselves on the same side in many a battle. Simkins, who was an outspoken critic of "exponents of the power structure," both black and white, saw Wright as "a vigilant and almost a radical spirit."

Unevenly and with varying degrees of difficulty, CIC women's committees materialized across the South. By 1924, eleven statewide groups had appeared. Although the organization tried to cross denominational boundaries and attract secular support, Methodist leaders dominated the organization and Methodist missionary societies continued to afford the major channels for white women's interracial activities. The Woman's Missionary Council, based in Nashville, instructed each local missionary society to form a committee charged with conducting a detailed survey of housing, sanitation, and recreational facilities in black neighborhoods and organizing a study group on black achievements and progress. Armed with this knowledge, local women were to work cooperatively with blacks on community improvement projects. The number of such Methodist committees grew from 100 in 1922 to 606 by 1927. Their activities consisted mainly of securing access for blacks to public services and upgrading segregated facilities. They helped establish dental and health clinics in public schools, secured library and hospital privileges, and set up municipal playgrounds.

The Woman's Committee, like the Interracial Commission in general, encouraged and coordinated the first stirrings of racial liberalism in the region. Here and there it helped ameliorate the worst injustices of segregation and break down the most blatant of racial stereotypes. It forwarded a growing spirit of regional self-criticism and rendered interracial work respectable in the urban South.

While individual perspectives broadened and friendships developed, however, tangible signs of organizational effectiveness were few. The weakness of interracial groups reflected the limitations of a reform movement dependent on the tactics of conciliation and moral persuasion. In addition, women faced the problem of defining a distinct role for themselves within a male-dominated organization. The Woman's Committee acquired neither autonomy nor adequate funding; it submitted its policy decisions and programs as recommendations to the Interracial Commission as a whole. Cut off from the exercise of political and economic power, women tended to substitute sentiment for strategy. Carrie Parks Johnson had begun her work confident in the belief that women's special religious sensibilities and maternal instincts would guide them to right action. Understanding would take place spontaneously: at the outset of the movement, she believed, "the silent anguish and the cry of the mother heart of the Negro race leaped the chasm and found response in the mother heart of the white race." But by the middle of the decade she was complaining that too often women assumed that once their emotions had been stirred their duty had been accomplished. They were willing to study "the history of the Negro" or "the Negro woman"; they might even issue a statement of principles calling for law and order and "racial integrity," but to adopt measures to which "publicity is attached" in the atmosphere of the early twenties required more vision and courage than any but the boldest few could muster.

The CIC Woman's Committee thus achieved only its most limited goals. Its efforts to bring southern women together on a "psychological basis" of motherhood, a shared religious heritage, and an outrage at masculine sexual behavior represented, in the context of a rigidly segregated society, a significant cultural breakthrough and a harbinger of things to come. Yet the Woman's Committee shared with the interracial movement in general an inability to address the systemic sources of sexual or racial oppression. Its internal affairs demonstrated both the bonds created by class, sex, and religion and the formidable barrier that race posed to a genuine women's alliance.

By the end of the 1920s, interracial gatherings had begun to lose their symbolic impact. Black leaders as well as whites were searching elsewhere for a more effective mode of operation, for more realizable goals. In 1929, Jessie Daniel Ames, a Texas business woman and suffragist, assumed leadership of the organization. Ames brought to the movement an instrumental approach to social issues that set her apart from her more religiously oriented co-workers. Spurred by a rise in racial violence at the onset of the Depression, this "person of practical mind" channeled the Woman's Committee away from interracialism and into an elaborately organized single-issue campaign against lynching. The Association of Southern Women for the Prevention of Lynching (ASWPL), which she founded in 1930, was for white women only. More effective by far than the Woman's Committee, it linked the language of evangelicalism with the pragmatism of the suffrage movement. But it also marginalized black women. Although black leaders continued to participate in the Interracial Commission, met with ASWPL organizers, and worked tirelessly to educate and influence its policies, the vision of an interracial women's movement faded along with the nineteenth-century ideals of morality and maternalism from which it sprang.

Questions for Study and Review

1. Compare the lives of immigrant women in the North and black women in the South during the decades surrounding 1900.

2. Compare the motivations, resources, tactics, and impact of Hull House residents, Jewish boycotters, and southern interracial advocates.

3. What were the relationships between the concerns of rural whites and blacks in the Farmers' Alliance and rural and urban blacks in community organizations in the late nineteenth century?

4. Trace the relationships between black and white women activists from the antislavery movement through the Reconstruction era and into the campaign against lynching.

Suggested Readings

John Patrick McDowell, *The Social Gospel in the South: The Woman's Home Mission Movement in the Methodist Episcopal Church, South, 1886–1939* (1982).

Thomas C. Holt, "The Lonely Warrior: Ida B. Wells-Barnett and the Struggle for Black Leadership," in John Hope Franklin and August Meier, eds., *Black Leaders of the Twentieth Century* (1982).

Beverly W. Jones, "Mary Church Terrell and the National Association of Colored Women, 1896–1901," *Journal of Negro History* (Spring 1982).

Rosalyn Terborg-Penn, "Discontented Black Feminists: Prelude and Prologue to the Passage of the Nineteenth Amendment," in Lois Scharf and Joan Jensen, *Decades of Discontent* (1983).

Cynthia Neverdon-Morton, *Afro-American Women of the South and the Advancement of the Race, 1895–1925* (1988).

PART FOUR

The

Critical Decades

The Progressive Era had not yet come to a close when new issues and new social visions began to emerge. Fostered by World War I, by the rise of consumer culture and commercial entertainment, and by a growing population of young, single city dwellers, social and economic forces began to reshape relations between immigrants and the native-born, blacks and whites, wealthy and poor, children and parents, women and men. Yet what at first appeared as a revolution in social and sexual relations turned out to be more a mild modification than a complete transformation of older attitudes and behavior.

Especially in the first two decades of the twentieth century, the cultures of progressivism and of a new urban order overlapped. Chicago's Hull House residents were still actively pursuing their municipal housekeeping chores, for instance, when young working women began pursuing economic autonomy and sexual excitement in the city's boardinghouse districts. Black club women continued to battle racial violence in the South while their sons and daughters migrated north for jobs and the promise of a better life. Jewish and Italian women were still employing neighborhood protests to protect family interests when nativism abruptly curtailed the flow of immigrants and Americanization programs demanded that those already here adhere to a single set of cultural norms. Most blacks, immigrants, and workers were still adjusting to the problems created by industrial expansion when affluent housewives began grasping at the "labor-saving" devices made available by technological progress.

World War I did not initiate these changes. Nonetheless, it did serve as a catalyst for a whole series of transformations in race relations, sex roles, consumerism, technological development, and political realignments. Immigrants and blacks probably felt the impact of the war most immediately and directly. Jim Crow laws, immigration restrictions, imperial ventures, agricultural depression, and labor unrest had heightened racial tensions throughout the late nineteenth and early twentieth centuries. The response

115

Symbol of progress and source of pride as well as means of transportation, the automobile resulted in greater geographic mobility for all classes. Mass production kept prices down so even some working-class families could buy an automobile. Owning an auto meant they could move out of the crowded cities into the suburbs, as well-to-do and middle-class families had done before them. Farmers and ranchers drove their new cars into small rural towns to conduct business and to socialize. Here, rows of Model Ts line the streets of Henderson, Texas.

among African-Americans and immigrants was organization—of ethnic clubs, unions, interethnic and interracial societies, neighborhood associations, and other self-help societies.

Still, World War I provided the best opportunity for blacks and immigrants to improve their economic status while proving their loyalty to country and community. Despite President Wilson's order to maintain segregated eating facilities and rest rooms in the armed services and a nationwide upsurge in anti-German and anti-Semitic attacks, large numbers of blacks and immigrants volunteered their services to aid the American cause. On the home front, black women and men headed north seeking industrial jobs, while Mexicans traveled across the border to fill the demand for agricultural workers. These and other groups excluded from the American mainstream purchased hundreds of millions of dollars in Liberty Bonds and stamps, often encouraged to do so by female-led campaigns.

Lynchings and other forms of racial violence continued during the war and escalated thereafter as native-born whites closed ranks against broadening democracy at home after the Allied victory abroad. Nativist sentiments that emerged prior to the outbreak of hostilities in Europe were also heightened by the war. Deeply held fears of foreigners expressed during the 1890s reemerged shortly after the war fueled by the Red Scare. The result was the passage of legislation requiring literacy tests for immigrants, restricting the number of those entering the country, placing quotas on European immigration, and prohibiting the settlement of all Asians.

At the same time, those seeking to ferret out Communists, socialists, and other radicals focused on native-born female activists as well as foreigners. In 1924, the Chemical Warfare Department of the federal government released a Spider-Web Chart that linked twenty-nine women leaders and fifteen women's organizations to "the Socialist-Pacifist movement in the United States" and to "International Socialism." The web included not only the Women's International League for Peace and Freedom and other overtly pacifist associations but also the National Federation of Business and Professional Women's Clubs, the Young Women's Christian Association, the National Consumers' League, the Women's Christian Temperance Union, the General Federation of Women's Clubs, the National League of Women Voters, the National Council of Jewish Women, and the American Home Economics Association. Ironically, women in some of the targeted organizations, through campaigns against "white slavery" or prostitution and for Americanization, voiced their own concerns about the dangers lurking both in and around foreigners.

Not surprisingly, then, resident immigrants were subject to increasing pressure to abide by "American" standards and values and to reject traditional foods, dress, and customs. Sarah Deutsch examines the process of immigration and Americanization among Mexicans and Hispanics in the Southwest during and after the war. She demonstrates how the economic needs of native-born farmers assured an open-door policy for Mexican migrants during the war while at the same time their cultural prejudices barred these newcomers from becoming full citizens in peacetime. She focuses particularly on the growing demand for migrant labor and the effects of this seasonal and transient employment on community development and family relations among the expanding Chicano population.

Not all migrants experienced the war as restrictive, however. For many, especially native-born whites and some blacks, geographical mobility promised escape from the prejudices and prohibitions of rural life or from domestic strife and forms of physical punishment we would now characterize as child abuse. Young women and men were on the move well before the war began, but increased job opportunities and wartime mobilization intensified the trend. By 1920, the census recorded for the first time that a majority of all Americans lived in cities.

Joanne Meyerowitz traces the path followed by young working-class women seeking refuge from conventional family bonds and traditional sexual mores in the boardinghouse districts of Chicago. These urban neighborhoods provided the young and mobile with access to cheap rooms, commercial entertainment, and a chance to experiment socially and sexually. Living outside the family—made possible for more affluent women through college life and settlement houses—became possible for "working girls" only when both housing and employment opportunities expanded in the early 1900s. Then, lured by the new urban culture of movies, department stores, dance halls, and dating, young women left home in unprecedented numbers to join their peers on the city streets.

The social and sexual liberation women sought was curtailed by low wages, long hours, and the high cost of living. Single women coped with these limitations by sharing rooms and meals, assisting each other in times of illness or unemployment, and finding male escorts to treat them to movies and meals. Organization was another way to cope with the problems of limited resources. Working girls' clubs, local branches of the Young Women's Christian Association, unions for factory workers, retail clerks, and waitresses, and middle-class women's associations with an interest in cross-class organizing, such as the Women's Trade Union League and the National Consumer's League, offered some support for working women. Yet associations composed solely of female wage earners often lacked the resources for extensive activities in urban neighborhoods; unions found themselves on the defensive as the postwar conservative reaction took hold; and middle-class and cross-class organizations gave increasing attention to protective legislation and woman suffrage in the same period.

The one form of organizing that working women may have needed the most and with which they had the least contact was the birth control movement. The lack of information and of affordable contraceptive devices increased the economic and sexual vulnerability of this segment of the population. Most women in the boardinghouse districts and other working-class neighborhoods were not aware that Emma Goldman, Margaret Sanger, and other birth control pioneers could provide means by which to reduce the dangers of venereal disease and the likelihood of pregnancy. State and federal laws against the dissemination of such information created formidable barriers to public discussions of the subject, but the taboos and prohibitions were already crumbling when war erupted.

Women challenged the prevailing sexual mores from a variety of directions. Anarchist and socialist women, including labor organizers such as Elizabeth Gurley Flynn, started to write and lecture on the topic in the 1910s. In 1916, Sanger founded the New York Birth Control League, which five years later expanded into the American Birth Control League. Wartime concern within the armed forces simultaneously led to increased recognition of the problems caused by sexual ignorance and encouraged scientific studies of venereal disease and birth control. Thus, as young women and men motivated by personal desires began testing the restraints of the Victorian era, a host of other groups were launching movements that would culminate in women's greater control over their bodies.

Sexual experimentation in urban centers, increased awareness of birth control, and the emergence of sexual subcultures that rejected traditional definitions of family—such as gay and lesbian circles and bohemian opponents of monogamy—inspired a new wave of attention to preserving domestic ideals and marital bliss. Promoted by groups as diverse as ministers, advertising executives, cosmetic company founders, movie producers, and beauty pageant sponsors, the "heterosexual imperative" was proclaimed in sermons, magazines, and popular lectures and on billboards, radio programs, and theater marquees across the country.

By attaching sexual attractiveness to new products and appliances, advertisers channeled seemingly dangerous sexual energy into the capitalist marketplace. Ruth Schwartz Cowan traces this development and its impact on housewives' consumption of household appliances from the 1910s to the 1930s. She reveals how new sexual values and new technology could be harnessed to reinforce women's traditional domestic role. This role was further enhanced by the rise in the same period of social science and home economics. The efficiency that Frederick Winslow Taylor and his followers brought to industry in the early 1910s, domestic science experts extended to housework at the end of the decade. Improvements in the standard of living, greater emphasis on the mother's responsibility for child nurture, and a decline in the availability of domestic servants assured that neither "labor-saving" appliances nor scientific management would lessen women's domestic labors, only modify them.

In the decades surrounding World War I, African-Americans, Mexicans, and other immigrant groups found their lives transformed by geographical mobility but still restricted by racist and nativist sentiments and economic exploitation. Young, mostly native-born, women and men of the working classes eagerly entered a new urban scene where they became subjects for social science investigators and models for more affluent bohemians. Yet most would continue to live on the margins, both economically and socially, despite the general prosperity of the postwar period. Moreover the technological ingenuity that was reshaping single women's occupational alternatives—electric lights and cash registers in department stores and restaurants, typewriters and telephones in offices—was also being used to reinforce married women's domestic obligations. These were critical decades for women, families, and communities, but the long-term significance of the changes occurring were little clearer in 1929 than they had been in 1899.

Suggested Readings

Maurine Weiner Greenwald, *Women, War, and Work: The Impact of World War I on Women Workers in the United States* (1980).

Carroll Smith-Rosenberg, *Disorderly Conduct: Visions of Gender in Victorian America* (1985).

Lois Banner, *American Beauty* (1983).

John D'Emilio and Estelle Freedman, *Intimate Matters: A History of Sexuality in America* (1988).

Glenna Matthews, *"Just a Housewife": The Rise and Fall of Domesticity in America* (1987).

EIGHT

Transforming Hispanic Communities: World War I and Americanization in the Southwest

Sarah Deutsch

World War I raised hopes of many African-Americans who dreamed of escaping southern segregation and brutality by migrating north for industrial jobs opened to blacks by military mobilization. Over 450,000 blacks left the South between 1916 and 1918, bound for Detroit, St. Louis, Chicago, and other industrial centers. They were not the only group to migrate. Mexicans also headed north, pushed by civil war at home and pulled by labor demands in the United States. When Congress passed legislation restricting immigration in 1916, southwestern employers eager to boost agricultural production successfully sought exemptions for Mexicans. These Mexican-born immigrants joined Spanish-Americans, or Hispanics, settled in the region since before 1900.

Still, economic necessity did not mean social acceptance for Mexicans in the Southwest any more than it did for African-Americans in the North. Indeed, as the Mexican and Hispanic population increased, barriers to acceptance and assimilation also increased. Across the country, native-born whites hopped aboard the bandwagon of Americanization, insisting that immigrants speak English, adopt Anglo-American life-styles and values, and pledge undying allegiance to the American flag and nation. Yet Anglo-Americans in the Southwest were never convinced that they wanted Mexicans to assimilate. Viewing the immigrants in racial as well as in ethnic terms, many Anglos advocated segregation, drawing on Jim Crow models from the South rather than acculturation efforts from the North as the most appropriate means of addressing Mexican migration.

Deutsch traces the impact of labor recruitment and Americanization initiated during the war and segregation policies instituted in its aftermath on Mexican and Hispanic communities. Focusing specifically on the increased transiency among these groups, whether long-settled in the United States or newly arrived, Deutsch demonstrates the devastating effects on family life. The status of women, for instance, traditionally rooted in food production and child care, was undermined when mothers and daughters were forced into casual labor along with other migrants. Nonetheless, even as villagers migrated to find labor, they remained bound to their villages by ties of kinship and mutual dependence, creating a community that came to span the entire region.

In the conservative atmosphere of post-World War I America, Mexicans, Hispanics, and African-Americans suffered a variety of abuses, most dramatically revealed in the race riots of 1919 but also evident in Anglos' increasing economic and political domination of the Southwest. Over the long term, the destruction of traditional familial and communal structures and lifeways may have been more devastating than the sporadic outbursts of violence. Still, as Deutsch demonstrates, Mexican and Hispanic villages retained their cultural distinctiveness despite the twin pressures of Americanization and economic upheaval fostered by war.

The coming of the war stood on its head one basic premise of the regional community. Government indifference, at least for the moment, vanished. The government now needed to make soldiers and loyal citizens of the villagers. In addition, producers in the region demanded seasonal labor on a new scale. Just as elsewhere producers drew southern blacks and rural folk to the cities to replace a European immigration cut off by the war, in New Mexico and Colorado they drew Hispanics from the villages and added to them Mexicans from south of the border.* From 1914 to 1921, the resulting massive migration movements and unprecedented federal interference threw competing cultures and groups into a new intimacy; it gave a new twist to the dynamics of intercultural contact on the Anglo-Hispanic frontier.

The new pressures threatened the delicate balance of opportunity and isolation on which the regional community depended. Not only was there a sudden surge of Mexican aliens with whom, in Anglo eyes, Hispanics were identified, but the sudden entry and withdrawal of federal funds, personnel, and the draft affected the regional community at its very core, the Hispanic villages. By the time the dust of all the mobilization settled, and federal interference with the regional community receded, the picture of that community had changed, in some ways, permanently.

※

From *No Separate Refuge: Culture, Class, and Gender on an Anglo-Hispanic Frontier in the American Southwest, 1880–1940* by Sarah Deutsch. Copyright © 1987 by Sarah Deutsch. Reprinted by permission of Oxford University Press, Inc.

* Chicano or Chicana is the modern term used to designate both Mexican-born residents of the United States and United States-born people of Mexican or Spanish-Mexican descent.

Mexican immigration to the United States had begun well before 1914. The war with Mexico in the 1840s barely interrupted Mexican migration to the north, despite the fact that the area now lay under the United States' instead of the Mexican flag. Mexican laborers manned the region's mines, railroads, and commercial farms, and homesteaded occasionally. Between the mid-nineteenth century and 1910, Anglo migrants from the East, Midwest, and Europe overwhelmed this relatively modest Mexican migration. Then, in 1910, the Mexican revolution began. As civil war raged through Mexico year after year, increasing numbers of Mexicans fled the war's chaos and its destruction of life and land.

The Southwest's employers generally welcomed these new immigrants in the same way they welcomed Hispanics—as cheap labor. The war in the Balkans, home of many railroad laborers, had forced western railroads to rely increasingly on Mexican labor. Small farmers along the new irrigation developments also looked to this labor as they continued to expand their acreage in sugar beets and cotton despite the declining profitability caused by the general economic slump in 1913 and the threat of gradual removal of all tariff protection on sugar.

In just a few years, however, the situation changed drastically. With the onset of a wider conflict in Europe came an unparalleled increase in industrial and agricultural activity throughout the United States to meet European belligerents' demands. The slump was gone and so was the abundant cheap labor. The specter of a free market in sugar receded as United States producers eagerly strove to fill the gap created by the withdrawal of central Europe's beet sugar from circulation. The corresponding disappearance of European labor from the United States markets meant that new employers began to recruit actively and vie for

Mexican and Spanish-American labor, formerly their labor of last resort. It was in 1916 that the Great Western Sugar Company of northern Colorado, on behalf of the small farmers whose beets it needed, began for the first time not simply hiring but recruiting Hispanic workers in southern Colorado and New Mexico. As cotton and beet growers in California, Arizona, and Texas and railroad and mining enterprises increased the competition for this labor, increasing numbers of recruiting agencies, processing companies, and farmers' associations sought labor directly from Mexico.

So it happened that, although the New Immigration Act of 1917 seemed to the Commissioner-General of Immigration "an eminently satisfactory piece of legislation . . . of great benefit to the country," the act provoked, in the Commissioner's own assessment, "no little hysteria" on the part of southwestern employers. The law contained a literacy test as well as a doubled head tax. It threatened to halt the immigration of impoverished and largely illiterate Mexicans, at a time when southwesterners planted record sugar and cotton crops and when resident Mexicans fled the United States in droves, spurred by threats of conscription. Beet-sugar companies warned of lost harvests, while railroad employees claimed that with half their summer construction workers barred, disrepair of tracks could endanger troop and supply movements.

In response to such employer agitation, a series of administrative decrees temporarily exempted Mexican agricultural labor from the head tax and literacy test and even from much older contract labor provisions. From the start, the exemptions converted Mexican immigration from a regional to a national issue. As interest increased, such widely distributed publications as the *New York Times* and the *Literary Digest* devoted more space to the issue. In this arena, Spanish Americans became dangerously entangled with Mexicans as older stereotypes combined with the issues of recent United States relations with Mexico, labor unrest in the Southwest, and rising nativism to create a more negative response to both Mexicans and Spanish Americans than that of southwestern employers.

Relations with Mexico since the revolution began were less than cordial, and the portrayal of the Mexican Revolution in the United States did little to erase popular pictures of Mexicans as lawless, short-sighted, treacherous bandits. Just as it seemed that little more was needed to convince the United States public that Mexicans were enemies, whether by virtue of United States aggression or their own, on March 1, 1917, less than two months after Pershing's withdrawal from Mexico, the newspapers printed the famous "Zimmerman telegram." Sent by the German foreign secretary to his ambassador in Mexico, the telegram proposed that Mexico join Germany in a war against the United States to gain back the "lost territory" of the Southwest.* Setting the seal to the distrust, the telegram raised the specter of a possible fifth column: the stubbornly persistent Spanish-speaking community of that same Southwest.

Chicano labor unrest gave body to this specter of a fifth column. In June and July of 1917, large strikes broke out in the mines of both Arizona and New Mexico. In June, at Bisbee, Arizona, where a Western Federation of Miners organizer had recorded "a great deal of discontent" back in 1915, the strike was led by that bugbear of World War I nativism and antiradicalism, the Industrial Workers of the World.

The violence of these mining strikes and of United States-Mexican relations made Mexicans and Spanish Americans in the United States vulnerable to the same repressed nativistic trends

---

* Revolution in Mexico and the attendant fears of U.S. businessmen with investments in the country led to demands for invasions by U.S. troops in 1914 and General Pershing's massive "punitive expedition" against Pancho Villa and his followers in 1916.

as enemy aliens were. Discontent was defined as disloyalty and alienation, and the cure for alienation, of course, lay in Americanization. As it did elsewhere in the United States and for other ethnic groups, Americanization became intimately tied to the war effort, and "100 percent Americanism" became the only way to prove loyalty and ensure national security.

"Redeeming" this internal Mexico clearly required turning its inhabitants into Americans, unhyphenated. That "Spanish-Americans" were "terribly insulted if called Mexicans" did not remove them as alien targets of the new nativism. The majority of Americanizers were unable or unwilling to draw the distinction. Despite Hispanic service records and repeated testimonials to the loyalty of the Spanish Americans, church woman Katharine Bennett was not alone in her thoughts that "in this day when hyphenated Americans are unpopular it is a curious fact that here in the Southwest the form Spanish-American is constantly used." *Literary Digest* declared the "hyphenate issue" the most vital of the day, and Woodrow Wilson, who had made Americanism an issue in his re-election campaign, later proclaimed, "Any man who carries a hyphen about with him carries a dagger that he is ready to plunge into the vitals of this Republic." In this context, the retention of not only a hyphen but the Spanish language and a distinct culture as well seemed to Anglos evidence of divided loyalty on the part of United States-born Hispanics, evidence of a continued inability "to forget the wrong which they consider the United States inflicted on their country" in 1848.

✳

If the war brought the federal government to Hispanic villages through an increased Americanizing fervor, it also came in less rhetorical ways. The government needed these hyphenated citizens to act. The government had to call upon them for food and for fighting men. In the process of this call, the government reached into every village, plaza, and town, "bringing the war home" to the non-migrants.

The darkest way in which the war reached into Hispanic enclaves was conscription. While little boys in these villages as elsewhere played soldier, approximately 10,000 of their older brothers, making up 65 percent of New Mexico's contingent, served in the war. Spanish Americans in southern Colorado also volunteered in numbers, one Anglo resident recalled, "much greater in proportion than any other class of volunteers." Almost every New Mexican village was tapped, and the call seemed to reach in particular the few relatively well educated, the graduates of mission schools and the teachers.

As the nation discovered, however, there were immediate difficulties in the government's attempt to call on village resources, even on its manpower. Not only had some villages never heard the Pledge of Allegiance; in the first conscription of 1917 thirty-eight of forty-six draftees from Taos and Mora counties, New Mexico, could not understand "enough English to attempt to drill." Moreover, closer investigation revealed this situation was no passing phase in the Hispanic hinterland. For some Spanish Americans, conscription provided their first contact with the United States government. A few, in good faith, claimed exemption on the grounds of non-citizenship. Their parents sometimes found the call even harder to comprehend. It was not simply a question of divided loyalty and hyphens. In villages impoverished in terms of both cash and government services, reactions to the war itself, according to contemporary observers, ranged from people "much opposed" on whom the food regulations worked real hardship, to "great indifference" among others who seemed focused on "how to avoid going or allowing others to go into the service."

At the same time, the revelations gleaned in the war effort spurred government action and brought new Anglo attention and services to the villages. Government-aided studies exposed to many Anglos for the first time the conditions in Hispanic villages. As the investigators, usually women, found "the death rate appallingly high," they brought the villages a new allotment of health services. Similarly, in Hispanic villages the lack of commercial farming meant that stimulating agricultural production there often had more in common with welfare work than it did on more profitable and usually Anglo acreages. The government's desire for increased food production opened new horizons to besieged Hispanics. To compensate for the previous year's poor grain crop and the unpromising spring, New Mexico encouraged lessees to plant crops on state land, offered seed at cost or on mortgage, and, with the help of newly enlarged federal appropriations, vastly expanded its agricultural extension and home demonstration services to include Hispanic as well as Anglo agents who would disseminate new technology and methods in the plazas.

[Yet] Hispanic farmers in many villages could not reap the benefits of the more than doubled price of wheat and corn or the boom in livestock prices that resulted from war-torn Europe's rising demand for United States foodstuffs. A two-year drought so severe that it, rather than the events of the war, became the marker for that time dessicated much of northern New Mexico. By the end of 1917, one missionary reported, "There is nothing to feed the chickens. . . . There are no eggs, no milk and no fresh meat." Many commercial farmers and stockraisers lost their land. They and the erstwhile semisubsistence farmers found themselves forced to buy food at the newly inflated prices.

As the economics base of the village dwindled still further, these hungry migrants swelled the number of those who already traveled the paths of the regional community. Like rural migrants across the country, they found the increased wages for common labor during the war an additional drawing factor. Beetwork wages, for example, rose by 50 percent. Some villages which had sent five or ten migrants north before the war now lost up to 60 percent of their population, at least seasonally.

Hispanic women in the villages, like women elsewhere during World War I and as they always had, took over the men's tasks on the farms or filled jobs left empty by male recruits and migrants. Young bilingual Spanish American women increasingly found employment as clerks, stenographers, and teachers. In 1916 only 20 percent of all teachers and 26 percent of Hispanic teachers in Rio Arriba County had been Hispanic women, but by the 1918/19 academic year, Hispanic women provided over 30 percent of all teachers and over 40 percent of Hispanic teachers. With a dwindling land base, Hispanic women, like the men, sought a livelihood from the Anglicized aspects of the economy, but they did so within the villages instead of outside them.

Despite the continuing overall pattern of village women and migrant men, a significant minority of the villagers ceased their peregrinations and began, in new parts of Colorado, to form an increasingly persistent contingent, a series of more permanent outposts on the Chicano frontier. Sugar-beet companies anxious to cut recruiting costs erected more labor colonies as Hispanics increasingly dominated the state's sugar-beet labor force. By 1920 even in northern Colorado, Chicanos, half from New Mexico and southern Colorado and half from Mexico, formed 40 percent of the hand labor and 90 percent of the migrant labor. Although the Great Western Sugar Company in northern Colorado did not begin building beet colonies until the mid-1920s, the number of Hispanic families who stayed year after year on the same site in both mining and beet areas in northern

Colorado grew to about one-quarter of the Chicano laborers, again half Mexicans and half Spanish Americans.

*

The end of the war brought many Hispanic veterans home to their villages and northern settlements. They brought with them a desire for modern facilities, from gymnasiums to bathrooms. But as the veterans brought home their dreams of improvement, the federal services and support that had in wartime finally begun to reach the villages quietly slipped away. In two or three northern New Mexico Hispanic communities a few domestic science and agricultural courses resulted from new funding for vocational education, but the agricultural extension service's outreach program, with its touring demonstrators, literature, equipment, and drastically reduced staff, retreated to its former Anglo focus until the 1930s. Red Cross nurses also vanished from the scene, as had the funds which supported them. At the same time the Medical Association of New Mexico secured a legislative act requiring certification of anyone providing medical services, including *parteras* [midwives], despite the "quite outspoken denunciation . . . of the law" by many villagers. The villagers' moment in the spotlight was over almost before it had begun, and the Protestant missionaries who remained found themselves once more at impoverished and isolated outposts. The World War had exacted a heavy price from the villagers in money and in educated youths. It had left them with few lasting benefits, and with little sense of continuous participation in a larger American community.

After the war some Anglo club women continued to believe that Americanization numbered among "the great problems of the day." Others, by 1920, were disillusioned. Their disillusionment brought further withdrawal of resources devoted to the cause. The president of the Colorado State Federation of Women's Clubs confessed:

> [W]e took up the work of Americanizing the foreigner with much enthusiasm and were brought after some discouraging experiences to realize that Americanization is not a plan of instruction which can be worked out systematically and concisely but it is a state of mind which, like Charity, must begin at home.

These women, across the nation convinced of the failure of Americanization because of the enduring difference and cultural strength of immigrant and migrant groups, turned their attention instead to "citizenship" among their own ethnic groups, community service, and a "thrift" movement.

Neither had that other war, the suffrage campaign, succeeded in smoothing over ethnic differences among women at any but the most elite levels. The campaign finally gained momentum in New Mexico in 1917, three years after that state became the only western state without woman suffrage. In an effort to reach the Hispanic population of the state, the suffragists printed leaflets in Spanish and cultivated Spanish American speakers and leaders, including Aurora Lucero and Adelina Otero-Warren, both members of families well entrenched in the social and political elite. But the vast majority, approximately 90 percent, of the organized movement in the state remained Anglo.

At elite levels among women as among men, the war and its aftermath witnessed a continued alliance between Spanish Americans and Anglos based on mutual respect for ethnic difference. But on less than elite levels, suspicion and distrust prevailed. Alice Corbin Henderson's picture of "the English, Spanish and Indian women who met over the canning kettle, or across the Red Cross table where a common impulse moved them and a common purpose obviated the need of an interpreter," was charming but inaccurate. On the contrary, mobilization agencies in the state had found that "it is not possible to combine demonstrations for English and Spanish-speaking people even when they can all be reached by one language," because, as one county agent revealed, "the Spanish-speaking people will not come to a meeting called for both."

✳

In the first year after the war, the number of Mexicans entering the country under the exemptions for immigrant agricultural labor increased over 100 percent and continued to grow. The Great Western Sugar Company, for example, turned to Mexican labor only in 1919, requesting 700 laborers that year and projecting a need for several times that number for the following year. By 1920, the estimated number of Mexican laborers needed for sugar beets was 14,200, a not overwhelming but vital 20 percent of the crop's hand labor. The number of Mexicans headed for Colorado that year under the exemptions had more than tripled. It was the change in scale that struck the Anglos most forcibly. In Weld County, Colorado, the number of Mexican-born inhabitants had increased over 700 percent in ten years, from 90 to 756, and these were accompanied by an even larger number of Spanish Americans in this formerly almost entirely Anglo county. Anglos no longer spoke, as they had ten years earlier, of an Anglo invasion of the Southwest. Instead they voiced fears of "this invasion of aliens."

A rapidly escalating proportion of Hispanic village families also increased their reliance on wage labor or, like farm folk all over the country, left the villages altogether. Many headed for such larger towns of New Mexico as Grants and Albuquerque. Others departed for the state's coal-mining areas, Gallup and Raton, and for railroad shops and Colorado's coal mines. But the largest contingent set out for the beetfields, where push and pull came together.

Most of the farmers seemed to agree with Americanization teacher Alfred White, that "the peon has always lived like a pig and he will continue to do so." National Child Labor Committee investigator Charles Gibbons found that "the local people . . . feel they are giving the Mexican all he deserves; in fact one frequently finds the opinion that they (residents) are performing an act of charity in allowing the Mexican to work for them, and therefore any kind of house will do for them to live in." Most growers and even investigators were convinced that whatever the conditions in Colorado, they represented an improvement over Hispanic and Mexican villages.

Most Chicanos, on the other hand, saw little if any improvement. They had come north, to the margins of the Hispanic regional community, to better their condition. Though often bitterly disappointed in what they found, many could not afford to turn back. An exasperated Chicana living in a one-room shack with her family of twelve demanded, "How can you expect folks to live decently when given a place like that?" The Chicanas tried desperately to turn these shacks into homes, despite their long hours in the fields and the meager furnishings they could bring with them. The migrants used boxes as tables and cupboards, and often slept on the floor. Mary Vela remembered that her mother stayed up all night to clean when they moved. Another mother made her own paste and pasted a two-room shack with newspapers for decoration and warmth; her daughter remembered, "[W]e would lay there and read all the news there was in the newspapers."

As to the work itself, there were some Chicano school children and a few Chicano women who, not needing to provide their entire support from the beets, contracted small acreages, an amount easily managed in workdays of reasonable length. A local lawyer assured investigators that "children are in much better conditions in the open fields and the open air than they would be in their homes. In general," he asserted, "this summer outing is looked upon by the children as a frolic." But Mary Vela recalled beetwork as "backbreaking and heavy. During the harvest we'd work 18-hour days." At least one Spanish-speaking woman lost two sons to a kidney disease exacerbated by long hours of stooping over the fields. Thinning the beets in early summer required crawling, and topping them during the harvest required stooping, and was all, according to investigator Paul Taylor, "disagreeable . . . dirty . . . monotonous and repetitive."

When these Chicano colonists and settlers no longer disappeared each winter below some imaginary border, the Anglo townspeople erected their own borders. They used the burning crosses of the Ku Klux Klan, so popular elsewhere in Colorado in the 1920s, to mark the edges of the adobe colonies, and used signs in restaurants, barbershops, and movie theaters bearing such inscriptions as "White Trade Only" and "No Mexican Trade Wanted," which made it impossible for Hispanics in towns like Greeley and Brighton to buy so much as a hamburger. The rhetoric of a "Mexican invasion" continued virtually unabated both in the national popular press and in Colorado. And Hispanic colonists remembered vividly nearly sixty years later the indignity of having an Anglo doctor arrive unannounced to take blood samples for Wasserman tests to detect syphilis. "That's how bad they wanted to get rid of us," recalled one. Spanish Americans had difficulty registering to vote, and local Anglos continued to "wish the Mexicans were not there."

Many Chicanos resented the implications of such segregation. Some Hispanics remembered that people were considered "better" if they lived outside the colony, and that the colonies' lack of modern sanitary facilities helped give some colonists the attitude of "If I ever get a chance, I'll move out of this place." But the isolation from Anglo life, the Anglo prejudices, and the low wages reinforced each other and created, as one investigating team expressed it,

"a vicious circle." "From this circle," they concluded, "few can escape through their own efforts."

✳

Chicanas did not escape this structure of discrimination and marginalization. It altered their patterns of life within the Hispanic community and its contrast to village structures had enormous ramifications not only for the place they would hold in Anglo-dominated areas, but for the viability of an autonomous Chicano community in the north.

The Hispanic villages of northern New Mexico and southern Colorado in the 1920s continued in their flexible sexual division of labor and mutual decision making, along with their migratory element. Village women—single, married, and widowed—continued to own property and govern its disposal, run dance halls, clean school houses, butcher livestock, dry fruit and vegetables, take in laundry, weave rugs, lead religious services, participate in communal plastering and whitewashing, and barter labor with their neighbors. They also continued to plant, cultivate, and harvest gardens that provided an increasingly vital proportion of the families' subsistence; toward the end of the decade they came to the attention of at least one county agricultural extension agent who taught them to treat their seed with formaldehyde and to increase their yield in other ways. In addition, much as Anglo farm wives of day laborers did, Hispanic wives of migrants managed their husbands' duties on the farms with the help of their children. In fact, so completely had village life come to devolve on these women that by the end of the 1920s, as one Hispanic male recalled, "when the men came back, they were kind of like guests."

In cases where the men did not migrate and so could do the farm work, the women, in increasing numbers, performed wage work for

Anglos by taking in laundry, "babysitting," or doing other domestic service, to provide the cash their households lacked. The female wage workers, like the males, tended to view wage work as subordinate to their main object, the continuity of village life. As service to village welfare, the villagers accepted both the day work of the women and the sorties of girls to Santa Fe and Albuquerque with, as one male Chimayo inhabitant remembered, "a great pride."

The cash that male and female migrants brought home paid taxes, provided such modern necessities as gable or corrugated iron roofs and school supplies, and permitted villages to survive despite depleted resources. Some women who earned wages used their earnings to buy canned goods and sometimes even canning equipment, and many women in remote communities treasured their Montgomery Ward and Sears catalogs, continuing a selective adoption of Anglo culture.

The villages, however, continued to suffer high infant mortality rates, epidemics, and a lack of government health or other services. Some work in instructing midwives began with the allocation of the Sheppard-Towner funds, but only at the rate of one instructor for all of New Mexico, and one for the San Luis Valley. Because the price of Anglo doctors was prohibitive, sparsely scattered women missionaries still provided the major channel of modern health information and services, and Hispanic villagers in northern New Mexico and southern Colorado continued to rely most heavily on their "uninstructed" *parteras*.

Village life was far from ideal, but it provided a framework in which women had a certain degree of independence, a variety of duties, a supportive community of other women and kin, and a central and powerful role in community life. Chicanas in northern Colorado found themselves lifted out of that network of relations and provided with pallid substitutes for the village features that had given them strength and support.

Hispanic women in northern Colorado planted gardens when they could, but with over half the women working in the beetfields, even in the relatively rare instances when they had suitable land and water, they did not have the time to tend vegetables, and so often planted flowers instead. Less than 2 percent of Hispanic beet-labor families in northern Colorado produced even a minor part of their food, and at least 33 percent had no gardens at all. As in the villages, when the family had property Hispanic women could inherit and control it. But in northern Colorado that property provided sustenance for neither the women nor their families. Food had to be purchased; preparation was not shared among the community. In the Hispanic villages, women had often measured their value by their ability to provide and prepare food, both for their own and for neighboring families. As in other societies, food was more than sustenance; it carried emotional freight, bound villagers to one another, and defined their relations. Change in this arena would eventually shake all others. Women would have to find new ways to measure their value. As with the men, their relationship to the land and to what it produced, a relationship which had provided the key to village membership, had changed. Membership in the community, like women's own value, would have to be defined in other ways.

Religion could not provide the missing link. Hispanic women in the north as in the south attended church more regularly than did the men. For most Hispanic women in the north, church groups remained their only formal affiliation. But less than half the beetworking families attended church with any regularity. Hispanic civil marriages in the north continued to outnumber religious ones until the end of the decade. In addition, distanced from their own church, many Hispanics converted to Protestant sects when they reached northern Colorado, and others had converted before they came. Only about half the Chicano colonists at

Rituals, like the funeral shown here, helped maintain the community spirit of village life among the Mexican immigrants living in northern New Mexico and southern Colorado. In northern Colorado, most Hispanic women worked for wages in the beetfields in the summer and in factories or mines during the winter. The need to work for wages undermined the women's status as providers of food for their families and left them unable to re-create the interdependent networks of neighborhood and kin that had sustained them in their native villages.

Greeley, for example, were Catholic. While religious divisions did not necessarily lead to strife within the colonies, they did not encourage community spirit as village rituals had.

Nor did religion provide a gate to a new interethnic, Anglo-Hispanic community. The First Presbyterian Church in Fort Collins allowed Hispanic members to meet in their building, but only in the basement, and Greeley's Catholic church reserved one row especially for Hispanics. "Even religion," concluded Paul Taylor, "does not obliterate the line of social cleavage." Within the church, as in the larger community, Hispanics endured a marginal position.

Other areas proved equally flawed as foundations for the re-creation of Hispanic women's central role. In New Mexico and southern Colorado, Hispanic women in heavily Hispanic areas were achieving a variety of elective political offices, from county school superintendent to secretary of state. But in northern Colorado, they, like the men, had trouble proving citizenship and establishing residence of sufficient length to register to vote. Once eligible, they tended to vote in the same proportion as Hispanic men, but neither had the numbers nor the cohesiveness to achieve office or even leverage. And while *parteras* became itinerant politicians in New Mexico, they were simply one more sign of an increasingly tenuous female community in northern Colorado. Midwives had come with the Chicano migrants—"you couldn't survive without them," recalled Arthur Maes—but in the perambulating world of the beetfields, there was no assurance the *partera* would always be within call. One Hispanic woman had two of her children with the help of a *partera* in Greeley, but by the time she had two others, the *partera* had returned to New Mexico.

Residence in northern Colorado brought no compensation for the loss of *parteras* in improved health services. Hispanic infants died at a rate as much as twice that of other beetworking ethnic groups. And when, in the early 1930s, Hispanic women turned to Weld County's new free doctors they discovered a mixed blessing. The women found it "much better" during birth because they had ether for the pain, but found it harder afterwards. In New Mexico, relatives and neighbors had gathered round. All helped. In the north, remembered one mother, "[W]e didn't have nobody to do anything for us so we had to work up to the minute we had kids and then up immediately, no women around to help."

There were rare stories of interethnic friendship and even intimacy among women. At least one Hispanic mother learned English in an informal group of beetworking women, including Japanese and German Russian, which met in each other's kitchens and exchanged ways of cooking. She learned to make German bread and other German dishes, and cried when the German lady moved away. Maria Chavez remembered that "neighbors" never visited each other, but also that "white and brown" came to dances on the farms. And Paul Taylor related an incident of a female farm operator who cared for her Spanish American beetworking family's baby for three months when the mother went to the hospital with blood poisoning. There were even a few intermarriages: five in Weld County in 1926, or 8.6 percent of Hispanic and almost 1 percent of all marriages in the county that year.

For many Hispanic women, however, the loneliness and isolation experienced in a childbirth unattended by relatives permeated their lives. They remembered a life in New Mexico where families always got together, one night at one house, one night at another, and now

they spent months on isolated farms, scattered across the valley. Amelia Cordova's mother liked to melt the snow that piled in corners and wash her hair with it. When one night a chemical in the snow blinded her, Amelia had to quit school to take care of her mother. No women came to help. No community of women had arisen to replace that left in New Mexico.

The rejection many Chicanas in northern Colorado experienced was not simply by Anglo society as a whole, but in particular by Anglo women and girls. "American girls," reported Paul Taylor, "particularly expressed a prejudice against social intercourse with Mexicans." Margarita Garcia remembered that there were clubs in her school, but "they wouldn't even tell us about it." The Anglo mothers were little different. Taylor found it was the farmers' wives, not the farmers, who most adamantly opposed social mixing. Hispanic mothers like the one so determined to give her children an education that she had no "time to visit or do anything else except care for her family" and work in the fields, attended P.T.A. meetings where "The Americans made it so plain that they were unwelcome that they didn't come again." A superintendent even complained, "It is too much trouble to have Mexicans in the P.T.A."

Without the communal and exchanged labor of the village, the companionship of women in childbirth, the power bases of the garden and the church and of the village itself, Hispanic women in northern Colorado found their place in society altered indeed. No longer at the ordered center of village life, they were increasingly unable to affect the institutions, the church, the school, or the midwives they had controlled or helped to control at home.

Thoroughly dependent on a money economy, Chicanas in northern Colorado did not find in wage labor, when they could get it, a satisfactory replacement for their gardens as a means, or for their villages as an end. Performing agricultural labor for wages, unlike the nonwage labor in the garden or the village fields, provided neither the status of ownership or even necessarily the control of income produced. The farmer contracted with and paid the husband and not the wife for the family's labor.

Moreover, there was little in the off-season jobs available to them that would advance the status of women either in the Hispanic or the Anglo society. The winter occupations open to women were even more limited and poorly paid than those open to Hispanic men. Only about one-tenth of the Chicanos with winter wage work were mothers, and while the men with winter employment averaged sixty dollars a month income, the women averaged half of that. Domestic service, the largest category of jobs open to Chicanas, paid as much as ten or twelve dollars per week in Denver, but Maria Chavez remembered cleaning houses for fifty cents a day in the beet areas of Wyoming. And not all employers looked kindly on Chicana domestics, as one Spanish American girl, a United States citizen working her way through school, recalled. "A woman to whom I applied for work when I first came to x——— said, 'People of your nationality are just terrible; I can't stand them, they're so crude, lazy, and so uncultured.'"

Even Chicanas who managed to obtain teacher's certificates found the north an uncongenial environment for job seeking. One Anglo freshman told an aspiring Spanish American girl, "If I were you, I wouldn't waste my time here for they'll never permit girls of your race to teach in our American schools." Chicanas in northern Colorado found that even Denver lacked the Hispanic infrastructure necessary to provide more than a handful of clerical jobs. In Greeley no Hispanic clerked in the stores until after World War II. And Weld County, at the end of the decade, had only one Hispanic teacher.

Neither would the efforts of Americanizers help much in broadening horizons or advancing the status or centrality of Chicanas in northern Colorado. While Santa Fe and Albuquerque schools began to place emphasis on achieving independence and office skills for Chicanas, Fairview School in Denver, according to its president, was "placing special emphasis in its work with Mexican girls on homecraft, domestic science, care of the home, etc." The sentiment there seemed to echo the common wisdom of the time regarding minorities, that "the Mexicans show considerable aptitude for hand work of any kind," as one educator phrased it, and that "girls should be trained to become domestic servants, and to do various kinds of hand work."

These Americanizers, like social workers with other immigrant groups, displayed a desire to mold the behavior of women from another culture into standards acceptable to but not identical with their own middle-class, "American" standards and aspirations. They trained domestic servants and "mothers," not professionals. They continued to believe that in mothers they beheld "the channel through which to raise the standard of community along all lines." And what better way to train Chicanas in "American" mothering than by encouraging them to meet the demand for domestic servants?

Religious Americanization work also targeted mothers. It too, emphasized home care. But Protestants and Catholics focused more on the community than on the workplace, and strove actively to involve the women. In this largely woman-to-woman cross-cultural contact, Americanizers saw themselves as liberating Chicanas from their isolation. A Woman's Christian Temperance Union volunteer English teacher in Denver's Colfax area visited Chicano homes to reach "the mother of large families," a "slave and prisoner" in her home because she spoke no English. Presbyterians established two or three "Houses of Neighborly Service" in northern Colorado which replicated many village mission patterns; residents visited "the Mexican women" and invited them for English language study. Catholics, too, decided that women held the key, and the Mexican Welfare Committee of the Colorado Knights of Columbus gave rosaries "to women on their promise that they will gather two or three families into their homes at least one evening a week to recite it." In ignorance of the religious structure of the villages, the committee claimed, "[W]e make them leaders." In 1927, its first year of welfare work, the Denver Deanery of Catholic women also "decided to concentrate on Mexican Welfare," and set up a clinic and two "social centers" which resembled settlement houses. Striving to provide a community center, they sponsored boys' and girls' clubs, glee clubs, English lessons, and classes on sewing, household care, laundering, table service, sick care, wise spending, and physical culture.

This Americanization, although still bound by a somewhat one-dimensional view of Hispanic womanhood, was at least softened by a new sensitivity. Even the fictionalized versions of Hispanic life that emerged from this effort more closely resembled the truth than those from New Mexico a decade and a half earlier. Robert McLean, in charge of Spanish-speaking work for the Presbyterians, warned that "Mrs. Garcia resents it when a 'home visitor' comes to her little house, and makes friendly observations, however kindly, upon the subject of homemaking, care of babies or personal hygiene!" But Mrs. Garcia, McLean continued, was eager to learn English and was willing to sit through domestic messages embedded in language lessons at the teacher's home.

As it had in Hispanic villages, the assumption that women functioned as cultural bearers, that "the mothers frequently furnish a key to the situation" and so determine cultural survival or acculturation, ensured women, both Anglo and Chicano, a central role in the sphere of Americanization. They would comprise both target and teacher. But what had Chicanas to gain from the interaction? Learning English in and of itself would neither change their position from marginal to central in Anglo society nor return them to the center of Hispanic society; and neither would improved domestic care. Just as it would take more than isolated women missionaries to Anglicize New Mexican village

culture, so it would take more than isolated English, home, and health-care lessons to transform impoverished and transient women into an integrated, stable, multiethnic or even simply Hispanic community. The role of cultural transmitter remained, but it was a role on the margin of each culture, at the intersection between them, and so provided centrality in neither.

Both men and women suffered from narrowed opportunities, but the men's purview, in a permanent life on the Anglo frontier, had gained weight within the Chicano society, while the women's lost it. Contrary to what many sociologists and other observers believed, this marginality of women in the Chicano society was not something the Chicanos had carried with them from the villages, but was the result of adapting to life in a new, Anglo setting. In a sense, this development was an Americanization of gender roles, one echoing the experience of United States women during nineteenth-century industrialization and that of immigrant groups at the turn of the century. The institutions of female authority—the church, the garden, non-wage work, and the family—became for Chicanas as they had become in Anglo society, increasingly peripheral to the main concerns of subsistence in a centralized, male-dominated cash economy.

While their relationship to Anglo society became an increasingly vital force in altering relations between the sexes within their own culture and society, it is less clear whether and how it altered roles within Hispanic marriages. Both partners still participated in decision making and voted in elections when eligible. Women still asserted their right to full knowledge and often mutual control of financial matters.

※

With Chicanas unable to recreate the stable village core that sustained social harmony in the villages, and with Chicanos marginal economically and socially in the Anglo community, it was unclear what sort of community Hispanics could create on the northern Colorado frontier. Indeed, Anglos tended to be pessimistic about the ability of Chicanos to adjust to life in northern Colorado at all. Inheriting a legacy of disdain for seasonal workers and migrant laborers, which labeled their relationship to farm labor as "excrescences upon its fair face," Anglos were disposed to agree with a Weld County sheriff that "a Mexican is a 'natural born liar, thief, and gambler.'" Visions of lawless and irresponsible hordes, visions unanchored by statistics, floated in the public imagination. The colonies were seen as potential dens of iniquity, where "the dancing girl and the wine-cup are star attractions." Their inhabitants appeared in local papers almost solely in criminal context, with their ethnicity prominently featured.

Chicanos did commit some crimes. Most involved petty theft—stealing from coal bins— or revolved around prohibition: moonshining and drinking and selling liquor, activities popular among Chicanos in both New Mexico and Colorado, but hardly peculiar to them. Anglos, however, even those with the most direct contact with Hispanics, consistently and greatly distorted the scale of lawbreaking. The official line held that prosecution of Chicanos accounted for three-quarters of Weld County court cases. An investigation in 1924 revealed instead that even including appearances as plaintiffs, Chicanos accounted for only 6 percent of the total county court cases and 10 percent of the justice of the peace cases, a figure not disproportionate to their number in the county's population. Conspicuous in their "otherness" and their poverty, Chicanos found themselves subject to these myths and to arrest, according to contemporary investigators, "without a clearly defined case or cause against them." Where a fee system ruled, constables and other officers whose income depended on fines and costs advised their victims to plead guilty.

In terms of relief and family stability, fear had also exaggerated the reality. Hispanic divorces in Weld County occurred at a lower rate than either Anglo divorces in that country or Hispanic divorces in southern Colorado or New Mexico. Few Hispanic children spent time in either the state home for dependent children or the state Industrial School for Girls. And the proportion of relief accounted for by Hispanics, while slightly greater than their proportion of the population at large, remained well under 20 percent, less than the proportion of Hispanics among the lowest-income groups. On the whole, concluded one investigator, impoverished Anglos in northern Colorado "indicated a much poorer social adjustment proportionately than did the Spanish-speaking group." It is possible that, after northern trauma, divorcées, single and deserted mothers, and delinquent children all fled back to the Hispanic homeland. It seems more consistent with the evidence, however, that despite frequent migration, low income, and severe discrimination, solidarity and not disorganization characterized Chicano families in the Anglo north. These families proved stronger than the forces which buffeted them on the edge of the regional community.

As with racial and immigrant enclaves elsewhere, the colonies' homogeneity relieved some of the pressure to assimilate. Residents had, as one investigator found, "their own favorite dishes," and no one encouraged them "to abandon their native language for American." Though economically dependent on the Anglo world, they retained, as had the villages, some social and cultural autonomy. Here, perhaps, those who did remain year after year could recreate the regional community in truncated and more vulnerable form. The barrio could be a new core.

By the late 1920s, some colonies increasingly resembled the interrelated villages. Chicano couples met and courted there, among the "meticulously tended lawns, and the watered and swept earthen patios," that one colonist remembered. They held dances and even fiestas in the colonies. The women, recalled one early settler, "had their own clubs," and sewing, cooking, mutual aid, and church groups, and in January 1930, it was their efforts, in part, which culminated in a new Pentecostal Assembly of God Church built by colonists in the Greeley colony.

From this more cohesive base, colonists and other settlers began to shift to more aggressive strategies in intercultural matters. The regional community, with its migrant patterns, was in some sense a strategy of retreat, as was the high turnover that embodied Chicano protest at conditions in beetwork. In the same vein, Mexicans consciously decided against citizenship, rejecting the second-class status they believed it would bring. A Mexican in the South Platte Valley declared, "To hell with the United States. We don't have to be slaves in Mexico." But as retreat to the villages became increasingly impractical and more stable communities evolved, direct protests occurred. At least one Chicano in Weld County filed a civil rights case in 1927 against Greeley restaurant proprietors who ejected him on grounds that he was a Mexican. World War I veterans among the colonists also early asserted the colonists' rights in the community at large in regard to voting and discrimination. Their membership in local American Legion branches provided virtually the only organized non-charitable social link between ethnic groups and bolstered their legitimacy as spokesmen in each.

As the sense of neighborhood in the colonies grew, resistance began to take more collective forms. Chicano boycotts in Greeley and Johnstown led to the removal of discriminatory signs from the shop windows, at least temporarily, in 1927. Though less successful, a committee of Chicanos also protested the establishment of separate school rooms for Chicano children. By the end of the decade, like Denver, the colonies and mining towns had their own Hispanic groups and *mutualistas* [mutual aid societies]. Some accepted both Mexican and Spanish Americans, others only one or the other. Some of the colonies even organized into self-governing bodies under commissioners of their own choosing. In 1928 the Greeley colony, for example, drew up "articles of association for the management of colony affairs," including police and sanitary regulations, and filed them with the county police. This was, perhaps, the ultimate declaration of an autonomous community on the Anglo-Hispanic frontier. These Hispanics created room for themselves and committed themselves to permanent residence without committing themselves to assimilation.

Questions for Study and Review

1. How did World War I shape the long-term relations of Hispanics, Mexicans, and Anglos?

2. How did the Red Scare that followed World War I affect opportunities for minorities and women?

3. Compare the roles of women in northern Jewish, southern black, and southwestern Mexican families and communities.

4. Transiency shaped the lives of families like the Patches in eighteenth-century New England, of Cherokees in the nineteenth century, and of African-Americans and Mexicans in the twentieth. Compare the effects of transiency on women and men in each group.

Suggested Readings

Virginia Sapiro, "Woman, Citizenship and Nationality: Immigration and Naturalization Policies in the United States," *Politics and Society* (#1, 1984).

Maxine Seller, "The Education of the Immigrant Woman, 1900–1935," *Journal of Urban History* (May 1978).

Mario Garcia, "The Chicana in American History: The Mexican Women of El Paso, 1880–1920," *Pacific Historical Review* (May 1980).

Yuji Ichioka, "*Amerika Nadishiko:* Japanese Immigrant Women in the United States, 1900–1924," *Pacific Historical Review* (May 1980).

Vicki Ruiz and Susan Tiano, eds., *Women on the U.S.-Mexico Border: Responses to Change* (1987).

William Breen, "Black Women and the Great War: Mobilization and Social Reform in the South," *Journal of Southern History* (August 1978).

NINE

The Roaring Teens and Twenties Reexamined: Sexuality in the Furnished Room Districts of Chicago

Joanne Meyerowitz

Despite her long years of experience at Hull House, Jane Addams might well have been shocked had she toured Chicago's furnished room districts at night. She was aware, no doubt, that affluent Americans were seeking to forget wartime hardships by testing new forms of entertainment, consumption, and sexuality. Yet Addams and her peers might have been more upset than they already were regarding the new (lack of) morality had they understood the extent to which the privileged were now modeling their behavior on that of the poor, rather than the reverse.

The flapper—bold, emancipated, and carefree—was one of the foremost symbols of the postwar era. Novels and movies promised working girls the chance to join the ranks of the "new woman," to rise from rags to riches and take advantage of the pleasures of the new urban society. Not everyone, however, was unmindful of the old dangers that lurked behind these new pleasures. Reform-minded writers, scholars, and activists had long noted that the more typical path of the pleasure seekers was from riches to rags. Sexual experimentation could turn young women into moral outcasts, as was most eloquently portrayed in Theodore Dreiser's *Sister Carrie*. Settlement house residents sought to assist real-life Carries, but to do so, they finally had to admit that women had sexual urges and that overwork, commercial entertainment, poverty and alcohol encouraged the expression of these urges.

Historians who study the flapper era also waver between praise and criticism of the period's social and sexual freedoms. They generally agree, however, that the changes wrought were initiated by middle-class rebels and bohemians. When working women appear in such studies, they are portrayed most often as passive recipients—beneficial or not—of a culture forged by their social superiors.

By focusing on the furnished room districts of Chicago, Meyerowitz presents a different version of how change occurred, how social and sexual developments of the early twentieth century emerged and spread. In a city with an abundance of settlement house residents and social scientists, Meyerowitz finds a vibrant if sometimes precarious working-class subculture rooted in changing patterns of women's work and changing forms of family life.

Working women and men crowded into furnished rooms, seeking independence from parents and support from each other. Women's low wages combined with the lure of commercial entertainment to assure that courting would take on economic as well as romantic meaning. The bargain between escort and date might result in a free evening out, gifts of clothing or jewelry, lodging, or the exchange of sexual favors. Though differing by race, sexual preference, and neighborhood, working-class women collectively created new sexual standards that were then imitated by middle-class rebels, a process that calls into question the power of middle-class reformers as well as rebels to shape society to their vision.

The broad outlines of the early twentieth-century sexual revolution are now well known. From roughly 1890 to roughly 1930, sexual reticence gave way to public discussions and displays of sexuality in popular magazines, newspapers, and movies. At the same time, women began to adopt more sexual, or at least less modest, styles; shorter skirts, cosmetics, bobbed hair, and cigarettes, once the styles of prostitutes, all seemed evidence of a larger change in mores when adopted by "respectable" working- and middle-class women. Men and women mingled freely in new commercialized recreation industries and in workplaces. And surveys of the middle class revealed increases in premarital intercourse.

Historians have now written at least three versions of this sexual revolution. In the oldest and now standard account, young middle-class "flappers" rebelled against the repressive standards of their parents by engaging in shocking behavior, such as petting in automobiles, dancing to jazz music, and using bawdy language. A more recent version of the sexual revolution developed with the growth of the field of U.S. women's history. In this rendition, young feminist bohemians, or independent "new women," influenced by the writings of Freud and other sexologists, experimented sexually and rejected the homosocial sisterhood of earlier woman's rights activists. A third variation points to a working-class component. Urban working-class "rowdy girls" appear as early as the 1830's, but seem to enter center historical stage in precisely the same years that the middle-class "new women" and "flappers" self-consciously rejected Victorian mores. In the workplace and in dance halls, theaters, and amusement parks, young working-class women adopted an overtly heterosexual style that dismayed both their parents and middle-class reformers.

This article is a case study of working-class women's sexuality in the furnished room districts of turn-of-the-century Chicago. In a particular setting, how did women participate in the sexual revolution, and how was their behavior interpreted and publicized? This approach modifies the various versions of the sexual revolution. For one, it locates neglected geographical centers of urban sexual activity—the furnished room districts—and early active participants in the sexual revolution—the women lodgers. Second, it points to economic imperatives that motivated and shaped at least part of the sexual revolution. And, finally, it shows how middle-class observers reshaped the experiences of sexually active working-class women and broadcast them to a larger national audience.

Recently feminists have engaged in heated debates over the meaning of twentieth-century sexual expression. The debates are polarized between those who emphasize the sexual dangers, such as rape, that oppress women and those who focus on the sensual pleasures that await women. While this article does not enter these debates directly, it suggests the importance of studying sexuality in context. Sexual behavior, of course, is neither inherently dangerous for women nor inherently pleasurable. Like other socially constructed behaviors, its meaning derives from the specific context in which it is enacted. This study examines how and why a particular group of women adopted the freer modes of sexual

An earlier version of this article was presented at the Organization of American Historians Convention, April, 1986. Thanks to Estelle Freedman, Zane Miller, Leila Rupp, Christina Simmons, Bruce Tucker, and the anonymous *Feminist Studies* reviewers for their helpful comments.

The flapper, with her bobbed hair and short skirts, symbolized the trend toward more liberal sexual attitudes and behavior during the 1920s, but the image overlooked the reality that economic necessity often lay behind the bohemian life-style characteristic of the furnished-room districts of major cities.

expression that characterized the early twentieth-century sexual revolution. It finds that neither sexual danger nor sensual pleasure provides adequate explanation.

Most major American cities today have a distinct geography of sexuality. That is, one could locate districts and neighborhoods known as the institutional and social centers of various sexual subcultures. Take San Francisco, for example, a city known for its celebration of sexual variety. Upscale heterosexual swinging singles live in apartments and frequent bars in the Marina district. Downscale heterosexual men go to porn shops and massage parlors in the Tenderloin. Female prostitutes sell their services at the corner of 18th and Mission Streets; male prostitutes sell their services on Polk Street.

Gay men congregate in the Castro district, and lesbians meet in the bars and coffeehouses in the vicinity of Valencia Street.

A lesser-known geography of sexuality also existed in early twentieth-century American cities. In 1916, sociologist Robert Park identified what he called "moral regions" of the city, "detached milieus in which vagrant and suppressed impulses, passions, and ideals emancipate themselves from the dominant moral order." A moral region, Park wrote, "is not necessarily a place of abode. It may be a mere rendezvous, a place of resort." He included Bohemia, the half-world, and the red-light district among the more pronounced "moral regions" of the city.

At the end of the nineteenth century, a few urban investigators identified the furnished-room districts, or areas where rooming houses abounded, as "moral regions" of sorts, distinct neighborhoods where unconventional sexual behavior flourished. By the early twentieth century, reformers defined a "furnished room problem" more precisely. In 1906, for example, in a study of Boston's South End furnished room district, Albert Benedict Wolfe described and lamented the "contamination of young men, the deterioration of modesty and morality of young women, the existence of actual houses of prostitution in the guise of lodging-houses, the laxity of landladies, the large number of informal unions, the general loosening of moral texture." Later, in the late 1910's and 1920's, more dispassionate sociologists reported and explored "a new code of sex relationships" in the furnished room districts of Chicago. Evidence from newspapers, autobiographies, vice reports, and social surveys also suggests that the furnished room districts were indeed the centers of sexually unconventional subcultures.

By the end of the nineteenth century, most major American cities had furnished room districts. These districts often first appeared in the city center, and, later, as business displaced downtown housing, moved outside the center along major transportation lines. The large proportion of adult residents and the small proportion of children distinguished these districts demographically from other neighborhoods of the city. A residential street in a furnished room district usually resembled other residential streets in the city: a typical block would consist of single-family homes, buildings of flats, large tenements, or older mansions. The owners of the buildings, however, converted the interiors into one- or two-room dwellings. They might divide a flat into two or three smaller units or divide a large tenement into an "apartment hotel" with as many as one hundred furnished rooms.

In Chicago, three such districts emerged in the late nineteenth century. On the South Side, the furnished room district included major portions of the Chicago black community and also what was, before the 1912 raids, the segregated vice district of the city. On the West Side, the district housed a population of predominantly white service and factory workers. A transient male hobo population congregated on the inner boundaries. On the North Side, where rents were slightly higher, clerical and sales workers lived in rooming houses alongside white service and manufacturing workers, artists, bohemians, and radicals of all stripes. In the early twentieth century, the North Side district included substantial numbers of Irish and Swedish roomers.

These districts burgeoned in the early 1890's when migrants and visitors streamed to Chicago for the World's Columbian Exposition. They continued to grow in the first decades of the twentieth century. By 1923, the Illinois Lodging House Register reported over 85,000 lodgers in about 5,000 rooming houses in the three major furnished room districts. By 1930, residents of the new small unit apartments (with private bathrooms and kitchenettes) joined the lodgers in furnished rooms.

Several distinctive features of the furnished room districts fostered the development of extramarital sexual relationships. Most obviously, women and men lived together in houses where most people did not live in families. In these neighborhoods, lodgers found numerous opportunities to create social and sexual ties with their peers. Further, the high geographic mobility in the furnished room districts made informal, transient relationships the norm. One writer went so far as to claim that the entire population of Chicago's North Side furnished room district changed every four months. This high turnover rate created an atmosphere of anonymity in which lodgers rarely knew their neighbors well. Community pressures to conform to conventional familial roles were weaker than in more settled neighborhoods. And parental authorities were absent. Many rooming house keepers, eager to keep their tenants, refrained from criticizing or interfering with roomers' sexual behavior. In addition, the predominance of men in the North and West Side districts may have encouraged women to participate in extramarital heterosexual relationships: it must have been easy for women to meet men and difficult to avoid them.

In any case, the prevalence of prostitution in the furnished room districts created a climate where open expressions of sexuality were common. In the first decade of the twentieth century, the most prominent vice district of Chicago lay in the South Side furnished room district. Brothels were tolerated in sections of the West and North Side districts as well. In addition, on the South, West, and North Sides, some keepers of rooming houses and hotels rented rooms by the hour or night to prostitutes and their customers. After the municipal government closed the brothels in the 1910's, investigators in the furnished room districts repeatedly found rooming houses and hotels used for prostitution. A 1922 study concluded: "The furnished room situation in Chicago is particularly bad, especially on the South Side. Many of the women who operate upon the streets and in the cabarets utilize the rooming houses."

In addition to the hotels and rooming houses, the "bright light" centers of the furnished room districts provided settings in which men and women could socialize. Investors who hoped to profit from the market of lodgers opened cafeterias, cheap restaurants, tea rooms, soft-drink parlors, saloons, dance halls, cabarets, and movie theaters in the furnished room districts. Residents of the districts turned these institutions into social centers. As one observer noted: "Considerable companionship grows up around these resorts. One is struck by the fact that the same people visit and re-visit the same cabaret time and again."

On the North Side, Clark Street and, on the West Side, Halsted Street, were well known for their night life. In 1918, the section of Clark Street that ran through the North Side district housed 57 saloons, 36 restaurants, and 20 cabarets. In the South Side furnished room district, the State Street "Stroll" and, by the 1920's, 35th Street emerged as the "bright light" centers of the black community. Dance halls, restaurants, movies, and saloons for black customers coexisted with "black and tan" cabarets which offered racially integrated recreation. When young men and women who lived with their parents went out for a night on the town and when wealthier people went "slumming," they often went to the furnished room districts of the city.

The furnished room districts, it seems, were geographic settings where behavior considered unacceptable elsewhere was accepted matter-of-factly and even encouraged. In residential communities of Chicago, neighbors often stigmatized sexually active unmarried women. The case of Mamie, a young woman who lived with her parents in a working-class neighborhood of Chicago, is illustrative. Mamie first encountered problems in 1918 when a policewoman reported her for "unbecoming conduct with sailors." The unbecoming conduct continued, and, two years later, rumor had it that her neighbors talked of signing a petition to expel her from the neighborhood. Contrast Mamie's brief case history with the comment of a student of Chicago's South Side furnished room district: "It is said that an attractive woman who does not 'cash in' is likely to be considered a fool by her neighbors, instead of any stigma being attached to a woman who 'hustles' in this neighborhood."

By the early twentieth century, the furnished room districts of Chicago and other large cities were known as havens for women and men who chose to defy conventions. In addition to migrants and transients, they attracted women and men who wanted to have adventures and break taboos in a community without parental supervision. Here interested lodgers could enter peer-oriented subcultures that sanctioned extramarital sexual behavior. An account from a study of Chicago's North Side, written in 1918, shows the complexity and the casual nature of social and sexual relationships:

[J. and V.] went to the North Clark Street section where they posed as man and wife. They took a couple of furnished rooms . . . , and remained there for two years. Both of them worked, often bringing in as much as $30.00 a week together. They took their meals out and got along very well.

Then two of the girl's sisters came to Chicago to find work and rented rooms next to them. These girls had good intentions but not securing very lucrative positions, they soon learned how to supplement their wages by allowing young men to stay with them.

These girls struck up an acquaintanceship with another girl who used to remain overnight with them now and again when they had been out to a dance or cabaret. J. liked this new girl and as he put it could not "help monkeying with her" and when V. found it out she became extremely jealous and shortly afterwards left him. Her sisters and the other girl followed her.

Other accounts provide additional glimpses of how women formed social networks in the furnished room districts. In 1911, two women, seventeen and twenty years old, met at a South Side dance hall. The older woman persuaded the younger woman to leave her parents' home and room with her on Chicago's North Side. After they moved in together, they made "pick up acquaintances" with men at dance halls and on the street. Around 1913, Myrtle S., who roomed in the North Side furnished room district, made friends with a woman at the restaurant where she ate her meals. This woman introduced her to a man, Lew W., with whom she spent several evenings drinking beer in a North Side inn. Myrtle testified that she lost her virginity when Lew took advantage of her: "one night she lost consciousness after her drink of beer and awoke next morning in the Superior Hotel, 721 North Clark Street." Despite this betrayal, she returned to the hotel with Lew on two other occasions. Later, Myrtle met another man at a "chop suey" restaurant.

Several of the social circles that developed in the furnished room districts of Chicago were distinguished by unconventional lifestyles, sexual preferences, or political leanings. In the North Side district of Chicago, for example, a subculture of hoboes congregated in and around Washington, or Bughouse, Square. In her autobiography, hobo "Box Car Bertha" wrote, "Girls and women . . . seemed to keep Chicago as their hobo center. . . . They all centered about the Near North Side, in Bughouse Square, in the cheap roominghouses and light housekeeping establishments, or begged or accepted sleeping space from men or other women there before them." The women hoboes whom Bertha described engaged casually in sexual relationships. One woman, she wrote, had "a group of sweethearts," others lived and traveled with men "to whom by chance or feeling they had attached themselves," and still others engaged in "careless sex relations."

By the 1920's, lesbian communities were also visible in the furnished-room districts of Chicago. Among black women, blues singer Ma Rainey, a bisexual, suggested that lesbians frequented State Street, in the South Side rooming house area. In a song recorded in 1924, she included these references to State Street among other more sexually suggestive verses:

Goin' down to spread the news
State Street women wearing brogan shoes
Hey, hey, daddy let me shave 'em dry . . .
There's one thing I don't understand
Some women walkin' State Street like a man,
Eeh, hey, hey, daddy let me shave 'em dry.

According to Box Car Bertha, "several tea shops and bootleg joints on the near-north side . . . catered to lesbians." Bertha found a large number of lesbians among the Chicago hobo population. Another observer found lesbians in the somewhat less transient population of the Near North Side furnished-room district's bohemian circles. He, too, noted that homosexual women and men frequented the tea rooms of the area and held parties in their rented rooms.

The best-known subcultures of the furnished room districts were undoubtedly the bohemian subcultures of artists, intellectuals, and political radicals. In Chicago, black bohemians congregated in the South Side furnished room district, and some white socialists and anarchists lived in the West Side district. But the heart of Chicago's Bohemia was on the North Side where one study found that, "Most of the experimenters are young women." In most respects, Chicago's bohemians resembled the better-known bohemians of New York's Greenwich Village. Chicago, though, had its own distinctive institutions. On the North Side, for example, the informal Dill Pickle Club provided a setting for lectures, plays, and jazz performances. And the anarchist tradition of a soap-box oratory in Washington Square provided a public forum for bohemian speakers.

As in the other subcultures of the furnished room districts, women who joined the bohemian circles expected and often wanted to participate in extramarital sexual activities. For example, Natalie Feinberg, the daughter of working-class Jewish immigrants from Russia, expressed an interest in "free love" before she moved away from her family in Chicago, changed her name to Jean Farway, and "frequented the various gathering places" of the bohemians. According to the sociologist who described her, "She won the reputation of wishing to become a great courtesan."

Historians remember the furnished room districts primarily for the articulate, "emancipated" middle- and upper-class members of the bohemian communities. These bohemians are seen as vanguards of modern sexuality, women and men who experimented freely with new sexual possibilities learned from Sigmund Freud, Havelock Ellis, and other sexologists. The geography of sexuality helps to place the bohemians in context. They were only one subculture among several in the furnished room districts. The furnished room districts housed working-class women and men as well as middle- and upper-class bohemians. There is no evidence that the "revolution" of a bohemian and middle-class vanguard trickled down to the working class. In fact, it seems more likely that the bohemians learned of new sexual possibilities not only from the "highbrow" writings of the sexologists but also from the "lowbrow" behavior of their less intellectual neighbors.

The furnished room districts not only provide a setting for observing various participants in the sexual revolution; they also reveal the social and economic context that shaped sexual mores. Heterosexual relationships in the furnished room districts included "dating," "pick ups," "occasional prostitution," and "temporary alliances." Like professional prostitution and marriage, these were economic relationships as well as sexual and social ones. Because employers paid self-supporting women wages intended for dependent daughters and wives, many women lodgers worked in low paying jobs that barely covered subsistence. In an era of rapidly expanding urban consumerism, these women were forced into scrimping and self-denial. By entering sexual relationships, however, they could supplement their wages with free evenings on the town, free meals in restaurants, and sometimes gifts and money. In many cases, the new sexual expression allowed women to participate in the urban consumer economy.

Even in the most innocent dating, men customarily paid for the evening's entertainment. Women, in return, gave limited sexual favors, ranging from charming companionship to sexual intercourse. In 1910 a federal report on self-supporting women stressed the economic value of dating:

Even if most of the girls do not spend money for amusements, it is no proof that they go without them. Many of the girls have 'gentlemen friends' who take them out. 'Sure I go out all the time, but it doesn't cost me anything; my gentleman friend takes me,' was the type of remark heard again and again. . . . [G]irls who have 'steadies' are regarded as fortunate indeed.

A woman need not have a "steady," however, to benefit from dating. In "pick ups," women met male strangers casually on street corners or in dance halls, restaurants, and saloons. They then spent the evening and sometimes the night with them. The 1910 federal report suggested that a woman who wore attractive clothing could find men who would pay for her entertainment:

> the majority, even if they have no money to spend or no one to take them out, as long as they have clothes that are presentable, can have some entertainment. They can 'take a walk' on the street, go into the free dance halls, where they meet men who will treat them to the entertainment the place affords. . . .

Such was the case in Chicago. In the furnished room districts, women attempted to pick men up in dance halls and on the streets. In 1911, for example, a vice investigator in a dance hall in the North Side furnished room district encountered several women who asked him "to take them to shows or dances." Ten years later, in the heart of the South Side furnished room district, Gladys B., an 18-year-old black woman, "went cabareting" with James P. after she picked him up at the corner of 35th and State Streets. They ended the evening in a South Side hotel room. Presumably James paid for the cabarets, the hotel room, and perhaps for Gladys' sexual services. (In this case, he paid more than he bargained for: this mundane pickup became newsworthy only when Gladys escaped in the night with James' wad of money.)

In the early twentieth century, young working-class women who lived in their parents' homes also participated avidly in the new urban dating patterns promoted by commercialized recreation facilities. For many women lodgers in the furnished room districts, however, the necessity of supporting themselves on low wages added a special imperative. Lodgers themselves were highly aware of the economic benefits of dating. A waitress said bluntly, "If I did not have a man, I could not get along on my wages." A chambermaid in a hotel said, "If the girls are good and refuse invitations to go out, they simply have no pleasure." And a taxi-dancer stated, "It's a shame a girl can't go straight and have a good time but I've got to get what I get by 'Sex Appeal.'" One male resident of the North Side furnished room district concluded: "[women] draw on their sex as I would on my bank account to pay for the kind of clothes they want to wear, the kind of shows they want to see."

"Occasional prostitution" resembled dates and pick ups, but here the economic benefits were even clearer. Women asked men explicitly to pay for the sexual services provided them. These women worked in stores, offices, factories, and restaurants by day and sold their sexual services on occasional nights for extra money. While many women who dated probably exchanged only companionship, flirtation, and petting for evenings on the town, the smaller group of occasional prostitutes stepped up the barter, exchanging sexual intercourse for gifts or money. These women did not necessarily see themselves as prostitutes; they simply played the "sex game" for somewhat higher stakes.

Without watchful relatives nearby, women lodgers could engage in occasional prostitution more easily than working women who lived in their parents' homes. Accordingly, vice investigators in search of occasional prostitutes went to the furnished room districts to find them. In a North Clark Street saloon, for example, a vice investigator met two women who lived in the North Side furnished room district. They worked in a department store for $5.50 per week. "They can't live on this," he reported, "so they 'hustle' on the side." Another "occasional prostitute," a 19-year-old migrant from Indiana, lived in a furnished room on Michigan Avenue and worked in a South Side restaurant. The investigator stated: "Is not a regular prostitute, goes with men for presents or money. Is poorly paid at restaurant."

With pick ups and occasional prostitution, the relationships usually lasted for one night only. In a "temporary alliance," a woman maintained a sexual relationship with one or more "steady" boyfriends or lived with a man as if she were married. Amy, a 20-year-old woman who lived in the South Side furnished room district, worked as a cashier in a downtown restaurant until she met a streetcar conductor who agreed to "keep" her. He had given her a new fall hat and promised to buy her a new winter coat. Amy occasionally went out with other men "to get a little more spending money." Another account of temporary alliances in furnished rooms stated tersely, "For 10 months, Marion lived a hand-to-mouth existence, dependent upon the bounty of several men with whom she became intimate." As Albert Wolfe wrote in 1906, these alliances were motivated in some cases by "genuine and lasting regard," but in others, "the motive of the girl is simply to find support, and that of the man gratification."

From the limited evidence available, it seems that economic realities also shaped sexual relationships in the lesbian subculture. Some lesbians in the furnished room districts depended on men, earning money as prostitutes. Others found higher-paid or wealthier women to support them. For example, in the North Side district in the late 1920's, one lesbian, Beatrice, was supported by her lover Peggy who earned money as a prostitute. Peggy, wrote Box Car Bertha, "has had a dozen sweethearts, all lesbian, and has always supported them." Bertha also reported a form of gold digging or, more precisely, veiled blackmail among lesbians. After a North Side party, some lesbians persuaded the wealthier women attending to pay for their companionship: "The lesbians would get their names and addresses and borrow money by saying, 'I met you at . . . [the] party.'" Some lesbians also prostituted themselves to other women.

This emphasis on the economics of sexual relationships should not obscure the sexual dangers or the sensual pleasures that many women experienced. On the one hand, some women lodgers encountered undeniable sexual violence, such as rape, and others found themselves betrayed by false promises of marriage. On the other hand, many women clearly enjoyed the sexual relationships in which they found physical pleasure, excitement, and companionship. As one woman stated bluntly, "Frankly, I like intercourse!" Further, the economic dependency in these relationships was not necessarily more exploitative or more oppressive than wives' traditional dependence on husbands or daughters' traditional dependence on fathers.

The economic imperatives are important, though, for they point to a neglected political economy of the early twentieth-century sexual revolution. The exchange of sexual services for financial support moved beyond the marital bedroom and the brothel and into a variety of intermediate forms including dating, pick ups, temporary alliances, and occasional prostitution. The sexual revolution was not simply, as one historian has written, "prosperity's child." In the furnished room districts, economic need shaped sexual experimentation. "What I get is mine. And what they have is mine, too, if I am smart enough to get it," said one self-avowed gold digger, ". . . . I'll show you how to take their socks away." "Modern" sexual expression, then, not only threatened women with danger and promised women pleasure; in a variety of forms, it also offered financial reward.

Not surprisingly the sexuality of women lodgers captured public notice. In local and national media a variety of observers constructed conflicting interpretations of the unconventional sexual behavior of the furnished room districts. Reformers, manufacturers of popular culture, and sociologists dominated these debates.

In late 19th-century Chicago, conservative authors, often male, disparaged the working woman who lodged on her own. Because she had not chosen to live in a private family as a domestic servant, they wrote, she undoubtedly had "false notions of pride," tended toward laziness, and longed for finery. She was not, the conservatives found, of proper moral character, and they did not hesitate to cast aspersions. In 1888, for example, one letter to the editor of a Chicago newspaper asked, "Have we not seen these very girls in their finery and gay toggery on Saturday nights in the streets and on Sundays at the parks better dressed than many virtuous wives and daughters?" The letter argued that women who lodged should seek jobs as domestics where they might have the "home comforts and home influences of good, respectable people." The writer concluded: "These 'poor girls' are themselves to blame if they seek the filth of life instead of the purity of it."

Countering this conservative approach, middle-class reformers, primarily women, elaborated and spread a more sympathetic image of woman lodgers. In the late nineteenth and early twentieth centuries, Chicago reformers in the organized boarding home movement, in the antiprostitution crusade, and in the campaign to improve women's wages wrote with genuine concern for poorly-paid self-supporting women. With a sense of female solidarity, they deplored the economic hardships faced by most wage-earning women. Like the conservatives, though, they accepted middle-class Victorian views that lamented female sexual expression.

These writers, however, rarely blamed the sexually active woman. Following in the footsteps of earlier female moral reformers, they read sexual expression as a symbol of female victimization. These writers portrayed sexually active women lodgers as passive, pure, and impoverished orphans duped, forced, or unduly tempted by scheming men. While they occasionally criticized women lodgers for their "tendency . . . to drift away from sweet and tender home influences," most often they condemned the "vampires" who trapped "poor, innocent little girls." The reformers acknowledged that a woman lodger might enjoy the companionship she found in the furnished room districts, but "the glare of cheap entertainments and dangers of the street," they feared, would overpower her. In short, they adopted a stereotype of female weakness and innocence that absolved the woman lodger of responsibility for her own sexual behavior.

The reformers appointed themselves as maternal protectors. In Chicago and other cities, they opened subsidized boarding homes—"veritable virtue-saving stations"—to lure women from the commercial lodgings of the furnished room districts. By the 1920's, Chicago alone had over 60 organized homes managed by Protestant, Catholic, Jewish, Afro-American, German, Swedish, Polish, and Norwegian-Danish middle-class women for working women of these religious, racial, and ethnic groups. Reformers also established room registries that placed women lodgers with private families in residential neighborhoods. They campaigned for minimum wage laws because they saw the low pay of women lodgers as a major cause of "immorality." To "outwit evil agents, who would deceive the innocent," they placed charity workers in train stations and police matrons in public dance halls. While they helped women in need of support, they obscured the actions that women lodgers took on their own behalf and elaborated instead an image of weak-willed women in sexual danger. In fact, well after most reformers had acknowledged the competence of working women who lived in their parents' homes, the "woman adrift," who lodged on her own, remained a symbol of endangered womanhood.

A variant of the reformers' discourse reached into popular culture. In the late nineteenth and early twentieth centuries, popular "working girl" romance novels, printed as cheap paperbound books or story-paper serials, adopted the image of orphaned and innocent "women adrift." In these female versions of Horatio Alger stories, young, virtuous, native-born, white woman endured endless agonies when alone in the city and eventually married wealthy men. Here the language of female victimization reached its most sensational. Listen to Charlotte M. Stanley, the author of "Violet, the Beautiful Street Singer; Or, an Ill-Starred Betrothal": "Oh, what cruel fate was it that had so suddenly altered the safe, smooth current of her young existence and cast her adrift in this frightful, seething whirlpool of vice and crime?" In another story, "Alone in New York," the hapless heroine, "pretty little Bab," entreats her rescuer, "I have no friends, no home, no place to rest in this great, bad city, and I shall die if you leave me now!" This story, as its subtitle announced, hoped to attract readers with "A Thrilling Portrayal of the Dangers and Pitfalls of the Metropolis." The queen of the romance novels was probably Laura Jean Libbey, the author of over sixty novels in the last two decades of the nineteenth century. Libbey created especially naive heroines who endured unusually excruciating agonies. As Libbey wrote of one heroine, "She was like an infant torn from its mother's breast and thrust out upon the cold mercies of the pitiless world." Like the reformers, Libbey publicized the perils of life in the city and sympathized with the lone working woman whom she portrayed as passive, innocent, and endangered.

The reformers and romance novelists, though, were fighting a losing battle, in part because the women they hoped to help belied the image of helpless victim. In fact, some women lodgers themselves directly attacked the reformers who treated them as pathetic orphans. In 1890, several "self-respecting and self-supporting" residents of the Chicago YWCA home wrote a blistering letter to a local newspaper:

The idea seems to be in circulation that we who are unfortunate enough to be independent, are a collection of ignorant, weak-minded young persons, who have never had any advantages, educational or otherwise, and that we are brought here where we will be philanthropically cared for, and cold winds tempered for us. A matron is provided, and committee of women who happen to be blessed with a few thousand dollars worth of aristocracy, had charge of the matron.

The women also complained of the furniture and food, and referred to themselves as the "victims of the home."

By the early twentieth century, some reformers began to reassess their outlook. Managers of organized homes and other astute observers could not help noting that many women lodgers were competent, assertive, and sexual by choice. Using the fact-gathering methods of the new social science, social investigators met face to face with women who pursued companionship, adventure, and entertainment actively. While reformers' concern for the woman lodger continued, they dropped their earlier emphasis on her passivity. Some reformers also began to recognize that wage-earning women had sexual urges. In 1910, one Chicago anti-vice crusader, who described self-supporting women as innocent, naive, and unprotected, wrote in a distinctly modern passage, "it must not be forgotten that every normal girl or woman has primal instincts just as strong as her brother's." Jane Addams, Louise DeKoven Bowen, and other Chicago reformers rejected the earlier image of female passionlessness. Instead, they blamed overwork, commercialized recreation, and alcohol for bringing out natural yearnings and instincts that they preferred to see repressed.

As reformers observed women lodgers, their fears about women's sexual vulnerability diminished. They saw that women in the furnished room districts lived in a world that attached less stigma to female sexual activity. Reformers interviewed women who had given up their chastity without an inkling that they had chosen "a fate worse than death," and they saw a wage-earning woman might choose to sell or exchange sexual services without ruining her life. "The fact that she has earned money in this way does not stamp her as 'lost' . . . ," a 1911 federal report stated. "And the ease with which, in a large city, a woman may conceal a fall of this kind, if she desires to do so, also helps make a return to virtuous ways easy . . . occasional prostitution holds its place in their minds as a possible resource, extreme, to be sure, but not in the least unthinkable."

By the mid-1910's the observations of reformers coincided with broader changes in middle-class thought and behavior. In the years before World War I, increasing numbers of middle-class urban women adopted the more open sexual behavior of women in the furnished room districts. This change in middle-class morals further undermined the older image of female innocence and passionlessness, and challenged reformers' fear that female sexual behavior denoted female victimization. After World War I, in a conservative political climate, reformers suffered further from declining public interest and from government repression and indifference.

Ultimately the reformers' discourse on sexuality could not compete with a newer discourse

emerging in popular culture. In the early twentieth century, cabaret reviews and movies attracted audiences by using the woman lodger as an appealing symbol of urban energy, allure, and adventure. In this newer discourse, the woman lodger, headstrong and openly sexual, lived boldly in a fast-paced urban environment. In the earlier romance novels, unfortunate circumstance—poverty or death in the family—forced timid young women, soon to be victims, from happy parental homes. Or foolish young women left home and soon regretted it. In the newer scenarios, women, like Theodore Dreiser's Sister Carrie, chafed at the restrictions of domesticity and the dullness of the small town. As one writer concluded: "[The city] is her frontier and in it she is the pioneer." In the earlier discourse, the woman victim's suffering signified the high cost of urban living; in the newer discourse, the woman pioneer's pleasure pointed to its rewards.

The newer image appeared in the first decade of the twentieth century in the stories of chorus girls who achieved stardom and married wealth. These women strutted boldly across the stage, displaying their bodies and commanding attention through their sexual appeal. They won wide publicity in 1908 when the trial of Henry Thaw made sensational headlines and reached larger audiences still in a movie, *The Great Trial*. Thaw had murdered architect Standford White in a jealous rage over White's affair with Thaw's wife, Evelyn Nesbit. During the trial, Nesbit, a former chorus girl, told how wealthy men entertained, courted, and, in her case, married the sexually attractive dancers in cabarets and theaters. As she recounted her rise from the life of a hard-working chorus girl to a life of luxury and extravagance, she announced the material and romantic possibilities available to the sexual, independent wage-earning woman.

In the following years, as the number of movie theaters expanded rapidly and the size of the audiences grew, the woman lodger emerged as a central character in the new feature films. At first, in the early "white slavery" films, the heroines faced threats to their virtue and sometimes eventual victimization. At the same time, though, in the early serials—*The Perils of Pauline, The Hazards of Helen,* and *Dolly of the Dailies*—the heroines, independent from family, were "healthy, robust, and self-reliant." They met available and often moneyed men whom they attracted with their native allure. While they encountered dangers and difficulties, they also enjoyed the daring nightlife in cabarets and dance halls as well as the high life in opulent villas.

Soon the movies portrayed increasingly competent and more overtly sexual working-class heroines. By 1915, Mary Pickford, had made her career as the first major movie queen. In her films, Pickford, though always chaste, often portrayed women lodgers who flirted, danced, wore revealing clothing, and enjoyed energetic activities. She combined the purity of the Victorian orphan with the sexuality of the chorus girl. Her exuberance and spunk attracted male suitors, leading to upwardly mobile marriages. By the 1920's, the movies drew clear connections between separation from family, on the one side, and female sexuality and material gain, on the other. In some movies, the woman lodger was the stock heroine in rags-to-riches stories. The following description of *At the Stage Door* typifies the formula: "Mary leaves home to become a chorus girl in New York, and soon she achieves stardom. Philip Pierce, a young millionaire, is attracted to her."

As the heterosexual activities and the assertive behavior of the independent working woman became more explicit in the movies, so did the dangers she posed to men. The woman lodger as gold digger appeared at least as early as 1915. In *The Model; Or, Women and Wine,* wealthy young Dick Seymour pursues an independent working woman, Marcelle Rigadont, an artist's model. Marcelle, as one character advises her, wants to "play him for a sucker

. . . and bleed him for every cent he's got." In the end, she confesses, "I never loved you—It was only your money I was after." In the 1920's, at least 34 films included the gold digger with her "aggressive use of sexual attraction."

This new sexual image was not limited to the movies. Although unrecorded forms of entertainment are harder to document, it seems that the same image appeared in the chorus revues of cabarets and theaters. In "The Girl From My Hometown," for example, the opening number of the Midnight Frolic's "Just Girls," staged in 1915, "girls from 24 cities and one small home town came to New York for adventure, men, and a new life." "Sally," a Ziegfield revue staged in 1920, told the story of a working-class orphan who climbed from the "chorus to theatrical fame, wealthy admirers, and riches." By the 1920's, variations on these plot lines appeared repeatedly in the new monthly pulp romance magazines such as *True Story, Dream World,* and *True Romances.*

In the late 1910's and 1920's, the new image of women lodgers achieved academic legitimacy in the writings of the urban sociologists at the University of Chicago. Inaugurated in the 1890's, the academic discipline of sociology moved quickly from an anti-urban moralism to more rarefied theoretical questions. In Chicago, sociologists, predominantly male, undertook intensive investigations of urban life, using census data, interviews, and observation. They showed little interest in women or in sexuality per se; rather they used the sexual behavior of women in the furnished room districts to bolster their theories of "urban evolution." Sociologist Robert Park wrote, "Everywhere the old order is passing, but the new has not arrived. . . . This is particularly true of the so-called rooming-house area." In this view, the furnished room districts became the vanguard of urban change, characterized by "disorganization" and "individuation." As these terms suggest, some sociologists saw the furnished-room districts as disturbed, soulless, and lonely.

For the most part, though, the sociologists had a stronger faith in progress. As the vanguard of urban evolution, the furnished room districts were, in a sense, the most advanced development of urban life. With a marked ambivalence, the sociologists described the furnished room districts and their residents as "emancipated" as frequently as they called them "disorganized."

For the sociologists, the women of the furnished room districts represented the freedom of urban life. As in the movies, the sociologists found that the city released women from the "monotony of settled family life" in the small town. From a barren and restricted life, the woman moved to "a section of the old frontier transplanted to the heart of the modern city" where, competent and self-seeking, she could pursue her individual desires and ambitions. One particularly blunt sociology student stated, "The homeless woman of modern cities is the emancipated woman." In all of the areas where earlier reformers had discovered exploitation of unprotected women, sociologists now found willing participation. Of dating for money, Frances Donovan wrote, "She is not . . . exploited nor driven into it, but goes with her eyes wide open." Another sociologist asserted, more dubiously, that prostitutes were no longer exploited by procurers or pimps. And, as in the movies, some of the sociologists depicted the sexually "emancipated" woman as an exploiter of men. "In the quest after the material equipment of life . . . ," sociologist Paul Cressey wrote, "the girl becomes not only an individualist but also—frankly—an opportunist." In earlier reformers' portrayals, men exploited naive women; in the sociologists' discussions of the "urban pioneer," women lodgers, like the gold diggers in the movies, exploited naive men.

No less than the earlier image of the innocent victim, the new image of the urban pioneer reduced women in the furnished room districts to stereotypes. It exaggerated certain features of women lodgers' lives and neglected others. The sociologists used self-supporting women as examples of uniquely urban personalities, and, accordingly they emphasized those aspects of women's lives that supported their theories of urban evolution: individualism, unconventional sexual behavior, transient personal relationships, and freedom from social control. Their commitment to the idea of evolutionary progress encouraged them to accept these urban features as at least somewhat positive and liberating. At the same time, they downplayed the negative constraints of low wages, sexual harassment, and economic dependence that many women lodgers continued to face. With the new stereotype, the sociologists undermined reform efforts to alleviate female poverty.

The reformers and romance novelists drew on a stereotype of women as passive, passionless, and imperiled, while the sociologists, moviemakers, and pulp magazine writers tapped an older stereotype of women as active, pleasure-seeking, and potentially dangerous. The changing discourse marks the waning influence of moral reformers and the rise to cultural power of manufacturers of mass entertainment and academic social scientists. It also highlights a larger change in the portrayal of women in America, from the Victorian angel to the sexy starlet. In the late nineteenth century, women lodgers, alone in the city, epitomized the purity of endangered womanhood; in the early twentieth century, the same women were among the first "respectable" women broadcast as sexual objects.

The sexual behavior of women in turn-of-the-century furnished room districts is not an isolated episode in U.S. women's history. Other historians also describe sexual experimentation among women lodgers. From at least the 1830's to at least the 1960's, women who supported themselves in the cities sometimes explored the boundaries of sexual convention.

In turn of the century Chicago, the volume of migrants led entrepreneurs to invest in restaurants, furnished rooming houses, theaters, cabarets, and dance halls where lodgers could eat, sleep, and socialize. Woman and men flocked to and shaped these institutions, creating new peer-oriented subcultures in specific urban districts. In these districts, most women could not afford to view sex solely in terms of sexual danger or sensual pleasure, for sexual expression was also tied inextricably to various forms of economic support. In this context, the sexual revolution was, most likely, sometimes oppressive, sometimes exciting, and often an exchange.

The history of the woman lodgers in the furnished room districts is important, for these women helped chart the modern sexual terrain. In fact, they may have set patterns that other women later followed. In the furnished room districts themselves, middle- and upper class bohemian "new women" may have observed and learned from the unconventional behavior of the working-class women who were their neighbors. Middle-class pleasure seekers and "flappers" may have copied the blueprints of "sexy" behavior they observed while slumming in the cabarets and dance halls of the furnished room districts. And movie-goers and magazine readers may have learned from the portrayals of women lodgers, as the new movies and romance magazines used the sexuality of independent wage-earning women to attract and titillate viewers and readers.

Questions for Study and Review

1. What does this article suggest about the relative roles of working-class women and men and middle-class bohemians in the shaping of a new social and sexual order?

2. What does life in Chicago's furnished room districts suggest about the changing dynamics of the family?

3. Among Mexican, Jewish, African-American, and native-born working-class women, what were the relationships between the work they performed and their roles in shaping their families and communities?

4. What do you think the response of furnished room residents would have been to settlement house residents or nineteenth-century moral reformers?

Suggested Readings

Joanne Meyerowitz, *Women Adrift: Independent Wage Earners in Chicago, 1880–1930* (1988).

Kathy Peiss, *Cheap Amusements: Working Women and Leisure in Turn-of-the-Century New York* (1986).

Susan Porter Benson, *Counter Cultures: Saleswomen, Managers and Customers in American Department Stores, 1890–1940* (1986).

Ruth Rosen, *The Lost Sisterhood: Prostitution in America, 1900–1918* (1982).

Sumiko Higashi, *Virgins, Vamps and Flappers: The American Silent Movie Heroine* (1978).

Leila Rupp, "'Imagine My Surprise': Women's Relationships in Historical Perspective," *Frontiers* (Fall 1980.)

TEN

Two Washes in the Morning and a Bridge Party at Night: Consumer Culture and the American Housewife Between the Wars

Ruth Schwartz Cowan

If the new consumer culture helped to produce a revolution in sexual mores and to sweep single, working-class women out of the family and into furnished rooms, it also accelerated technological and cultural transformations in family life that intensified married, middle-class women's commitment to domesticity. Arguing that marriage and family were the "natural" desire of "normal" women, social scientists, magazine editors, and advertising executives combined to establish a new era of fulfillment through housework. With domestic service declining as an occupational choice among all groups of women, and with children packed off to school and husbands off to work, women were encouraged to believe that household chores were "an expression of the housewife's personality and of her affection for her family."

New appliances—electric irons, vacuum cleaners, and washing machines—and new commercial products—cake mixes, soap flakes, and cold cereals—provided the means by which housewives could indulge their creative talents and maintain new and higher standards of cleanliness, nutrition, and child care. Failure to achieve these standards, and to smile while doing so, was a failure to be truly feminine and a source of potential guilt. Advertisers preyed on the anxieties of housewives and measured the success of their campaigns by the increase in new items developed and sold.

Cowan analyzes the economic and demographic changes that underpinned the cultural and ideological transformations she so artfully describes. In an era when divorces were up, children left home earlier, and fewer families lived near relatives, heightening domestic ideals was one way of binding the familial fabric. Moreover, as more items were produced in factories and fewer in households, the reorientation of the housewife's work away from economic and toward emotional sustenance seemed essential if large numbers of women were to stay focused on family concerns. The impact of the consumer-oriented "feminine mystique" of the 1920s was diminished by the economic crisis of the 1930s. As a result, the activities and ideals described by Cowan reached only a small percentage of American women before World War II. Still, they set the course for a second postwar surge of domesticity and a return to the "feminine mystique" in the 1950s.

The "feminine mystique" has been part of American cultural life for quite a long while, far longer than Betty Friedan and others have believed; its origins go back to the period after the First World War, not the Second. Political tracts very often idealize the past, and *The Feminine Mystique* was no exception; the norms for American women between the wars were not nearly as bold and adventurous as Betty Friedan would like to think. The cult of true womanhood—that marvelous Victorian combination of Christian sentimentalism and sexual repression—had indeed died by the early 20's, but the ideology that replaced it was, to all intents and purposes, the same "feminine mystique" that Friedan attributes to the 40's and 50's. Whatever it was that trapped educated American women in their kitchens, babbling at babies and worrying about color combinations for the bathroom, the trap was laid during the roaring 20's, not the quiet 50's.

In the advertisements, the informative articles and the advice columns of the *The Ladies' Home Journal, McCall's, American Home* and other similar magazines, a careful reader can watch the feminine mystique descending upon the minds and hearts of American women during the two decades between the wars.

That mystique, like any system of cultural norms, was a complex and subtle affair, continuous with previous ideologies, yet clearly different from them. The mystique makers of the 20's and 30's believed that women were purely domestic creatures, that the goal of each normal woman's life was the acquisition of a husband, a family and a home, that women who worked outside their homes did so only under duress or because they were "odd" (for which read "ugly," "frustrated," "compulsive," or "single") and that this state of affairs was sanctioned by the tenets of religion, biology, psychology and patriotism. Hardly a surprising ideology to be found between the covers of women's magazines, past or present. The feminine mystique differed from previous value systems in its prescriptions about the detail— who might reside in that household, how many children that happy family might contain, what the relationship between husband and wife, mother and children, housewife and household ideally might be.

The ideal housewife of the 20's and 30's did not have servants, or to put it another way, the servants she had were electrical, not human. In *The Ladies' Home Journal* for January 1, 1918, "The Householder's Dream of a Happy New Year," had been a cartoon: "Mandy Offers to Stay for Life and Takes Less Wages." Throughout the monthly issues that year, in advertisement after advertisement, Mandy was repeatedly depicted: if you wanted to sell flannel baby's clothes to the readers of *The Ladies' Home Journal* you drew a baby held by a nursemaid; if you wanted to sell fabric, you drew a maid pinning up hems; shampoo—a maid washing her mistress's hair; talcum powder—"Nurse powders baby"; washing soap— a laundress hanging up clothes. All this in a year when, according to the editorial columns of the magazine, domestic help was scarce because of the wartime restrictions on immigration and the attractive salaries offered to women in industry. By the time a decade had passed Mandy had retreated from the advertisements; by 1928 she had almost entirely disappeared into the realms of fiction. In that year if you wanted to sell radiators to the readers of *The Ladies' Home Journal* you drew a housewife

Are You Sure
they're free from Goiter?

Many mothers make the mistake of believing that their children are free from goiter merely because they can detect no fullness of the neck.

Yet goiter can and often does exist even though there is no noticeable enlargement.

Thus mothers must be more than ever on their guard against this common cause of physical and mental backwardness. In many localities 2 out of every 3 children are victims of simple goiter.

The surest, safest and easiest way to protect children from goiter is to use Morton's Iodized Salt on the table and in cooking. It is a preventive which has been endorsed by health authorities everywhere.

Morton's Iodized Salt is not a medicine, but is merely our famous salt that pours with a trace of tasteless iodine added for goiter prevention. Get it from your grocer at once and use it for every salt purpose.

MORTON'S SALT

IODIZED OR PLAIN

When it rains it pours

Revolutions in household technology helped foster the consumer culture of the 1920s, and the housewife who ran her own home and cared for her children without the help of servants became the family's chief consumer. Housewives could find instructions about their duties and responsibilities in the advice columns, in the informative articles, and even in the advertisements featured in women's magazines.

playing on the floor with her children; if you wanted to promote supermarkets, women were shown doing their own shopping; cleansing powder—a housewife wiping her own sink; floor wax—an elegant lady polishing her own floor; hand cream—"They'll never know you mopped the floor yourself"; washing machines—" "Two washes in the morning and a bridge party at night."

Even before the Depression struck, at a time when prosperity was widespread, American advertisers idealized the woman who was going to buy their product as a housewife, well dressed, to be sure, neatly coiffed and elegantly manicured, but a housewife who cheerfully and resolutely did her housework herself. The only servant in a full-page ad depicting every aspect of housework, an ad for Ivory Soap which appeared in *The Ladies' Home Journal* in 1933, was a confinement nurse. Mandy had not disappeared entirely. She was still an important character in women's magazine fiction. *American Home* still published house plans that included a maid's room, and *Parent's Magazine* still worried about the ways in which servants influence children, but the days when a housewife of moderate means fully expected that she would have at least a maid of all work, and probably a laundress and nursemaid, were clearly over.

On the matter of servants the feminine mystique was a reversal of older attitudes. The servantless household had once been regarded as a trial and a tribulation; now it was regarded as a condition dearly to be wished. Adequate household help had always been a problem in America and women's magazines had repeatedly offered advice to housewives who were, for one unfortunate reason or another, coping with their homes singlehandedly. The emphasis in those articles was often on the word, "unfortunate"; the housewife was told, for example, that if help is scarce, it is easiest to serve children the same food the adults are eating, and at the same time—although clearly it would be better for their digestion and your temperament if they ate with a nursemaid in the nursery; hopefully the servant shortage would soon pass. Occasionally a lone voice (often male) would remind the housewife of her patriotic obligations (wouldn't it be more democratic to fire the servants and have the family pitch in and do the work?) or would appeal to the higher reaches of her intellect (think how much chemistry you could learn if you would only do the cooking yourself!) but the housewives apparently managed—somehow—to resist such blandishments. Housework was regarded as a chore, albeit a necessary one, and if it could be palmed off on someone else, so much the better. If one can gauge from the content and tone of advertisements, advice columns and letters to the editor, the American housewife clearly preferred to employ servants whenever economic and demographic conditions permitted her to do so.

This attitude began to change in the years after the First World War. Housework was no longer regarded as a chore, but as an expression of the housewife's personality and of her affection for her family. In past times the housewife had been judged by the way she organized her servants; now she would be judged by the way she organized her kitchen. If she were strong and proud of herself her work room would be filled with labor-saving devices, meticulously cleaned and color coordinated; if she were insecure, frustrated and lonely, woe to her kitchen—it would be disorderly, dim and uninviting. When the kitchen had been dominated by servants it had been a dreary room, often in the basement of the house. Now that the kitchen had become the housewife's domain it had to be prettied up.

> Time was when kitchens were big and dark, for keeping house was a gloomy business. . . . But now! Gay colors are the order of the day. Red pots and pans! Blue gas stoves! . . . It is a rainbow, in which the cook sings at her work and never thinks of household tasks as drudgery.

Laundering had once been just laundering; now it was an expression of love. The new bride could speak her affection by washing tell-tale gray out of her husband's shirts. Feeding the family had once been just feeding the family; now it was a way to communicate deep seated emotions.

> When the careful housekeeper turns from preparation of company dinner to the routine family meals, she will know that prime rib roast, like peach ice cream, *is a wonderful stimulant to family loyalty,* but that it is not absolutely necessary for every day.

Diapering was no longer just diapering, but a time to build the baby's sense of security; cleaning the bathroom sink was not just cleaning, but an exercise for the maternal instincts, protecting the family from disease.

Clearly, tasks of this emotional magnitude could not be relegated to servants. The servantless household may have been an economic necessity in the 20's, as the supply of servants declined and their wages rose, but for the first time that necessity was widely regarded as a potential virtue. The servantless housewife was no longer portrayed as "unfortunate"; she was happy, revelling in her modern home and in the opportunities for creative expression that it provided.

The fact is that the American home was never a more satisfying place than it is today. Science and invention have outfitted it with a great range of conveniences and comforts. . . . All this is, in the main, women's work. For the first time in the world's history it is possible for a nation's women in general to have or to be able to look forward to having homes and the means of furnishing them in keeping with their instinctive longings. The women of America are to be congratulated, not only in the opportunity but because of the manner in which they are responding to it. When the record is finally written this may stand as their greatest contribution.

And what opportunities there were! In earlier years American women had been urged to treat housework as a science; now they were being urged to treat it as a craft, a creative endeavor. The ideal kitchen of the prewar period had been white and metallic—imitating the laboratory. The ideal kitchen of the postwar period was color coordinated—imitating the artist's studio. Each meal prepared in that ideal kitchen was a color composition in and of itself: "Make Meals More Appetizing by Serving Foods that Have Pleasing Contrast of Color." Ready made clothes could be disguised by adding individual hand sewn touches; patterned towels could be chosen to match the decorative scheme in the bathroom; old furniture could be repainted and restyled. The new housewife would be an artist, not a drudge.

The new housewife would also be a consumer, not a producer.

A woman's virtue and excellence as a housewife do not in these days depend upon her skill in spinning and weaving. An entirely different task presents itself, more difficult and more complex, requiring an infinitely wider range of ability, and for these very reasons more interesting and inspiring.

That task was, of course, buying. The words come from an article about shopping for linens, but they could have been taken from any one of the numerous articles on wise buying—clothes, sheets, rugs, blankets, silverware, appliances—that began to appear regularly in women's magazines through the 20's. In earlier days the young housewife had to be taught to make things well; in the 20's she had to be taught to buy things well. Magazines and manufacturers created new devices to teach her how to be a "professional" buyer: product testing services, gadget buying services, home shopping guides, home demonstrators, new packages, new grading systems. Apparently the devices worked; scores of sociologists and economists have noted that consumption is now the most important social function still performed by families. Unlike so many familial functions, consumption has been expanding, not contracting; the 20's appear to be the decade in which the expansion began.

In her physical appearance the new housewife looked quite different from her older counterparts. In earlier days the ideal American matron had been plump; corset makers were happy to send her garments that would add inches to her *derrière* if she were unfashionably skinny. After World War I the corset makers changed their tune; the emphasis was on reducing, not increasing. By the end of the 20's advertising campaigns were predicated on the American woman's passion for slenderizing: Sunkist oranges are nutritious, and non-fattening; Fleischman's yeast will aid your digestion and prevent constipation if you are dieting; Postum should be substituted for coffee while dieting because it calms the nerves. By the end of the 20's articles about exercising to keep fit had become a regular feature in *The Ladies' Home Journal;* before the war they had been unknown.

She was thin, this ideal lady, and she was also elegant; her hands were long and well manicured, so were her legs. If she worked hard at her housework during the hot weather, she remained "personally irreproachable"— thanks to cream deodorants. She wore a fashionable wool suit with a fur collar to visit her local A & P and applied Pompeian Night Cream to keep from looking tired after an exhausting night of bridge. If life was creating problems for her she knew that one or two dabs of Raquel Orange Blossom Fragrance would guarantee eternal bliss. This particular form of hidden persuasion, the notion that cosmetics can guarantee happiness, seems to have been invented in the 20's. The cosmetics industry must have entered a boom phase after World War I—if the number and size of its advertisements are any gauge of its economic well-being.

Child rearing was the single most important task that this new housewife had to perform. Experts agree that a child raised by nursemaids was a child to be pitied. The young boy tended by servants would never learn the upright, go-getting resourcefulness of the truly American child, would never become a useful member of the egalitarian republic, and would—horror of horrors—probably fail in the business world. His sister, deprived of the example of her mother, would not know how to manage the myriad appliances of the modern kitchen; she would never learn how to decorate a pineapple salad, or how to wash silk underwear in an electric machine, and consequently—horror of horrors— she would never attract and keep a truly American husband. Even more worrisome was the thought that children raised by nursemaids might never reach adulthood because they would not be tended by persons who were familiar with the latest medical and nutritional information. American mothers, anxious about infant mor-

tality, were advised not to leave their offspring in the care of illiterate, untutored servant girls. In 1918, the editor of *The Ladies' Home Journal* rejoiced in the knowledge that, if present trends continued, the postwar generation of American children would be the first generation to be raised by its mothers; they would be healthy in mind and body and, as a result, they would lift the sagging fortunes of the race. There was very little Freudianism in this new child psychology; mothers were to take over the rearing of their children, not because of the psychological traumas of separation, but because mothers were likely to be better informed and better educated than nursemaids.

Spending time with her children seems to have been as much a moral imperative for the housewife of the 20's as spending time on Christian good works was for her mother. There were no more socks to be knitted for missionaries, or elderly sick relatives to be visited, or Bible classes to attend; instead there were basketball games to watch with her children, card games to play with them, and piano lessons to help them with. Togetherness had become a fact for middle-class Americans long before the editors of *McCall's* coined the term in 1954.

I accommodate my entire life to my little girl. She takes three music lessons a week and I practice with her forty minutes a day. I help her with her school work and go to dancing school with her . . .

There are now never ten days that go by without my either visiting the children's school or getting in touch with their teacher. I have given up church work and club work since the children came. I always like to be here when they come home from school so that I can keep in touch with their games and their friends . . .

I certainly have a harder job than my mother did; everything tends to weaken the parents' influence. But we do it by spending time with our children. I've always been a pal with my daughter, and my husband spends a lot of time with the boy. We all go to basketball games together and to the State Fair in the summer . . .

We used to belong to the Country Club but resigned from that when the children came, and bought a car instead. That is something we can all enjoy together.

The advent of the Depression apparently accelerated this trend. Magazine editors noted that families were being forced to rely upon their own devices for entertainment; the end of prosperity meant the end of meals in restaurants and parties in hotels. *American Home* published essays on turning basements into playrooms; *The Ladies' Home Journal* discovered the barbecue; *Parents' Magazine* began denoting with an asterisk the articles that would be of interest to progressive fathers (i.e. those who wished to take a hand in rearing their own children).

Life was not always a bed of roses in the model American household, but if the lady of the house had any complaints, she refrained, whenever possible, from discussing them with her husband. "She must never bring her troubles to the table"; dinner time was a moment of sweetness and light in her husband's weary day; he came home from the office to be greeted with a cheering cup of Steero bouillon; his children were scrubbed ("Self respect thrives on soap and water") and anxious to tell him about their day in school (they have done well because they did not forget to have hot cereal for breakfast). Woe unto the housewife who would mar this scene by reminding her husband that he had failed to clean his hair out of the sink that morning—or other domestic trivia. She was almost always cheerful, this modern housewife; in fact, the constellation of emotions that she was allowed to display in magazines was really rather limited. She could be

happy, loving, tender or affectionate; occasionally she was worried, but she was never, never angry. What, after all, did she have to be angry about?

Only one anxious emotion ever creased her brow—guilt, she felt guilty a good deal of the time, and when she wasn't feeling guilty she was feeling embarrassed: guilty if her infant didn't gain enough weight, embarrassed if her friends arrived to find that her sink was clogged, guilty if her children went to school in soiled clothes, guilty if she didn't eradicate all the germs behind the bathroom sink, embarrassed if her nieces and nephews accused her of having body odor, guilty if her son lagged in school, guilty if her daughter was not popular with the crowd (her mother having failed to keep her dress properly ironed). In earlier times a woman could have been made to feel guilty if she had abandoned her children or been too free with her affections. In the years between the wars American women apparently began to feel guilty if their children were seen in public in scuffed shoes. Between the two sources of anxiety there seems a world of difference. Advertisers may have stimulated these guilt feelings, but they could not have created them singlehandedly; the guilt must have been there or advertisers would not have found that they could be successful by playing upon it.

In 1937 Emily Post coined a name for the new American housewife: Mrs. Three-in-One, the lady who is cook, waitress and hostess at her own dinner parties. She was fairly well educated and somewhat sophisticated. Her family was smaller than her mother's but more attention was lavished upon it. Her infants were weighed every day and their nutritional intake carefully planned. The development of her youngsters was carefully watched and social affairs of her adolescents carefully—but discreetly—supervised. She drove a car, played bridge and took vacations. She had very few servants, or none at all. In the morning she served her family a light breakfast; lunch was a can of soup for herself. She shopped by telephone, or in a small supermarket, bought most of her clothes ready-made, wore silk stockings, and tied her hair in a neat scarf when doing housework. She could nurse a child through measles, repair a dripping faucet, decorate a kitchen, discourse on vitamins, give a speech before her ladies' club or entertain her husband's business associates—all with equal facility. She was always cheerful, healthy, up-to-date, and gracious, never angry, frustrated, sick, old-fashioned or—perish the thought—gainfully employed. She was content with her life and had no doubts about her femininity; if she wished for anything it was another appliance or a better rug for the living room. She had the vote, but rarely discussed politics; believed in divorce, but was not herself divorced; practiced birth control but did not discuss sex with her daughter.

Social ideologies are responsive to change in economic and demographic conditions. The advent of the feminine mystique was a major ideological change and there must have been social and economic changes that produced it. One crucial aspect of the new ideology was its emphasis on the servantless household; changes in the supply of domestic servants are likely, therefore to have been an important precondition.

Household labor was generally performed by five different types of workers in the early years of the 20th century: the housewife herself, her children (primarily her daughters), other female relatives (a maiden aunt perhaps, or a grandmother), dayworkers, and servants who lived-in. Data on changes in the number of any of those types of labor are rather hard to come by, or are likely to be quite unreliable when we have them. Domestic servants are one of the most difficult categories of workers to enumerate as their labor is often transient, or part-time, or unreported. In the early decades of this century social commentators believed that in every category (except the housewife herself) the

supply of labor was declining, and the data that are available tend to support this conclusion. Certainly wages paid for household employees were rising. [The Lynds] estimate that in 1890 a live-in cook received about $4.00 a week in wages (this does not count the expense of the room and board); in 1920 this would have increased to $25. The Lynds estimate that in 1924 a single day's work for a day laborer cost the Muncie housewife approximately what a week's labor would have cost her mother. Similarly the Lynds found that the business class housewives in Muncie had roughly half the number of household servants that their mothers had had; according to the Federal Census for Indiana, the number of families per servant increased from 13.5 in 1890 to 30.5 in 1920. Using nationwide statistics as a guide, it appears that most of this increase occurred in the decade from 1910 to 1920; the number of families per servant was roughly 10 in 1900, 10 in 1910 and 16 in 1920. These data do not, of course, tell us anything specific about the *supply* of labor, but they are suggestive; if wages were rising and the proportion of workers to households falling, contemporary social critics may have been right in their assumption that the supply of household servants was declining because of the twin pressures generated by fewer immigrants and more attractive industrial wages. Data on the other two categories of household help, children and female relatives, are, to all intents and purposes, nonexistent, but here again the remarks of social critics may be suggestive. Many observers noted tendencies toward less available labor from those sources as well: grandparents were not as frequently moving in with their married children (in part because houses were smaller); grown daughters seemed inclined to have apartments and jobs of their own before marriage; maiden aunts, like their unmarried nieces, were apparently living alone and liking it more.

The odd thing about these social commentaries is that they are recurrent American themes.

Household help has always been a sore point in American life; servants were constantly disappearing from the labor market or otherwise behaving recalcitrantly, and the daughters of middle classes, if they weren't actually out working at Macy's, were often balking at household labor. Yet none of the other periods in which this scarcity of household labor was proclaimed produced an ideology like the feminine mystique, an ideology which put a premium on the servantless household. Consequently we must assume that the declining supply of servants (paid or unpaid) although it must have been part of the preconditions leading to that ideology, was by no means the whole story.

The story becomes more complete if we look at what was happening to domestic technology during those years. For the first time in the history of the republic there was, after 1918, a viable alternative to the labor of housewives, domestic servants, maiden aunts and adolescent daughters—the machine. It was a classic American solution: when in doubt try a machine. For several years before the war, home economists had been pressing for the rationalization of household labor. After the war, as electrification and assembly-line production of consumer goods increased, that rationalization seemed to be at hand.

Almost every aspect of household labor was revolutionized during the 20's; in good part this was due to electrification. In 1907 (the first year for which data are available) only 8% of dwellings in the U.S. had electric service; by the time we entered the war this had risen to 24.3% and by 1925 more than half the homes in America (53.2%) had been wired. If we consider the data for urban and rural non-farm dwellings the figures are even more striking: almost half of those homes had been electrified by 1920 (47.4%) and more than two-thirds by 1925 (69.4%). During this period the price of electricity fell from 9.5 cents per kilowatt hour to 7.68 cents (for an average monthly use of 25 kilowatt hours, which is the order of magnitude then used in homes). The amount of money spent on mechanical appliances grew from $145 millions in 1909 to $667 millions in 1927, an increase of almost 500%, while at the same time expenditure on clothing increased only 250% and on furniture, 300%; similarly the dollar value (in current prices) of electric household appliances produced for domestic consumption soared from $11.8 millions in 1909 to 146.3 millions in 1927.

With the spread of electrification came the spread of electrical appliances: a small motor to power the family sewing machine, a fan, an electric iron (the earliest models had no thermostats, but they were still easier to use than the irons heated on cooking stoves), a percolator, perhaps a toaster, a waffle iron or a portable heater. Automatic refrigerators went on the market in 1916 (at roughly $900); in 1921, 5,000 units were sold, but by 1929 that figure had risen to 890,000 units and the price had fallen to roughly $180. A study of 100 Ford employees living in Detroit in 1929 revealed that 98 families had an electric iron, 80 had electric sewing machines, 49 had electric washing machines, and 21 had electric vacuum cleaners. The benefits of technology were clearly not limited to the upper middle classes.

As household habits were being changed by the advent of electricity so eating habits were being changed by the advent of the metal can, the refrigerated railroad car and new notions about diet. Before World War I an average American family ate three extraordinarily hefty meals a day.

Steak, roasts, macaroni, Irish potatoes, sweet potatoes, turnips, cole slaw, fried apples, and stewed tomatoes, with Indian pudding, rice, cake or pie for dessert. This was the winter repertoire of the average family that was not wealthy, and we swapped about from one combination to another, using pickles and chow-chow to make the familiar starchy food relishing. . . . Breakfast, pork chops or steak with fried potatoes, buckwheat cakes, and hot bread; lunch a hot roast and potatoes; supper same roast cold.

In 1908 an article appeared in *The Ladies' Home Journal* describing an ordinary family lunch; were that meal to be served today it would be regarded as a state banquet. By the middle of the 20's such meals were no longer the rule: breakfast had been reduced to eggs and/or cereal; lunch was essentially one course, or perhaps soup and a sandwich; dinner was usually no more than three. Commercially canned fruits and vegetables made variations in the classic winter menu possible. Some canned goods (primarily peas and corn) had been on the market since the middle of the 19th century, but by 1918 the American housewife with sufficient means could have purchased almost any fruit or vegetable, and quite a surprising array of ready-made meals, in a can: Campbell's soups Heinz's spaghetti (already cooked and ready to serve), Libby's corned beef and chili con carne (heated directly in its package), Stokeley's peas, corn, string beans, lima beans, tomatoes, succotash, LaChoy's bean sprouts, Beechnut's chili sauce, vinegar, and mustard, Purity Cross's creamed chicken, welsh rarebit, lobster à la newburg, Van Camp's pork and beans, Libby's olives, sauerkraut and Vienna sausages, DelMonte's peaches, pineapples, apricots and plums. In the morning the American Housewife of the 20's could have offered her family some of the new cold cereals (Kellogg's Corn Flakes, or Krumbles, or Post's Grape Nuts Flakes); if her family wanted pancakes she could have prepared them with Aunt Jemima's pancake mix. Recipes in the women's magazines in the 20's utilized canned goods as a matter of course: canned peaches in peach blancmange, canned peas in creamed finnan haddie. Very often the recipes did not even include the familiar rubric, "canned or fresh," but simply assumed that "canned" would be used. By the middle of the

20's home canning was on its way to becoming a lost art; the business-class wives of Muncie reported that they rarely put up anything, except an occasional jelly or a batch of tomatoes, whereas their mothers had once spent the better part of the summer and fall canning. Increased utilization of refrigerated railroad cars also meant that fresh fruits and vegetables were appearing in markets at reasonable prices all through the year. Fewer family meals were being taken at home; restaurants and businessmen's clubs downtown, cafeterias in schools and factories, after-school activities for teenagers—all meant that fewer members of the family were home for meals. Cooking was easier, and there was less of it to be done.

Part of the reason that cooking became easier was that the coal or wood-burning stove began to disappear. After World War I the women's magazines only carried advertisements for stoves that used natural gas, kerosene, gasoline or electricity; in Muncie in 1924 two out of three homes cooked with gas. The burdensome chore of keeping a coal stove lit and regulated—and keeping the kitchen free of the resultant soot—had probably been eliminated from most American homes by the 30's. The change in routine that was predicated on the change from coal stoves to oil or gas stoves (electric stoves were inefficient and rarely used in this period) was profound; aside from the elimination of such chores as loading the coal and removing the ashes, the new stoves were simply much easier to regulate. One writer in *The Ladies' Home Journal* estimated that kitchen cleaning was reduced by one-half when coal stoves were eliminated. As the coal stove disappeared from the kitchen, the coal-fired furnace also started disappearing from the basement. By the late 20's coal furnaces were no longer being advertised in home equipment magazines and home owners were being urged to convert to oil or gas or electricity, "so that no one has to go in to the basement anymore." A good number of American homes were centrally heated by the mid-20's; in Zanesville, Ohio, 48% of the roughly 11,000 homes had basement furnaces in 1924.

As the routines of meal preparation became less burdensome in the 20's so did the routines of personal hygiene. The early 20's was the time of the bathroom mania; more and more bathrooms were installed in older homes and new homes were being built with them as a matter of course. Sixty-one per cent of those 11,000 homes in Zanesville had indoor plumbing and bathrooms in 1924. In Muncie in 1890 ninety-five out of every hundred families took baths by lugging a zinc tub into the kitchen and filling it with water that had been pumped by hand and heated on the stove; by 1924 three out of four Muncie homes had running water. The rapid increase in the number of bathrooms after World War I was the result of changes in the production of bathroom fixtures. Before the war those fixtures were not standardized and porcelain tubs were routinely made by hand; after the war industrialization swept over the bathroom industry: cast-iron enamelware went into mass production and fittings were standardized. In 1921 the dollar value of the production of enamelled sanitary fixtures was $2.4 million, the same that it had been in 1915. By 1923 just two years later, that figure had doubled to $4.8 million; it rose again, to $5.1 million, in 1925. The first one-piece, recessed, double-shell cast iron enamelled bathtub was put on the market in the early 20's; by the time a decade had passed the standard American bathroom had achieved its standard American form: a small room, with a recessed tub, tiled floors and walls, brass plumbing, a single-unit toilet, and an enclosed sink. This bathroom was relatively easy to clean, and—needless to say—it helped revolutionize habits of personal cleanliness in America; the body-odor fetish of the 30's can be partly attributed to the bathroom fetish of the 20's.

Similarly, the "tell-tale gray" syndrome of the 30's had its roots in the changing technologies of clothes washing. Soap powders and flakes arrived on the market in the early 20's, which meant that bars of soap no longer had to be scraped and boiled to make soap paste. Electric washing machines took a good part of the drudgery out of the washing process, although they required a considerable amount of time and attention to operate, as they did not go through their cycles automatically and did not spin dry. There was more variation in methods of handling household laundry than in any other domestic chore; the Lynds noted that on the same street in Muncie, families of the same economic class were using quite different washing technologies: hand washing, electric machines, commercial laundries, laundresses who worked "in," and laundresses who worked "out." Advertisements in the women's magazines do not give a uniform picture either: sometimes showing old-fashioned tubs, sometimes depicting machines. Commercial household laundries entered a boom period in the 20's; they began to expand their services (wet wash, rough dry, etc.) and began to do more personal laundry (as opposed to flat work) than they had in past years; nationwide, the number of power laundries doing more than $5,000 business a year rose from 4,881 in 1919 to 6,776 in 1929, and their receipts more than doubled.

While the processes of cooking, heating, cleaning, lighting and washing were revolutionized, other processes—just as much a part of the housewife's daily routine—were changing, but not quite as drastically. The corner grocer, the door-to-door merchant and the curbside market were slowly being replaced by the telephone and the supermarket. In 1918 *The Ladies' Home Journal* referred to supermarkets as "The New Stores Without Clerks"; by 1928 there were 2,600 Piggly Wiggly markets across the country. Telephone shopping had become routine in many households by the end of the 20's. Instead of purchasing whole cases of canned goods or bushels of apples and onions to be stored and used over the months, housewives were now telephoning daily orders and having them hand-delivered. 1 head of lettuce, 1 pat of cream cheese, 1 can of string beans, 1/4 pound of mushrooms. Hardwood floors were replaced by linoleum; instead of tedious hand polishing, only a mop, soap and water was now required. Heavy cast iron pots and pans were giving way to aluminum and Pyrex. Ready-made clothes were no longer thought "poorfolksy"; by 1928 a good part of each monthly issue of the better women's magazines was devoted to photographs and drawings of clothing that could be bought off the rack. Home sewing, home mending, the once ubiquitous practice of making over dresses—all became vestigial crafts; young women were now being taught how to shop for clothes, not how to make them. Home baking also disappeared; the bakers in Muncie estimated that, depending upon the season, they supplied between 55% and 70% of the city's homes with bread.

Many factors must have contributed to the revolution in household production that occurred during the 20's. On the whole those were prosperous years and prosperity made it possible for many people to buy new equipment for their homes. Vast industrial facilities which were created during the war were converted to the production of consumer goods during peacetime. The apparent shortage of servants and the rise in their wages must have encouraged households to try the new appliances more readily than they would otherwise have done. The growth of magazines devoted to the interest of modern housewives no doubt encouraged the trend as did the growth of consumer credit arrangements. Whatever the causes were, the event itself seems indisputable; profound changes in household technology occurred between the end of the First World War and the beginning of the Depression— whether we measure those changes by the number of individual innovations or by the rate of their diffusion. Certain changes did occur after the Second World War: the standard American kitchen achieved its present form,

with standardized fixtures and continuous counter space; the automatic washing machine (which could spin and go through its cycles itself) became widespread; the laundromat replaced the commercial laundry; the supermarket replaced the grocery store; frozen foods to some extent replaced canned foods; the dishwasher and the home dryer became more reasonable in price; the ranch home with its open room plan became more popular. However, all those changes pale to insignificance when compared to the change from oil lamps to electric lamps, coal stoves to gas stoves, coal furnaces to gas and oil furnaces, kitchen heating to central heating, outdoor plumbing to indoor plumbing, not having a bathroom to having one, canning tomatoes to buying canned tomatoes, making dresses to buying them, baking bread to buying it, living with servants and living without them.

Thus, a fundamental productive process was revolutionized by the introduction of new technologies; almost simultaneously an ideology developed which insured that those new technologies would be used in very specific and rather limited ways. In early days the new technology could have been used to communalize housework. The first vacuum cleaners were large mobile units; they were brought into a home by a team of skilled operators to take over the housewife's cleaning chores. The new washing machines could have been placed in communal laundries where paid employees would take over the housewife's washing chores, and the editors of *The Ladies' Home Journal* advocated that this be done. Those same editors also advocated retention of the wartime communal kitchens, so that the wasteful process of cooking each family's meals separately would be eliminated. Many of the early luxury apartment houses had, along with elevators, communal nurseries on their roofs. Within a very few years, needless to say, those visions of communal housekeeping had died a not very surprising death; this was America, after all, not

Soviet Russia. The new domestic technology, communalized or not, could have freed American women to do productive work outside their homes; the growth of the feminine mystique insured that they would not do it.

The advertising industry cooperated in this endeavor, even if it did not invent it. As the size and number of women's magazines increased in the 20's, the amount and the variety of advertising increased also. The American woman was becoming the American consumer *par excellence;* automobile manufacturers, cigarette producers, life insurance companies (not to speak of the advertisers whose wares were of traditional interest to women) all discovered the virtues of the women's magazines. The magazines, of course, found ways to encourage this custom. They used their non-advertising space to advertise in subtler ways: listing new products by their brand names, adopting editorial policies that encouraged women to buy, creating "shop at home" columns for mail order purchases, sponsoring consumption oriented contests.

> Home building, home decoration and furnishing, *home making,* in fact, is the most outstanding phase of modern civilization. . . . The magazines of today have played an important part in this; they have carried on an intensive sincere campaign for better homes. But an even greater part has been that of the manufacturers. . . . Not only has beauty and convenience and efficiency of home equipment been carefully studied to meet the demand of the modern housewife . . . but back of all this stands the guarantee of the maker of his goods.

Late in the 20's those earnest manufacturers (and their sincere advertising agents) discovered that they could sell more gadgets by appealing to the housewife's fears than by appealing to her strengths; advertisements stopped being informative and started pandering to status-seeking and guilt. An advertisement for soap in 1908 was likely to talk about the clean factory in which the soap was produced and the pure ingredients from which it was made; a similar advertisement in 1928 was likely to talk about psychological trauma experienced by children who go to school with soiled clothes. It would be difficult to prove that manufacturers and advertising agencies invented the feminine mystique, but it would be equally difficult to deny that they did everything they reasonably could to encourage it.

In a quite different way the proponents of the child health movement also helped to encourage the mystique. The infant mortality rate in the United States in 1915 was 100 for every 1,000 live births, one of the highest in the world. There were very few families who were not touched, in some way, by the specter of infant death. After the war, with its discouraging reports about the health of young recruits, various public agencies began a concerted effort to improve the health and the physique of American's young people, particularly by disseminating information about proper nutrition and proper care of children during illness. The women's magazines were prime agents in dissemination of this information; *The Ladies' Home Journal,* for example, started a Babies Registry so that mothers of registered babies could receive monthly instructional booklets. Professional organizations, such as the Child Study Association (which organized child study groups in cities across the country and began publishing *Parents' Magazine* in 1926), and the federal government were also active in the campaign to improve the health of the young. By the end of the 20's advice to parents on the physical care of their children could be had at every turn: in magazine articles, in thousands of new books, in advertisements, in government pamphlets. The health of children became an overriding, perhaps even a compulsive concern for parents; they were urged to buy GE Mazda Sunlamps to provide Vitamin D for their children, to learn which foods would be most helpful in preventing anemia, to keep Vicks VapoRub on hand in case congestion should develop, to wear masks when they entered a sick child's room, to cleanse their bathrooms with BonAmi because the other (scratchier) cleansers would leave places for germs to breed, to guard against "pink toothbrush," to watch for the signs of eczema, to use Castoria for constipation, Listerine for sore throats, and VapoCresoline for whooping cough.

This new concern for the health of children was no doubt necessary, and some of it no doubt worked; the infant mortality rate fell to 65 per 1,000 live births by 1930, before the age of the miracle antibiotics—but the burden that it placed upon the new American housewife was immense. Children had to be kept in bed for weeks at a time; bedpans had to be provided and warmed, "since even the slightest chilling is to be avoided carefully"; in some diseases excrement had to be disinfected before being discarded; food had to be specially prepared; leftovers had to be burned after the sick child's meal; utensils had to be boiled, alcohol baths administered, hands scrupulously washed, mouths carefully masked—and through all this the nursing mother was expected to "get plenty of rest and outdoor recreation," and remain unrelentingly cheerful, "for cheerfulness is needed in a sickroom and the attitude of a mother nursing an ailing child largely influences the speed of recovery." Needless to say, mothers had to remain at home in order for all this nursing to be done; the death of a child whose mother had gone out to work was a recurrent theme in women's magazine fiction. In this sense, the child health movement was paradoxical; many women made careers out of convincing other women to stay at home and tend their children.

The feminine mystique, the social ideology which was formed during the 20's and solidified during the 30's, was quite a functional solution to real economic and demographic conditions. Servants were scarcer and their wages higher. Electricity could save burdensome labor and washday was unquestionably easier to face when the washing was done by machine than when it was done by hand. Infants' lives could be saved if care were taken to sterilize their bottles and balance their diets. In fact the feminine mystique worked; it kept women at home to do jobs that, in one way or another, American society needed to have done.

Questions for Study and Review

1. What was the relation of the new consumer culture to the opposing images of women—flappers versus homemakers?

2. How did technological developments related to housework differ from those related to industry in their effects on women?

3. If technological improvements coincided with increased standards of cleanliness and nutrition, then to what extent were domestic appliances truly labor-saving devices?

4. How did the family and community roles of the technologically sophisticated housewife of the 1920s differ from that of the Jewish immigrant housewife of the early 1900s or the midwestern farm wife of the mid-nineteenth century?

Suggested Readings

Ruth Schwartz Cowan, *More Work for Mother: The Ironies of Household Technology from the Open Hearth to the Microwave* (1983).

Susan Strasser, *Never Done: A History of American Housework* (1982).

Stuart Ewen, *Captains of Consciousness: Advertising and the Social Roots of the Consumer Culture* (1976).

Dorothy Hayden, *The Grand Domestic Revolution: A History of Feminist Designs for American Homes, Neighborhoods and Cities* (1981).

Joann Vanek, "Time Spent in Housework," *Scientific American* (November 1974).

Faye Dudden, "Experts and Servants: The National Council of Household Employment and the Decline of Domestic Service in the Twentieth Century," *Journal of Social History* (Winter 1986).

PART FIVE

The Great Depression and World War II

Women were among the foremost chroniclers of the Great Depression. Hired by the Works Progress Administration (WPA) and other government agencies to collect folktales, compile city guides, index local archives, and interview and photograph ordinary women and men, they documented the meaning of economic crisis for families and communities across the country. Dorothea Lange's *Migrant Mother* may be the most widely recognized of these Depression portraits, but it is only one of thousands that captured the pain and fortitude of common folk with many burdens and few resources.

Those whose lives were chronicled—whatever their region, race, ethnicity, or sex—shared some common problems. Unemployment, crowded quarters, family stress, personal anxiety, and limited options were the daily concerns of millions of Americans throughout the 1930s. Women who were bombarded during the 1920s with messages extolling the virtues of sexual attractiveness and a happy home faced the Depression from a slightly different stance than men, who perceived their role as that of family provider and household head. These differences were intensified by the alternatives offered each sex for coping with the collapse of their family's financial security.

As more individuals lost their jobs and fewer found new jobs, employers, politicians, and private citizens suggested a range of causes and offered a variety of cures for the crisis. One common theme was that women should not work if men lacked jobs. As Earl Leiby of Akron, Ohio, wrote to Franklin Roosevelt in 1933:

> You and we all know that the place for a wife and mother is at home, her palace. The excuse is often brought up that the husband cannot find employment. It is the writers' [sic] belief that if the women were expelled from places of business, . . . these very men would find employment.

Though most Americans seemed to accept the necessity of women working if they were the sole support of a family, legislators followed Leiby's logic in

During the Depression, popular sentiment still held that woman's proper place was in the home. Unfortunately, for many "home" might be a ramshackle hut, a cardboard box, or a canvas lean-to. Dorothea Lange's *Migrant Mother* captures the grim reality of family life for migrant workers during the Great Depression.

forbidding married women to work in certain occupations, such as teaching, or in government jobs where husbands were already employed.

Whatever the popular sentiment, however, women did work during the Depression, and in large numbers. At the level of national leadership, more women than ever held high government posts. Many, like Secretary of Labor Frances Perkins, traced their political roots to the Progressive Era. Nearly all found in Eleanor Roosevelt a model and an advocate for women's expanded political influence. At the local level, women's work was less glamorous but just as important. Ironically, as a result of the sex-typing of jobs, "total female labor force participation rose in the period from 1930 to 1940 more than in any previous decade in the twentieth century." Not only did the number of jobs in such female-dominated occupations as nursing, domestic service, and typing decline less than jobs in those areas typically reserved for males, but most men refused to take "women's work" even if no other employment was available.

The effects of these employment patterns on everyday life were often both dramatic and traumatic. Families in which men lost their breadwinning role to women suffered considerable economic and emotional stress. Women generally continued to perform the bulk of domestic work, perhaps to ease men's fear of a complete role reversal. With more children living at home, keeping up with housework and maintaining family harmony placed unusually heavy burdens on adult females. Families adjusted to these difficulties in different ways. In some cases, children and husbands took on added household chores, men accepted their new roles, and family members actually formed tighter bonds in response to crisis. In other cases, conflict, violence, and abandonment resulted from family tensions too deep to resolve.

The patterns of women's work varied as always by region, race, ethnicity, and age. Most notably, black women as well as younger and older women regardless of race were pushed out of the work force as native-born white women aged twenty to twenty-five sought jobs they once considered undesirable. African-American women, who had long contributed to family well-being through paid employment, found themselves forced out of work alongside male kin. In addition, black and other minority families were discriminated against in the distribution of public assistance meant to alleviate their hardships. Some of these women joined the intensified union struggles of the period, participated in unemployment councils, or joined popular political movements that offered wide-ranging solutions to the crisis. Others appealed for help on an individual basis, many directly to Franklin and Eleanor Roosevelt, whom they viewed as especially sympathetic to their plight. Pinkie Pelcher of Greenwood, Mississippi, pursued this latter path:

> "We are wondering," she wrote, "what is going to become of this large number of widow women with and without children. These white women at the head of the PWA [WPA] is still [telling us] colored women when we go to the office to be certified for work to go hunt washings. . . . The white people dont pay anything for their washing. [We] cant do enough washing to feed [our] family."

Entering the labor force, doing double duty at work and home, carrying both economic and emotional responsibilities for the family, joining unions and other protest movements, and appealing for a fair share of public assistance, women pursued a variety of strategies to combat poverty. Julia Kirk Blackwelder examines these strategies and women's part in them among Anglos, blacks, and Hispanics in San Antonio, Texas. She chronicles both the common roles played by women as women in crisis-ridden families and the distinct opportunities and barriers confronting them as members of different class, racial, and ethnic communities.

In San Antonio, as elsewhere, preparation for war ended the Depression. Beginning in the late 1930s, employment opportunities increased, this time more quickly for men than for women as heavy industry received the first infusion of federal money. Though World War II eventually brought minority, married, and older women into the work force, and into industry, the process began slowly. Only the attack on Pearl Harbor, the mass mobilization of men that followed, the promise of government subsidies to industries hiring women, and a nationwide recruitment campaign finally brought the symbol of "Rosie the Riveter" to life.

From 1942 to the end of the war, millions of women entered the work force. Most had worked before or would have sought paid work in the period with or without a military crisis. Only a small percentage, moreover, lived out the Rosie the Riveter image of "making history working for victory" by "working overtime on the riveting machine." Far more women were employed in traditional female jobs that also expanded during the war, such as food preparation, laundry, sewing, and nursing. And whatever the type of work performed, sex-segregation and sex-stereotyping continued.

Despite these limits on women's wartime opportunities, significant changes did occur. Black and Hispanic women found not only more but much better chances for employment. Married women over thirty-five with children entered the work force in record numbers. Automation installed in munitions and aircraft factories to facilitate female employment transformed heavy industry forever. Female workers joined unions in unprecedented numbers; some headed women's locals, a few became unionwide leaders.

In addition, stores stayed open later to accommodate working mothers; short hair, which was safer and less time-consuming to fix, became fashionable; rationing of items such as sugar and stockings altered habits of cooking and dress; and, perhaps most important, a range of family issues such as publicly funded child care became matters of national concern. Alan Clive analyzes both women's recruitment into wartime industries in Detroit, Michigan, and its impact on the household, the workplace, and the marketplace. By following the city's women through the period of demobilization, he illuminates both the short- and long-term effects of the war on female wage earners and their families.

Demobilization generally meant that women who had been working in heavy industry lost their jobs or were relegated to traditional female jobs. Though women left high-paying jobs reluctantly, many saw peacetime as providing the opportunity to start families long postponed. Nonetheless, during the baby boom years (1946–55), the proportion of women in the work force did not decrease. Rather, it continued to rise as new sex- and race-typed jobs opened in the service sector and as families began to rely on two incomes to take advantage of the expanding consumer economy that allowed them to enjoy a middle-class life style.

Both wartime experience and the far-reaching economic changes that followed assured that prewar sexual and racial patterns would never be completely reinstated. Government intervention in the economy—and in many other areas of life—that seemed so necessary during depression and war continued to expand after 1945, reshaping relations between individuals, families, employers, unions, communities, and the state. At the same time, in everyday life, the effects of two decades of upheaval could not be erased. Ordinary women and men had coped with economic, familial, communal, and military crises. They had taken on new roles, changed their expectations, traveled to different areas of the country and the world, formed new relationships and networks, and experienced previously unknown risks, responsibilities, and accomplishments.

Fanny Christina Hill, a black woman born in Texas who labored in domestic service until the age of twenty-four, landed a job at North American Aircraft during the war and was one of a small percentage of female wage earners to return to work there in peacetime. Commenting on the effects of wartime experiences on black women, she concluded:

> It made me live better. I really did. We always say that Lincoln took the bale off of the Negroes. . . . Well, my sister always said . . . "Hitler was the one that got us out of the white folks' kitchens."

As Hill's statement makes clear, the lives of all Americans changed dramatically as a result of the Great Depression and World War II.

Suggested Readings

Susan Ware, *Holding Their Own: American Women in the 1930s* (1982).

Joan Hoff-Wilson and Marjorie Lightman, eds., *Without Precedent: The Life and Career of Eleanor Roosevelt* (1984).

Lois Scharf and Joan Jensen, eds., *Decades of Discontent: The Women's Movement, 1920–1940* (1983).

Susan M. Hartmann, *The Homefront and Beyond: American Women in the 1940s* (1982).

Karen Anderson, *Wartime Women: Sex Roles, Family Relations, and the Status of Women during World War II* (1981).

ELEVEN

Women of the Depression: Anglo, Black, and Hispanic Families in San Antonio

Julia Kirk Blackwelder

If the flapper and the feminine mystique competed for female attention in the 1910s and 1920s, economic crisis and family survival refocused women's vision in the 1930s. Daughters and sons who had eagerly left home in the earlier era often returned—with spouses and children in tow—in the depression decade. Family strain took other forms as well: Husbands and fathers fought the economic and psychological burdens of unemployment and lower income, extended families sought to share small houses, and more women were pushed into positions as breadwinners.

Not all women and men experienced the Great Depression in the same ways. Some of the affluent escaped relatively unscathed. Middle-class families, who had the high expectations that came with prosperity, suffered emotionally as well as financially. Working-class families, who had fewer resources at the beginning of the crash, were pushed to the margins more quickly. Farmers of all races and ethnic backgrounds and African-Americans, Hispanics, and other minorities regardless of occupation were perhaps the hardest hit. Within each of these class, racial, ethnic, and occupational groups, women and men often were affected differently as traditional expectations, the sexual division of labor, and federal relief programs shaped the hopes and opportunities for each sex.

By focusing on San Antonio, Texas, Blackwelder reveals the ethnic and racial variations in the ways that Anglo, black, and Hispanic communities survived the depression decade. At the same time, she notes similarities in the roles played by women in all three groups. In the absence of the massive and militant union relief drives staged by the Congress of Industrial Organizations in some cities, San Antonio residents were forced to rely on family resources, community charity, and federal relief. The first of these differed according to the long-term economic and social status of each group; the last two differed according to federal legislative and local bureaucratic assumptions about ethnicity, race, and gender.

By following the female life-cycle before and during the depression and comparing the private and public labors of Anglo, black, and Hispanic wives and daughters, Blackwelder shows how women in different racial and ethnic communities faced problems, both distinct and common, and how they reshaped their own roles in the family to address the economic crisis. Overall, economic necessity seems to have pushed women into more unconventional roles in the family and the work force at the same time that the existing sexual division of labor and federal relief programs reinforced traditional expectations. The legacy of the Great Depression for women and the family was ambiguous and cannot be isolated from the effects of the war that finally revitalized the economy. What is clear is that women were simultaneously asked to take on new responsibilities and to remain within acceptable parameters of behavior for their sex, race, class, and ethnicity.

As San Antonio women articulated their concerns during the Depression and as they remembered the past, their thoughts ran first and last to family. Social worker Adela Navarro remembered her mother's watchful supervision of her children's education and her insistence on respectful behavior. Homemaker Ruby Cude recalled how hard her husband worked, sometimes holding down two jobs at one time, to make a comfortable life for his family. Store clerk Beatrice Clay reminisced about neighborhood sharing and backyard picnics that helped and cheered each of the families in her community. Family commanded deepest personal loyalties and constituted the primary economic unit in which a woman participated.

Marriage and the arrival of children were events that the average young girl expected in her life as well as the circumstances that most narrowly defined the roles she played in adulthood. Most girls coming of age in San Antonio in the 1920s married before or after a period of paid employment, stayed at home to rear the children, and did not enter the paid work force after marriage. The well-being of wives and of daughters living at home usually depended on the labors of male wage earners. For women who did not enter the work force, the vagaries of the labor market and the wage cuts of the 1930s were experienced second-hand in the form of sharply reduced household budgets, the sometimes awkward presence of husbands and fathers at home during their usual working hours, and male depression. The first responses of wives and daughters to financial setbacks

were to adapt to a life-style of leftovers and hand-me-downs and to show support for male family members who felt shame for economic problems not of their making. As Navarro remembered of her father and her brothers, "I could see what had happened in my own family, that they just couldn't bear it."

Regardless of their family status, women's experiences during the Depression were not individual or solitary experiences. Their dependence on male wage earners profoundly influenced most women's perceptions and roles during the Depression. Women saw the Depression through the filter of emotional concerns and attachments that affect wives, mothers, and daughters in prosperous times as well. A woman did not achieve independence by remaining single and entering the work force; life was more comfortable if economic resources were pooled, and regard for parents or siblings was paramount if the woman had neither spouse nor child. The composition of the family and family changes over time defined the responsibilities of women as they moved through the Depression decade, but for most women family concerns of one kind or another were ever present. Women who wished or needed to work weighed their household responsibilities and attitudes of family members in the balance with the benefits of market labor and the difficulty of finding work.

In 1930 and in 1940 the vast majority of adult women were married. Marriage patterns were not the same for all population groupings, however, and marriage did not bring the same responsibilities to all women. Among San Antonio women blacks married earliest, 22 percent of all black women between the ages of fifteen and nineteen being married, widowed or divorced in 1930. Mexican-American and native born Anglo women married slightly later than blacks. As women reached their early twenties, life-cycle patterns manifested their greatest differences by ethnicity, though only among foreign-born Anglos was the majority single. After age twenty-five, differences in the percentages of the population who were married began to even out, but Anglo immigrant women remained the least likely to have married.

The age of marriage increased slightly between 1930 and 1940 with women in all age brackets somewhat more likely to be single at the end of the decade. Black women, a small percentage of the total female population, recorded a decline in both the number and the percentage of women reporting themselves as divorced, but the chances of other women experiencing divorce increased. Both the number and the percentage of women in the total population who were widows [also] increased over the course of the Depression.

The Depression exacerbated emotional as well as economic stress on the family, and either kind of stress might lead to the dissolution of the family unit or temporary separation of its members. Admissions of men and women to the state mental hospital in San Antonio increased dramatically during the early 1930s. Suicide increased, though it remained rare among women. The tensions created by poverty and overcrowded living conditions proved overwhelming to Janie Brown Katlan, who lived with her husband, two sisters, and four nieces in a two-room apartment. In 1938, after nine months of marriage, the twenty-year-old woman shot herself through the heart. Another San Antonio woman, Kate Clark, poisoned herself. She left a note in which she explained that she knew it was wrong to take her life but that she could not find work and suicide was "the only way out."

Abandonment was more likely to break up families than was mental illness or suicide. Unemployed fathers deserted their wives and children, who often had nowhere to turn for support. There were also instances of mothers abandoning their children. In May, 1936, an unemployed single mother left her three-month-old infant on the steps of the Salvation Army headquarters. The baby wore a note in which the mother said that she had gone to Austin in hope of finding a job. She promised, "I will send money every week if I have it."

In 1930 the state of Texas tried to minimize the effects of desertion by a spouse or parent in a law that facilitated support suits. As the law took effect in Bexar County, local officials reported encouraging signs that the legislation was slowing desertion. The county tried to counsel husbands, who were the primary targets, to keep families together. County-court records reveal, however, that mediation failed in many cases as wives took to the courts in hopes of forcing payments from their spouses or former spouses.

The reactions of Hispanic women to the new law reveal the limitations of cultural values in the depths of economic crisis. Despite cultural proscriptions that forbade wives from publicly shaming their husbands or even admitting that they had left home, Hispanic women were prominent among nonsupport plaintiffs. While they were unlikely to violate their husbands' authority as long as they remained at home, wives exercised considerable autonomy if their spouses deserted them.

Female family heads in all ethnic groups faced frightening circumstances during the Depression. When unemployment threatened the survival of their families, many women beseeched members of the Roosevelt administration to help them in some way. One mother wrote to Eleanor Roosevelt:

Aug 23—1939
San Antonio, Tex

Dear Mrs. Roosevelt:

I am trying hard to get on W.P.A. I'm a typist and just can't seem to find work. I have four little children depending on me. And I have no home and no money to buy food or pay rent. The relief has rejected me for W.P.A. work, because I have a three months old baby girl. The oldest boy is 6 and will go to school this year, but I don't know how I can send him if I dont get work.

My little baby needs milk and I can't buy it. Am living in one room in a basement which is warm and damp. . . .

Mrs. Roosevelt I'm begging you with all my heart to *please* help me if you can. I love my babies dearly and won't submit to them being put in a home away from me. I would simply die apart from them.

Mrs. Renee Lohrback

Despite the pressures of the Depression, most San Antonio families remained intact. In all ethnic groups most parents of young children stayed together during the Depression, but there were significant differences in family composition among Anglo, black, and Hispanic families. Overall, Anglo girls had greater chances than other San Antonio females of growing to adulthood in a family composed of two parents and their children and of imitating this pattern in their adult lives. Throughout the Depression the Anglo family was more stable than the minority family. The black family was the most likely of all San Antonio families to be broken by separation or abandonment, and the Mexican-American family was the most likely to be broken by death of a parent or child.

Mexican-American families were both larger and younger than other families, black families being the smallest. In 1930, Mexican Americans accounted for less than one-third of San Antonio families, but constituted three-fourths of families with three or more children under ten years of age and nearly two-thirds of families with four or more children under age twenty-one.

The San Antonio Health Department reported a decline in the birthrate during the Depression, especially during the early 1930s. The postponement of marriage and the practice of birth control were obvious factors in the declining birthrate, but abortion also persisted throughout the Depression as a means of family limitation. When undertaken without proper medical assistance, abortion was dangerous. Each year a few San Antonio women died at the hands of untrained abortionists. The story of Mrs. Antonia Mena illustrates both the desperation of poor wives and the crude conditions under which abortionists operated. When she discovered that she was pregnant, Mrs. Mena, aged twenty-eight, sought the aid of an abortionist. With her sister she went to the home of Mrs. Leota Mowers, who told them that she had performed many abortions and that her clients had suffered no ill effects. Mrs. Mena paid Mrs. Mowers her last ten dollars and gave her a radio as security for the additional twenty-five dollars that Mrs. Mowers required. After the abortion had been performed, police were called to Mrs. Mowers's home, where Mrs. Mena was found dead on the living-room floor.

The declining birthrate that characterized the Depression, especially its early years, did not necessarily mean that household size decreased as well. The Depression discouraged persons in their late teens and early twenties from leaving home to begin their own households either as newlyweds or as single persons. Carmen Perry's brothers postponed marriage and remained in the parental home longer than they wished. A young single women named Schild lost her clerical job early in the Depression and returned to her parents' home after a period of independence. Married children might also share quarters with their parents. Ruby Cude and her husband and children moved in with her parents after a period of being on their own. As the Depression neared its end, large numbers of young adults found themselves in the same situation as Miss Schild and the Perrys.

One of the most common concerns of women who wrote letters to Eleanor Roosevelt and New Deal administrators asking for help was the reality that poverty could interfere with the education of their children. Few families considered allowing children to drop out of school to seek employment because almost no jobs were available for teenagers as the Depression deepened. Many mothers, however, confronted the prospect or the reality of children leaving school because they could not pay for books and supplies or because they did not have enough clothes to leave the house. One mother laid off from WPA employment wrote to Eleanor Roosevelt that "in September when school starts it will be impossible for mine to attend, they will have no shoes & there clothing is no better than rags."

In 1930 one in every ten San Antonio families included lodgers, who might be live-in servants, guests, boarders, or rent-paying family members. Beatrice Clay described the economic circumstances under which homeowners took in family members as boarders:

I think there were some people who had a very very tough time because I had an uncle who lived almost on the same block that I lived. [He] was buying his home and he had not had a job for almost six months. And we were renting and he was buying so he came to me and asked me if I would move in with him. And he had his mother which is my grandmother and another nephew whose parents were both dead. And he said that they could make room and we could move in and what money we were paying for rent could pay the interest on his note to keep him from losing his house, which we did.

Black households like Clay's were the most likely to include boarders, and Mexican-American families were the least likely. While black San Antonians suffered residential segregation, they never experienced the intense overcrowding and slum conditions of the Mexican West Side. As Mexican immigrants flooded into the city in the 1920s, houses in the Mexican community were subdivided, and new one-room shacks were thrown up to accommodate the newcomers. Such close quarters discouraged adding outsiders to the household.

Regardless of the reasons, black households included more lodgers than did Mexican-American households. Since both the income from boarders and the responsibilities of caring for them may have discouraged married women from seeking work outside the home, it is surprising that black married women were both most likely to be in the labor force and most likely to keep lodgers. Conversely, married Hispanic women were least likely to seek work and least likely to have lodgers in their homes. Lodging arrangements are but one facet of the interaction between culture and economic conditions in San Antonio. The economic situation of the black family encouraged married women to bring money into the home in either wages or rent. Cultural values supported these economic motivations in black families. Female protectiveness in Hispanic families discouraged similar responses to need.

As mothers, both Anglo and black women worked with different goals from those of Mexican-American wives. Whereas a Hispanic mother taught her child obedience and devotion to family, an Anglo or black mother educated her child to "be somebody." In their adult lives Anglo women had a broader range of social contacts than either black or Hispanic women had and less emotional reliance on the extended family. Unlike Mexican-American wives, black wives frequently had close relationships with a few nonrelated women that involved some mutual dependence. Beatrice Clay, a black employee of Washer Brothers Department Store, maintained a mutually supportive friendship with a coworker that allowed both women to maintain steady incomes during the early years of the Depression. Anglo women, who were less likely to be employed, formed their extrafamilial friendships through churches, neighbors, social clubs, and their husbands. Even in the Depression years entertainment among Anglo women focused more around peer groups than around family. An evening's entertainment with other couples was an expected social activity of most wives, though the Depression may have reduced outings to a covered-dish supper at a friend's home. As an unmarried office clerk, May Eckles participated in similar activities with other unmarried friends or with a group of friends and relatives. Such get-togethers and group outings were not unknown to black and Mexican-American women, but they were less likely to center in relationships outside the family.

Women's understanding of their roles and responsibilities as daughters, wives, and mothers and as Anglos, blacks, or Hispanics predisposed them to cope with the realities of the Depression in different ways. A Hispanic mother ideally stayed at home to protect her family and her reputation, but there was no social disgrace for either her or her daughters if they sought pay for sewing or other tasks that they could undertake in their own homes. Black wives, accustomed to some autonomy in decision making, found employment outside the home easier to accept. Native-born Anglo wives generally felt the least economic pressure to enter the work force, and most had not expected to work after marriage. Nevertheless, work outside the home did not carry the same stigma for the Anglo wife as for a Mexican-American wife. Regardless of marital status or cultural role definitions, women weighed a number of familial considerations in reaching their decisions about seeking employment. In such deliberations the pull of the labor market increasingly won out over the pull of the home, but the transition involved changes in the work lives of all family members, not just wives or daughters and not just the members of one racial or ethnic group.

[Family strategies for survival moved beyond purely private decisions as government programs began to offer new economic opportunities to women and men by the mid-1930s. Yet even these alternatives varied according to one's gender, ethnicity, and race.] The WPA educational programs in San Antonio offered hope and economic assistance, but the programs reflected local racial and ethnic preju-

dices as well. The vast majority of students and teachers were Anglo, but Mexican-American residents enrolled in some courses alongside Anglos and in other courses for Spanish-speakers. Adult classes in English, citizenship, and trade skills were offered through the "Americanization" program at the Sidney Lanier School, a Hispanic secondary school. Anglo and Hispanic women in San Antonio's education projects studied business and clerical subjects with the goal of gaining white-collar jobs. They also enrolled in such classes as furniture making that were created primarily to teach housewives to "make do" with home furnishings that could be constructed from scrap materials. Graduates of the home-improvement courses were expected to pass on their newly learned skills to female friends and neighbors. Under the WPA Anglo and Hispanic women were also employed in domestic work in the Housekeeping Aid Projects, programs to assist in home and child care when parents were ill or otherwise incapable of managing by themselves. The Housekeeping Aid Projects were totally separate from the Household Workers Project, the only educational program for black women, which taught them to be "capable domestics."

The first large public relief project for San Antonio women was a federally funded canning plant, which employed 900 women in the summer of 1934. Project administrators expected to double the plant payroll by the end of the year, but in January, 1935, only 450 women were employed. The second large project was a WPA sewing room. The first sewing room opened with 278 employees in October, 1935, and within a year sewing projects had expanded to employ 2,300 persons. The sewing rooms were the largest WPA projects for women, though various other programs employed lesser numbers of blue- and white-collar female workers. Women with clerical or administrative skills worked on all programs sponsored by the Federal Emergency Relief Administration and the WPA within and outside the Division of Women's Work, but more than half of all female WPA

Racial discrimination and ethnic bias were evident in the various educational, employment, and financial aid programs in San Antonio. The Housekeeping Aid Project, for example, trained Anglo and Hispanic women in home management and child care and placed them in temporary positions as live-in helpers to assist mothers who were ill or otherwise unable to manage by themselves. The Household Workers Project was a separate program for black women, designed to teach them skills related to their "appropriate" role as domestic servants.

administrators in San Antonio worked with the sewing projects as supervisors or in some other administrative capacity.

While public works programs generally discriminated against women in a variety of ways, WPA projects offered a few women an unprecedented opportunity to develop and apply executive skills as project and agency administrators. In Texas as elsewhere women headed the offices and nearly all the projects of the Division of Women's Work. A second category of white-collar jobs for women under emergency work programs was recordkeeping, both as administrative functionaries of public agencies and in special projects such as the Historical Records Survey and local proj-

ects to organize city ordinances and criminal records. Women in San Antonio served in various publicly funded positions as clinical aides, hospital workers, school cafeteria workers, and nursery-school workers. Librarians, editors, writers, artists, and musicians found work in the WPA professional programs. Women appeared regularly in WPA musical and theatrical performances in San Antonio and participated in arts programs under both the WPA and the National Youth Administration. Early in 1936 the San Antonio WPA office reported that 1,280 women and 2,739 men were employed in local professional projects.

In a city like San Antonio, where the Depression reached so broadly and deeply, the FERA

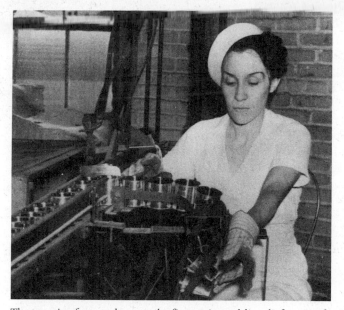

The canning factory that was the first major public relief project for San Antonio's women failed to provide lasting assistance. Within six months the number of women employed there fell from 900 to 450. In 1935 when the expected shipment of beef failed to arrive, the plant was forced into a temporary shutdown.

and the WPA provided the margin of survival for many women and their families, though there was always more demand for work than either agency could begin to meet. Public works projects were late in coming to San Antonio, and women had an especially long wait for their meager share of emergency employment. Before the arrival of federal public assistance the legions of hungry and unemployed residents had few places to turn for help. Since neither San Antonio nor Bexar County dispensed local public relief funds, the unemployed could turn only to private charities during the early years of the Depression. The Salvation Army, the Junior League, the International Institute, Catholic and Protestant churches and convents, settlement houses, and other organizations helped feed and clothe destitute local residents and transients. The Bexar County Red Cross provided food, clothing, and shelter, and their relief expenditures increased 300 percent from

1928 through 1931. As San Antonian Veda Butler recalled, the relief commodities dispensed by the Salvation Army to the East Side black community were insufficient and barely edible, but people waited in line for hours for these handouts because of their desperate need.

There were virtually no Anglo-financed private social services other than the Salvation Army to which blacks could turn in times of need. However, a history of steady employment and the strong economic base of black churches provided the black community with some weapons to fight the ravages of the Depression. The Mexican-American community lacked the overall economic strength to see its members through hard times. A few private charities dispensed food and clothing on the West Side, but they could do little to mitigate the widespread starvation and disease. The concentration of poverty in San Antonio and its consequences are revealed in health statistics of the

Depression years. In 1937, after public relief had alleviated some of the city's health problems, Mexican Americans suffered a death rate from tuberculosis of 310 per 100,000, blacks 138 per 100,000, and Anglos 56 per 100,000, giving San Antonio the worst record of any major American city. The infant death rate was 144 per 1,000 live births among Hispanics, 105 among blacks, and 51 among Anglos. For Mexican Americans housing conditions were as severe a threat as starvation. The high incidence of infant diarrhea and enteritis among Hispanic children testified to environmental dangers. Hundreds of mothers watched helplessly each year as their young children sickened and died.

Throughout the Depression local politicians and relief administrators discriminated against blacks and Hispanics. Racism was at the heart of the resistance to locally funded public relief, but early in the Depression, San Antonio leaders moved to improve the dispersal of private relief assistance. At the end of 1931, Mayor C. M. Chambers announced the formation of the Central Unemployment Relief Committee (CURC), which was authorized to collect private funds for relief efforts and to certify workers for the few public jobs funded by a recent bond issue. Encouraging charity was as far as either the city or the county would go in ameliorating local problems, The CURC exemplified Anglo antagonism to Hispanics in announcing that no aliens would be hired for jobs funded through contributions to the committee. The committee began providing make-work the following January, but the funds and foodstuffs the CURC could distribute made little impact, and by March the funds had been exhausted. During its three months of operation CURC distributed about $55,000 in money and food among the unemployed. The committee reported that "about 5,000 heads of families have registered with the committee and it is estimated that an additional 1,000 white families, who having been placed in such circumstances for the first time in their experience, due to a sense of humiliation and pride, have not registered."

Throughout 1932 stories of tragedy and suffering abounded. The *San Antonio Express* reported "five motherless children, living with a sick father in an old storebuilding, had no bed clothes and practically nothing to eat. Such instances of dire need are encountered frequently enough in normal times, but unemployment conditions have multiplied them." Private charities were unable to meet the demand for assistance during the same months that CURC offered relief. The Milk and Ice Fund, which had been established to provide a supply of sanitary milk to needy San Antonio children, assumed broader relief responsibilities early in the Depression. At the beginning of 1932 the fund warned that it could not continue its efforts through the remainder of the year without additional contributions, and in 1935 all fund activities terminated. The failure of public agencies to allocate general relief funds handicapped the city and county utilization of outside assistance. The Federal Farm Board's donation of 300,000 pounds of wheat flour nearly went unused because many families had no stoves and no funds were available to bake bread from the flour. The San Antonio Federation of Women's Clubs raised funds to bake 10,000 loaves of bread, and the rest of the flour was distributed to the needy.

Despite the obvious inadequacy of private funds to meet the local emergency, some civic leaders continued to oppose public relief. Commenting on President Hoover's plea in 1932 that relief administrators "make sure that no American this winter will go hungry or cold," the *San Antonio Express* argued that "Responsibility for that achievement rests, first of all, upon the individual citizen, who cannot evade his 'God-imposed obligation to look after his neighbor.' When that debt shall have been discharged, it will be time to appeal for government assistance, through the Reconstruction

Finance Corporation." In fact, some RFC funds had already flowed into Bexar County, and in the fall of 1932 the city sought a $300,000 loan from the new corporation. The chamber of commerce estimated that twice that amount would be needed to sustain the unemployed through the winter.

Both the city and the county [also] benefited from expenditures of the NRA, the CWA, and the WPA. The CURC became a countywide committee under the guidance of the Texas State Relief Commission. In early August the committee, now federally funded, began making cash disbursements to relief clients. On August 5 more than one thousand persons lined up outside the Bexar County Courthouse to receive their payments of $4.50 per household head in exchange for two days' labor on relief projects.

Relief administrators heavily criticized cash payments as encouraging workers to refuse the jobs that were available. A. W. Greene, manager of the U.S. Employment Service office in San Antonio, asserted that he had been unable to meet requests for cotton pickers because of the cash payments. Greene insisted that hundreds of pickers, who had left San Antonio for the fields, turned back to the city when they learned that relief cash would be dispersed. A few days after Greene's statement to the press, police were called in to disperse a crowd that had besieged the farm-employment office on the West Side. The *San Antonio Light* reported that the crowd was composed of job applicants who had rushed to find picking jobs after hearing that all local work projects and cash relief payments would be suspended.

In September the relief committee, now known as the Bexar County Board of Welfare and Unemployment, replaced one central office with nine neighborhood relief offices. While bringing services closer to the clients, the decentralization also effectively segregated Anglo, black, and Mexican-American clients from each other. State and federal evidence of mis-

management of relief funds in Bexar County forced a second reorganization of the relief board in the late fall of 1933. Local work funds were cut back in February, 1934, when the CWA closed down. Relief rolls again rose to more than 17,000 families. The termination of work relief prompted disorder at the Mexican-American welfare office on the West Side.

The WPA and the NYA provided the major sources of help for the unemployed from 1935 through 1939. Federally funded relief provided the margin of survival for thousands of San Antonians, but there were never sufficient resources to meet the needs of all who qualified for assistance, and per capita relief expenditures in the city were low. In New Orleans, a city also hard-hit, monthly emergency relief expenditures under the FERA averaged $29.68 for a family of four, while in San Antonio the average was $15.74. Women workers in San Antonio, whether family heads or supplementary workers, faced special obstacles in obtaining emergency jobs.

Despite the establishment of women's divisions and the prominence of women in some New Deal agencies, women were second-class citizens under most work relief programs. Under the operating procedures of the WPA and other agencies, job preference was given to male family heads. Separated or widowed female family heads received first-priority ratings only if there were no adult male children in the household. A married woman whose husband was present in the home achieved first-priority certification only if her husband was disabled. An applicant of second-priority status stood no reasonable chance of employment in public works. Although the NYA created jobs for the youthful female workers who had been denied employment in the CCC, boys received preference over girls in NYA placement.

Overall, men dominated the better-paying emergency jobs. Among women the superior status of Anglos is revealed in statistics showing that a disproportionate number of women's jobs went to whites rather than blacks and no black or Hispanic women were prominent in the administration of federal programs for women in San Antonio. The general pattern of discrimination against women in the allocation of public or private relief jobs throughout the Depression also emerges in direct relief statistics. While needy men were given jobs, needy women were frequently extended only commodities. While men received most of the relief jobs in San Antonio, women comprised most of the direct relief clients.

As scholarly studies of the New Deal alphabet agencies have documented, the federal government accepted and reinforced southern laws and traditions of segregation in the administration of relief and public works programs. In San Antonio separate relief projects were maintained for blacks and whites. Mexican Americans and Anglos were not administratively segregated from each other in the work programs of the FERA or the WPA, but Anglo and Mexican-American clients rarely crossed paths in applying for relief commodities or emergency jobs. A relief office on the West Side served most of the Mexican-American clients, channeling Mexican-American men and women into unskilled work and reserving the few white-collar positions for Anglos. Similarly, federal and local relief agencies respected the tradition of occupational segregation by gender. The establishment of the women's division under both the FERA and the WPA generated segregation by sex in federal emergency job programs throughout the nation.

Particularly in San Antonio relief administrators regarded women as temporary workers whose primary role was in the home. Relief programs were structured to equip female clients with domestic skills that they could utilize after the Depression had passed. Relief programs developed around the assumption that additional women had been propelled into the labor market by declining male employment and that these women would retire to the home when

the work of fathers and husbands returned to normal. Administrators recognized that some women would always be in the work force, and these workers were rigorously segregated into "appropriate" occupations. As the Texas relief director reported in 1935, "We believe our projects for women, in addition to keeping them from the despair of idleness, provide the more lasting benefit of permanently equipping these women to meet responsibilities in the home and to accept industrial opportunities as they develop."

Federal New Deal administrators demanded local support before they approved individual works projects. The refusal of San Antonio and Bexar County to appropriate relief funds presented a special problem in obtaining federal relief. Local support had to be obtained through private donations, usually of building use and supplies, or the allocation to federal projects of employees already on city or county payrolls and the use of space in city or county properties. Even after these initial barriers were overcome, lack of equipment and supplies frequently delayed or interrupted approved projects. The relief canning plant was forced to shut down for a period in 1935 because beef shipments failed to arrive. Shortages of machines and material in the sewing rooms caused especially severe problems because the sewing projects employed the most women.

Although sewing projects were created primarily as an appropriate alternative to direct relief for female family heads, Texas officials recognized the value of the workers' efforts in providing relief commodities. In 1935 the director of the WPA women's work division in San Antonio wrote the Washington office seeking continued support for sewing rooms:

There is a most widespread and pressing need for garments for indigents, both for the unemployable of the Texas Relief Commission and also for those who are really employable but who have yet not been put to work. We feel that in operating these sewing rooms we can not only occupy our women profitably but can also do something of great value, particularly in clothing the school children of relief families, many of whom cannot attend school until such clothing is provided.

Texas officials frowned on any works project that employed women at tasks that they perceived as nontraditional. Although Texas women had worked as migrant agricultural laborers for generations, the state WPA head vetoed projects that required heavy outdoor labor. The WPA employed women on grounds improvements in several southern cities, but the Texas office refused to approve a similar project in the state, and the WPA in Texas also objected to federal funding of laundry work for women, though women were already extensively employed in commercial laundries throughout the state. Women's projects of the CWA, the FERA, and the WPA in Texas were largely confined to sewing, food processing, and domestic service or health care.

Programs for black women functioned on the assumption that the destiny of the black woman was domestic work. In an economic environment in which opportunities for the employment of domestic workers in homes were declining, the FERA and the WPA reinforced occupational segregation and participated in a discriminatory educational system that denied black women the skills to compete for the few areas of female employment that expanded during the Depression. In 1937, Mary Katherine Dickson, a local administrator, pointed out that a black church in San Antonio had been conducting a training program for black domestic workers and argued the need for such a program through the WPA adult-education program. Dickson reasoned that domestic training was the most suitable education for black women because "between 75% and 85% of persons employed in household service are

black." In elaborating on her justification, Dickson revealed her personal perspective that the best interests of blacks and whites would be served by educating black women to function in an inferior place:

> In fact, the majority of housewives in San Antonio have a very real servant problem on their hands and, at present, no means of solving it satisfactorily. The public school system here, as elsewhere, has provided, in the past, essentially the same curriculum for the negroes as for the whites, in spite of the fact that their environments, their economic expectations, and their places in the social scale are mostly different.

The proposal went forward to federal officials in Washington with a supporting letter from Maury Maverick, the new congressman from San Antonio, whose election campaign had been marked by racist undercurrents. Maverick worked for household-worker projects through the following year. After an initial period of funding in 1938, Maverick cited the regional significance of the WPA Household Workers Training Project, noting that it was "the first attempt by the government to actually train these people for the jobs they are now performing. In the South . . . the field of labor for Negroes is restricted." Black women had a more difficult time than others in securing certification for WPA jobs. WPA supervisors and employees of the county employment office told black women that they should seek employment in private homes. As Lula Gordon complained to Eleanor Roosevelt, black women were forced into accepting domestic jobs, though such work often proved of short duration. Their employment in this manner might remove them from immediate consideration for any WPA jobs opening up, but if they refused the work, they would be taken off the WPA rolls altogether.

Justifiably, relief administrators in San Antonio were concerned about the possibility of charges of racial or ethnic discrimination, especially in the black community, which was better organized politically than the Hispanic West Side. Mary Taylor, the local WPA woman's work supervisor, sought to head off such charges in the face of budget cuts by publicizing programs for San Antonio blacks that had continued to function. In 1936 she wrote to her regional supervisor:

> As you know I had given considerable thought to developing good Negro projects—for obvious reasons! As soon as quota reduction was announced I asked Mr. Drought if he would approve my having a series of articles on such projects prepared and sent to the big Negro newspaper in Pennsylvania. I thought it might forestall criticism as to racial discrimination.

WPA officials in San Antonio faced charges of racism not only because they did discriminate against blacks but also because San Antonio blacks had articulate spokesmen and organizations working on their behalf. Blacks in San Antonio suffered discrimination under the WPA that was unequaled in other parts of the state. Although Anglo and Hispanic garment workers were almost entirely segregated from each other in the private sector, no administrative decisions by the FERA or the WPA mandated separate public sewing rooms for the two groups. Nevertheless, officials assigned black women exclusively to separate projects. J. E. Thompson, a black San Antonio clergyman, supervised one project for black women in the city. In 1939, Thompson, who had conducted a private domestic-worker training program at the church he pastored, was fired as coordinator of the Household Workers Training Project. The National Association for the Advancement of Colored People and other groups unsuccessfully protested the dismissal. WPA administrators in San Antonio argued that blacks would not respect the authority of a member of their own race, though black supervisors had been successfully employed elsewhere.

WPA officials took a broader view of the occupational possibilities of Mexican-American women than of black women. The adult-education program of Sidney Lanier School, which enrolled more than three hundred Hispanic men and women, had Americanization as a unifying goal but presented various training and educational programs. Women were offered training in nutrition and home and child care. Clerical skills were another area of study, and some graduates of the school obtained employment as stenographers and bookkeepers. However, the majority of Hispanic WPA clients found jobs in sewing rooms and did not enter WPA classes.

Discrimination on the basis of marital status added to the liabilities of gender and ethnic origin that many women bore as they sought employment in Depression San Antonio. As Lois Scharf has documented with regard to the nation as a whole, the work rate among married women increased dramatically, but the increase occurred despite the disapproval of husbands, societal pressure, and some legal measures taken to deprive wives of employment. The Depression elicited unprecedented public pressure to drive women, particularly married women, from the work force. It did not matter that men were unlikely to prepare for or accept jobs as teachers, nurses, or secretaries; society demanded that married females withdraw from the work force. In 1931 the American Federation of Labor adopted a position endorsing discrimination in hiring against women whose husbands earned a decent wage.

Nationally the unfounded fears that women competed with men for a limited number of employment openings and that they displaced employed male workers was translated into a law prohibiting a husband and wife from simultaneous employment by the federal government. Section 213 of the Economy Act of

1932 did not specify which partner in a marriage would be hired or continued on the federal payroll, but since wives almost universally had less earning power than husbands, it was women who gave up federal jobs. Only a few states adopted similar legislation during the 1930s. Most states left the matter of working wives to local governments. At the local level female public employees were most visible in the schools, and married women teachers were the most common targets of discrimination.

Depression San Antonio was a city without a strong voice for women's rights. Although women in Atlanta, Georgia, and some other cities successfully fought policies preventing the employment of married female teachers, the dismissal of married women from the San Antonio schools met little opposition. In August, 1931, the San Antonio school board announced that married women would receive low priority in the hiring of new teachers. In June, 1932, all previously hired married women whose husbands earned a minimum of two thousand dollars a year were terminated. In 1931 offices in the Bexar County Courthouse began dismissing married women, a practice apparently opposed only by the victims. May Eckles noted in her diary: "There has been a mess stirred up in Jack Burke's office over cutting out the married women and Mrs. Achs is sure on the warpath, she says she is going to give Mr. Burke a piece of her mind at four o'clock this afternoon." Eckles registered her lack of sympathy with her coworkers when she noted, "Well all the married women are missing this morning and I aint sorry, for I certainly am not in favor of married women working unless they have to, there are too many unmarried ones without jobs." It did not trouble Eckles that there were three adult workers in her household while other households were being reduced to one or possibly no workers.

San Antonio's union voice was unsympathetic to the plight of the married female work-

ers. William B. Arnold, editor of the pro-labor *San Antonio Weekly Dispatch,* accepted the fallacious argument that the firing of married women would create jobs for men, and he also argued that home and family suffered when wives went out to work. In 1939 he wrote:

> The wife is inescapably the builder of the home and the guardian of its children. These duties are necessarily neglected by working wives. We want no dictators telling women what to do; but the country cannot ignore the deterioration of the home, due to the pressure of married women in industry.

In drafting emergency employment programs for women, Texas relief officials were wary of drawing in married women. Texas officials balked at setting up household-worker projects in the state if second-priority female workers—women living with employed or employable fathers, husbands, or sons—were to be recruited. A Texas administrator reported that several organizations in San Antonio would donate space for conducting WPA training programs as long as no woman with an outside source of income was certified for entrance, because "the general feeling in this part of the country is that her husband and father should earn the livelihood for the family."

Although married women were discriminated against by the school board and had difficulty obtaining emergency jobs, personal influence in local administrative offices could break down the barriers that had been erected against their hiring. Anglo women, of course, were much more likely to have pull in city and county offices than black or Hispanic women. In 1933 an investigation by the Texas Senate of the Bexar County Board of Welfare and Employment involved accusations that wives of city and county employees were receiving emergency work wages while other San Antonians went hungry. The secretary of the welfare board presented evidence substantiating the complaints to the senate. Subsequent reorganization of the board eliminated the advantages that some wives had had, but complaints that privileged women received jobs to the detriment of the needy continued throughout the remainder of the Depression.

Women workers understood that their only competitors for emergency work were other women. The most likely critics of working women were unemployed women. Late in the Depression a widow with two dependents wrote Eleanor Roosevelt that her WPA salary had been cut while wives with no real need had experienced no reduction:

> I have been on the W.P.A. at a salarie of $57.60 per month for the past few years. Recently I was cut to a $40.00 a month salarie. Instead of cutting the women who had other income and husbands to support them, they have cut the widow women with children and no other income. If the W.P.A. had made this cut after an investigation to prove that people did not need their jobs, it would have been different, but they are taking the jobs away from the little people, while they have increased their own salaries. Why? Because the little fellow had no pull. It is not efficiency or education or refinement or need that counts in San Antonio, it is pull.

Throughout the New Deal era women in supervisory positions were special targets of accusation that they did not need jobs or that they had obtained their positions through personal connections. Both the men and the women most likely to have influence were persons with white-collar skills. When supervisory positions on women's projects were filled, different criteria of selection were applied from those used in selecting women to perform the sewing, canning, cleaning, or inventorying that the projects involved. Mary Taylor wrote to Ellen Woodward that in the matter of supervisory personnel her office had not "made it a point to employ only needy people" but that

when there were two equally qualified candidates the candidate with greater need was given preference.

In San Antonio as elsewhere in the nation, the administration of both public and private relief entailed endless bureaucratic red tape. Caseworkers were viewed with suspicion; almost all of them were Anglos and few were bilingual, though Mexican Americans comprised more than half the relief population. When Ruth Kolling was appointed to oversee local relief operations, she was characterized by the Bexar County Protective League as well seasoned in "the kind of charity where a poor woman is asked a bunch of impertinent questions and given a bunch of carrots and a bunch of beets and told not to eat it all at once."

Adela Navarro was the first Hispanic appointed as a caseworker in San Antonio, and it was more than a year before the second was hired. Often frustrated by official procedures or policies, she found ways to circumvent the rules when it seemed necessary. She refused to report to her superior that among her cases was a couple living together out of wedlock because she knew that they would be stricken from relief rolls if the information was divulged. However, said Navarro, someone was "so damn mean" that the information reached the relief office despite her silence on the issue. When her supervisor asked whether she knew that a particular couple were not married, she answered that she did not consider it her place to sit in moral judgment and that what she did know was that the people were hungry, and she could get them food. Satisfied with her response, the supervisor no longer interfered with her case reports.

Although public and private relief work was inconsistently administered and always inadequate to meet women's needs, clear patterns of preference and discrimination characterized the programs. Women were regarded merely as temporary and secondary workers who needed help getting by in hard times. The content of training programs generally militated against occupational advancement for women and was frequently unsuited to the local economy. Although black women were perceived as permanent workers, they received the fewest opportunities for training. Mexican-American women fared better than blacks in the variety of public works that employed them, but many Hispanics were turned away from relief and employment offices because of their alien status.

Questions for Study and Review

1. What was the impact of the Great Depression on the social, sexual, and technological developments of the preceding two decades?

2. How did women contribute specifically to coping with the depression, and how did depression-era policies affect women's role in the family and community in the long run?

3. Compare the family and community roles of San Antonio's Anglo, black, and Hispanic women with those of furnished room residents, southern black activists, and Mexican migrants in the Southwest during the 1910s and 1920s.

4. Economic crises often call into question the relation between women's paid labor and their domestic responsibilities. How did responses to such concerns differ during the depression, in seventeenth century Salem, in nineteenth-century New England factory towns, and in the South during Reconstruction?

Suggested Readings

Ruth Milkman, "Women's Work and the Economic Crisis: Some Lessons from the Great Depression," *Review of Radical Political Economics* (Spring 1976).

Lois Rita Helmbold, "Beyond the Family Economy: Black and White Working-Class Women During the Great Depression," *Feminist Studies* (Fall 1987).

Ann Banks, ed., *First Person America* (1980).

Gerald Markowitz and David Rossner, eds., *"Slaves of the Depression": Workers' Letters about Life on the Job* (1987).

TWELVE

The Home Front and the Household: Women, Work, and Family in Detroit

Alan Clive

Rosie the Riveter is perhaps the most well-known symbol of women's contributions on the home front during World War II. Drawn by Norman Rockwell for *Saturday Evening Post* magazine, the original Rosie was more tomboy than temptress, more fun loving than feminine. She suggested that a woman in industry could indeed become one of the boys. Yet when the federal government began actively recruiting women for industry in 1942 and 1943, it was less interested in transforming traditional images of women than in reassuring women that traditional images could be maintained even as the nation waged total war.

Just as happened in the Great Depression, drastic alterations in work life and home life and in women's and men's roles occurred during World War II, and a substantial share of the changes were initiated or shaped by federal policies. At the same time, the federal government had no more interest in using military preparedness than it had in using economic crisis to reorganize gender relations and the sexual division of labor. Industrial expansion, labor migration, hopes for racial and sexual equality, huge increases in government spending, and the promise of peacetime prosperity reshaped American society in fundamental ways. Yet the war left behind a legacy of hardship as well as hope, with automation, deskilling of jobs, and the failure to address adequately racial and sexual discrimination proving the fodder for future struggles on the home front.

In his study of female war workers in Detroit, Michigan, Clive provides a complex portrait of the benefits offered and barriers facing women on one home front. Focusing on both industrial and domestic settings, he traces the gradual movement of women into Detroit's factories and its effects on the sexual and racial composition of the labor force, levels of production, training programs, the attitudes of union leaders and employers toward women, and women's attitudes toward employment, unions, and domesticity. By focusing on provisions for child care, he provides a case study of the different and often conflicting assumptions and needs of those seeking to mobilize women for war.

Clive also follows, more briefly, the movement of women out of heavy industry at war's end when, despite the desire of many to remain in their jobs, government, unions, and employers sought to reinstitute the prewar sexual division of labor. As Clive concludes, women "could return to being waitresses, shop clerks, or maids, but they could not remain in industry."

World War II did not revolutionize gender or race relations. Nonetheless, it provided many women and minorities with their first high-paying, skilled jobs, pulled older and married women and mothers into wage-earning in large numbers, raised such issues as public-supported day care and equal pay for equal work, and raised expectations in black and white women and men that life could be better. In these ways, it set the stage for great changes to come in the following decades.

The war's impact on working women reveals much about the scope and limits of change in American society. The most obvious indicator of the wartime change is the great increase in female employment that took place during the conflict. From 14,600,000 in 1941, the number of employed women in the United States had increased by 1944 to 19,370,000, far more than a third of the labor force. Women took jobs of all descriptions and skills in war industry. But what did the rise in the female labor force signify, beyond the fact that more women were at work? Did the war experience generate new attitudes toward women and their status?

Chester W. Gregory declares affirmatively that "women employed in defense plants demonstrated such skill and praiseworthy performance that a kind of social, economic, and psychological equality between men and women which had not existed before in American society was evolved. . . . As a result of the war crisis . . . women were able to emancipate themselves socially and psychologically and to establish a greater degree of social and economic independence than they had ever known before." Looking back at the 1940s, William Chafe notes somewhat less optimistically: "There was no question that economic equality remained a distant goal but the content of women's lives had changed, and an important new area of potential activity had opened up to them, with side effects which could not yet be measured." Eleanor Straub flatly asserts that "World War II permanently altered concepts of welfare, industrial technology . . . the relationship of the individual to the state, and the role of interest and minority groups in politics, but no comparable changes in the status of women in American society are visible."

These discussions of women and World War II, with their contradictory findings, are based on surveys at the national level. An examination of women and war in a single state affords the opportunity of testing national-level generalizations on a specific test community. Few states better qualify for such a study than Michigan. With 4 per cent of America's population, the state obtained better than 10 per cent of the nearly two hundred billion dollars in prime war supply and facilities contracts awarded by the US government and the Allies from 1940 to 1945. Only New York state outranked Michigan in this category. Hundreds of companies in dozens of communities across the state fashioned every conceivable item required by an embattled nation. The automobile industry, which had made the name Detroit world-famous in a more peaceful era, naturally led all Michigan manufacturers in the output of war goods. Most of the automakers' national total of twenty-nine billion dollars worth of vehicles, engines, guns, shells, and additional assorted material was produced in such prewar industry centers as Detroit, Pontiac, Flint, Lansing, Saginaw, and Muskegon.

Manpower constituted an essential element in Michigan's industrial triumph. State manufacturing employment peaked at 1,226,000 persons in November 1943, a 60 per cent rise over the annual average of 721,000 industrial workers employed statewide in 1940. Total employment in the Detroit labor market area obtained a wartime high during the same month in 1943, more than doubling to 867,000 persons from the 396,000 at work three years earlier. The size of Michigan's labor force gradually declined during the last twenty months of war, but as late as December 1944, 1,075,000 people—

From "Women Workers in World War II: Michigan as a Test Case" by Alan Clive, *Labor History,* Winter 1987, Volume 28, Number 1. Copyright © 1987 by The Tamiment Institute. Reprinted by permission.

one out of every five inhabitants of the state— were directly engaged in war production.

The extent to which women might figure in this enormous manpower increase was in part conditioned by bitter depression experience. Female emancipation had received a severe setback during the 1930s, when mass unemployment lent new emphasis to the long-cherished belief that the woman's place was in the home, not in the office or on the assembly line, where her presence might deny work to a man supporting a family. The 1932 Michigan state legislature requested that local governments fire all but one member of a family where more than one member worked in a department, a measure clearly aimed at removing married women from payrolls. The proportion of women in the Michigan labor force rose from 18.7 per cent in 1930 to 21.5 per cent in 1940, but females remained clustered in the occupations traditionally reserved to them—storeclerk, stenographer, maid, and so forth. The notion of additional female employment in industry had been discussed at the outset of the defense program but had not been implemented to any great extent. Few women entered defense training courses, and an October 1941 analysis of sixteen major industrial groups in the state found that defense work "still is predominantly a man's job."

But the increasing labor demands of Michigan war industry after Pearl Harbor, combined with the exactions of the draft, compelled the hiring of women workers in great number. The proportional rise of female employment in the state ultimately was more striking than that for the nation; from 391,600 in March 1940 (24.8 per cent of the nonfarm workforce), the number of employed women in Michigan more than doubled by the war peak in November 1943 to 799,100 (34.8 per cent of the nonfarm workers). The proportion of males employed in manufacturing in the Detroit labor market area rose from 56 per cent to 71 per cent between 1940 and 1943, but the percentage of Detroit women in industry increased from 22 per cent to 53 per cent of all employed females in the area during the same period. In October 1940 there were only 5.7 women per one hundred production workers in the automobile industry; four years later, the rate reached 24.4. Examining Detroit war plants in March 1943 investigators for the United Automobile Workers (UAW) found that women composed 30 per cent of the workforce at Briggs, 32 per cent at Bendix's Wayne division, and 27 per cent of all persons employed at Willow Run.

A Women's Bureau survey disclosed that fully 51 per cent of the 387,000 women at work in Detroit during late 1944 and early 1945 had been employed before Pearl Harbor. They had shifted from jobs as waitresses, sales clerks, and maids into manufacturing and, to a lesser extent, into government work. The war years also witnessed the emergence of a new female worker: the same study reported that 28 per cent of the Detroit female labor force were housewives, and 18 per cent had been students prior to the declaration of war (the remaining 3 per cent were then seeking work). The demographic balance of the female labor force altered radically with the entrance of these new workers in vast numbers. Once dominated by single women under thirty years of age, the female labor force now contained substantially larger proportions of older and married women. The Women's Bureau found Detroit's female workers evenly divided at 45 per cent each between single and married women, the remaining 10 per cent being widowed or divorced. Only 44 per cent of the women were in the prime employment age group of twenty-nine years [or below], in contrast to the 41 per cent of women workers over thirty.

A complex set of trends and demands dictated the shape of the wartime women's workforce. Long-term demographic tendencies within the national female population resulted

Labor shortages during World War II prompted the hiring of women workers away from such traditionally "female" jobs as waitresses, clerks, stenographers, and maids and into the wartime manufacturing industries. Despite the large increase in female labor force participation, developments in the years immediately following the war suggest there was little lasting change in women's status or in traditional attitudes toward women and their role.

in a reduction of the age at marriage and an increase in the number of older women in relation to all women. The coming of war provided a further stimulus to marriage; the number of Michigan weddings performed in December 1941 set a state record for a single month. The marriage rate declined during the next four years, but rose sharply again with the coming of peace. Seeking a perspective on wartime changes in female employment, Chafe observes: "At the turn of the century, the young, the single and the poor had dominated the female labor force. Fifty years later, the majority of women workers were married and middle aged, and a substantial minority came from the middle class. In the story of that dramatic change, World War II represented a watershed event."

Government manpower policy also influenced the nature of the female labor force, but that policy left much to be desired both in conception and execution. At no time did the War Manpower Commission (WMC) give women more than an advisory voice in decision-making, and usually the Commission ignored proffered advice. At first paying little attention to the potential of women workers, the WMC abruptly plunged into an unproductive round of female recruitment drives at the end of 1942, nowhere more fruitlessly than in Detroit.

The genesis of the drive was Detroit's surprisingly poor performance in the early months of the war. Conversion was taking longer than had been predicted, and munitions output lagged in many areas. A serious labor shortage also contributed to the problem. By mid-year, local industrialists had grown fearful that Detroit might lose additional contracts and that the War Manpower Commission might step in to take control of hiring practices. Business and union representatives met with government officials at the Detroit office of the War Production Board on June 26 to discuss the manpower crisis. Frederick Harbison, economist and consultant to the WPB's Labor Supply Branch, put the matter bluntly to the assembled group: "If you start to meet some of your problems, you are going to be in the position to tell the Manpower Commission what Detroit is going to do . . . to meet its labor shortage, and you will not be in the position of having policies dictated to you by people who may know nothing about Detroit or the particular . . . problems that affect Detroit. . . ."

The solution both to the problem of contract removal and the threat of federal interference, Harbison suggested, lay in the employment by Detroit industry of upward of eighty thousand women, a figure that would have approximately doubled the number of women then employed in local manufacturing. The June 26 meeting approved a program for the recruitment of women into Detroit industry. Of the some two score persons who attended this conference largely concerned with female employment, only one person, Irene Murphy—the Wayne County Office of Civilian Defense's specialist on the day care of children—was a woman.

On August 10, mailmen delivered some 650,000 postcards to households in Wayne, Oakland, Macomb, and Washtenaw Counties; area women, whether interested in factory employment or not, had been asked to fill out and return the cards to the Detroit branch of the United States Employment Service (USES). The USES classified the applications according to availability, experience, and potential work capacity, and, as production demands warranted, the agency scheduled interviews with those women who had offered their services. An encouraging 265,009 cards were returned, but by January, 1943 only 2,290 women had been placed in jobs, and only 1,742 in factory posi-

tions. Manpower planners had failed to reckon with female resistance to industrial employment. Many women had not yet decided whether to work and others did not comprehend the seriousness of the labor supply problem. Employers, moreover, persisted in their customary reluctance to utilize the services of the USES.

During 1943 the WMC largely failed in its efforts to persuade Michigan women to take vital but low-paying civilian service jobs in stores and other businesses. Throughout the war, the Michigan state government refused to allow substantial changes in the regulations governing hours of employment and working conditions for female labor. No Michigan manufacturer could employ a woman for more than nine hours a day or for more than fifty-four hours a week, nor could a woman work in a variety of hazardous occupations, especially those that endangered her "capacity for motherhood." Thus women poured into the war plants as often as not in spite of, rather than because of, government policy.

Women worked for many reasons. Some responded to propaganda that stressed the link between their jobs and the lives of their men in combat. "Since I have found the place where I can serve my country best, I should feel as if there were blood on my hands—his blood—if there were no oil on my hands today," a begrimed woman worker proclaimed from a 1943 recruiting advertisement.

Women took jobs out of patriotism or as a way of escape from the tedium of separation from husband or fiancé. They sought to enlarge their economic opportunities, but in many instances, women worked simply to maintain a standard of living equivalent to or even lower than that to which they had become accustomed before the war. Service wives often experienced long delays in receiving government allotment checks or found that the monthly stipend did not stretch far enough. The Women's

U. S. ARMY
OFFICIAL POSTER

SOLDIERS *without guns*

To recruit women to the war effort, the government launched an intensive propaganda campaign that appealed to women's personal patriotism. On posters and billboards, on the radio, and in magazines and newspapers, women war workers were advised that their efforts would help shorten the war and save the lives of their soldier husbands, brothers, and sons.

Bureau estimated that more than 70 per cent of Detroit's married female workers contributed at least 50 per cent of their earnings toward the maintenance of a family group. The majority of the women worked to live.

Despite the declared manpower emergency, Michigan industry welcomed women with something less than enthusiasm. Manufacturers insisted that women simply were not the equal of men in factory work. Women did not understand machinery and were not trainable.

Employers complained of the added costs of adjusting equipment used by women and of providing such facilities as separate washrooms and the like.

Such negative attitudes, however, could not bar the new female workers from the shop floor, and once the women arrived, recalcitrant employers discovered that the necessary accommodations did not bring on bankruptcy and often promoted productivity. Observers noted that women's absentee rate was generally lower than that of men and that female motivation was generally higher. Briggs and Packard were among the many firms that hired women to act as counselors to the female workers. The counselor's mandate varied from plant to plant, but her duties usually included advising women of company policy and assisting them with personal or work-related problems. The UAW trained female stewards to take on similar responsibilities in several factories. Experience convinced management that women, after all, could learn quickly and well. Much was made of the ability of tiny feminine hands to deal with intricate components and of women's presumed aptitude for dull, repetitive tasks. "There isn't a thing women can't do here when we divide a job into small parts," said a superintendent at Cadillac. Such an assessment, of course, applied to many a raw male recruit as well, and not infrequently the praise bestowed by management on women workers carried a condescending undertone implying that women would never match men in industrial competition.

Employers made no secret of their unwillingness to hire black women, whom management often regarded as so many refugees from *Porgy and Bess* or Harlem's Cotton Club. The first major breakthrough in black female hiring in Detroit did not come until the end of 1942, when, after a vigorous campaign by black protest organizations, token numbers of black women began work at Willow Run, Kelsey-Hayes, and Murray Body. The total black female labor force in the four-county Detroit Metropolitan area rose from 20,170 in 1940 to 50,215 in 1944, a rise of 150 per cent and a rate of increase triple that of white female workers. Thousands of black domestics abandoned their positions as household servants for more lucrative factory work. Black women eventually constituted between 35 and 75 per cent of the workforce in certain small Detroit plants. Black females, however, remained concentrated in such low-wage positions as janitors, sweepers, and material handlers. And employer discrimination continued: in early 1944 a Detroit firm hired black females in order to demonstrate their incompetence as industrial employees, only to discover that the new workers were equal to their tasks.

Women workers of all races faced a variety of discriminatory practices. Industry upgraded and promoted women much more slowly than men. Separate seniority lists often confined a woman's upward occupational mobility within a single all-female department. It was the wage issue, however, that caused the most controversy. Manufacturers customarily placed women in the lowest-paying jobs and paid them less for the performance of work traditionally done by men. Michigan state law guaranteed women equal pay for "similar" work, but the statute was so vague that it was virtually unenforceable. "In the plant I come from, we have thousands of women who in the past have been working in jobs that are practically identical with men's work, and yet because there was the word 'similar' in there, we have never been able to break this thing down," complained Irene Young, a worker from the General Motors (GM) Ternstedt plant in Detroit, in 1942. In late September of that year, the War Labor Board (WLB) ruled against GM in an equal-pay case brought by the UAW and the United Electrical Workers, and WLB General Order 16, issued in November, permitted companies to equalize male and female pay on a voluntary basis without reference to Washington.

The voluntary clauses of the WLB's order, together with qualifications later placed on the original GM decision, vitiated the Board's original initiative. Organized labor failed to mount a sustained campaign on the equal-pay issue. Employers proved adept in maintaining the sexual pay differential by such means as giving different titles to similar jobs or by changing job classifications from skilled to semi-skilled. The Michigan Regional WLB issued a murky directive in August 1944 forbidding employers to pay lower rates to women because of slight changes in job content, but the same ruling stated that women were not entitled to equal pay *per se,* especially when costs were increased in order to hire them. Despite government laxity, union indifference, and employer evasion, women's average weekly wages in Michigan rose $14.40 between October 1942 and August 1944, while male wages increased only an average of $9.90 per week. By August 1944 women in the state's engine turbine industry earned 94.3 per cent as much as men, and females in the automobile industry had closed to within 89 per cent of the male wage average. But the weekly wage gap at that time favored males by $15.22, or more than seven hundred dollars a year.

Male workers and union leaders did not go out of their way to welcome women employees. Men vociferously protested and sometimes went on strike against policies favorable to women, such as the movement of women to better shifts that they were not entitled to by strict seniority. Speaking before a New York City meeting of female unionists in October 1943, UAW president R. J. Thomas scored women for an alleged inability to think through problems; for their "ingratitude" in refusing to support unions, which were responsible for their high wages; and for their dependence on men for leadership.

Many women, however, undoubtedly agreed with May McKernan, a delegate to the 1942 UAW convention from a Detroit Plymouth local, who told her fellow unionists: "I should [not] like for the brothers to forget that when the subject of women comes up, they shouldn't say, 'Well, that's the woman's problem.' We are getting tired of men saying 'Well that's the woman's problem.'" In his 1943 scolding of women, Thomas had described the equal-pay issue as "a woman's problem," forgetting that much hung on the issue: the pay of thousands of returning veterans who might be forced to accept a "woman's wage" in order to reclaim jobs temporarily held by women; and the ability of the UAW to convince its members that it could win critical tests against management.

Belatedly, the UAW took steps to bring itself into closer touch with its estimated 250,000 dues-paying female workers. In early 1944 the union established a Women's Bureau within its War Policy Division to offer counseling and other forms of aid. Mildred Jeffrey, an experienced organizer in the clothing industry serving at the time on the staff of the War Production Board (WPB) in Washington, was chosen to head the new department. Under the Bureau's auspices, a group of women delegates held the UAW's first Women's Conference on December 8-9, 1944 in Detroit. The conferees voted against special seniority rights for women, followed the CIO line by denouncing the Equal Rights Amendment then pending in Congress, and prodded the UAW International Executive Board to take more vigorous action on the equal-pay issue. The establishment of the Women's Bureau and the calling of the Women's Conference indicated a willingness on the part of Michigan's largest union to assist its female workers; the extent to which they were accepted, however, is indicated by the fact that R.J. Thomas began his 1944 annual report to a union one-fifth female in membership with the customary salutation, "Dear Sirs and Brothers."

The woman worker may not have been the beloved of labor and management, but she was the undoubted darling of the press and public. According to a typically gushing newspaper report of mid-1943, every Rosie who riveted at Detroit's N.A. Woodworth Company looked "like a cross between a campus queen and a Hollywood starlet." The press closely scrutinized "the girls," their parties, and their late-night meetings with male coworkers at local bars. Such glamorization may have served a useful purpose insofar as it attracted women to war work by assuring them that they would not lose their "feminine" qualities in so doing. But some of the publicity, with its constant emphasis on beauty and its sexual innuendo, deprecated the woman worker as a person.

Much of the excitement surrounding women workers was created by their special wearing apparel. For safety, industry forbade most female production workers to wear jewelry, nail polish, make-up, dresses, or Veronica Lake hair styles. Snoods, low-heeled shoes, and slacks were "in." In the early 1940s, however, slacks were still garments to be worn only by a Marlene Dietrich or by the most chic of society trendsetters. In 1941 the *Detroit News*'s fashion writer had cautiously suggested to her readers: "If you have a truly adventurous spirit, you might pioneer in introducing slacks on city streets. Try wearing them around your neighborhood. . . . Report to us how the neighbors take to the idea."

On the right figure, a pair of slacks could cause a sensation; supervision at the Ford Highland Park plant docked a young woman a half-hour's pay for wearing a pair of red slacks. The article of clothing in question, management claimed, created safety and production hazards because of the potential for distraction of male workers. The case ultimately reached Harry Shulman, the umpire of grievances under the Ford-UAW contract, who decided in favor of the woman in June 1944. Noting the absence of a company rule against vividly colored garments, Shulman opined, "It is common knowledge that wolves, unlike bulls, may be attracted by colors other than red and by various other enticements in the art and fit to female attire."

Management often feared that the introduction of women workers would set off a sexual explosion. General Motors adopted a strict policy of firing any male supervisor and female employee who were discovered to be "fraternizing." The company justified its position on the grounds that improper sexual conduct by either party could impair labor-management relations and might expose the policy of hiring women to unfair criticism. In a 1944 decision, the GM contract arbitrator upheld the dismissal of two women and two foremen from the Flint AC plant who had been seen together in after-hours spots. Unions sometimes proved as puritanical as management on the subject of sex; Flint UAW Local 599 voted in April 1943 to instruct committeemen to ignore grievances brought by any woman "indecent in her wearing apparel or actions." The minutes of the meeting offer no clue as to how the female members of the local divided on the issue. Here and there, a woman gained a nickel an hour more with a sultry glance, and a foreman conditioned the promotion of a woman on sexual considerations, but despite rumors of illicit affairs and illegitimate pregnancies, moral standards in war industry remained remarkably impervious to propinquity.

The working woman of World War II was concerned with far more than the decency of her dress. An employee in plant or office, she was, in many instances, also the manager of a household. She shared with other citizens the discomforts of crowded housing and transportation, but manpower and supply shortages particularly frustrated her efforts to maintain a home. Too often, she found empty shelves or locked doors at neighborhood groceries. A WPB study of August 1943 estimated that 75 per cent of female absenteeism in one plant could be attributed to inadequate laundry service. The Detroit WPB office announced in February 1943 the appointment of local socialite and President-in-law Dorothy Kemp Roosevelt as special coordinator for both female recruitment and for women's out-of-plant problems; little, however, was ever heard from her. In seeking to solve war-related community problems, the federal government rarely distinguished between matters of concern to the entire community and those that impinged especially upon women. This attitude was described by Mary Anderson, one of the wartime directors of the Women's

Bureau, who noted "a great tendency among governmental officials to speak about 'the people' as a whole, but when they spoke of the 'people,' they meant the men."

The sudden entrance of thousands of women into industrial life raised many issues, and none carried more far-reaching social implications than the question of whether mothers should work, and the subsidiary problem of care for their children. Some mothers had always worked outside the home, but *Detroit News* women's adviser Nancy Brown stated the prevalent opinion about the practice in a 1940 reply to a woman undecided about seeking a job: "Your children are still of school age. In spite of your assertion to the contrary, they do need you. It would not be possible for you to carry on two jobs, one outside your home and one inside."

Throughout the war, government agencies, social workers, educators, and politicians echoed this statement in varying words. Mothers who worked, it was maintained, might do enormous psychic harm to their young children and irreparable damage to the family, the primary social unit. The WMC released its first official statement on the working-mother question during the spring of 1942: "The first responsibility of women with young children in war, as in peace, is to give suitable care in their own homes to their children."

Even when the state reached the height of its manpower demand in November 1943, Governor Harry Kelly observed: "I have yet to find any emergency that should call mothers away from home to the detriment of our youth. For the good of the Michigan of tomorrow, I ask mothers of young children to pause and consider before they seek outside employment. . . . Consider your children."

Among the arguments mustered on behalf of working mothers was the contention that their employment in war industry might reduce migration into congested areas (there is no evidence, however, that such a relationship actually developed). The economic imperative certainly weighed heavily upon the woman who had to support her family while her husband was in the service. Even the 1942 WMC directive cited above insisted that no bar to employment be placed in the way of mothers with young children and that "the decision as to gainful employment should, in all cases, be an individual decision made by the woman herself. . . ." When certain Michigan factories attempted to exclude younger mothers, management invariably discovered that many women lied about their family status rather than lose the chance for work. Since women workers were being recruited and since an increasingly large number of mothers intended to work in spite of pleas to the contrary, something had to be done about their children, from whom they would be separated for a large part of each working day.

A few isolated schools and centers had pioneered the concept of day care. Detroit's Merrill-Palmer School, founded in 1920 to instruct young women in home management and child development techniques, opened the state's first nursery school in 1922. During the depression the Federal Emergency Relief Administration and the Works Progress Administration (WPA) introduced day care on a nationwide basis by opening centers for the children of mothers receiving government assistance. The WPA centers were closed to regularly employed women.

With the onset of the defense boom in the spring of 1941, officials in the Michigan Department of Social Welfare (DSW) grew anxious about the "haphazard and undesirable day nurseries" that were springing up. State welfare officials began to plan for the establishment of a committee to coordinate day care service in hard-hit Wayne County. Such a committee began work in Detroit in January 1942, its leadership and expertise supplied in large part by Irene Murphy, a social worker and lecturer at Wayne University, and Dr. Edna Noble White, for twenty years director of Merrill-Palmer.

Thirty-seven communities across the state eventually organized more or less active counterparts of the Wayne County body. There was a need for a complementary state organization and in November 1942 the Michigan government asked Dr. White to chair a State Day Care Committee (SDCC) under the sponsorship of the MCD.

Although Michigan took the initiative in setting up an administrative structure for day care, no network of nursery centers could be organized without federal assistance. Various government agencies, including the United States Children's Bureau (USCB) and the Federal Works Agency (FWA), examined the day care question throughout 1941, and in February, 1942 the FWA received permission to use Lanham Act funds for the construction and maintenance of child care centers for children of working mothers. Enacted in 1940, the Lanham Act authorized federal aid to defense-impacted communities. The first such project, however, did not win final certification until August 31, 1942. The FWA could pay all expenses for nursery projects under certain circumstances, but it generally adhered to the standard Lanham funding formula that required localities to contribute half of all costs. Washington eventually spent nearly fifty-three million dollars for hundreds of day care centers, established primarily in major production areas. Shortly after Pearl Harbor, the WPA opened its centers to children of working mothers and to youngsters with a parent in the armed forces, and this expanded program continued until the agency's demise in mid-1943.

The Detroit, Highland Park, and Hamtramck boards of education agreed to supervise separate federally sponsored nursery programs, and the necessary documents were sent to Washington for approval in October 1942. The FWA assented to the plans in March 1943, agreeing further to take over the twenty-three Wayne County WPA centers, which were due to close within a matter of weeks. By the end of January 1945 twenty-eight Michigan communities, most of them in the four-county Detroit area, were sponsoring 179 child care centers at an estimated cost for the first six months of the year of $1,694,828, 60 per cent of which was provided by the FWA.

The most popular type of facility was the day nursery for two- to five-year-old children. Practices varied from area to area, but most centers operated continuously for twelve hours, from six-thirty or seven o'clock in the morning onward. They served three meals a day, offered organized recreation directed by nursery teachers and volunteers, and provided cots or beds for afternoon naps. Extended school services allowed mothers to leave children six to fourteen years of age for care immediately before and after school. These centers or "canteens" usually were located within the school building itself. A center for night care proved unsuccessful in Detroit; but similar centers apparently worked well in Ypsilanti and Saginaw. Several communities sought to obtain care for infants by encouraging nonworking women to become foster mothers, taking perhaps three or four infants into their homes for more individualized attention. In addition to sponsoring such programs, four Michigan cities ran counseling services to guide mothers to the best available child care, and the Wayne County committee organized an elaborate information clearing house, the Children's War Service (CWS), in April 1943.

Day care advocates supported their demands with a flood of statistics suggestive of a great unmet need. The Wayne County committee estimated in early 1943 that local war plants and civilian industry employed some sixty thousand mothers, who had forty-five thousand children potentially in need of care. On the basis of this and other surveys, the Michigan WMC devised a formula that calculated that one child required day care for every seven women employed in Michigan industry (the ratio was projected to be 1:5 for women entering manufacturing for the first time). The friends of day care also noted many pathetic instances of individual deprivation. Thousands of children roamed the streets of industrial communities unable to enter homes locked for the day by their war-worker parents. More fortunate youngsters carried the house key on a string fastened around the neck.

A need clearly existed, yet day care centers were strikingly underutilized both in Michigan and across the country. Nationally, Lanham Act programs served a mere hundred thousand children, perhaps a tenth of those eligible, and far fewer than the total of youngsters served by Great Britain's more elaborate system of child care. To be sure, the number of day care children in Michigan steadily increased, reaching 6,024 in early 1945 (4,501 in metropolitan Detroit), while the number of employed women steadily declined. But the same surveys that seemed to affirm the necessity for day care consistently reported that no more than 5 to 10 per cent of the presumably needy youngsters were actually enrolled in nursery school programs.

An analysis of the Michigan day care failure casts light on the underlying forces on society that actively or unwittingly placed limits on wartime change. Bureaucratic in-fighting and political opposition at the national level hobbled the day care program from the outset. The Children's Bureau, the Office of Education, and Federal Security Administration (FSA) waged guerrilla war against the FWA for control of day care policy and funds. On the one hand, the FSA and its allies favored a state-controlled program that placed emphasis on foster homes and a high quality of care; the FWA, on the other hand, looked upon a federally controlled system of rapidly constructed group centers as the best answer to the problem of child care in a temporary crisis. The struggle came to a climax when the contending parties clashed over a day-care bill introduced in Congress earlier that year by Senator Elbert Thomas of Utah. The Thomas bill gave the Children's Bureau final jurisdiction over day care and revamped

the entire program to suit foster-care proponents. Passed by the Senate, the measure died in a House committee. Neither the Lanham Act nor its supplementary titles mentioned day care, and the entire nursery program was generally unpopular on Capitol Hill. President Roosevelt finally arranged a cease-fire in August, 1943 that left the FWA's authority intact.

Bickering and buckpassing concerning Michigan day care rivalled the fighting in Washington. In several communities, the local Council of Social Agencies, which favored day care, fought with the county MCD committee, which did not. During a special session in 1944 the state legislature defeated a program sponsored by the State Day Care Committee to establish counseling centers and to provide state-funded child care services in war-impacted areas wherever local initiative failed to do so. State lawmakers enacted bills authorizing boards of education to set up nursery facilities and bringing private day care centers under state licensing authority, but these statutes did not represent a fundamental state commitment to day care. Charged with the major responsibility for the financing and operation of day care centers, local school boards, usually strapped for cash, objected to paying for a program so costly and so socially questionable.

Administrative and legal problems also dogged day care in Michigan. A federal regulation prohibited school districts from asking for Lanham Act funds until schoolbuildings reached 200 per cent of capacity, by which time most such schools no longer had room for a day care center. Once a locality applied for government assistance, it had to surmount seven separate state and federal reviews before approval was granted. A 1943 study of Detroit day care needs revealed that many of the centers were poorly located (it was not unusual for waiting lists to lengthen at one nursery while other centers remained half-empty), improperly staffed, and inadequately administered. A cumbersome Detroit licensing ordinance made it all but impossible for individual women to offer foster care in their homes. Illegal foster homes inevitably appeared, and the press reported that a three-month old baby had suffocated at one such home in Detroit and that children had been beaten in others.

The statistics of need the day care defenders cited were subject to wild fluctuations: the Census Bureau's sample survey of the Detroit-Willow Run area in 1944 counted only half as many children eligible for day care as previous compilations had indicated, and the state WMC thereafter revised its ratio of needy children to employed mothers upward to one in nine. Reflecting on the vicissitudes that beset the state's child-care effort, the supervisor of the DSW's Children's Division, Gunnar Dybwad, concluded in a November 1945 letter that "Michigan has no reason to be particularly proud of its day care program."

Michigan industry did little to accommodate the working mother. As the great Detroit female recruitment drive began in the fall of 1942, local manufacturers stated that they had no plans to provide day care facilities. A UAW woman told the Senate Education and Labor Committee considering the Thomas bill in June 1943 that many mothers had been forced to quit war jobs for lack of adequate nursery centers. It was not until September 1943 that the Automotive Council for War Production began to circulate information throughout Detroit war plants publicizing available facilities. Hudson established a center for the children of mothers employed in all three of its Detroit plants, but nowhere in Michigan were there day care services equal to the highly publicized programs in the West Coast shipbuilding industry. Although Michigan organized labor generally supported day care and Irene Murphy credited UAW as the driving force behind her Wayne County committee, the unions apparently allowed their female members to carry on alone the battle for expanded child care services, the struggle being seen as only another "woman's problem." Neither labor nor management seemed eager to take the steps, admittedly complex, required to assign working mothers with young children to convenient shifts.

Day care centers constituted what might have been, in Eleanor Straub's words, "the most significant social experiment of the war years." Child welfare specialists learned through their wartime experience much about the aims and realities of day care. A sufficient number of Detroit mothers became interested in the service to support a small program into the late 1940s, and the DSW reappointed a state day care consultant in 1947, the post having been vacant since the legislatures's rebuff of the SDCC's statewide nursery plan three years earlier. Limited, well-run nursery schools gained a measure of acceptance among the postwar middle class, but the concept of large-scale day care for the children of working mothers never caught on. Nothing happened during World War II to warrant abandonment of the belief that the mother—and the mother alone—bore the principal responsibility for the upbringing of her children.

The failure of working mothers to make sufficient use of nursery facilities eventually relegated the question of day care to a position of secondary importance. A problem of greater import, and one that could not be swept aside, was the postwar status of working women. Even as Detroit manpower officials readied postcards for distribution to area women in the opening phase of the August 1942 recruitment drive, the author of a letter to the *Detroit News* mused: "We have quite a number of intelligent men devising ways and means of getting women in on all the factory and war jobs so we boys can go knock off a Jap and a Heinie, but I really want to meet the chap who is intelligent enough to get them out again when we boys come back."

The army of newly employed women added greater uncertainty to already uncertain postwar economic calculations, as evidence accumulated to document female intentions of remaining at work. The Woman's Bureau reported in May 1945 that 75 per cent of all Detroit working women desired some form of postwar employment. The percentage rose to 80 per cent among women employed before Pearl Harbor and fell to no less than 60 per cent among former housewives.

Such surveys, of course, indicated only what women wished to do, not what they would do after V-J Day. Many female workers probably wanted to remain in their high-paying industrial jobs but did not really expect to do so. A large number of women declared against future employment if their husbands could support them or if men were in need of work. A national consensus, moreover, developed rapidly and strongly in support of the contention that women should not remain at work in their wartime numbers once peace returned. Opinion polls found solid majorities opposed to female employment that jeopardized jobs for men. The Federal government took pains to emphasize the temporary nature of war work and did nothing to encourage women in their aspirations for peacetime jobs. A spate of books and articles appeared, increasing in volume as victory neared, picturing a happy future for women in wedded bliss and in homes chock-a-block with long-unavailable consumer goods.

Betty Allie, chairwoman of the Michigan Unemployment Compensation Commission, spoke for the majority when she said in November 1943: "When the period of postwar adjustments comes, and their men come home, . . . you will see women returning naturally to their homes. A woman's first interests are her home, her husband, and their children. . . ." Women without family ties or who lost husbands during the war were entitled to employment, Allie continued, "but there need

be no fear that all (women) will compete for the postwar job. They will look on this period in their lives as an interlude. . . . Women will always be women."

When production cutbacks accelerated during the spring and summer of 1945, women were severed from employment at a rate approximately double that of men. Women composed one of the largest elements in the low-seniority pool ordinarily laid off first, but management had other ways of ridding itself of unwanted females. A government survey of conditions in Michigan as of September noted that some employers were shuffling work assignments to give women the sort of heavy-lifting jobs that they were either legally barred from performing or that they might not want. One GM plant in Flint violated seniority altogether to put all women on the midnight shift. The majority of women who worked prior to the war could return to being waitresses, shop clerks, or maids, but they could not remain in industry.

Those women who turned for help to their unions found little comfort. The UAW was preoccupied with assimilating the returning veterans and with its forthcoming confrontation with General Motors. Walter Reuther warned the Women's Conference in 1944 that women could expect no "special privilege" to enable them to hold on to their jobs; rather, they must fight for a full employment economy. By November 1945 Michigan's nonfarm female workforce stood at 525,000, a quarter of a million less than the wartime peak, but still higher both proportionally and absolutely than in 1940. Female manufacturing employment in Detroit, however, fell from 124,000 in March 1945 to sixty-six thousand by year's end, one-quarter of the wartime high and a mere twenty thousand more than in 1940. Only a handful of women workers protested the treatment accorded them.

When America entered the war, leaders of some of the prominent women's organizations expressed cautious optimism that the nation would respond to the female contribution to victory with the grant of equality. As V-J Day dawned, however, it was difficult to determine the actual extent of change. The volume of female employment had risen, but women's status had not. The government, so generous in its praise of female America, still evinced no willingness to grant women an effective voice in political or economic decision-making. Neither business, labor, nor any other organized segment of society supported a significant change in women's role based on wartime accomplishments. There had been no revolution in attitudes, only a series of expedient measures, often implemented grudgingly in the face of national emergency. The genteel club leaders and lady college presidents who functioned as spokeswomen for their sex submitted, with more or less grace, to male notions of women's place.

Women of other nations made no more progress toward equality during the war than did their American sisters. British women had received the vote in partial reward for their contributions during World War I but secured no comparable concession after 1945. Since Nazi ideology enshrined women as childbearers, Hitler vetoed plans put forth in 1942 for the increased employment of German-born women in munitions plants, preferring slave labor. Thomas R. H. Havens found that the status of Japanese women rose little between 1937 and 1945. Despite enormous strains placed on the Japanese economy by mobilization and American aerial assault, the tradition-bound military regime opposed the utilization of large numbers of women in war industry. "It is moot," Havens concludes, "whether total war more greatly ossifies or transforms a people in response to national crisis."

This observation was no less true of the United States than of its enemies, especially in light of the objectives for which America fought. Save for the Four Freedoms address and the Atlantic Charter, both of which predated Pearl Harbor, President Roosevelt shied away from the high-flown patriotic rhetoric that marked World War I. At one point, he recorded his wish that the new global conflict be known simply as "the Survival War." What Roosevelt and the American people wished to see survive was the existing social and political order. The depression of the 1930s had caused millions to question the justice of that order. The New Deal had tinkered with the problem of economic collapse for years without satisfactory solution. Dictators abroad and doubters at home sneered at American institutions and saw the nation sliding toward social catastrophe.

The war offered Americans the chance to vindicate their system. Michigan's governor, Murray D. Van Wagoner, expressed a belief held by many when he told his fellow state chief executives in August 1942:

> When Hitler sneered at democracy, and when we ourselves began to wonder if perhaps we were incapable of uniting to do the job that had to be done, the war gave us the chance to prove to ourselves that America still has the best economic and political system on earth, a system that creates, that offers hope for a better and more prosperous world tomorrow, . . . a system that we can all believe in and work for, and fight and die for.

Americans wanted affirmation, not change. The pride of the nation before 1929 had been its industrial machine, exemplified best by the automotive factories of Detroit and Michigan. To that machine, and not to a transforming doctrine, the nation turned in 1941 for the key to victory. Among the most hallowed of American institutions to be protected and affirmed was the traditional concept of womanhood. It was during World War II that the apotheosis of the unliberated woman, Miss America, rose to national prominence and respect. At times it appeared that every nubile young woman was competing for a place in the pinup parade.

Most women failed to grasp whatever opportunity for emancipation the war afforded. As Straub observes, they "saw it as a matter of production and military strategy rather than a contest of values and ideals." Women perceived World War II very much as men did, and by and large, expected no more than a better life for themselves and their families in a nation renewed and once more confident.

Questions for Study and Review

1. The Great Depression and World War II were periods of massive upheaval. What were the differences in their effects on relations within the family and between families and the state?

2. To what extent did heavy industries undergo permanent changes as they sought to recruit and accommodate women for war work?

3. Both Britain and Germany developed government-sponsored day care programs that were far more comprehensive than those in the United States. Why was this so, and what were the consequences?

4. Compare the politicization and mobilization of women during World War II with that of women during the American Revolution and the Civil War. To what extent did each war transform women's roles over the long term?

Suggested Readings

Ruth Milkman, *Gender at Work: The Dynamics of Job Segregation by Sex during World War II* (1987).

D'Ann Campbell, *Women at War with America: Private Lives in a Patriotic Era* (1884)

Sherna Berger Gluck, *Rosie the Riveter Revisited: Women, the War, and Social Change* (1987)

Karen Anderson, "Last Hired, First Fired: Black Women Workers during World War II," *Journal of American History* (June 1982).

Valerie Matsumoto, "Japanese American Women during World War II," *Frontiers* (#1, 1984).

Maureen Honey, "The Working-Class Woman and Recruitment Propaganda during World War II," *Signs* (Summer 1983).

PART SIX

Postwar
Society

In many ways, World War II was "a milestone for women in America." However, in the years immediately following war's end, the obstacles of discrimination, sex-segregation, the double day, and the "feminine mystique" reappeared to narrow the paths women might pursue. The relative peace and prosperity of the 1950s translated into domestic affluence for many, allowing families to fulfill their desires for more children, larger homes, "labor-saving" appliances, and new cars. Of course, beyond the scenes of suburban bliss existed a far more complex reality where middle-class mothers struggled to give substance to their dreams and minority and working-class women struggled to gain security for their families. In the following decades, moreover, the contradictions of the baby-boom era inspired daughters of the 1950s to join political crusades in an attempt to recast class, race, and sex roles and relations.

Ironically, the decade of the 1950s, when the mass media began documenting cultural trends and political developments in fine detail, continues to elude historical understanding. The images that remain dominant, revived by nostalgia buffs just as they were being revised by scholars—rock 'n roll, Elvis Presley, happy homemakers, auto-bound vacationers, television "sitcoms," Ozzie and Harriet, Ike and Mamie—still often overwhelm more poignant and critical reflections on the decade. Battle-scarred Korean landscapes, the Army-McCarthy hearings, Richard Nixon's Checkers' speech, the Montgomery bus boycott, racial turmoil in Little Rock, Arkansas, the melancholy television drama *Marty,* the angry "Beat" writers, and rising cold war tensions in Southeast Asia, the Middle East, and the Caribbean were also realities in this supposedly bland decade. It is perhaps the jarring effect of juxtaposing these two series of images that best captures the dilemmas and contradictions of the period.

The concern with image and reality is especially crucial to an analysis of female experience in the 1950s. More than for men, a single version of postwar reality for women remains fixed in our minds. The young, white,

During the postwar era mass media, particularly television, played a predominant role as purveyor and reinforcer of cultural attitudes. Television situation comedies, even slightly offbeat programs like *The Honeymooners,* emphasized woman's proper place in the home and her proper role as helpmate to her spouse.

middle-class mother, coffee-klatching with her suburban neighbors and laughing, self-deprecatingly, at the foibles of Harriet, Ozzie's wife, is the popularly accepted depiction of fifties womanhood. Perhaps the portrait is harder to dispel because large numbers of women did live out parts of this scenario. Nonetheless, overall during the decade, more women and more married women with children went to work than ever before. Most minority and working-class women remained crowded into deteriorating inner city neighborhoods. Rural women, too, struggled to sustain the promises of wartime prosperity while the prices and the prestige of the family farm fell.

Despite the accent on domesticity, women of all classes and races also expanded their public organizational efforts. The Women's Peace Party, the Women's Joint Congressional Committee, the Women's International League for Peace and Freedom, and similar organizations protested the arms race and challenged cold war policies. The National Woman's Party kept alive the struggle for an Equal Rights Amendment in the face of opposition from a host of other women's organizations, such as the League of Women Voters and the National Council of Catholic Women. Local women's groups campaigned on behalf of issues as varied as national defense, civil rights, and the environment. Individual women—such as Ethel Rosenberg, Rosa Parks, and Betty Freidan—proclaimed their personal visions of the new society and in doing so became important symbols of their age.

The meshing of mass media with cultural symbolism complicates our perceptions of the period. Did the media create or reflect popular opinion? Did it select or merely project newsworthy events? When television cameras zoomed in on the hearings of the House Un-American Activities Committee (HUAC), were viewers impressed or horrified? Did Ruth Crane's show featuring "The Equal Rights Review," a pageant enacted by members of the National Women's Party, affect popular perceptions of the Equal Rights Amendment? Did viewers identify with, seek to emulate, or perceive as fantasy the images conveyed in *Father Knows Best, I Love Lucy, Our Miss Brooks,* and *The Honeymooners?* James West Davidson and Mark Hamilton Lytle explore these issues, arguing that the roles of women and men in situation comedies and the relationship between mass media and the audience were in flux throughout the fifties, as were the roles and relations of women and men in society at large.

Out of this turgid decade emerged the mass movements of the 1960s and 1970s. In the case of civil rights, demands for change were first voiced in the midst of postwar adjustments. *Brown* v. *the Board of Education* (1954), the Montgomery bus boycott (1955), and the desegregation of Little Rock's Central High (1957) are only the most well-documented of the challenges to continued racism. In each of these episodes, female figures—Linda Brown; Rosa Parks and Jo Ann Gibson Robinson; Carlotta Walls, Thelma Mothershed, Melba Pattillo, Gloria Ray, Minnijean Brown, and Elizabeth Eckford— were in the front lines and on the front pages of national periodicals. They were not alone. Rather, they symbolized, with their dual burden of race and gender, the despair, anger, and hope of ordinary African-Americans of both sexes. David Garrow captures women's central roles in one of these events, the Montgomery bus boycott, and thereby suggests their significance in the civil rights movement as a whole.

The struggle for black equality sparked a range of social movements in the 1960s, but perhaps none drew more heavily on its ideas, tactics, and rhetoric than women's liberation. Two white women—Casey Hayden and Mary King— involved in the 1964 Freedom Summer in Mississippi carried the message of liberation, modified to encompass women's grievances, into the antiwar movement. That movement and its New Left leaders provided women with another source of political ideas and practical experience. Women in the antiwar movement were attracted by the ideal of participatory democracy. Yet the male leaders of Students for a Democratic Society (SDS) who so eloquently articulated the concept still assumed that sexual hierarchy would prevail within their own organization. When a small group of women challenged sexism in SDS, they were confronted with boos, jeers, and profanity.

Inspired in a variety of ways by experiences in the civil rights and antiwar movements, a generation of young women formulated their own critique of the social and sexual order, one in which seemingly personal problems were recognized as political issues. The enthusiasm of these radical feminists converged, and at times conflicted, with proposals offered by older, more affluent women who combined frustration over the "feminine mystique" with political and professional savvy in organizational matters. With Betty Freidan's *Feminine Mystique* as their "bible" and President Kennedy's Commission on Women as their model, more moderate feminists forged an agenda and an association to implement it—the National Organization for Women, or NOW.

Both NOW and its radical counterparts in local communities—rape crisis centers, spouse abuse shelters, women's health clinics, and similar organizations—were rooted in and reinforced the dramatic social, economic, and political transformations of the decades from 1960 to the present. Massive expansions in service sector occupations, a huge influx of women into the labor force (resulting in almost as high a proportion of white as black women working for wages), the establishment of new types of workers' organizations, increased numbers of college-educated and professionally trained women, a heightened awareness and perhaps incidence of rape, spouse abuse, and incest, the promise of control over reproduction through contraception and abortion, declining marriage and birth rates, increasing numbers of women and men living alone and women and children living in poverty, and the fears produced by such sweeping changes placed women's issues at the center of contemporary political debate.

Divided as always by class, race, region, ethnicity, and age, and increasingly by religion, ideology, and sexual preference, women disagreed over both the definition of and the solution to the problems caused by postwar transitions in values, life-styles, and opportunities. Jane Mansbridge traces the debates among women in Illinois over one of the most controversial issues of the period, the Equal Rights Amendment (ERA). Her close examination of the divisions among its supporters and between supporters and opponents reveals the social and cultural cleavages that continue to divide American women and men. The defeat of the ERA did not eliminate a source of contention. Rather, the defeat simply intensified debate over other issues, such as sexual harassment, comparable worth, subsidized daycare, and abortion. By the 1980s, the feminist slogan "the personal is political" had been taken up by the New Right as well. Now, both sides sought to translate their cultural experiences and political preferences into socially sanctioned and even state-regulated practice.

The postwar world is the society in which we live. It is, as one historian has written, an "unfinished journey." It is a journey in which blacks and whites, immigrants and native-born, working-class and wealthy, women and men still vie for control over the paths to follow and the speed with which those paths will be covered.

Suggested Readings

William Chafe, *The American Woman: Her Changing Social, Economic, and Political Role, 1920–1970* (1972).

Anne Moody, *Coming of Age in Mississippi: An Autobiography* (1968).

Rosalind Pollack Petchesky, *Abortion and Women's Choice: The State, Sexuality and Reproductive Freedom* (1984).

Louise Kapp Howe, *Pink Collar Workers: Inside the World of Women's Work* (1977).

Karen Brodkin Sacks, *Caring by the Hour: Women, Work, and Organizing at Duke Medical Center* (1988).

THIRTEEN

From Rosie to Lucy: The Mass Media and Changing Images of Women and Family

James West Davidson and Mark Hamilton Lytle

Compared to the depression and war that preceded it and the "Sixties" generation that followed, the decade of the 1950s seems tame. Prosperity and patriotism reigned supreme as Americans settled back into the traditional refuges of family and community. In the fifties, a resurgent "feminine mystique" spread deep into the middle class. It even began to affect working-class images of an ideal life as communities such as Levittown promised a suburban life-style to every hard-working family. Magazines, movies, advertising, and, perhaps most powerfully, television produced images of femininity for millions of postwar mothers to emulate.

Behind the tranquil image of suburban affluence and the Sylvania picture tubes that occupied center stage in suburban homes lurked another reality. Postwar labor unrest, renewed racial violence, McCarthyism, and inflation all threatened domestic equilibrium just as cold war tensions threatened the international balance of power. Civil rights activists, scholarly critics of consumerism and anti-Communist hysteria, and nonconformist "Beat" writers and musicians slowly brought a generation's unease to light.

Still, the light that glowed most brightly on American mass culture was that of the television set. From it emanated vivid images against which women and men, parents and children, could measure their own lives, their own families and communities. In trying to explain the developments that transformed Rosie the Riveter into the Happy Housewife, Davidson and Lytle analyze the ways that television shaped and was shaped by American ideals about sex roles and sexual relationships. Setting the popular images broadcast in situation comedies against the backdrop of economic and demographic change, the authors examine the portrayal of women and men in a variety of shows. Davidson and Lytle find that despite the many "sitcoms" in which the "feminine mystique" was reinforced—such as *The Adventures of Ozzie and Harriet* and *Father Knows Best*—some of the most popular series—*Our Miss Brooks, I Love Lucy,* and *The Honeymooners*—featured "unconventional characters and unusual plot situations."

Recognizing the difficulty of determining the relationship between media and reality, the authors nonetheless conclude that the popularity of shows in which nontraditional women or battles of the sexes were central to the series was rooted in part in the discontent among women that would blossom a generation later into feminism. The diverse representations of femininity and of family described here remind us just how complicated the decade of the 1950s was and how central conflict and controversy were to this era of supposed consensus.

It was 1957. Betty Friedan was not just complaining; she was angry—for herself and uncounted other women like her. For some time, she had sensed she was not alone. Now she was certain, as she read the results of a questionnaire she and about 200 graduates of Smith College had completed. The alumni office, no doubt, had been seeking responses designed to show how well a college education fitted Smith students for their roles in later life. But many of the women who answered, it seemed, were frustrated with their lives. They resented the wide disparity between the idealized image society held of them as housewives and mothers and the realities of their daily routines.

True, most were materially well off. The majority had families, a house in the suburbs, and the amenities of an affluent society. But amid that good fortune they felt fragmented, almost as if they had no identity of their own. And it was not only college graduates. "I've tried everything women are supposed to do," one woman confessed to Friedan; "hobbies, gardening, pickling, canning, being very social with my neighbors, joining committees, running PTA teas. I can do it all, and I like it, but it doesn't leave you anything to think about—any feeling of who you are. . . . I love the kids and Bob and my home. There's no problem you can even put a name to. But I'm desperate. I begin to feel I have no personality. I'm a server of food and putter-on of pants and a bedmaker, somebody who can be called on when you want something. But who am I?" A similar sense of incompleteness haunted Friedan. "I, like other women, thought there was something wrong with me because I didn't have an orgasm waxing the kitchen floor," she recalled with some bitterness.

A growing sense of doubt led to a period of questioning. Why, she wondered, had she chosen fifteen years earlier to give up a promising career in psychology for marriage and motherhood? What was it that kept women from using the rights and prerogatives that were theirs? What made them feel guilty for anything they did in their own right rather than as their husbands' wives or children's mothers? Women in the 1950s, it seemed to Friedan, were not behaving quite the way they had a decade earlier. During World War II the popular press extolled the virtues of women like "Rosie the Riveter"—those who left homes and families to join the work force. Now, Rosie was no longer a heroine. The media lavished their praise on women who devoted themselves to family and home. In the closing scene of one 1957 *Redbook* story, the heroine, "Junior" (a "little freckle-faced brunette" who had decided to give up her job), nurses her baby at two in the morning sighing, "I'm glad, glad, glad I'm just a housewife." What had happened? "When did women decide to give up the world and go back home?" Friedan asked herself.

That question might engage a historian in the 1980s, but it was not one housewives of the 1950s were encouraged to ask. For a red-blooded American to doubt something as sacred as the role of housewives and mothers was to show symptoms of mental distress rather than a skeptical or inquiring mind. Whatever the label attached to such feelings—neurosis, anxiety, or depression—most people assumed that women like Friedan needed an analyst, not a historian, to explain their discontent. The malaise was a problem with individuals, not with society. To cure themselves, they needed only to become better adjusted to who and what they were.

Friedan, however, was no ordinary housewife. Before starting her family, she had worked as a newspaper reporter; even after her chil-

By 1947 many women laborers were back in the home full time and the baby boom was underway. *Life* magazine celebrated the labors of a typical housewife by laying out a week's worth of bedmaking, ironing, washing, grocery shopping, and dishwashing for a family of four. An incomplete tally shows over 250 plates washed and 35 quarts of milk consumed.

dren came, she wrote regularly for the major women's magazines. By 1957 she was fed up with the endless stories about breast-feeding, the preparation of gourmet snails, and similar domestic fare that was the staple of *Redbook, McCall's* and *Ladies' Home Journal.* She had noticed, too, that many women like herself who worked outside the home, even part time, felt guilty because their jobs threatened their husbands' roles as providers or took time away from their children. Thus Friedan began to wonder not only about herself as a woman, a wife, and a mother but also about the role society had shaped women to play.

Having seen the results of the Smith questionnaire, Friedan's reportorial instincts took over. She sensed she was onto a story bigger than anything she had written. But when she circulated an article describing the plight so many women were experiencing, the male editors at the women's magazines turned it down flat. It couldn't be true, they insisted; women could not possibly feel as guilty or discontented as Friedan claimed. The problem must be hers. "Betty has gone off her rocker," an editor at *Redbook* told her agent. "She has always done a good job for us, but this time only the most neurotic housewife could identify."

Friedan was not deterred. If the magazines would not print her story, she would do it as a book. For five years, she researched and wrote, describing the "feminine mystique" that she saw American culture promoting.

The new mystique makes the housewife-mother, who never had a chance to be anything else, the model for all women . . . it simply makes certain concrete, finite, domestic aspects of feminine existence—as it was lived by women whose lives were confined by necessity to cooking, cleaning, washing, bearing children—into a religion, a pattern by which all women must now live or deny their femininity.

By the time Friedan was finished, the book had become a crusade. "I have never experienced anything as powerful, truly mystical, as the forces that seemed to overtake me as I wrote *The Feminine Mystique*," she later admitted. Published in 1963, the book soon joined the ranks of truly consequential books in American history. What Harriet Beecher Stowe did for slaves in *Uncle Tom's Cabin,* Jacob Riis for the urban poor in *How the Other Half Lives,* Upton Sinclair for public health in *The Jungle,* or Rachel Carson for the environment in *Silent Spring,* Friedan did for women. No longer would they bear their dissatisfaction in silence as they confronted the gap between their personal aspirations and the limited avenues society had left open to them. Friedan helped inspire a generation of middle-class women to demand the equal rights and opportunities men routinely claimed. Together with other activists, she founded the National Organization for Women (NOW) in 1965 to press for reforms on an institutional level, donating royalties from her book to support it. . . .

Many of the questions Friedan raised were the sort that historians are trained to explore. Why hadn't women followed up on the gains in employment they experienced during World War II? What caused society in postwar America to place so much emphasis on home and family? What was the image of women that the mass media, scholars, and other opinion makers presented? . . .

What is striking is that by 1945, despite all the gains women had made [during World War II], most attitudes about women and work had not changed substantially. Surveys showed that Americans, whether male or female, continued to believe that child rearing was a woman's primary job. Thus the marked demographic shift of women into the work force was revolutionary in import, but it brought no revolution in cultural attitudes toward sex roles. . . .

Despite the general expectation that women would return to the home after the war, female laborers did not simply drop their wrenches and pick up frying pans. Many continued to work outside the home, although mostly to support their families, not to find career alternatives. As peace came in 1945, polls indicated that over 75 percent of all working women wanted to continue at their jobs. About 88 percent of high school girls surveyed said they hoped for a career as well as the role of homemaker. Though employment for women did shrink slightly, a significantly higher percentage of women were working in 1950 than in 1940 (28 percent versus 24). Even more striking, that figure continued to rise, reaching 36 percent by 1960. Those numbers included older women, married women with children, and women of all social classes.

Such statistics would seem at first to undercut Friedan's notion that the vast majority of American women accepted the ideal of total fulfillment through housework and child rearing. Some 2.25 million women did voluntarily return home after the war and another million were laid off by 1946. At the same time, 2.75 million women entered the job market by 1947, leaving a net loss of only half a million.

But if Friedan was mistaken in seeing a mass female exodus from the work force, a significant shift did take place in the types of work performed. When women who had been laid off managed to return to work, they often lost their seniority and had to accept reduced pay in lower job categories. Employment in almost all the professions had decreased by 1960. Despite gains in some areas, women were concentrated in jobs that were primarily extensions of their traditional responsibility for managing the family's physical and emotional well-being: they were nurses, not doctors; teachers, not principals; tellers, not bankers. Far more worked in service jobs (as maids or waitresses, for example) than in manufacturing. Overwhelmingly, job opportunities were segregated by gender. About 75 percent of all women workers held female-only jobs. In fact, gender segregation in the workplace was worse in 1960 than in 1900—and even worse than segregation by race. Thus, even though women's participation in the work force remained comparatively high, it did not inspire a corresponding revolution in attitudes about women's roles in society. . . .

Attitudes, of course, were at the center of Friedan's concerns in *The Feminine Mystique;* and the demographic profile we have sketched underlines the reason for her focus. If the percentage of women holding jobs continued to increase during the 1950s and young women, when polled, said they hoped to combine work in some way with motherhood, how did the cult of the "feminine mystique" become so firmly enshrined? If wartime laboring conditions produced a kind of revolution in fact but not in spirit, what elements of American culture reined in that revolution and kept it from running its course?

As Friedan was well aware, economic and demographic factors played a crucial role in renewing the concern with home and family living. During the war, millions of American men fought overseas, which meant that, correspondingly, millions of wives at home could not have children. Even before the war, the hard times of the depression had discouraged couples from starting large families. But in 1945, when the home front saw the return of peace and prosperity and GIs were eager to do more than kiss their wives hello, the well-nigh inevitable pressures set off a postwar baby boom. For the next fifteen years the United States had one of the highest birthrates in the world, ris-

ing from an average of 1.9 to 2.3 children for each woman of childbearing age. Large families became the norm. The number of parents with three children tripled, while those with four quadrupled. Women also married younger. The average age of marriage dropped from 22 in 1900 to 20.3 in 1962. With the highest rate of marriage of any nation in the world, American men and women clearly chose to organize their lives around family.*

Clearly, material conditions not only pushed women out of the workplace as GIs rejoined the peacetime economy but also pulled women back into the home as the birthrate rose. Friedan acknowledged these changes but noted that the birthrates of other economically developed nations—such as France, Norway, and Sweden—had begun to decline by 1955. Even more striking, the sharpest rise in the United States came among women aged fifteen to nineteen. In Great Britain, Canada, and Germany, on the other hand, the rise was more equally distributed among age groups. What was it that made so many American "teen brides" give up the chance of college and a career for early marriage and homemaking?

Friedan's answer was to look more closely at the mass media. Magazines, radio, movies, television—all these had come to play a predominant role in modern culture. They exposed Americans by the millions to powerfully presented messages conveying the standards and ideals of the culture. The media, observed sociologist Harold Lasswell in 1948, had come to perform many of the tasks that, in medieval Europe, were assumed by the Catholic Church. Like the church, the media possessed the capacity to send the same message to all classes at the same time, with confidence in their authority to

---

* At the same time, the United States had the world's highest divorce rate. Enthusiasm for marriage was apparently no guarantee of success.

speak and to be heard universally. Friedan, for her part, found it significant that in the postwar era the media's message about women—what they could dream of, set their sights on, and accomplish—underwent a marked shift. The purveyors of popular culture suddenly seemed determined to persuade women that they should not just accept but actually embrace the ideal ized image of women as wives and mothers.

Having written for the mass-circulation women's magazines, Friedan already knew the part they played in promoting the feminine mystique. What surprised her was how much the image of women had changed. In the 1930s, the woman most likely to appear in a magazine story had a career and was as much concerned with a goal of her own as with getting her man. The heroine of a typical *Ladies' Home Journal* story in 1939 is a nurse who has "strength in her hands, pride in her carriage and nobility in the lift of her chin. . . . She had been on her own ever since she left training, nine years ago. She had earned her way, she need consider nothing but her heart." And unlike the heroines of the 1950s, these women did not have to choose invariably between marriage and career. If they held strongly to their dreams, they could have both. Beginning in the 1950s, however, new heroines appeared. These, Friedan noted, were most often "young and frivolous, almost childlike; fluffy and feminine; passive; gaily content in a world of bedroom and kitchen, sex, babies, and home." The new women did not work "except housework and work to keep their bodies beautiful and to get and keep a man." "Where," Friedan asked rhetorically, "is the world of thought and ideas, the life of the mind and the spirit?"

Talking with some of the few remaining editors from the 1930s, Friedan discovered one reason for the change. "Most of the material used to come from women writers," one explained. "As the young men returned from the war, a great many women writers stopped writing. The new writers were all men, back from the war, who had been dreaming about home, and a cozy domestic life." Male editors, when queried, defended themselves by contending that their readers no longer identified with career women, no longer read serious fiction, and had lost almost all interest in public issues except perhaps those that affected the price of groceries. "You just can't write about ideas or broad issues of the day for women," one remarked.

Just as the image of women changed in mass magazines, so too did women's fashions follow Rosie the Riveter out of the factory. As historian Lois Banner has observed, in the 1930s only a movie star like Katherine Hepburn could get away with wearing slacks. During the 1940s, however, a boyish or mannish look for women became popular. Narrow skirts, padded shoulders, and suits all had a vogue. That ended in 1947, when Parisian designer Christian Dior introduced the "new look." Dior-inspired fashion emphasized femininity. Narrow waistlines drew attention to shapely hips and a fully defined bosom. Most women had to wear foundation garments to achieve the necessary look. The new styles reached their extreme in the "baby doll" fashions, with cinched in waists that set off full bosoms and bouffant skirts held out by crinoline petticoats. Women's shoes ushered in a bonanza for podiatrists. Toes became pointier and heels rose ever higher, until it became dangerous for women to walk. Banner concluded that "not since the Victorian era had women's fashions been so confining." That fashion was a male image of the ideal feminine look.

In the 1930s, magazines and movies had set the fashion. By the 1950s, both those media had begun to lose their audience to television. Women who had once gone to the matinee stayed home to watch the latest episode of *As the World Turns*. In 1951, cities with television networks reported a 20 to 40 percent decline in movie attendance. Almost overnight, television became the preeminent mass medium, carrying images—feminine or otherwise—of American culture into the home. By 1949 there were about a million sets and 108 licensed stations, most in large urban markets. By 1952, 15 million Americans had bought sets; by 1955, the figure had jumped to 30 million; by 1960, television had entered 46 million homes. In fact, more American homes had television sets than had bathrooms! Obviously, if we are to understand how the mass media of the 1950s shaped the image of women, television must be at the center of our focus.

And indeed, television portrayed women of the fifties in predictable ways. Most often they were seen in domestic dramas or comedies, in which Mom and Dad were found living happily with their two or three cute children and possibly a live-in maid or relative to provide additional comic situations. The homes in which they lived, even that of blue-collar airplane riveter Chester Riley (*The Life of Riley,* 1949–50, 1953–58), were cheerfully middle class, with the antiseptic look of a furniture showroom. As for Mom herself, she never worked outside the home and seldom seemed to do much more than wave a dust cloth or whip up a three-course meal at a moment's notice. Sometimes, as in *The Adventures of Ozzie and Harriet* (1955–66), she is competent, cool, and collected. Ozzie, in fact, often seems rather a lost soul when he is turned loose in his own castle, having to be guided gently through the current week's predicament by Harriet. In other series, such as *The Burns and Allen Show* (1950–58), women like Gracie Allen and her friend Blanche played more the role of "dizzy dames," unable to balance checkbooks and sublimely oblivious to the realities of the business world. When Harry Morton announces to his wife Blanche, "I've got great news for you!" (he's been offered a new job), Blanche replies, "When can I wear it?"

Perhaps the domestic comedy that best portrayed the archetypical family woman was *Father Knows Best* (1954–62). The title says it all: Robert Young, playing Jim Anderson, never lacks a sane head, while his wife Margaret is devoted, though something of a cipher. She lacks Gracie Allen's originality yet still can be counted on as a source of genial humor as she tries vainly, for instance, to learn to drive the family car. Warmhearted, attractive, submissive, competent only within the sphere of her limited domain, she is the fifties housewife personified. . . .

The mass media of the 1950s, television prime among them, saturated the American public with the image of the new feminine mystique. But to establish that merely raises a much thornier issue: What sort of relationship is there between the media and reality? . . .

What effect do the mass media have on real life? Obviously, that is a complex question. But in sorting out the possible answers, we can see that there are two sharply contrasting ways of responding. On the one hand, it is possible to argue that, in fact, the media have very little effect on the real world, since they merely reflect tastes and opinions that mass audiences already hold. Confronted with a need to attract the largest number of consumers, media executives select programs that have the broadest appeal. Advertisers seek less to alter values than to channel existing ones toward a specific choice. Americans already value romantic love; once Lever Brothers has its way, they brush with "Close-Up" to achieve it. In the most extreme form, this "reflection hypothesis" would see the media as essentially passive—a simple mirror to society. And in that case, a good deal of Friedan's examination of female imagery might be instructive but beside the point. Women of the fifties were portrayed the way they were because, for whatever reasons, they had been transformed by the conditions of postwar culture.

But that extreme form of the reflection hypothesis breaks down for several reasons. First, if we argue that the mass media are merely reflections, then what are they reflecting? Surely not "real life" pure and simple. Only in commercials do the people who brush with Close-Up make their mates swoon. The parents on *Father Knows Best* are happily married, with two children, hardly the statistical norm in

America even then. Divorced, single-parent mothers were unknown in sitcom land. Black families were virtually nonexistent. Obviously, while the media reflect certain aspects of real life, the reflection hypothesis must be modified to admit that a good deal of what is reflected comprises idealized values—what people would like to be rather than what they really are.

But if mass communications reflect ideals as much as reality, whose ideals are these? As Friedan pointed out, most of the editors, producers, directors, and writers of the 1950s were men. If male rather than female ideals and aspirations were being communicated (or, for that matter, white rather than black, middle-class rather than lower-class, or the ideals of any limited group), then it again becomes legitimate to ask how much the ideals of one segment of America are shaping those of a far wider audience.

Of course, many of the people involved in producing mass culture would argue that in the matter of dreams and ideals, they are not selling their own—merely giving the audience what it wants. But do audiences know what they really want? Surely they do sometimes. But they may also be influenced, cajoled, and swayed. Persuasion, after all, is at the heart of modern advertising. A fifties marketing executive made the point quite freely, noting that

> In a free enterprise economy, we have to develop the need for new products. And to do that we have to liberate women to desire these new products. We help them rediscover that homemaking is more creative than to compete with men. This can be manipulated. We sell them what they ought to want, speed up the unconscious, move it along. . . .

Obviously, if young girls learn week in and week out that father does indeed know best and that a woman's place *is* in the home, the potential for manipulation is strong. . . . But a young girl, no matter how long she watches television, is also shaped by what she learns from her parents,

schoolteachers, religious instructors, and a host of other influences. Given those contending factors, how decisive a role can the media play?

Content analysis of early television programming has led sociologist Gaye Tuchman to conclude that television practiced the "symbolic annihilation of women." By that she meant that women were "demeaned, trivialized, or simply ignored." Surveys of television programs revealed that women, who were over half the population, accounted for just 32 percent of the characters in prime-time dramas. Most of the women who did appear were concentrated in comedy series. Children's cartoons had even fewer female characters. Even where women appeared most often—daytime soap operas—they still held inferior positions. A 1963 survey showed, in fact, that men held 80 percent of all jobs in prime-time shows.

Women were demeaned in other ways. They were most often the victims of violence, not the perpetrators. Single women were attacked more frequently than married women. The most favorably portrayed women were either courting or in a family role. In the 1950s, two-thirds of all the women characters on television shows were married, had been married, or were engaged. Even in soap operas, usually set in homes where women might presumably be allowed to act as leaders, women's roles were trivialized, for it was usually men who found the solutions to emotional problems. . . .

The world of television drama was overwhelmingly white, middle-class, suburban, family-centered, and male dominated. In eighty-six prime-time dramas aired during 1953, men outnumbered women 2 to 1. The very young (under twenty) and the old (over sixty) were underrepresented. The characters were largely of courting or childbearing age and employed or employable. High white-collar or professional positions were overrepresented at the expense of routine white- or blue-collar jobs. Most characters were sane, law-abiding, healthy, and white (over 80 percent). Blacks, who accounted for 12 percent of the population, appeared in only 2 percent of the roles. Heroes outnumbered heroines 2 to 1; and since heroic foreigners were more likely to be women, that left three American heroes for each American heroine.

In these same eighty-six shows, male villains outnumbered female villains. On the one hand, feminists might take heart at this more positive presentation of women. On the other, villains had many traits that Americans admired. While more unattractive, dishonest, disloyal, dirty, stingy, and unkind, they were also brave, strong, sharper or harder than most heroes, and had inner strength. Thus they were effective even if undesirable. By minimizing women as villains, television denied them yet another effective role. Similarly, television dramas presented the most favorable stereotypes of professions in which men dominated. Journalists, doctors, and entertainers all had positive images, while teachers—a large majority of whom were women— were treated as the slowest, weakest, and softest professionals (though clean and fair). . . .

Since we are not in a position to undertake field research on how audiences of the fifties were affected by programs involving women, let us instead resort to a subjective analysis of television's product itself and see what its leading characters and dramatic themes reveal. . . . The most promising programs for exploring gender issues are the situation comedies, or "sitcoms." As we have seen, other genres popular in the 1950s—crime shows, westerns, quiz programs, and network news—tended to ignore women or place them in secondary roles. A majority of the sitcoms, however, take place in a domestic or family setting in which women are central figures. The plots regularly turn on misunderstandings between men and women over their relationships or the proper definition of gender roles. As a consequence, of all television programs, sitcoms had the most formative influence on the image of women.

As a genre, sitcoms had their roots in radio shows like *Jack Benny, Burns and Allen,* and *Amos 'n' Andy*—an influence that helps explain why their comedy came to be more verbal than that of film, which blended physical and verbal humor.* Sitcoms derived most of their laughs from puns, repartee, or irony. What the camera added was the visual delivery of the comedians: a raised eyebrow, a curled lip, or a frown. Thus closeups and reaction shots were key to the humor, especially since the small television screen limited the detail that could be shown. "You know what your mother said the day we were married, Alice?" grumps the obese Ralph Kramden on *The Honeymooners.* [A close-up, here, for emphasis; the double-chin juts in disdain.] "You know what she said? I'm not losing a daughter; I'm gaining a ton." Or another time, when Ralph's vanity gets the better of him, he brags, "Alice, when I was younger, the girls crowded around me at the beach." "Of course, Ralph," replies Alice, "that's because they wanted to sit in the shade." [Cut to Ralph's bulging eyes.]

From the historian's point of view, the more intriguing sitcoms are not the predictable ones like *The Adventures of Ozzie and Harriet* or *Father Knows Best* but those that do not seem to fit the standard mold. It is here—where the familiar conventions come closest to being broken—that the tensions and contradictions of the genre appear most clearly. In different ways, *Our Miss Brooks, I Love Lucy,* and *The Honeymooners* all feature unconventional characters and unusual plot situations. *Our Miss Brooks* stars Eve Arden as an aging, unmarried schoolteacher whose biting humor makes her a threat to the bumbling men around her. *I Love Lucy,* with Lucille Ball, follows the wacky attempts of Lucy Ricardo to break out of her narrow domesticity into the larger world of

---

* *Amos 'n' Andy,* a show about a taxicab company operated by blacks, presented a special crossover problem. The white radio actors who starred in the show were hardly appropriate for a visual medium.

show business or into some moneymaking venture. Though the Ricardos had a child midway through the series, he was not often featured in the show. *The Honeymooners* was perhaps the most offbeat sitcom of the fifties. It featured the Kramdens, a childless couple, who lived in a dreary Brooklyn flat with their neighbors Ed and Trixie Norton, also childless. Ralph, a bus driver, and Ed, a sewer worker, seem unlikely subjects to reinforce the middle-class values of Friedan's feminine mystique.

Despite their unusual formats, all three sitcoms were among the most popular shows of the fifties, and *Lucy* stayed at the top of the ratings for almost the entire decade. By looking at them, we can better understand on what basis a show could deviate from traditional forms and still remain successful.

As it happens, none of these shows is as exceptional as it might first seem. All incorporate elements of the traditional family show structure, with male authority remaining dominant, middle-class values applauded, and the proper order of society prevailing by the end of each episode. Still, there is more to them than the simple triumph of the feminine mystique. The three leading female characters—Connie Brooks, Lucy Ricardo, and Alice Kramden—reveal through the force of their comic personas certain tensions that slick production styles and pat plot resolutions cannot hide. We see glimpses of women's discontent as well as women's strength in coping with adversity.

The comic tensions in *Our Miss Brooks* arise from two primary sources: Connie constantly clashes with her authoritarian and pompous principal, Osgood Conklin, and—at the same time—has her amorous eye on the biology teacher, Mr. Boynton. He seems oblivious to her sexual overtures yet is the best prospect to save her from spinsterhood. In one show she walks in with her arms full of packages. "Can I hold something?" he asks. "Sure, as soon as I put these packages down," she cracks. He overlooks the sexual innuendo that she is forced to use in her constant attempts to stir his interest.

Miss Brooks is oppressed on several levels. She recognizes that society places little value on her role as a teacher. There is no future in her job, where she is bullied, exploited, and underpaid. Marriage offers the only way out, but since she is superior in intellect and personality to the men and no longer young and fresh, her prospects are dim. Thus she faces a future in which she cannot fulfill the feminine mystique. Her only hope is to use her wiles to trick Mr. Boynton into marriage. She must be passive-aggressive, because convention prevents her from taking the initiative. At the same time, she must accept an economic role that is far beneath her talents. Rather than challenge the system that demeans her, she survives by treating it as comical and transcending it through the force of her superior character.

The first episode of the series establishes many of those themes as well as a somewhat irreverent style. Connie gets an idea that she can arouse Mr. Boynton's interest by starting a fight. That leads to a number of laughs as Boynton ducks each of her attempts at provocation. Before she makes headway, she is called on the carpet by Mr. Conklin, the principal. In his office, he radiates authority, glowering from behind his desk and treating her with disdain. But Miss Brooks hardly folds before the onslaught. She tricks him into reminiscing about his youth and, as he becomes more mellow (and human), she assumes greater familiarity, until she is sitting casually on the corner of his desk. By the end of the meeting, Connie has sent Mr. Conklin on a wild goose chase that leads to his arrest by the police. In his absence, she becomes acting principal and clearly relishes the sense of authority she gains sitting in the seat of power. The duly constituted hierarchy has been bearded and stood on its head. Of course, all is set right in the end, but before order returns, we have had a glimpse of a world where women have power.

The liberties taken in the show, however,

amount to scarcely more than shore leave. Even if Miss Brooks is unmarried, the show does have a kind of surrogate family structure. Despite her relatively advanced age, Connie's real role is more that of an impish teen daughter. She lives in an apartment with a remarkably maternal housekeeper. One of the students at school, Walter (who these days would be classified as an eminent nerd), serves as a surrogate son, while Mr. Conklin, of course, is the father figure. That leaves Mr. Boynton to be paired off as Miss Brooks's reticent steady. As for Connie's challenges to Mr. Conklin's male authority, they are allowed only because the principal is pompous, arbitrary, or abusive of his position. And Mr. Boynton turns out not to be as dumb as he acts; indeed, at the end of the first episode, as Miss Brooks waits eagerly for a kiss that will demonstrate his interest, he holds back, his wink to the audience indicating that he can dish it out too. With Mr. Conklin back in charge and Mr. Boynton clearly in control, the male frame is reestablished, Connie has been chastened for her presumption, and the normal order of things restored.

Similar tensions operate in the *I Love Lucy* show. Lucy's efforts to escape the confines of domesticity threaten her husband Ricky and the well-being of the family. The plot generally thickens as Lucy cons her neighbor Ethel Mertz into joining her escapades. Ethel and Lucy then become rivals of their husbands. In an episode that could have generated biting commentary, Lucy and Ethel challenge Fred Mertz and Ricky to exchange roles. The women will be the breadwinners, the men the housekeepers. Both, of course, prove equally inept in the others' domain. Ethel and Lucy discover they have no significant job skills. After much frustration, they end up working in a chocolate factory under a woman who is far more domineering and arbitrary than Mr. Conklin ever was. In a parody of Charlie Chaplin's *Modern Times,* they fall hopelessly behind as they pack candies off a relentless conveyor belt. By the end of the day they are emotionally drained, humbled, and thwarted.

In the meantime, Ricky and Fred have virtually destroyed the apartment. How much rice do they need for dinner? They decide on several pounds, so that the kitchen is soon awash. Just as Ethel and Lucy are relieved to return home, Fred and Ricky are overjoyed to escape the toils of domestic life. Each side learns a new regard for the difficulties faced by the other.

Despite the schmaltzy ending, there is a real tension in the structure of this episode and the series as a whole. Within the orthodox framework (Lucy and Ricky are firmly middle class, worrying about money, friends, schools, and a house in the suburbs), the energy and spark of the show comes precisely because Lucy, like Miss Brooks, consistently refuses to recognize the male limits prescribed for her. Although Ricky manages to rein her in by the end of each episode, the audience realizes full well that she is too restless, too much restricted by four walls and a broom, and far too vivacious to accept the cult of domesticity. She will be off and running again the following week in another attempt to break loose.

The show's most successful moment might also serve as a model of 1950s family life. In its early years, television honored all the middle-class sexual mores. Even married couples slept in separate beds and the word "pregnant" was taboo (since it implied that a couple had been sexually active—at least once). The producers of *Lucy* thus faced a terrible dilemma when they learned that their star was indeed with child. What to do? They made the bold decision to incorporate Lucille Ball's pregnancy into the show. For months, television audiences watched Lucy become bigger and more uncomfortable. On January 19, 1952, the big day arrived. The episode "Lucy Has Her Baby" (filmed earlier in anticipation of the blessed event) scored the highest rating (68.8 percent) of any show of the decade. News of the birth of Desi Arnaz, Jr., rivaled the headlines for the inauguration of Dwight D. Eisenhower, which occurred the following morning.

More than any sitcom of the 1950s, *The Honeymooners* seems to deviate from middle-American stereotypes. As lower-class, childless couples living in stark apartments, the Nortons and Kramdens would scarcely seem ideal reflections of an affluent, family-centered society. Ralph and Alice struggle to get by on his $67.50 a week salary as a bus driver. Sewer worker Ed Norton and his wife Trixie live off credit. Whenever their appliances or furniture are repossessed, Ed starts over at another store. The Kramdens have no television set, telephone, vacuum cleaner, or other modern appliance. Their living room/kitchen, the main set for the show, had only a bureau, a table and chair, a standing sink, an icebox (literally), and a stove. It had the look of the depression era, not the 1950s.

The show turns on Ralph's obsession with money and status. He is forever trying to get rich quick, earn respect, and move up in the world. All that saves him from himself and disaster is Alice's stoic forbearance. She has had to live through all his efforts to assert his authority—"I'm the boss, Alice and don't you ever forget it!"—and to resist his harebrained schemes (diet pizza parlors, wallpaper that glows in the dark to save electricity). And it is Alice who cushions his fall when each new dream turns to ashes. Like most middle-class American couples, Ralph and Alice bicker over money. Ralph is a cheapskate, not by nature but to mask his failure as a breadwinner. Alice must use her feminine wiles to persuade him to buy anything, even a TV or a telephone. To protect his pride, Ralph accuses her of being a spendthrift. Their battles have far more bite than those seen in any other sitcom of that era. In no other show do the characters so regularly lay marriage, ego, or livelihood on the line.

Why, then, did the audience like this show? For one thing, it is very funny. Ed Norton's irrepressible deadpan is a perfect foil to Ralph's manic intensity. It is a delight to watch Norton take forever to shuffle the cards while Ralph does a slow burn. And Alice's alternately tolerant and spirited rejoinders complete the chemistry. In addition, there is a quality to the Kramdens' apartment that separates it in time and space from the world in which middle-class viewers live. The mass audience is more willing to confront serious questions if such issues are raised in distant times or places. Death on *Gunsmoke* does not have the same implications as a death on *Lassie*. Divorce for Henry VIII is one thing; even a hint of it for Ozzie and Harriet would be something quite different. Thus the Depression look of the Kramdens' apartment gives the audience the spatial and temporal distance it needs to separate itself from the sources of conflict between Ralph and Alice. The audience can look on with a sense of its material and social superiority as Alice and Ralph go at it:

Ralph: You want this place to be Disneyland.

Alice: This place is a regular Disneyland. You see out there, Ralph? The back of the Chinese restaurant, old man Grogan's long underwear on the line, the alley? That's my Fantasyland. You see that sink over there? That's my Adventureland. The stove and the icebox, Ralph, that's Frontierland. The only thing that's missing is the World of Tomorrow.

Ralph (doing his slow burn): You want Tomorrowland, Alice? You want Tomorrowland? Well, pack your bags, because you're going to the *moon!* [Menaces her with his raised fist.]

Underneath it all, however, *The Honeymooners* is still a middle-class family sitcom. Alice and Trixie don't have children; they have Ralph and Ed. In one episode Trixie says to Alice, "You know those men we're married to? You have to treat them like children." A trick of social class makes this arrangement work without threatening the ideal of male authority. Since the middle classes have always equated the behavior of the poor with that of children—and Ralph and Ed are poor—no one is surprised by their childish antics. Trixie and Alice, both having married beneath them, maintain middle-class standards. At the end of almost every episode, Alice brings Ralph back into the fold after one of his schemes fails. Surrounding her in an embrace, he rewards her with his puppydog devotion: "Baby, you're the greatest."

One episode in particular reveals the price Alice paid to keep her man-child, marriage, and selfhood intact. A telegram arrives announcing, "I'm coming to visit. Love, Mom." Ralph explodes at the idea of sharing his apartment with his dreaded mother-in-law, for her disapproval and insults wound his brittle pride whenever she visits. There are numerous jokes at Ralph's expense as well as some cutting commentary on mothers-in-law, after which Ralph moves in with the Nortons upstairs, where he sparks a similar fight between them. Finally, marriage and family prevail over wounded pride. An unrepentant Ralph returns home, only to find out that "mother" is Mother Kramden, whom Alice, of course, is treating with the very warmth Ralph denies *her* mother. He is once again reduced to a shamefaced puppy.

Alice's victory is so complete that it threatens to destroy her relationship with Ralph. As if to soften the blow, she sits down to deliver her victory speech. She lowers her eyes, drops her shoulders, and speaks in tones of resignation rather than triumph, finally reading to Ralph a letter in praise of mothers-in-law, who have the "hardest job in the world." It turns out to be a letter Ralph wrote fifteen years earlier to Alice's mother. The sentiments are so sappy that they virtually destroy the comedy. Like Ralph, the producers must have thought it better to eat crow than leave a residue of bitterness or social criticism. They must have recognized that their material had been too extreme, the humor too

sharp, and the mother-in-law jokes too cruel for middle-American tastes.

Even after its apology, the show ends with what appears to be an unintentional image of Alice in a domestic prison. Mother Kramden has gone off to "freshen up." A penitent Ralph admits his defeat, then announces he is going out for some air—in essence to pull himself back together. But what of Alice? She is left holding nothing more than she had before—dominion over her dreary kitchen. Her responsibility to Ralph's mother prevents her from escaping also, and she is no better off than before the battle began. Her slumped posture suggests that she understands all too well the hollowness of her triumph. We must believe that many women in videoland identified with Alice.

The Honeymooners, I Love Lucy, and *Our Miss Brooks* all suggest that, while the male characters in the series maintain their ultimate authority, the "symbolic annihilation" of women that Gaye Tuchman spoke of is, in these comedies at least, not total. A battle between the sexes would not be funny unless the two sides were evenly matched; and setting sitcoms in the home placed women in a better position to spar. Further, where men's roles gave them the advantage in terms of social position, rank, and authority, women like Connie, Lucy, and Alice vied equally through the sheer strength of their comedic personalities. The producers, of course, were not closet feminists in permitting this to occur; the circumstances simply made for popular shows. And their ratings were high, we would argue, partly because they hinted at the discontent felt by many women, whether its strength was recognized or not. . . .

If the mass communications industries simply reflected public taste and never influenced it, they would become nonentities—multimillion-dollar ciphers in any explanation that seeks to account for change. On the other hand, if we assign too manipulative a role to the media, it becomes difficult to explain any change at all. How was it that hundreds of thousands of girls who watched themselves being symbolically annihilated during the 1950s supplied so many converts to the women's movement of the sixties?

The mass media, in other words, while influential forces in modern society, are perhaps not as monolithic in outlook as they sometimes seem. The comparison to the medieval church is apt so long as we remember that the church, too, was hardly able to impose its will universally. Even where orthodoxy reigned, schismatic movements were always springing up. Today's heretics may be feminists rather than Anabaptists, but they are responding to pressures growing within society. From a feminist point of view, we may not have reached utopia merely because, by 1984, a female television producer could launch the series *Cagney and Lacey,* in which two female career police officers energetically catch murderers as well as live through the traumas of being diagnosed for breast cancer. All the same, there is change. Lucy is not Lacey, any more than Rosie was Gracie. And the same mass culture industry that threatened women with symbolic annihilation also published *The Feminine Mystique.*

Questions for Study and Review

1. Given the upheaval in gender roles and family life during the depression and war years, how can one explain the seeming return to tradition in the 1950s?

2. The "feminine mystique" first appeared in the 1920s according to Ruth Cowan. How did television affect the dissemination of such cultural ideals in the post-World War II period?

3. What does the popularity of *The Honeymooners*—a blue-collar sitcom set in an urban tenement—tell us about the attitudes and ideals of suburban television viewers?

4. How did technological developments in an area such as entertainment affect women and families differently from changes in industry, agriculture, or even household appliances?

Suggested Readings

Betty Friedan, *The Feminine Mystique* (1963).

Elaine Tyler May, *Homeward Bound: American Families in the Cold War Era* (1988).

Amy Swerdlow, "'Ladies' Day at the Capitol': Women Strike for Peace versus HUAC," *Feminist Studies* (Fall 1982).

Eugenia Kaledin, *Mothers and More: American Women in the 1950s* (1984).

Nancy Walker, "Humor and Gender Roles: The 'Funny' Feminism of the Post-War World II Suburbs," *American Quarterly* (Spring 1985).

FOURTEEN

The Origins of the Montgomery Bus Boycott

David J. Garrow

As middle-class Americans moved to the suburbs, those left behind in the inner cities found themselves increasingly isolated from the affluent society. Black Americans, whose hopes had been raised by the economic opportunities and democratic promises of wartime, found themselves caught in the same web of segregation, discrimination, poverty, and disfranchisement when peace was proclaimed. In the South, violence and cross burnings were the most vivid signs of postwar reaction. Attempts at collective action through such organizations as the NAACP led to charges of communism and, in at least a few cases, to assassinations of local and statewide leaders. In the 1950s, such incidents generally failed to rouse the nation; indeed, most Americans remained ignorant of the virulent racism that flourished amid postwar prosperity.

African-Americans, however, were fully aware of the problems and continued to organize. In local communities across the South, women and men joined forces to confront restrictions on their rights and opportunities. In 1954, the Supreme Court ruling in *Brown* v. *the Board of Education* spurred efforts to end school desegregation and similar affronts to black equality.

One of the most dramatic local campaigns was the Montgomery bus boycott of 1955–56. Often cited as the beginning of the modern civil rights movement and of Dr. Martin Luther King, Jr.'s career as its most renowned leader, the boycott began when Mrs. Rosa Parks refused to give up her bus seat to a white rider. A seamstress and a member of the NAACP, Mrs. Parks's action was prompted by both personal courage and collective preparation; it was the catalyst for a decade of protest.

December 1, 1955, the day of Rosa Parks's arrest, is a useful moment for historians seeking to pinpoint the emergence of a new form of black activism, yet that single event should not obscure the years of preparation that allowed this episode to take on national, even international, significance. Both black women and men formed political organizations in postwar Montgomery. The Woman's Political Council (WPC), along with men's political clubs, the NAACP, and the black churches, had sought justice for those previously harassed or arrested on city buses and had campaigned in support of white racial moderates for local office.

Only the WPC, however, had planned a full-scale bus boycott. Rosa Parks's arrest led Jo Ann Gibson Robinson and other council leaders to put that plan into effect and thereby reshape the lives of black and white, women and men, in Montgomery and the nation. Garrow captures those beginnings by focusing on the women who formed the WPC and planned and executed the boycott. Mrs. Robinson, "the instigator of the movement to start that boycott," refusing any special credit for herself, looks back on that pivotal moment in the civil rights movement and concludes, "the black women did it."

Jo Ann Gibson Robinson moved to Montgomery, Alabama, in the late summer of 1949 to join the English Department at all-black Alabama State College. A thirty-three year old native of Culloden, Georgia, twenty-five miles from Macon, she was the twelfth and youngest child of Owen Boston Gibson and Dollie Webb Gibson, land-owning black farmers who prospered until Owen Gibson died when Jo Ann was six years old. As the older children moved away, operating the farm grew more difficult for Mrs. Gibson, who eventually sold the property and moved into Macon with her younger offspring. Jo Ann graduated from high school there as the class valedictorian, and went on to earn her undergraduate degree at Fort Valley State College, the first member of her family to complete college. She took a public school teaching job in Macon and married Wilbur Robinson, but the marriage, heavily burdened by the death in infancy of their first and only child, lasted only a short time. Twelve months later, after five years of teaching in Macon, Jo Ann Robinson moved to Atlanta to take an M.A. in English at Atlanta University and then accepted a teaching position at Mary Allen College in Crockett, Texas. After one year there, Mrs. Robinson received a better offer from Alabama State, and moved to Montgomery.

Mrs. Robinson was an enthusiastic teacher and responded energetically to her new position at Alabama State. She also became an active member of Dexter Avenue Baptist Church, which many Alabama State professors attended, and she joined the Women's Political Council, a black professional women's civic group that

one of her English Department colleagues, Mrs. Mary Fair Burks, had founded three years earlier when the local League of Women Voters had refused to integrate.

It was a blissful fall, Mrs. Robinson later remembered. "I loved every minute of it." Just prior to Christmas she made preparations to visit some relatives in Cleveland for the holidays. Storing her car in a garage, she boarded a Montgomery City Lines public bus for the ride to Dannelly Field, the municipal airport. Only two other passengers were aboard, and Mrs. Robinson, immersed in holiday thoughts, took a seat towards the front of the bus. Suddenly, however, she was roused from her thoughts about her family by angry words from the driver, who was ordering her to get up.

"He was standing over me, saying 'Get up from there! Get up from there,' with his hand drawn back," she later recalled.

Shaken and frightened, Mrs. Robinson fled from the bus. "I felt like a dog. And I got mad, after this was over, and I realized that I was a human being, and just as intelligent and far more trained than that bus driver was. But I think he wanted to hurt me, and he did . . . I cried all the way to Cleveland."

That experience convinced Mrs. Robinson that the Women's Political Council ought to target Montgomery's segregated bus seating for immediate attention. "It was then that I made up . . . my mind that whatever I could add to that organization that would help to bring that practice down, I would do it," Mrs. Robinson recalled. "When I came back, the first thing I did was to call a meeting . . . and tell them what had happened."

Only then did Mrs. Robinson learn that her experience was far from unique, that dozens of other black citizens, primarily women, had suffered similar abuse from Montgomery bus drivers. Over the previous few years several black women, Mrs. Geneva Johnson, Mrs. Viola

White, and Miss Katie Wingfield, had been arrested and convicted for refusing to give up their seats. Earlier in 1949, two young children, visiting from the north and unfamiliar with Montgomery's practice of reserving the first ten seats on each bus for white riders only, even if black passengers were forced to stand over vacant seats, also were hauled in for refusing a driver's command to surrender their seats. Some oldtimers in Montgomery remembered how the black community had mounted a boycott in the summer of 1900, when the city had first imposed segregated seating on Montgomery's street cars, a boycott that had won a refinement of the city ordinance so as to specify that no rider had to surrender a seat unless another was available. Nonetheless, drivers often made black riders who were seated just behind the whites-only section get up and stand so that all white passengers could sit.

Mrs. Burks thought black toleration of those seating practices and other driver abuse, such as forcing black passengers to pay their dime at the front, and then get off and board the bus through the rear, side door, was scandalous. "Everyone would look the other way. Nobody would acknowledge what was going on," Mrs. Burks remembered. "It outraged me that this kind of conduct was going on," and that so far no black community organizations had done anything about it.

Black activism did exist in Montgomery, even though it had not yet focused upon bus conditions, despite the widespread complaints. Several years earlier Arthur Madison, a New York lawyer who came from one of black Montgomery's most prominent families, had returned home and tried to stimulate black voter registration, but white legal harassment had forced him to return to New York. The outspoken pastor of Dexter Avenue Baptist Church, Rev. Vernon Johns, who had come to Montgomery in 1948, regularly denounced the bus situation, but many blacks viewed Johns as too unpredictable and idiosyncratic to assume a leadership role in the community. The brutal rape of a black teenager, Gertrude Perkins, by two white policemen earlier in 1949 had led Rev. Solomon S. Seay to repeated efforts to obtain justice in the case, but white officials had brushed off his complaints.

Another visible black activist was Pullman porter Edgar Daniel Nixon, a member of A. Philip Randolph's Brotherhood of Sleeping Car Porters and a local leader of the National Association for the Advancement of Colored People (NAACP). Nixon served as Alabama state president of the NAACP in 1948–1949, and also devoted much time to his Alabama Progressive Democratic Association, a black alternative to a state Democratic Party that continued to discourage black participation despite the 1940s' demise of the "white primary." Nixon regularly mounted one initiative after another; in 1954 he succeeded in winning 42 percent of the vote in a losing race for a seat on the party's Montgomery County Democratic Executive Committee, a tribute not only to the more than 1,500 black voters that Nixon and other activists like businessman Rufus A. Lewis had helped register, but also to the grudging respect that many whites felt for Nixon's tireless efforts.

Lewis, a well-known former football coach at Alabama State College, had been especially active not only in encouraging black registration but also in trying to unify black Montgomery's civic activism. Although some colleagues viewed Lewis and Nixon as low-key rivals for top leadership, Lewis' Citizens Club served as a regular hang-out for politically-minded blacks; his Citizens Steering Committee, formed in the fall of 1952, looked to find ways to exert some black political influence over Montgomery's city policies.

Equally if not more important to the political life of black Montgomery than Nixon's Progressive Democrats, the NAACP branch, or Lewis' Citizens Committee, however, was Mrs. Burks and Mrs. Robinson's Women's Political Council. By the early 1950s Robinson had succeeded Burks as president, and the core membership of regularly active participants numbered at least thirty women such as Thelma Glass, Mary Cross, Irene West, Euretta Adair, Elizabeth Arrington, and Zoeline Pierce, who were either faculty members at Alabama State, teachers in the local, segregated public schools, or wives of relatively well-to-do black professional men. More than either Nixon's circle or Lewis', these middle-class women were the most numerous, most reform-minded group of black civic activists in Montgomery.

The first notable opportunity for black political influence to make itself felt came in November, 1953, in a special election to fill one vacant seat on the three-member Montgomery City Commission. The black-supported victor, Dave Birmingham, a genuine racial liberal, won fifty-three percent of the vote in a contest that involved little discussion of race and allowed Birmingham to construct an electoral coalition of blacks and lower-class whites.

Impressed by their success in representing the balance of power, black civic activists, led by the WPC, met in late 1953 with Birmingham and his two racially moderate colleagues, Mayor W. A "Tacky" Gayle and George Cleere, to voice three complaints about the racial practices of the municipally regulated and chartered bus company, Montgomery City Lines. Blacks having to stand over empty, white only seats on crowded buses was a constant insult and problem. So was most drivers' practice of forcing blacks to board through the rear door. Additionally, while buses stopped at every block in white sections of town, it was only every other block in black neighborhoods.

The three commissioners, Birmingham in particular, listened politely, but nothing came of the session.

Undaunted, Mrs. Robinson, who served as the WPC and black community's principal spokesperson, obtained another audience with the commission in March, 1954, and reiterated the three complaints. The WPC, which historian of Montgomery J. Mills Thornton III has accurately termed "the most militant and uncompromising organ of the black community" in pre-1956 Montgomery, also presented the commission with specific details of driver abuse of black passengers. This time the city officials agreed to alter the bus company's practice of stopping only at alternate blocks in black areas, but they and the city's lawyers insisted there was no way, under Alabama's state segregation statutes, that any changes or improvements could be made in bus seating practices. Robinson and other black representatives contended that elimination of the reserved, whites only seats, and a halt to the practice of making blacks surrender seats to whites on overcrowded buses would eliminate the most serious problems, but the white officials rejected the WPC's proposal that the front-to-back seating of whites, and back-to-front seating of blacks, with no one having to stand over an empty seat or give one up after being seated, would in no way offend the state segregation law.

Mrs. Robinson and her colleagues were unhappy over the city's refusal to show any flexibility. In early May, the Commission did approve the hiring of Montgomery's first four black police officers, but many black Montgomerians attached greater importance to the ongoing prosecution of a black teenager, Jeremiah Reeves, who faced the death penalty for the supposed rape of a white woman in 1951.

Mrs. Robinson was already thinking of how to put more pressure on the Commission to improve bus conditions when, on May 17, came a news announcement that strengthened her determination. The United States Supreme Court, in *Brown* v. *Board of Education of Topeka* and five companion cases challenging racially segregated public schools, ruled that governmen-

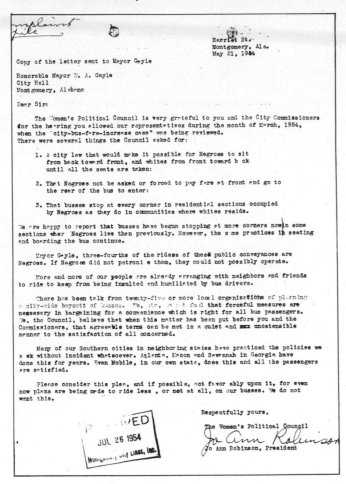

Copy of the letter sent to Mayor Gayle

Honorable Mayor W. A. Gayle
City Hall
Montgomery, Alabama

Dear Sir:

The Women's Political Council is very grateful to you and the City Commissioners for the hearing you allowed our representatives during the month of March, 1954, when the "city-bus-fare-increase case" was being reviewed. There were several things the Council asked for:

1. A city law that would make it possible for Negroes to sit from back toward front, and whites from front toward back until all the seats are taken:

2. That Negroes not be asked or forced to pay fare at front and go to the rear of the bus to enter:

3. That busses stop at every corner in residential sections occupied by Negroes as they do in communities where whites reside.

We are happy to report that busses have begun stopping at more corners now in some sections where Negroes live than previously. However, the same practices in seating and boarding the bus continue.

Mayor Gayle, three-fourths of the riders of these public conveyances are Negroes. If Negroes did not patronize them, they could not possibly operate.

More and more of our people are already arranging with neighbors and friends to ride to keep from being insulted and humiliated by bus drivers.

There has been talk from twenty-five or more local organizations of planning a city-wide boycott of busses. We, sir, do not feel that forceful measures are necessary in bargaining for a convenience which is right for all bus passengers. We, the Council, believe that when this matter has been put before you and the Commissioners, that agreeable terms can be met in a quiet and unostensible manner to the satisfaction of all concerned.

Many of our Southern cities in neighboring states have practiced the policies we seek without incident whatsoever. Atlanta, Macon and Savannah in Georgia have done this for years. Even Mobile, in our own state, does this and all the passengers are satisfied.

Please consider this plea, and if possible, act favorably upon it, for even now plans are being made to ride less, or not at all, on our busses. We do not want this.

Respectfully yours,

The Women's Political Council

Jo Ann Robinson, President

tally-mandated school segregation was unconstitutional and that the sixty-year-old doctrine of "separate but equal" was no longer valid.

Four days after the landmark *Brown* decision, Mrs. Robinson typed a letter to Montgomery's Mayor Gayle, with a copy to Montgomery City Lines manager J. H. Bagley. She thanked Gayle for the March meeting and for the change in the buses' alternate block stopping practice, but reiterated the WPC's great unhappiness at the ongoing seating policies. Then she politely voiced the threat she had quietly been recommending to her black leadership colleagues.

Mayor Gayle, three-fourths of the riders of these public conveyances are Negroes. If Negroes did not patronize them, they could not possibly operate.

More and more of our people are already arranging with neighbors and friends to ride to keep from being insulted and humiliated by bus drivers. There has been talk from twenty-five or more local organizations of planning a city-wide boycott of buses. We, sir, do not feel that forceful measures are necessary in bargaining for a convenience which is right for all bus passengers. We, the

Council, believe that when this matter has been put before you and the Commissioners, that agreeable terms can be met in a quiet and unostensible manner to the satisfaction of all concerned.

Mrs. Robinson pointedly noted that many Southern cities, including Mobile, already were using the front-to-back, back-to-front segregated seating plan that Montgomery refused to implement. "Please consider this plea, and if possible, act favorably upon it," she concluded, "for even now plans are being made to ride less, or not at all, on our buses. We do not want this."

Despite the extremely gentle and tactful language she employed in her letter to Gayle, Mrs. Robinson was hoping that black community sentiment would support a bus boycott to force the Commission's hand. Another meeting with the white officials on June 1 registered no progress, but Mrs. Robinson found only modest interest in her boycott idea throughout much of the black community, and placed the idea on a back burner for the time being.

Next to bus conditions, the second civic concern troubling the WPC and other black activists was the decidedly inferior quality of the segregated parks and recreation facilities available to black Montgomerians. One step the WPC had identified as a partial remedy was the appointment of a black member, such as WPC member Mrs. Irene West, to the city's Parks and Recreation Board. Mrs. Robinson voiced this request at a January, 1955, meeting of the City Commission, but despite supportive comments from Birmingham and Mayor Gayle, nothing happened. Instead, attention turned to the upcoming mid-March city elections, and a public candidates' forum that E. D. Nixon's Progressive Democratic Association held on February 23 at the black Ben Moore Hotel.

All three incumbents, plus their major challengers, Harold McGlynn for Gayle, Frank Parks for Cleere, and Sam Sterns and Clyde Sellers for Birmingham, attended the first-of-its-kind event and faced questions about bus conditions as well as the Parks and Recreation appointment. A majority of the contenders endorsed a black appointment to the Parks Board, while others avoided any specifics on either topic. Although the open soliciting of black votes by so many white candidates seemed impressive, one of Birmingham's challengers, former Auburn University football star and state highway patrol officer Clyde Sellers, saw the convocation, and Birmingham's sympathy for black concerns, as just the opening that was needed to cut into Birmingham's previously solid white working class electoral support.

Sellers' strategic desire to make race an election issue got a coincidental boost on March 2 when a fifteen-year-old black girl, Claudette Colvin, refused to give up her bus seat, well toward the rear of the vehicle, so as to accommodate an overflow of newly-boarding white passengers.

Police officers were able to drag Colvin from the bus only with considerable force. The incident immediately sent the black leadership into action. Mrs. Rosa Parks, a seamstress and long time NAACP member who was adult adviser to the NAACP Youth Council, to which Claudette Colvin belonged, immediately began soliciting financial assistance for her legal defense, as did Mrs. Parks' good friend Virginia Foster Durr, one of Montgomery's few racially liberal whites.

Rufus Lewis' newly formed Citizen's Coordinating Committee, yet another leadership unity organization which included E. D. Nixon and the WPC's Thelma Glass among its top officers, quickly sent out a mimeographed letter, "To Friends of Justice and Human Rights," seeking Colvin's acquittal, a reprimand of the bus driver involved, and clarification of the oft-ignored city provision that no rider had to give up a seat unless another was available.

Nixon and Mrs. Robinson, thinking that Colvin's case might supply an opportunity for a court challenge to the constitutionality of Montgomery's bus seating practices, interviewed the young woman, but concluded that her personal situation and the particulars of the arrest precluded using the incident as a test case. Robinson and others met, unsuccessfully, with city and bus company officials to seek dismissal of the charges.

Claudette Colvin was quickly convicted for both assault and battery and violating the segregation statute at a March 18 trial, only three days before the city election. When Colvin's attorney, young Montgomery native Fred Gray—who had been one of Mrs. Robinson's Alabama State students before attending law school in Ohio—filed notice of appeal, the prosecutor indicated that he would pursue only the assault and battery charge, not the segregation issue.

On the 21st, Sellers narrowly bested Dave Birmingham, who declined a possible runoff because of bad health, while Frank Parks, who had received black support, defeated Cleere. Disappointed both by the Colvin outcome and Birmingham's loss, the black leadership hoped for other opportunities.

In June, Mrs. Robinson, Gray and other black representatives met once again with city and bus company officials. Despite Gray's observations about Mobile's practices, the white officials, particularly bus company lawyer Jack Crenshaw, adhered firmly to their contention that no changes could be made legally in bus seating practices. Popular complaints about the seating situation and driver abuse remained at high levels, but no further organized initiatives were undertaken.

One relative newcomer to the city, Rev. Martin Luther King, Jr., who had succeeded Vernon Johns as pastor of Dexter Avenue Baptist Church in mid-1954 and accompanied Robinson's delegation to the early March meeting with the city, attributed a good part of the inaction to what he later termed "an appalling lack of unity among the leaders" and a "crippling factional-

ism." More of a problem than competition among the active leaders, King thought, was the pervasive indifference of many middle-class black Montgomerians to any political or civic concern. Economic vulnerability and fear of white retribution understandably inhibited some, but "too much of the inaction was due to sheer apathy," King later wrote.

Although Mrs. Robinson still husbanded her hope that the WPC could at some point launch a boycott of the buses, the late summer and fall of 1955 passed with relative quiet; the October 21 arrest of one black woman, Mrs. Mary Louise Smith, for refusing to surrender her seat became known to most of the black leadership only several months later.

On Thursday evening December 1, Mrs. Rosa Parks, the NAACP activist who had assisted Claudette Colvin's defense, felt tired and weary from her seamstress work at the Montgomery Fair department store when she boarded one of the Cleveland Avenue route buses at Montgomery's Court Square for her regular ride home. One stop later, after taking a seat in the first row behind the ten whites-only seats, Mrs. Parks and the three other black passengers in that row were ordered by the driver, J. F. Blake, to get up so that one newly-boarding white man—who could not be accommodated in the front section—could sit. Although the other three people complied, Mrs. Parks silently refused, and two police officers were summoned to place her under arrest and transport her to the city jail.

Word of the incident spread quickly. E. D. Nixon called the jail to learn about the charges, only to be refused an answer by the officer on duty. Knowing that attorney Gray was out of town for the day, Nixon called white lawyer Clifford Durr, who like his wife Virginia, already knew Mrs. Parks. The Durrs and Nixon drove to the jail to sign the bond for Mrs. Parks' release. A Monday trial date was set for the charge of violating the city's segregated seating ordinance.

```
                          POLICE DEPARTMENT
                          CITY OF MONTGOMERY

                                          Date   12-1-55        19

Complainant     J.F.Blake  (wm)
Address         27 No. Lewis St.                    Phone No.
Offense    Misc.                       Reported By   Same as above
Address                                             Phone No.
Date and Time Offense Committed      12-1-55      6:06 pm
Place of Occurrence    In Front of Empire Theatre  (On Montgomery Street)
Person or Property Attacked
How Attacked
Person Wanted
Value of Property Stolen                   Value Recovered

            Details of Complaint (list, describe and give value of property stolen)

       We received a call upon arrival the bus operator said he had a colored female
       sitting in the white section of the bus, and would not move back.
       We (Day & Mixon) also saw her.
       The bus operator signed a warrant for her. Rosa Parks, (cf) 634 Cleveland Court.
       Rosa Parks (cf) was charged with chapter 6 section 11 of the Montgomery City Code.

            Warrant #14254


THIS OFFENSE IS DECLARED:
UNFOUNDED              □     Officers   + S Day
CLEARED BY ARREST      ⊠
EXCEPTIONALLY CLEARED  □              D. W. Mixon
INACTIVE (NOT CLEARED) □
                                     Division   Patrol            Time   7:00 pm
                                                                         12-1-55
```

While attorney Durr explained to Nixon and Mrs. Parks that they could win her acquittal since there had been no other seat available for her to take when driver Blake demanded hers, Nixon argued that the arrest of Mrs. Parks, a widely-known and well-respected person in black Montgomery, was precisely the opportunity the black leadership had long-awaited for challenging the entire bus seating situation. With some hesitance Mrs. Parks agreed, and Nixon went home to plan his next steps.

Later that evening Fred Gray returned to town, learned of Mrs. Parks' arrest and immediately called Mrs. Robinson, who he knew to be the "real moving force" among the black leadership. Mrs. Robinson in turn called Nixon. They quickly agreed that the moment for launching the long-pondered boycott of the buses was at hand.

Nixon would make the calls to set up a black leadership meeting Friday evening; Mrs. Robinson and her WPC colleagues would immediately start producing and distributing handbills calling upon black Montgomerians to stay off the buses on Monday, December 5. "We had planned the protest long before Mrs. Parks was arrested," Mrs. Robinson later emphasized. "There had been so many things that happened

The Women's Political Council (WPC) of Montgomery, an organization of middle-class black women, was instrumental in organizing the 382-day-long Montgomery bus boycott. The boycott was prompted by the arrest of Rosa Parks, a widely respected NAACP activist, who had refused the bus driver's order to surrender her seat to a white rider. WPC leader and spokesperson Jo Ann Gibson Robinson, who had previously protested Montgomery's bus segregation policies, took advantage of the opportunity to mobilize the black community in a boycott of the city's bus system.

that the black women had been embarrassed over, and now they were ready to explode." They knew immediately that "Mrs. Parks had the caliber of character we needed to get the city to rally behind us."

Wasting not a moment, Mrs. Robinson sat down at her typewriter with a mimeograph stencil and typed the same message on the sheet several times:

This is for Monday, December 5, 1955

Another Negro woman has been arrested and thrown into jail because she refused to get up out of her seat on the bus for a white person to sit down.

It is the second time since the Claudette Colbert [sic] case that a Negro woman has been arrested for the same thing. This has to be stopped.

Negroes have rights, too, for if Negroes did not ride the buses, they could not operate. Three-fourths of the riders are Negroes, yet we are arrested, or have to stand over empty seats. If we do not do something to stop these arrests, they will continue. The next time it may be you, or your daughter, or mother.

This woman's case will come up on Monday. We are, therefore, asking every Negro to stay off the buses Monday in protest of the arrest and trial. Don't ride the buses to work, to town, to school, or anywhere on Monday.

You can afford to stay out of school for one day if you have no other way to go except by bus.

You can also afford to stay out of town for one day. If you work, take a cab, or walk.

But please, children and grown-ups, don't ride the bus at all on Monday. Please stay off of all buses Monday.

The stencil complete, Mrs. Robinson called one of her Alabama State colleagues, business department chairman John Cannon, who had access to the school's mimeograph room and readily agreed to join her for a long night of work. By daybreak they had run off thousands of sheets, cut them into single copies, and organized the brief flyers into batches for distribution to dozens of WPC members and their friends. After teaching her first morning class, Mrs. Robinson and two students set out in her car, dropping off the bundles to helpers all across Montgomery. Thousands upon thousands of the leaflets went from hand-to-hand throughout black Montgomery.

While the WPC's network put the boycott into effect, E. D. Nixon made dozens of phone calls to assemble the black leadership. Like Robinson and her WPC colleagues, Nixon knew that for their protest to win mass support, the city's ministers, not always in the forefront of black civic initiatives, would have to be convinced to give the effort their full and active support. The WPC's post-haste distribution of the announcements, Robinson and Nixon knew, ought to short-circuit any arguments that now was not a good time for a boycott, even before they could be voiced. As Fred Gray later emphasized, "the ministers didn't know anything about those leaflets until they appeared."

Although the Friday evening leadership caucus had some difficulties in overcoming the autocratic style of one black pastor, agreement was reached on further publicizing the Monday boycott and on holding a Monday evening mass rally to assess the first day's success. The leadership would meet again Monday afternoon to plan the rally, and amidst scores of weekend phone conversations between the various black activists, a consensus gradually emerged that perhaps a new, all-encompassing

community organization ought to be created to oversee this unique effort.

Mrs. Robinson and the WPC membership knew that with the protest going public, their state-payroll positions at Alabama State, and the budgetary vulnerability of the college to white political retaliation, required that they remain in the background. As Mrs. Burks later noted in explaining why the origin of the boycott leaflets was treated as a closely-guarded secret well into the 1960s, "the full extent of our activities was never revealed because of the fact that we worked at State."

Monday morning the amazing success of the protest was readily apparent as onlooker after onlooker observed no more than a handful of black bus riders on Montgomery's largely empty vehicles.

Also on Monday, Mrs. Parks, in a very brief trial, was convicted of failing to obey the driver's command to surrender her seat. Hundreds of black Montgomerians, in a remarkable scene, gathered at the courthouse to show their support. That afternoon, when the black leadership assembled, Rufus Lewis—to be certain that leadership did not fall into unskilled hands—quickly nominated his pastor, Rev. Martin Luther King, Jr., to be president of their new community group, the Montgomery Improvement Association. A surprised King hesitantly accepted, and the leadership agreed to make continuation of the boycott beyond their one day success, contingent upon mass sentiment at the evening rally.

A huge and enthusiastic turnout for the evening event quickly and convincingly answered that question. Now the community leaders turned their efforts to organizing substitute means of transportation for the thousands of black Montgomerians eager to forsake a transportation system that most had assumed was an unpleasant but unavoidable fact of daily life.

Thursday morning, with the boycott four days old, more than half a dozen MIA representatives, including King, Robinson and Gray, met with city and bus company officials under the auspices of the bi-racial Alabama Council for Human Relations. Even though King emphasized to the whites that "we are not out to change the segregation laws," but only to win the driver courtesy and first come, first seated front-to-back and back-to-front seating policy that the WPC had been requesting for well over a year, the white officials would not budge from their insistent refusal that no changes in seating practices could be implemented.

The whites' complete intransigence, in the face of a black community effort of such impressive proportions, surprised the black leadership, who had entered into those first negotiations believing that their modest demands ought to make for a quick settlement. Since "our demands were moderate," King later recalled, "I had assumed that they would be granted with little question." Only in the wake of that unproductive meeting did the MIA leaders begin to realize that it was the very fact of their challenge, and not the particulars of their demands, that had meaning for white Montgomery.

To the city and bus company officials such as Commissioner Clyde Sellers and attorney Jack Crenshaw, the real issue was not which precise seating plan was legally permissible, but the defense of segregation's policies as an exemplar of the underlying doctrine of white racial supremacy. On that question no compromise could be possible; there either was superiority or there wasn't. "They feared that anything they gave would be viewed by us as just a start," Mrs. Robinson later reflected. "And you know, they were probably right."

An often shy and resolutely self-effacing person, Jo Ann Gibson Robinson is now almost seventy and lives quietly by herself in retirement in Los Angeles. Only with some gentle encouragement will she acknowledge herself as "the instigator of the movement to start that boycott." Even then, however, she seeks to avoid any special credit for herself or any other single individual. Very simply, she says, "the black women did it." And she's right.

Questions for Study and Review

1. How do social movements emerge out of periods of apparent conservatism and conformity?

2. How did the media, and television in particular, change the national impact of the Montgomery bus boycott and other civil rights protests in the South?

3. How did the family, work, and community roles of black women converge to give Rosa Parks's act its particular potency in Montgomery, in the nation, and in the arena of cold war politics?

4. The civil rights movement is often called the Second Reconstruction. What were the similarities and differences between black women's family and community roles in the two Reconstruction periods?

Suggested Readings

David Garrow, *The Montgomery Bus Boycott and the Women Who Started It: The Memoir of Jo Ann Gibson Robinson* (1987).

Sara Evans, *Personal Politics: The Roots of Women's Liberation in the Civil Rights Movement & the New Left* (1979).

Mary King, *Freedom Song: A Personal Story of the 1960s Civil Rights Movement* (1987).

Carl M. Brauer, "Women Activists, Southern Conservatives, and the Prohibition of Sex Discrimination in Title VII of the 1964 Civil Rights Act," *Journal of Southern History* (February 1983).

FIFTEEN

Embattled Women: The Defeat of the Equal Rights Amendment in Illinois

Jane J. Mansbridge

Like the abolitionist movement of the nineteenth century, the civil rights campaign of the twentieth century inspired women as well as blacks to demand the equality promised by American democratic traditions. Also as in the earlier era, questions of racial and sexual equality coincided with issues of war, though in the 1960s the war was overseas and the "rebels" were on the side of peace. Drawing on the language, lessons, and tactics of the civil rights and antiwar movements, young women attacked obstacles to their personal emancipation at the same time that they challenged racism, militarism, and sexism in society at large. These radical feminists sought to transform the entire social, economic, and political system.

Another group of women sought instead to promote women's entrance into that system on an equal basis. Beginning in the early 1960s, these women, many with experience as workers, wives, and mothers, rebelled against the "feminine mystique." Hoping to reform rather than revolutionize the existing system, Betty Friedan and other older, professional women formed the National Organization for Women (NOW) to promote economic, political, and social equality between the sexes. Relatively successful in its early campaigns, often building on legislation initially drafted

to end racial discrimination, NOW formed tenuous relationships with their radical feminist counterparts on behalf of such issues as the Equal Rights Amendment.

Feminists of the 1960s and 1970s were never as unified as were the early civil rights activists. Among the latter, a combination of racial solidarity and residential segregation allowed blacks to draw on strong communal bonds when mobilizing for social change. White supporters, initially at least, accepted black leadership and fit themselves into the contours of a movement shaped by those most oppressed by racism. Women lived in no such shared communities, and differences in styles, strategies, and goals thus appeared earlier and cut deeper.

Only in the early 1970s, however, in response to feminist campaigns to legalize abortion and ratify the ERA, did the true fault lines among women emerge. Then a third group of women, led by Phyllis Schlafly and backed by powerful male-dominated institutions, forged an antifeminist front. Anticipating the conservative backlash of the 1980s that would threaten advances for both blacks and women, female conservatives mobilized both the mass media and local women's organizations to oppose the ERA and the revolution in gender relations it had come to symbolize.

Mansbridge focuses on the battle for the ERA's ratification in Illinois in order to detail the economic, political, and cultural forces that led groups of women to oppose one another as each claimed to represent women's welfare. Women who pitted themselves against each other in the Illinois ratification fight were only slightly less hostile to one another than they were to those who claimed to be on the same side yet were in constant conflict over tactics and strategies. Each of these groups represented different visions of justice and of gender relations, visions that would shape women's and men's lives through the 1980s.

In 1962, only 37 percent of all wives worked for pay outside the home. The wives of high school- and college-educated men were hardly more likely to work for pay than the wives of men with only a grade school education. Between 1962 and 1978 the proportion of wives working for pay rose from 37 to 58 percent. This growth was concentrated among wives with highly educated husbands, for whom the economic pressures to work were lowest. Among women whose husbands had only a grade school education, 34 percent worked for pay both in 1962 and in 1978. Among women whose husbands had attended college, 38 percent worked for pay in 1962, but this had grown to 65 percent by 1978.

The growing class divergence in whether a married woman worked for pay was matched by a growing class divergence in how women felt about housework. Between 1957 and 1976 there was no change in the percentage of homemakers with a grade school education who said they "enjoyed" housework. In both years it was about 76 percent. Among those who had attended high school, the percentage who said they enjoyed housework fell from 66 to 54 percent. Among homemakers who had attended college it fell from 67 to 38 percent. The same pattern emerges when one looks at career aspirations. Among grade school-educated homemakers, the percentage who said that they had at some point wanted a career actually fell from 30 percent in 1957 to 15 percent in 1976. Among high school educated homemakers it rose only slightly, from 37 to 40 percent. Among college-educated homemakers it rose from 48 to 60 percent.

From *Why We Lost the ERA* by Jane J. Mansbridge. Copyright © 1986 by The University of Chicago. Reprinted by permission of The University of Chicago Press and the author.

The rise of careerism and the declining attraction of housework among educated women was partly a response to changes in job opportunities. For a woman with only grade school education, homemaking was usually a more pleasant, autonomous, growth-inducing profession than waitressing, cleaning other people's houses, or working as a factory operative, and these alternatives did not improve during the 1960s and 1970s. For women with a college education, homemaking was often more attractive than teaching school or being a secretary, which were the main alternatives in 1960. But homemaking was often far less attractive than the options that had opened up by the late 1970s.

These changes meant that women became less likely to share the same common experiences. At the beginning of the contemporary women's movement, in 1968, women of all classes found themselves in something like the same boat. Their structural positions either as homemakers or as lower-level employees were similar, and they expressed much the same feelings about their work and their home lives. By 1982, when the ERA went down to defeat, one of the bonds of sisterhood—a common experience in the home—was breaking. When employers opened good jobs to women, the beneficiaries were highly educated women who had decided not to become full-time homemakers. The more educated a woman was, the more she benefited from these changes. For less-educated women, homemaking remained the job of choice, but it lost social standing as high-status women abandoned it.

The decision of most college-educated women to pursue careers other than homemaking raised to public consciousness the many disadvantages of work in the home. Highly educated women were tastemakers for their sisters. In the 1950s, to preserve their own self-esteem, they extolled the virtues of work in the

National Rally for Equal Rights

The struggle for ratification of the Equal Rights Amendment in Illinois was hampered by factionalism, which eventually undermined the efforts of thousands of people who supported the amendment. In the Stop ERA campaign, Phyllis Schlafly and her Eagle Forum preyed on women's fears that passage of the ERA would hurt women by denying them child support, forcing them to work and place their children in federally funded day-care programs, legalizing homosexual marriages, making abortion mandatory, and instituting unisex toilet facilities.

home. By 1980, they saw matters quite differently. A job once perceived as noble now seemed distinctly plebeian. Thus, homemakers suffered a tremendous loss in social prestige in two decades. Sociologists call this phenomenon "status degradation." It had happened to these homemakers through no fault of their own.

Homemakers not only lost a lot of status in the course of the decade preceding the ERA struggle, they lost a number of their traditional protections as well. The divorce rate was increasing, and alimony was decreasing. Many states had instituted "no-fault" divorce laws, which reduced social blame on the husband who tired of his family, and even put pressure on some nurturant women to go along with

their husband's desire to abandon ship. A new ethic had arisen for men, in which hedonistic egoism was no longer encumbered by responsibility. Society was beginning to condone a man leaving his family on the sole grounds that living with them and providing for them made him unhappy.

The old common-law contract between the sexes held that if a woman did the housework, raised the children, and obeyed her husband, he had to support her. As we have seen, this contract had little practical force, but the ERA would have undermined its symbolic force as well. It was the ERA's symbolic meaning that frightened the opposition. When Phyllis Schlafly said of loveless marriages, "Even though love may go out the window, the obligation should remain. ERA would eliminate that obligation," any reader would assume she meant the ERA's legal effect. But she spelled out her concerns more clearly when she "insisted that the ERA would say. '[B]oys, supporting your wives isn't your responsibility anymore,' and then they could no longer see it as their duty." It is what the ERA would "say," not what it would do, that really concerned Schlafly and the rest of the opposition. In this deep sense the struggle over the ERA was indeed a "struggle over symbols."

Homemakers have always been somewhat more conservative than men or working women, perhaps partly because they are less exposed to a cosmopolitan world. This conservatism does not show up on all issues, but on matters that involved sexual relations, the family, and women's roles, homemakers were noticeably more conservative than either men or working women in the years from 1974 to 1982. Furthermore, on interracial marriage, homosexuality, and abortion, the gap between homemakers and working women increased markedly over these years.

These concerns meant that homemakers were less likely than working women to join feminist organizations like NOW. When NOW did a sample survey of its members in 1974, only 17 percent described themselves as homemakers, whereas 52 percent of all women over eighteen in the United States described themselves that way in that year. During 1973 and 1974 NOW launched five direct-mail campaigns to solicit funds. Of these five, the only one that failed to pay for itself involved subscribers to *Redbook* and *McCall's,* both of which are aimed at homemakers.

While feminist groups found it hard to restructure their thinking to appeal to homemakers, the homemakers' precarious social position made them a natural resource for groups that wanted to turn back the clock on the sexual,

legal, and labor-force trends that had undermined the patriarchal basis of the family in the decades before the ERA struggle. Indeed, the resurgence of the New Right in the 1970s was based largely on "women's issues" such as abortion and the ERA.

Many people who followed the struggle over the ERA believed that the Amendment would have been ratified by 1975 or 1976 had it not been for Phyllis Schlafly's early and effective effort to organize potential opponents. Schlafly seems to have stumbled on the ERA issue almost by accident. In 1964 she had written a campaign biography of Barry Goldwater (*A Choice, Not an Echo*) that attacked the elite East Coast Republican establishment for selling out to the Russians and neglecting American defense. In 1972 she was writing a monthly newsletter, the *Phyllis Schlafly Report,* which focused mainly on military preparedness and the dangers of Communism. Her first attack on the ERA appeared in February 1972, before the Amendment passed the Senate, but did little more than damn the Amendment by association with *Ms.* and "women's lib" while praising the privileges women had derived from the Christian Age of Chivalry. In this first article, Schlafly urged women who did not like their lot to "take up your complaint with God."

After the Senate passed the ERA, Schlafly entered the fray in earnest. She devoted her entire November 1972 *Report* to an attack on the ERA, stressing the substantive changes that the ERA might make in men's and women's lives. To her potential audience of homemakers, she began by arguing that the ERA would abolish the husband's duty to support his wife. She concluded that if the ERA were passed, and if child-care centers were made available, "a wife with small children would no longer be 'unable' to support herself through employment, and so . . . would lose the right of support from her husband." [These claims were substantially untrue.]

While her focus was clearly on the concerns of the homemaker, Schlafly also touched on other substantive changes that she knew were likely to appall a conservative, or even mainstream, audience. Added Schlafly, "the Equal Rights Amendment will positively make women subject to the draft and for combat duty on an equal basis with men. Most women's libbers admit that this is what they want."

According to Schlafly, [Paul] Freund [Harvard Law School] concluded that the ERA (1) might make separate athletic competitions for men and women illegal; (2) would "presumably" reduce certain Social Security retirement benefits for women to the same level as those available to similarly situated men; (3) might abolish freedom of choice between boys' schools, girls' schools, and coed schools; (4) might eliminate separate physical education classes for girls and boys in public schools; (5) might abolish separate prison cells for men and women; and even (6) might make illegal separate public rest rooms for the different sexes. [Again, these claims were either exaggerated or false.]

Schlafly ended her *Report* with another pitch to homemakers, pointing out that the Civil Rights Act of 1964 already guaranteed equal pay for equal work. She concluded by describing the "two very different groups of women lobbying for the Equal Rights Amendment":

> One group is the women's liberationists. Their motive is totally radical. They hate men, marriage and children. They are out to destroy morality and the family. They look upon husbands as the exploiters, children as an evil to be avoided (by abortion if necessary), and the family as an institution which keeps women in "second-class citizenship" or even "slavery."

The second group was business and professional women who "have felt the keen edge of discrimination in their employment. Many have been in a situation where the woman does most of the work, and some man gets the bigger salary and the credit." Citing her own experience with this kind of discrimination, she said she supported this group in their effort to eliminate injustice, but she argued that everything necessary could be done through the Civil Rights Act and the Equal Employment Opportunity Act, which would not "take away fundamental rights and benefits from the rest of women."

This issue of the *Report* was aimed at homemakers (and their husbands), and the tactic was a startling success. To be sure a majority of homemakers in the United States continued to support the ERA, as did a majority of every other major demographic group. But the anti-ERA forces drew much of their active support from homemakers. Just as an exaggeration of the ERA's effect on working women became the major argument for the proponents, because it appealed not only to the general public but to a particular large and angry constituency, so an exaggeration of the ERA's effect on homemakers became, for the same reasons, the first major argument of the opponents.

While Phyllis Schlafly's exaggerations regarding the husband's duty of support and other "family" issues may well have helped her cause, the exaggeration that hurt her most, and became a major weapon in the hands of her enemies, was the issue of unisex toilets. Schlafly devoted only one sentence to the "toilet" issue in "The Right to be a Woman," but the wording of that sentence was crucial. Professor Paul Freund, she wrote, "indicates that [if the ERA is adopted] we must assume that rest rooms segregated by sex would be prohibited by the courts just as the courts prohibit color-segregated rest rooms." [The legislative history of the ERA, however, made it clear that this would never happen.]

Yet the unisex toilet issue fed the fervor of the anti-ERA forces by giving them something absolutely outrageous to focus on. It could conjure up visions of rape by predatory males. It could symbolize the stripping away of all traditional protections in an androgynous society where women could no longer claim special treatment from the more powerful male simply on the grounds that they were women. In the South it recalled vividly the historical trauma of racial integration. Indeed, as we shall see, unisex toilets became one of the four major themes that activists speaking to reporters and writing in the newspapers stressed as central to their opposition.

But while this issue strengthened the morale of the activists, it had mixed results among the public and backfired in the legislatures. Among the public nationwide, the argument was probably counterproductive. While there is no way of proving that this or any other argument hurt the opposition, the fact that in another survey 76 percent of the public thought that the ERA would not even increase the likelihood of integrated toilets suggests a widespread skepticism that normally would undermine credibility.

In the four key unratified states of Illinois, Oklahoma, Florida, and North Carolina, the overall effect on public opinion of the opposition's focus on toilets is less clear. Having lived through the racial integration of public toilets, the citizens of Florida and North Carolina may have been psychologically more susceptible to claims that the ERA would integrate toilets sexually, with the connotations of rape, defilement, and vulnerability that that image implies. But so few people anywhere gave integrated toilets as a reason for opposing the ERA that it is hard to see this issue as a frequent source of opposition even in the key unratified states. It is more likely to have appealed almost exclusively to the already convinced.

In the legislatures, the issue served to solidify the conviction of middle-of-the-road legislators that the opposition was irrational. In Illinois, pro-ERA legislators, aware of the effects on opinion of the toilet issue, were the only legislators to bring it up. They used unisex toilets over and over to imply that all other arguments against the ERA were equally exaggerated. Indeed, the pro-ERA forces jumped on the unisex toilet issue as quickly as the anti forces jumped on combat. This one massive and obvious distortion of the truth allowed them to label all the opponents' arguments as lies, irrelevancies, and scare tactics not worthy of serious consideration.

Schlafly herself came to understand the negative effect of this issue in the course of the ten years between 1972 and 1982. After her early salvos, she rarely mentioned unisex toilets again. After she entered law school in 1975, her speeches became a little more careful in other respects as well. She was learning, both from her new training and from experience, what worked with the mainstream audience. As one Illinois legislator commented, "I heard her in her first arguments, which were sloppy at times—incendiary, you know, not very, very good. She is so smooth now, I mean, she's got it down to an art form. I think she is totally unbeatable."

The STOP ERA forces were relatively hierarchically organized, with Schlafly herself at the apex of the hierarchy, but, in managing the activists who volunteered to help oppose the ERA, Schlafly still had to contend with the decentralized character of all social movements. Local groups could and did mount actions that highlighted the common toilet issue, and Schlafly could do little to stop them without diminishing their enthusiasm. This decentralization of responsibility was probably helpful with the public on some issues, because local groups could raise completely false arguments against the ERA without anyone having to take responsibility for them. (Schlafly herself, faced with some extreme anti-ERA propaganda, demurely told state legislators, "That is not one of my arguments against the ERA. . . . I think I can back up anything I write. And I am also very tolerant. I let people be against ERA for the reason of their choice.") Yet the opponents' cause must have suffered somewhat with middle-of-the-road legislators when proponents could testify that more than 90 percent of the allegations in some anti-ERA pamphlets were false.

Anti-ERA legislators usually avoided the most inflammatory charges, advanc[ing] reasons quite different from those of the anti-ERA activists. The opposition legislators' most frequent point in these newspaper stories was that the ERA would remove powers from the states. Their next most frequent point was that the Amendment was not needed. They were also worried about unforeseen consequences, including the draft and combat. They practically never mentioned toilets. In these same newspapers, activists' opposition to the ERA focused on four issues: first, that women would be drafted; next, that husbands would not be solely liable for the support of their families; third, that the ERA would threaten the family in general; and, finally, that public restrooms would become sexually integrated. In short, except for the draft and combat, opposition legislators and activists were worried about different issues.

While the parallels are not exact between the proponents' use of "59 cents" and the opponents' use of the husband's right to support, or between the proponents' exaggerations regarding combat and the opponents' exaggerations regarding toilets, these issues illustrate similar dynamics operating within both pro- and anti-ERA movements. Yet the opponents' exaggerations cost them less in the political struggle.

First, public support for the ERA rested not so much on a calculation of particular costs and benefits as on a generalized commitment to abstract rights. Given this kind of public commitment, almost any move from principle to substance tended to hurt the Amendment's chances. Consequently, once opponents turned public attention to the Amendment's effects, they were already well on their way to winning. Their exaggerations, while incurring some

costs in credibility, succeeded in making the substantive effects of the Amendment a central issue in the debate.

Second, because the amendment process requires a near consensus, the opponents had only to create enough doubt about the Amendment to prevent a consensus from forming. As in slander, only some of the dirt had to stick. The ERA's opponents had the framers of the Constitution on their side. Without proving anything, they had only to create an atmosphere of distrust in order to win.

❋

Both the pro-ERA and STOP ERA organizations always had to pursue two goals: surviving as organizations, and either passing or defeating the ERA. These goals often conflicted. The requirements of organizational survival forced both sides to recruit and retain activists for whom passing or defeating the ERA was only one of many goals, and whose activities occasionally did their cause more harm than good. Maintaining the commitment of these activists also required the organizations themselves to do things, like exaggerating the Amendment's probable effect, that sometimes hurt their cause. The need to maintain the activists' commitment to the organizations, moreover, shaped the day-to-day political tactics of the organizations on both sides, sometimes even bringing them into conflict with their nominal allies.

To attract and keep their activists, the different pro-ERA organizations chose different ways of mobilizing public opinion and changing legislative votes. NOW, a national organization that had come to rely heavily on direct mail contributions, leaned toward tactics that would generate national media coverage—mass rallies, demonstrations, and television ads aimed at a national audience. Local groups picked other strategies. In Illinois, the statewide umbrella organization, ERA Illinois, depended on the energies of women who had long-standing interest in state politics. Accordingly, it leaned toward tactics that involved its members in the things they liked most—district-based local organizing, and building personal relationships with state leaders in the two political parties. Both strategies had their weaknesses and strengths. But in Illinois, as in the other states, those who practiced one tended to see the other as at best self-serving or deluded and at worst undermining the cause.

In 1982, NOW organized a mass demonstration at the Illinois state capitol in Springfield. Thousands upon thousands of women in white surged down the wide streets toward the capitol dome that towered against the blue midwestern sky, chanting over and over, "What do we want?" "ERA!" "When do we want it?" "*Now!*" Yet, far from rejoicing at this massive show of support, the members of ERA Illinois, who talked every day to the legislators, wrung their hands and agonized over the cumulative anger that these demonstrations were building up, even among sympathetic legislators.

May and June are always the best times for a demonstration. There is time for preparation over the fall and winter, and the demonstration provides a kind of culmination to the year's activities, which always dissipate during the members' scattered vacations during the summer and resume in the fall. More important, the warm weather of the oncoming summer will always lure outside many whose spirits have congealed during the winter months. But late spring and early summer are also frantic days for state legislators, whose work is underpaid and part-time, and who inevitably postpone the most difficult issues—budget, roads, taxes—until the last moment before they themselves go back to their neglected families and jobs for the summer.

So when another ERA demonstration loomed on the horizon, the legislators grumbled and cursed, building up vengeful feelings against the "goddamned women" who were invading their citadel again, bringing no new insights or information with them, just endless pestering and emotional displays. ERA Illinois members, with their fingers on the pulse of the few wavering legislators, worried desperately at the possibility that each new demonstration might be the last straw.

For their part, NOW leaders ground their teeth in frustration when the president of ERA Illinois (a Republican) and the vice-president (a Democrat), wearing ERA buttons, attended a fund-raising dinner for Governor Thompson at which President Reagan was the principal speaker. NOW members were picketing outside the dinner, as they had picketed Reagan everywhere they could throughout the state when he came to support Republican candidates for reelection. They were picketing to draw attention to the President's opposition to the ERA and to his many national policies that hurt the poor, who were primarily women. They had no qualms about picketing Governor Thompson's fund-raising dinner, even though he was a liberal Republican who nominally supported the ERA, because he had also chosen a conservative Republican and arch opponent of the ERA, George Ryan, as his running mate for lieutenant governor. Ryan was the second speaker at the dinner. Illinois was reducing the size of its legislature, which meant that many incumbents would lose their seats. If Thompson and Ryan won the upcoming gubernatorial election, Ryan would play a pivotal role in redistricting, and thus in determining which legislators lost their seats. No legislator in any but the safest seat wanted to be on the wrong side of George Ryan, and Ryan had let it be known for a long time that he detested the ERA. What, then, were the ERA Illinois president and vice-president doing attending a $250-a-plate fund-raising dinner for Thompson at which both President Reagan and George Ryan would be honored speakers?

Members of ERA Illinois, on the other hand, believed that picketing Reagan would only generate national publicity and would never persuade any Illinois legislator to vote for the ERA. They had gotten the tickets to the fund-raising dinner free, they protested, and had distributed pro-ERA literature around the tables. Most important, it seemed clear to them that since the Republicans were the majority party in the Illinois house, making the ERA a straight Republican-Democratic issue would surely kill it. As one said,

> [NOW's leaders have] worked only with the Democrats and have simply almost ignored the Republicans, who are the majority party, and the leadership of the Republican Party, which has every prerogative to use the gavel in dozens of different ways to frustrate their efforts. . . .

The two tactics developed quite naturally from the different membership needs of the two groups. Each group attracted people with different political sympathies, ages, and ways of life. ERA Illinois, a nonpartisan body, had for several years had a Republican president. When the president of ERA Illinois ran for state senate in 1982, her campaign literature pledged her to work for "public assistance only for those truly in need," and "a balanced state budget." The next president of ERA Illinois, a school teacher, commented at a meeting, "If the parents would teach their kids responsibility, respectability and religion . . . at home, we'd have no problem with them at school!" NOW, on the other hand, had a membership of liberals and radicals who were almost exclusively Democrats. Indeed, as one Illinois NOW leader put it, "Most of our members would identify themselves as social-ist, without knowing what it meant." NOW, working with Democratic politicians, developed ERA strategies that tended to benefit the Democrats, while ERA Illinois worked with Republicans.

In part, the differences had to do with style. NOW members often thought of ERA Illinois as composed of ladies who sat with their hands in their laps expecting the Republican leadership to change because the ladies were so nice. The members of ERA Illinois were mostly over forty and thus older than most active members of NOW. ERA Illinois was also more sedate: in the first ERA Illinois meeting that I attended none of the women wore jeans, one wore a matched polyester pantsuit, and exactly half wore skirts—compared to half jeans and half slacks at my first local NOW meeting. More than half the women at ERA Illinois wore some kind of makeup compared to only one of the women at my NOW meeting. Ranging from the dumpy to the classically coiffed and tailored, the ERA Illinois women saw themselves as representing the grass roots. They laughed together, as they traded recipes during a potluck lunch, at the contrast their homey activity presented to the image they imagined state legislators had of the average ERA activist.

But notwithstanding the conservative senti-ments of their presidents and their older, more local backgrounds, these women were genu-ine feminists. ERA Illinois meetings almost always began with someone passing around a news item about women or the ERA that had made them mad or telling a joke that spoke to women's plight. They welcomed a member's newborn to "his first feminist meeting," and in my later interviews every woman I talked with identi-fied herself as a feminist. They simply had a different natural style. One ERA Illinois leader responded with irritation to the charge of "niceness" by saying,

> I don't think niceness makes anybody change. But there is only one way to keep a rapport going with the people who are in a position to make or break a piece of legislation, and that is to keep communicating, to be sensi-tive to that person, to keep relaying what you know, what you hear, to other people in the party who have your best interest in mind, your issue in mind. And look for the

moment when you might use some devious tactics to get what you need done.

But the NOW activists, eyeing the activities of some of the members of ERA Illinois, concluded that they were only trying to advance their careers in the Republican party.

Not only the age and style but the members' backgrounds in politics were quite different within the two groups. The typical NOW member had not been born in Illinois and did not necessarily expect to spend her life there. In my local NOW chapter, many of the members were recent migrants to the city, at least half were under forty, several were lesbians, and many were unmarried. Recognizing their ignorance of state politics, one woman suggested at my first meeting that the chapter set up a "legislative task force" to learn more about the state legislature. One NOW leader summarized her constituency: "We have a lot of people who know about reproductive rights, affirmative action, and all the feminist issues—but they don't know a thing about street lights." While these NOW members might eventually settle in Illinois and become local political leaders, right now they were "cosmopolitans" who had joined the organization primarily to share their feminism in an atmosphere of mutual support.

This generalized feminist ideology made NOW a multi-issue organization. As a result, many legislators tied the ERA to other feminist causes, especially legal abortion. The NOW leadership was aware of this dilemma. In the major ratification push of 1980, NOW's national office set up its ERA ratification project office in Illinois several blocks away from the main NOW office, specifically to insure that literature, posters, and other reminders that NOW was a multi-issue organization would not be present. But while the new direct-mail members of NOW often joined because of the ERA, the active chapter membership was still concerned with the full range of feminist issues. They had joined

the organization to find companions as well as to support the cause, and they often resented the fact that NOW's national office was devoting time and money to the ERA that they would rather have seen devoted to preserving abortion rights or other feminist causes. Occasionally, these members even responded to questions about the ERA's effect on abortion by defending a woman's right to abortion rather than taking the official NOW position that there was no connection between the two issues. ERA Illinois, on the other hand, prided itself in having engaged in its coalition a number of Roman Catholic organizations, which opposed abortion as a matter of principle. The leaders of ERA Illinois saw both NOW's support for abortions and the generally distracting effect of other issues as hurting the ERA.

The active members of NOW did have a larger goal in mind than simply ratifying the ERA. For many new members of NOW, working for the ERA was a radicalizing experience. It opened their eyes to the underlying attitudes of many of their legislators, friends, families, colleagues, and bosses. For many, the ERA provided their first political activity. In a NOW bus going to Springfield in 1980 I interviewed one woman who had driven from Colorado to Illinois, using her entire yearly vacation from her secretarial job to work for the ERA. She had come in touch with the women's movement for the first time at her second job, when "the first issue of *Ms.* had come out, and someone was sharing the issue around the office." With no NOW chapter or any other women's group in her town, she became a direct-mail member of NOW, and for years was politically active only by sending postcards to legislators when the *NOW Times* sent out a call. But when the ERA began to falter, she moved into a political activity that absorbed her evenings, her weekends, and now her one vacation. An older black woman told me that she had watched on television the ERA demonstration organized by

NOW in Chicago and had wanted to join in then, but this was the first time she had had the time to participate. Like almost everyone else on the bus, she had never been to Springfield before.

Knowing that work for the ERA was often the first step to committed feminism, both the leaders and most of the active members of NOW saw the ERA as only one battle in an ongoing, much longer war. They valued each demonstration, each phone call soliciting support, and each television ad, not just for its effect in passing the ERA itself but for its value in sensitizing all women to feminist political issues. Moreover, NOW was not just a local but a national organization, resting even more on its direct-mail membership than on its constituent chapters. Its political strength lay in attracting new members and in giving the present ones the feeling that the organization was doing something important. Once NOW became visibly involved in the national ERA struggle, its direct-mail membership began to increase dramatically. This meant that the organization naturally leaned toward activities that had a national impact, like television ads and massive demonstrations that would get national media coverage rather than toward local organizing in districts with wavering legislators, many of which did not even have a NOW chapter.

While NOW had to rely on a group of people who had joined the organization for a broad range of feminist reasons, ERA Illinois depended largely on the energies of a few women who in their unions, churches, or League of Women Voters chapters had followed state politics the way a fan follows baseball. At the first ERA Illinois meeting I attended, the president spent more than two hours giving an update on each of the state legislators, with a style so informal in its references that at least half the time I did not understand which legislator was being discussed. She caught the meeting up on the legislators' personal and political fortunes, who

had said what to whom at what restaurant, who was getting divorced, who had a hard race ahead in the next election, who was being maneuvered out of power by a group of local committeemen, and how that all affected the probable line-up of votes on the ERA in the upcoming legislative session.

During a break in another meeting, I turned to a nurse from the south side of Chicago who had been almost as quiet as I, and who I thought might be almost as confused. Hoping to begin a tentative alliance of the unsophisticated, I asked where she lived. "District 28," she replied, leaving me as ignorant as I was before. At a NOW chapter meeting, it is inconceivable that anyone would have described where she lived by naming her legislative district. Indeed, few would even have known the number of their legislative districts, much less expecting other people to know where a district identified by a number really was. For the ten or fifteen people who were extremely active in ERA Illinois, this kind of response was second nature. As one member of the board put it, they were "political animals."

Organizationally weak, ERA Illinois kept its larger membership by offering a nonradical way of supporting the ERA, and by acting as the coalition that brought together all the state supporters of the ERA—from unions to business. It attracted the energies of its most active members by giving them a chance to live and breathe intrigue, high drama and history-in-the-making, while also doing good. Such a strategy produced active members who engaged in what some ERA sponsors in the legislature considered counterproductive and naive meddling with the sponsors' legislative planning. And in spite of the enthusiasm of its most active members, ERA Illinois was not equipped to organize at the district level. It was an unexciting, frequently disorganized umbrella organization, with few individual members. While its organizational membership included a number of large groups, none of these groups had much interest in trying to mobilize its membership to enter active politics in their home districts. There were simply not enough "political animals" to go around.

Within the anti-ERA movement, the need to attract members also influenced tactics. But here the tensions between groups recruited in different ways were not as visible, at least on the surface, partly because the movement did not have to be as large (and therefore heterogeneous) and partly because of Phyllis Schlafly's dominant role.

At the beginning of the anti-ERA campaign, Schlafly relied primarily on the highly committed conservative subscribers to *The Phyllis Schlafly Report* and on the Eagle Forum, a group formed from her supporters in the National Federation of Republican Women after the Republican establishment, suspicious of her extreme views and populist tactics, had maneuvered her out of NFRW leadership. The women in the Eagle Forum had experience in local electoral campaigns and with state legislators. They also had an effective, though top-down, means of communication in *The Phyllis Schlafly Report,* and they had a war chest that Schlafly set up to receive donations for causes she took up in her newsletter. But these women were widely viewed as extremists, and they were far too few to launch a national movement. When Schlafly tried to organize more widely among homemakers, she shifted her tactics to include activities that homemakers could do in interrupted time, like phoning talk shows, sending letters to the editor in local papers, and writing state legislators. But so long as the STOP ERA movement was composed primarily of the Eagle Forum and a few homemakers, it could not mount an impressive demonstration at the state capitol. In the early days of anti-ERA organizing, the STOP ERA women who went to Springfield were, by and large, older women whose children had left the home.

Beginning around 1976, however, the STOP ERA movement acquired a third constituency, as fundamentalist groups began to enter politics and focus on "women's issues" like the ERA. Many of these fundamentalist women were full-time homemakers. But unlike most homemakers, their church activities had given them experience speaking in public and approaching strangers. Their churches and their own convictions demanded an interventionist, missionary stance toward anyone who had not accepted Jesus Christ as a personal savior. While most Americans confronted with someone who does not share their religious or political views avoid the subject, missionary fundamentalists deliberately bring the controversial subject into conversation, challenge the unbeliever, present personal testimony, and work actively for conversion. These skills and the evangelical enthusiasm that gave them life made it relatively easy for such women to enter the political arena. Moreover, the churches were already organized. They had preexisting meeting places, buses, and claims on their members' time and money.

Neither the media, the American public, nor most legislators were aware that most of the women who demonstrated against the ERA at state capitols around the country in the last years of the ERA struggle were fundamentalists brought there by their pastors. While the male ministers and bus drivers sat outside in the yellow buses, the women did their work under the rotunda. There was enough central coordination so that the pamphlets the women brought with them were usually official STOP ERA literature, but in conversation they readily gave witness to their extreme fundamentalist beliefs. When I took part in NOW's June 1980 ERA demonstration at Springfield, for example, I had no way of telling visually that the counterpickets—some young, some grandmothers, all wearing white and red dresses and sporting the traditional red hexagonal Stop sign of the "anti" forces—were there under the auspices of their church. But when I asked them my introductory question of why and how they had become involved in activity against the ERA, all but one gave me some version of the response:

Christian beliefs, mainly. I believe God made us different. . . . My religion strictly says women should submit to their husbands. It says so in the Bible, and you can't believe part of the Bible but not all. . . . So many people ask us why we do what we do—it's because of the Bible. Others don't know about the Bible, about the truth.

Or, as another explained,

It was through a church group. . . . and of course there was a religious reason—I know that God gave men certain responsibilities and He gave women responsibilities. The men were to take care of the women. . . . "The husband is the head of the wife, as Christ is head of the Church."

Only one of the women I talked with that day was not from a fundamentalist church group, and she was firmly convinced that the ERA was a Communist plot sponsored by the Trilateral Commission.

Until I interviewed these women myself I had had no idea that the basis for their action was a literal belief in the Pauline passages from the Bible stipulating that women must be subject to men. Nor did any of the reporters from national television or the Chicago newspapers who covered the demonstration that day know this, since they did not ask. Even a feminist reporter from one of the major television networks missed the religious motivation of the STOP ERA demonstrators. She had spent her time interviewing Phyllis Schlafly, and she, like everyone else, had assumed that the STOP ERA forces in the rotunda were the kinds of women Schlafly liked to claim as her troops—simply homemakers threatened by the potential loss of their special legal "protections" under the ERA.

The organizational base in church groups that developed about halfway through the ERA campaign gave the opposition an advantage in perceived longevity, at least among legislators who were aware of it, because these groups were all local and relatively stable. The legislators knew that they wouldn't go away, that they felt intensely, and that they would act politically on their feelings.

The people who are anti-ERA in my district feel very, very intensely about it. And they will go out and they will work for or against people that are anti-ERA [sic]. . . .

. . . I have a district that contains a lot of very basic conservative religious groups. For example, the bastion of anti-ERA feeling in my district is concentrated mainly in "the Bible Belt of the North." I have areas in my district where some women do not even exercise their right to vote.

—*Anti-ERA legislator*

However, the church groups, like NOW, had their own agenda, of which stopping the ERA was only a small part. As a result, while their tactics against ratification usually filled their own members' needs, they were often less effective with wavering legislators than NOW's activists. As we have seen, Phyllis Schlafly could not control what the fundamentalists said to legislators. Fundamentalist women sometimes told their legislators they would literally go to hell, or must have been inspired by the devil, if they voted for the ERA. The legislators, in turn, became furious at having their religious commitment questioned.

The Illinois experience was never exactly duplicated in other states. But the patterns of behavior I have described are not peculiar to Illinois or even to the struggle over the ERA. For example, few unratified states had as many problems as Illinois within their pro-ERA coalitions. But every state had some coalitional problems, and those problems were often related to the kinds of incentives the different organizations offered their memberships.

Illinois was also atypical because Phyllis Schlafly lived there. Schlafly's organizing tactics, however, were no different in Illinois, only stronger and more visible. If in Illinois, despite Schlafly's long term contacts in the state Republican party, STOP ERA still had to rely heavily on the fundamentalist churches, this was likely to be even more true elsewhere.

Finally, unlike most states, Illinois had a rule requiring a three-fifths majority in both houses to ratify constitutional amendments—a require-ment that was dropped soon after the ERA had died. Without the three-fifths rule, Illinois quite early would have become the thirty-sixth state to ratify the ERA. But the rule did not change the dynamics within the legislature or in the districts. It simply gave more power to the "downstate" and rural districts, making the balance of power on this issue closer to that in intrinsically more conservative states like Oklahoma and North Carolina. Thus, while the political situation in Illinois was certainly not typical, the processes at work in the state were probably quite typical.

Questions for Study and Review

1. To what extent was the battle over the ERA the last gasp of "sixties" activism and the first whisper of a conservative resurgence?

2. What were the similarities and differences in the conditions of blacks and women in postwar America and in the ways in which they pursued social change?

3. For a generation raised on *I Love Lucy* and other television "sitcoms" and indoctrinated through advertising and other means with the "feminine mystique," what were the forces that transformed some of them into activists, and specifically feminists?

4. To what extent did women's social activism in the 1960s and 1970s continue to draw on techniques and ideas employed by their counterparts in the 1830s and 1840s or at the turn of the century?

Suggested Readings

Mary Frances Berry, *Why the ERA Failed: Politics, Women's Rights and the Amending Process* (1986).

Joan Hoff-Wilson, ed., *Rights of Passage: The Past and Future of the ERA* (1986).

Winifred Wandersee, *On the Move: American Women in the 1970s* (1988).

Susan D. Becker, *The Origins of the Equal Rights Amendment: American Feminism Between the Wars* (1981).

Pamela Johnston Conover and Virginia Gray, *Feminism and the New Right: Conflict over the American Family* (1983).

APPENDIX

A Statistical Portrait

Ruth Milkman

To recapture the historical experience of women, scholars have pursued a host of new methods and turned to a variety of sources. Some famous or elite women left letters, diaries, and family papers, which historians have used to recreate these women's relations with their fathers and husbands as well as with female kin and friends. These documents also provide information about women's activities in churches, schools, and voluntary organizations as well as intimations of their attitudes toward children. A smaller number of poor, working-class, and minority women also wrote about their lives or had their spoken testimony transcribed by others. Yet uncovering and understanding the daily lives and thoughts of these nonelite and less well known women, and their male kin and neighbors, requires investigation of more than the conventional literary sources. Examinations of physical artifacts such as housing or dress, the use of visual and aural documents in the form of photographs or recordings, the gathering of oral histories, and the analysis of quantitative data all provide new means of illuminating the past.

The use of statistical information is especially important for reconstructing the objective boundaries of people's lives. Such data might include the relative numbers of women and men in a community, the average number of children borne by an adult women, the likelihood of a woman working for wages, the types of jobs she might hold and her average earnings, the life expectancy of women and men, and how each of these varied by region, race, class, and ethnic background as well as over time.

For most women, the size and makeup of their household, the amount and type of domestic labor they performed, and their access to paid employment set the framework of their lives. These factors shaped their relationships with relatives, neighbors, and the larger community and powerfully affected the opportunities open to them for education, recreation, and participation in public activities or institutions. For most of our nation's history, women of all regions, races, classes, and ethnic backgrounds shared certain experiences. More than 90 percent of all women did housework, were married, or lived in marriage-like relations, and bore children at some point in their lives. Yet more often it was not these broad similarities but rather the differences among women that were important in shaping the contours of individual, family, and community history. Thus, it is critical to locate women in place as well as in time and to chart change over time both for women as women and in relation to men.

Since the late nineteenth century, several new factors have emerged as significant in shaping the lives of women and men. Before this time, it was the death of one of the partners that ended most marriages. But with the dramatic increase in life expectancy after 1900, more and more marriages were ended by separation and divorce. This, in turn, created new types of households and placed different demands on women and men in terms of providing for themselves and their children. Over the same period, women's fertility rate declined, though more slowly for some groups than for others. The size of the average household shrank, and more women graduated from high school and college and entered the paid labor force. At the same time, women were still relegated to certain types of jobs, and black and immigrant women faced an even narrow range of choices than native-born white women. The gap between men's and women's wages remained remarkably consistent, although the gap between the wages of blacks and whites, especially for women, closed significantly after World War II.

In the tables, figures, and graphs that follow, Ruth Milkman provides quantitative portraits of women from a range of families and communities and across the expanse of American history. Though limited by the amount, types, and quality of data collected in past centuries, these statistical snapshots allow us to view our ancestors with a new clarity and to compare their experiences—their life expectancy, the size of their families, the racial and sexual balance in their communities, their opportunities for paid work, and their participation in various occupations—with our own.

The articles in this volume describe women in specific times and places and engaged in a variety of activities—childbirth and childrearing, slave labor, factory or farm work, wartime service, or political or religious pursuits. Consulting the graphs and tables provided here as you read the articles will help you place the women you read about within the larger context of the American experience. The statistical information will help you grasp better the different relationships between native-born white and immigrant women and men in early twentieth-century families. You will see, for example, that in the first group, there were roughly equal numbers of women and men, but in the second, there were substantially more men than women. You can perceive the importance of bearing children, rearing children, and earning wages for both white and black women, as well as how these experiences differed between the two groups. Fertility rates (the average number of births per woman) declined much more quickly for white than black women in the twentieth century, yet the percentage of black women in the paid labor force was much higher than that for whites until 1970.

You can begin to imagine what dramatic changes in individual and family life occurred as the average woman bore fewer and fewer children over the course of the century, with a woman of the 1970s bearing only half the number of children borne by her turn-of-the-century grandmother. And that granddaughter, born in the "baby boom" of the 1950s, had a much better chance than any of her foremothers of attending high school or college, working for wages at some time in her life, and joining a union. She was also likelier, however, to get a divorce, become head of a household, or live alone for some part of her life. These changes in family and work life give us a new perspective on what a political movement like feminism might mean to different generations of women, or to black women who by the 1960s had long been in the paid labor force in large numbers versus white women who were just entering paid labor in large numbers.

These statistical portraits throw into sharp relief the outlines of women's lives across the last century of our nation's history. Tracing the common as well as the quite different experiences of women of various ethnic backgrounds, classes, and races across both time and place, the charts, graphs, and tables included here set the contours of our own lives in a larger context and help us understand the conditions and the constraints under which earlier Americans carved out their individual, familial, communal, and national identities.

Suggested Readings

W. Elliott Brownlee and Mary M. Brownlee, *Women in the American Economy* (1976).

Richard A. Easterlin, "Population Change and Farm Settlement in the Northern United States," *Journal of Economic History* 36 (1976).

Michael Gordon, ed., *The American Family in Social-Historical Perspective* (3rd ed., 1986).

Joni Seager and Ann Olson, *Women in the World: An International Atlas* (1986).

Helen L. Sumner, *History of Women in Industry in the United States* (1910).

U.S. Bureau of the Census, *Historical Statistics of the United States, Colonial Times to 1970* (1975).

U.S. Bureau of the Census, *Negro Population, 1790–1915* (1918).

U.S. Department of Labor, *History of Wages in the United States from Colonial Times to 1928* (1934).

U.S. Department of Labor, Women's Bureau Bulletin 198, *Time of Change: 1983 Handbook on Women Workers* (1983).

Robert V. Wells, "Women's Lives Transformed: Demographic and Family Patterns in America, 1600–1970," in Carol Berkin and Mary Beth Norton, eds., *Women of America, A History* (1979).

In the twentieth century, life expectancy has increased dramatically for the entire U.S. population. However, women's longevity has increased substantially more than men's, among both whites and blacks. Whites of both sexes have significantly higher life expectancy than their black counterparts, but the extent of this difference has been reduced greatly over the course of the century. The following line graph shows the rise in life expectancy by gender and race from 1900 to 1985.

Life Expectancy (in Years) at Birth, by Gender and Race, 1900–1985

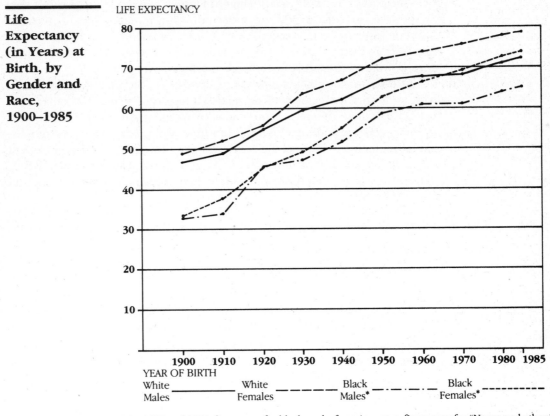

LIFE EXPECTANCY

YEAR OF BIRTH

White Males _____ White Females — — — Black Males* —·—·— Black Females* — — —

* For 1980 and 1985, figures are for blacks only; for prior years, figures are for "Negro and other."
Source: U.S. Bureau of the Census, *Historical Statistics of the United States, Colonial Times to 1970* (Washington: GPO, 1975), 55; U.S. Bureau of the Census, *Statistical Abstract of the United States: 1988* (Washington: GPO, 1987, 108th ed.), 71.

Fertility rates (the average number of births per woman) have fluctuated significantly in the past century, falling gradually in the period from 1890 to the Great Depression of the 1930s, reviving during World War II and in the "baby boom" of the postwar period, and then falling again after 1960 to reach a new low in the 1970s. Fertility rates have been consistently higher for blacks and other minorities than for whites; however, the trends over time are similar in direction for both groups. The line graph below shows the fluctuations in births per woman for whites from 1890 to 1984 and for blacks and others from 1940 to 1984. Data are not available for fertility rates for blacks and others from 1890 to 1939.

Fertility Rates (Births per Woman) for Women in the United States, by Race, 1890–1985

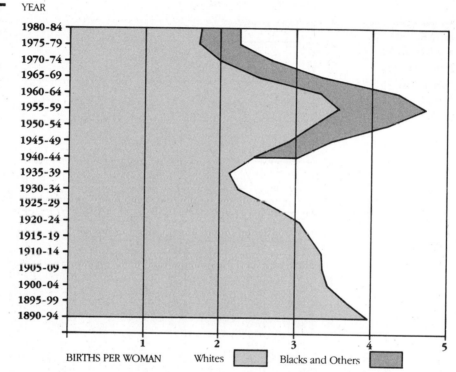

Source: Ansley J. Coale and Melvin Zelnik, *New Estimates of Fertility and Population in the United States* (Princeton: Princeton University Press, 1963), 36; U.S. Bureau of the Census, *Statistical Abstract of the United States: 1988* (Washington: GPO, 1987, 108th ed.), 59.

A major source of population growth in the period before World War I and in the period from the 1960s to the present has been immigration. However, the two waves of mass immigration differ in important ways. In the pre-World War I era, men outnumbered women among immigrants, whereas more recently the opposite has been true. Sex ratios have shifted in favor of women in the U.S. population as a whole in the course of the last century (due largely to the relatively greater increase in female longevity). The shift has been most pronounced among the foreign-born, reflecting the disproportionate growth of female immigration. A second difference between the two waves of immigration is that in the pre-World War I era, the vast majority of immigrants were Europeans; in the recent period immigrants have come predominantly from Asia and Latin America. .

Sex Ratios in U.S. Population, Foreign-born and Total, 1890–1980

WOMEN PER 100 MEN

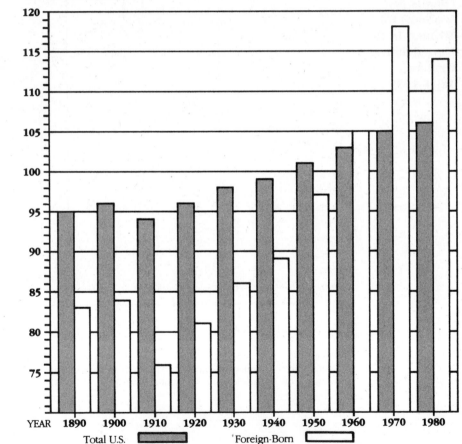

Total U.S.   Foreign-Born

Source: U.S. Bureau of the Census, *Historical Statistics of the United States, Colonial Times to 1970* (Washington: GPO, 1975), 14, 15, 117; U.S. Bureau of the Census, *Statistical Abstract of the United States: 1988* (Washington: GPO, 1987, 108th ed.), 38; U.S. Bureau of the Census, *1980 Census of Population,* vol. 1, Chapter D, Part 1 (PC80-1-D1-A), 9, 10; U.S. Census Bureau, Press Release #CB84-179, October 17, 1984.

Note that the figures shown in the graphs on these two pages (254-55) are for the *foreign-born population* rather than for *immigrants* entering the United States in a given year. This creates a time lag effect: The sex composition of immigrants changed sooner than that of the foreign-born population shown in the graph on the previous page; similarly, the change in the representation of immigrants of various national origins occurred sooner than the data in the graph below might appear to suggest. We use the figures for the foreign-born here, however, because they are much more reliable than those for immigration itself for the recent period, due to the difficulty in counting the large numbers of undocumented or illegal immigrants. In addition, figures for the foreign-born are more meaningful in the long run because there is substantial re-migration back to the home country among many groups. However, although they are better than the available figures for immigrants entering the nation, the census data that these tables are based on are widely believed to have undercounted recent immigrants. Thus, these figures should be interpreted with caution.

U. S. Foreign-born Population, by Region of Birth, 1890–1980

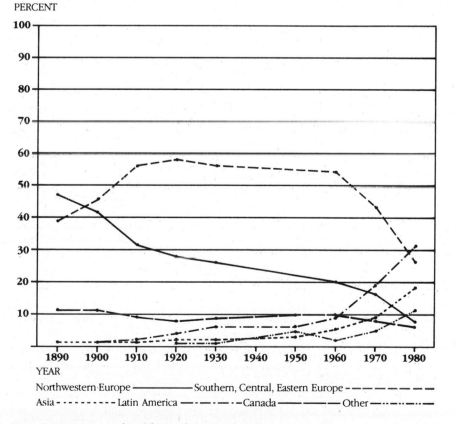

Note: Percentages are of total foreign-born population.

Source: U.S. Bureau of the Census, *Historical Statistics of the United States, Colonial Times to 1970* (Washington: GPO, 1975), 14, 15, 117; U.S. Bureau of the Census, *Statistical Abstract of the United States: 1988* (Washington: GPO, 1987, 108th ed.), 38; U.S. Bureau of the Census, *1980 Census of Population,* vol. 1, Chapter D, Part 1 (PC80-1-D1-A), 9, 10; U.S. Census Bureau, Press Release #CB84-179, October 17, 1984.

Another characteristic of the twentieth-century United States was enormous internal migration, especially the movement of population from rural to urban areas. Here there were no significant differences in the behavior by sex, but the implications of urbanization were nonetheless profound for women. The following graph shows the pattern of urbanization from 1890 to 1980, which mainly involved shifts from rural to small- and medium-sized urban settlements (including suburbs, which grew dramatically in the post-World War II years).

Percent of U.S. Population Living in Rural and Urban Areas, by Size of Urban Territory, 1890–1980

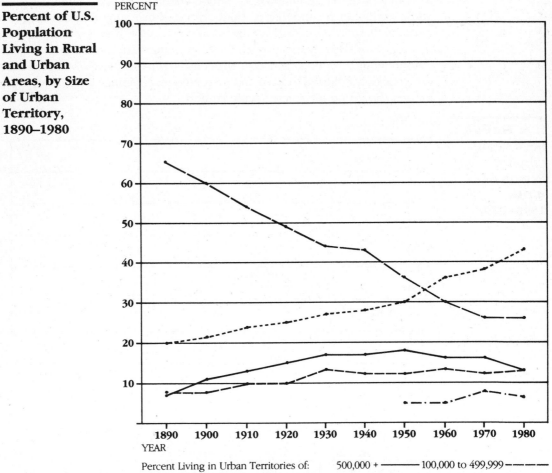

PERCENT

YEAR

Percent Living in Urban Territories of: 500,000 + ———— 100,000 to 499,999 – – – –
Less Than 100,000 · · · · · Other Urban* – · — · Percent Living in Rural Territories ————

* This category was introduced in the 1950 census; hence, no figures appear for earlier years.

Source: U.S. Bureau of the Census, *Historical Statistics of the United States, Colonial Times to 1970* (Washington: GPO, 1975), 11–12; U.S. Bureau of the Census, *1980 Census of Population*, vol. 1, Chapter A, Part I (PC80-1-A1), 37.

The average size of households in the United States was nearly twice as large a century ago as it is today, as the first graph below shows. This trend reflects not only lower fertility but also the increasing diversity of household types. Many more people live outside of traditional families today than in the past. The U.S. government refers to such people as "primary individuals," a group which includes people living alone as well as those living in households whose members are unrelated by kinship or marriage. In addition, there are more single-parent households today than in the past—most of them headed by women. The second graph below summarizes the changes in the distribution of household types from 1940 to 1987.

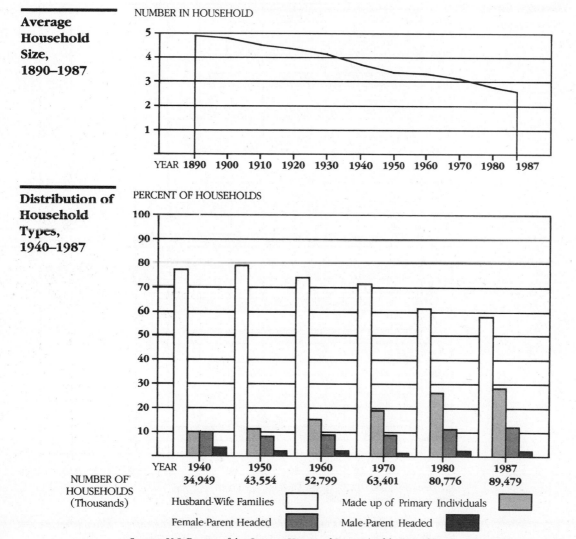

Average Household Size, 1890–1987

NUMBER IN HOUSEHOLD

Distribution of Household Types, 1940–1987

PERCENT OF HOUSEHOLDS

YEAR	1940	1950	1960	1970	1980	1987
NUMBER OF HOUSEHOLDS (Thousands)	34,949	43,554	52,799	63,401	80,776	89,479

Husband-Wife Families   Made up of Primary Individuals

Female-Parent Headed   Male-Parent Headed

Source: U.S. Bureau of the Census, *Historical Statistics of the United States, Colonial Times to 1970* (Washington: GPO, 1975), 41; U.S. Bureau of the Census, *Statistical Abstract of the United States: 1988* (Washington: GPO, 1987, 108th ed.), 43.

A major factor contributing to the declining proportion of traditional husband-wife households is the dramatic rise in divorce rates. The bar chart below shows the rates of marriage and divorce for selected years between 1920 and 1984. Both rates rose sharply immediately after both world wars; and both declined during the early 1930s, as a result of the Great Depression. In the late 1960s, the divorce rate rose sharply and has continued to climb. Marriage rates, however, have been falling over the same period.

Marriage and Divorce Rates, 1920–1984

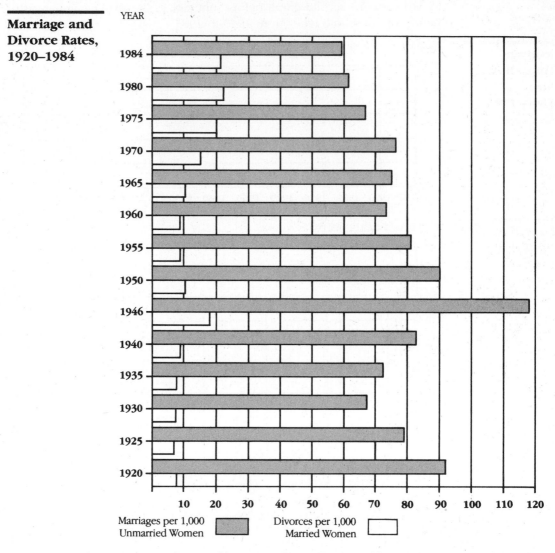

YEAR

Marriages per 1,000 Unmarried Women

Divorces per 1,000 Married Women

Source: U.S. Bureau of the Census, *Historical Statistics of the United States, Colonial Times to 1970* (Washington: GPO, 1975), 64; U.S. Bureau of the Census, *Statistical Abstract of the United States: 1988* (Washington: GPO, 1987, 108th ed.), 83.

Another way to look at divorce and marriage rates is to consider the long-term experiences of individuals, rather than the annual rates of marriage and divorce. The bar chart below shows the frequency of marrying, divorcing, remarrying, and redivorcing for three generations of women: those born between 1910 and 1914, between 1930 and 1934, and between 1950 and 1954. The figures vividly illustrate how much more common divorce has become in the course of the century, as well as the fact that while most people who divorce do eventually remarry, many of them later redivorce.

Percentage Ever Marrying, Divorcing, Remarrying, and Redivorcing for Women Born Between 1910–14, 1930–34, and 1950–54

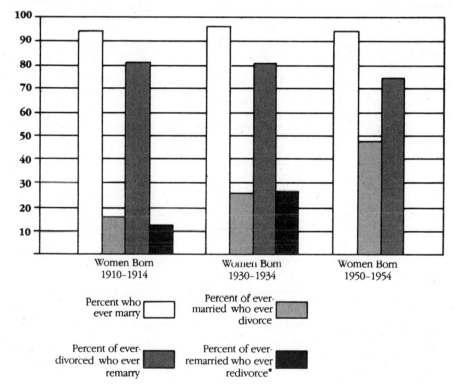

* Data for 1950-54 not available.
Source: Andrew J. Cherlin, *Marriage, Divorce, Remarriage* (Cambridge: Harvard University Press, 1981), 122–23.

Perhaps the single most dramatic change for women in the twentieth century has been the increased extent of their involvement in the paid labor force, especially since World War II. While in 1890 only 18 percent of women were employed outside the home, by 1986 over 55 percent were so employed. Meanwhile, male labor force participation has declined significantly over the same period.

Labor Force Participation of Women and Men, 1890–1987

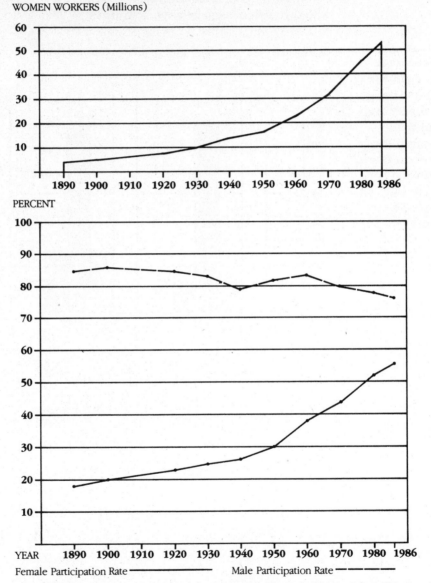

WOMEN WORKERS (Millions)

PERCENT

YEAR

Female Participation Rate ——————— Male Participation Rate — — — —

Source: U.S. Bureau of the Census, *Historical Statistics of the United States, Colonial Times to 1970* (Washington: GPO, 1975), 131–32; U.S. Bureau of the Census, *Statistical Abstract of the United States: 1988* (Washington: GPO, 1987, 108th ed.), 365. For 1890–1950 this table uses government data from the decennial census; for 1960–1987, the source is the Current Population Survey. These two sources use slightly different enumeration methods; thus, the two sets of figures are not strictly comparable.

The feminization of the work force has been accompanied by feminization of labor union membership. However, since the mid-1950s, while labor union membership has become increasingly feminized, unionization levels in the U.S. work force as a whole have declined. With few exceptions, the absolute number of women union members has increased steadily over the course of the twentieth century. From 77,000 female union members in 1910, the number grew to 260,000 in 1930; 800,000 in 1940; 3,000,000 in 1944 (at the height of women's wartime employment); 3,304,000 in 1960; and 7,191,000 in 1980. In recent years, the number of female unionists has begun to drop, along with union membership generally, leaving only 6,907,000 women union members in 1987.

Feminization of U.S. Labor Union Membership, 1910–1987

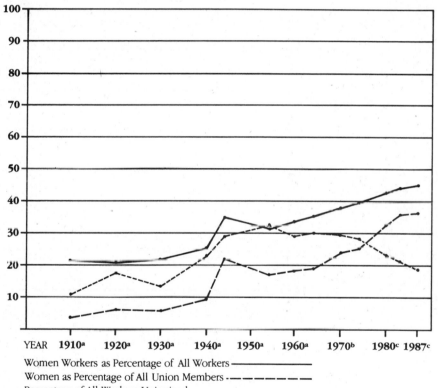

PERCENT

Women Workers as Percentage of All Workers ————————

Women as Percentage of All Union Members · — — — — — —

Percentage of All Workers Unionized - - - - - - - - - - - - - - - -

[a]Union

[b]Unions and employee associations

[c]Represented by unions and employee associations (including nonmembers covered by contracts)

Source: Gladys Dickason, "Women in Labor Unions," *The Annals of the American Academy of Political and Social Science,* 251 (May 1947), 70–71; U.S. Department of Labor, Women's Bureau, Bulletin 298, *Time of Change: 1983 Handbook on Women Workers* (Washington: GPO, 1983), 49; U.S. Bureau of Labor Statistics, *Employment and Earnings,* 32, no. 1 (January 1985), 208; U.S. Bureau of Labor Statistics, *Employment and Earnings,* 35, no. 1 (January 1988), 159–222; Leo Troy and Neil Sheflin, *U.S. Union Sourcebook* (West Orange, NJ: Industrial Relations and Information Services, 1985), A-1, A-2.

Black women had much higher rates of labor force participation than white women during most of the twentieth century, although in recent years the gap has been nearly eliminated. Similarly, foreign-born white women had higher participation rates than their native-born counterparts in the pre-World War II years, although by 1950 the difference was insignificant.

Women's Labor Force Participation by Race and National Origin

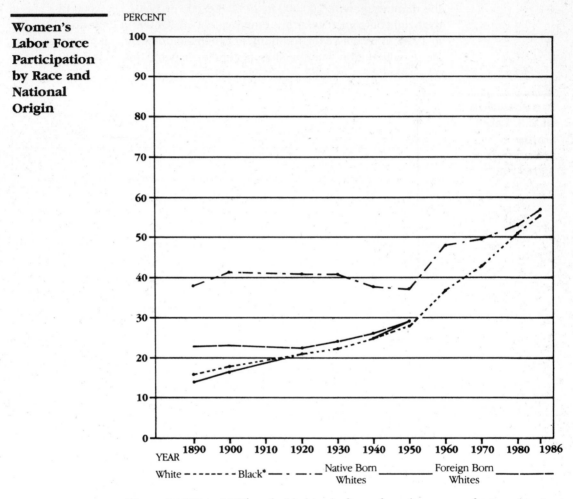

*Figures for 1980 and 1986 are for blacks only; figures for earlier years are for "nonwhites" or "Negro and other." Data for 1910 are not available.

Source: U.S. Bureau of the Census, *Historical Statistics of the United States, Colonial Times to 1957* (Washington: GPO, 1960), 72; U.S. Bureau of the Census, *Historical Statistics of the United States, Colonial Times to 1970* (Washington: GPO, 1975), 133; U.S. Bureau of the Census, *Statistical Abstract of the United States: 1988* (Washington: GPO, 1987, 108th ed.), 366; Clarence D. Long, *The Labor Force under Changing Income and Employment* (Princeton: Princeton University Press, 1958), Table A-4.

There has been a dramatic change in the pattern of female employment over the life cycle as large numbers of married women and mothers have begun working outside the home in the postwar era. In 1940 only 15 percent of married women with husbands present were in the paid labor force; by 1987, 56 percent of this group of women worked outside the home. While single (never married) women are still more likely to be employed than married women, the gap has narrowed considerably over time. And since the late 1960s, widows and divorced women actually have had a lower labor force participation rate than married women, reversing the previous pattern.

Women's Labor Force Participation, by Marital Status, 1890–1987

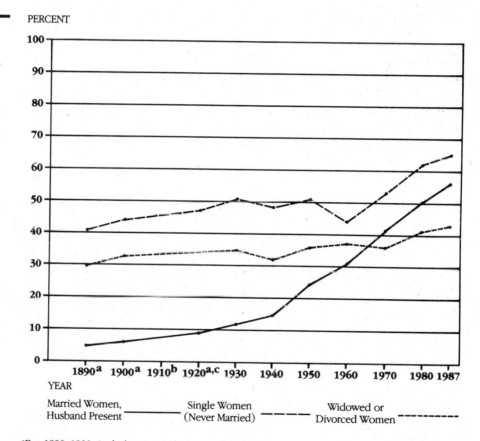

ᵃFor 1890–1930, includes married women, husband absent.

ᵇData for 1910 are not available.

ᶜFor 1920, widowed and divorced women are included with single women.

Source: U.S. Bureau of the Census, *Historical Statistics of the United States, Colonial Times to 1970* (Washington: GPO, 1975), 133; U.S. Bureau of the Census, *Statistical Abstract of the United States: 1988* (Washington: GPO, 1987, 108th ed.), 373.

The labor force participation rate of married mothers has increased dramatically since World War II, especially since 1970. A majority of married women with children under age 6 are now employed, and today married mothers of children aged 6 to 17 are more likely to be employed than married women with no children. As recently as 1950, married women without children were more likely to work outside the home than married mothers. The table below provides further details about the labor force participation of married mothers, showing that the majority of those with very young children (1 year old or younger) are now employed outside the home and that black married mothers have much higher labor force participation rates than white married mothers, whose rates are themselves high. These figures do not include single mothers, who also frequently work when their children are young.

Labor Force Participation Rates of Married Women, Husband Present, by Presence and Age of Own Children, 1950–1987

PERCENT IN THE LABOR FORCE

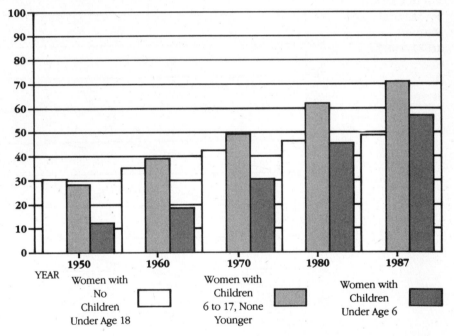

Labor Force Participation Rates of Married Women, Husband Present, by Age of Youngest Child and by Race, 1975–1987

	WHITE MARRIED WOMEN Youngest child aged:			BLACK MARRIED WOMEN Youngest child aged:		
	1 year or less	*3–5 years*	*6–13 years*	*1 year or less*	*3–5 years*	*6–13 years*
1987	51.2	59.3	69.6	70.3	77.9	80.7
1980	37.7	49.4	61.4	52.9	72.3	71.8
1975	29.2	40.3	50.8	50.0	61.7	64.9

Source: U.S. Department of Labor, Women's Bureau, Bulletin 298, *Time of Change: 1983 Handbook on Women Workers* (Washington: GPO, 1983), 18; U.S. Bureau of the Census, *Statistical Abstract of the United States: 1988* (Washington: GPO, 1987, 108th ed.), 374.

Throughout the past century, more women than men graduated from high school, although more men than women went on to graduate from college. The sex ratio in higher education gradually narrowed in the period before World War II, but after the war it suddenly widened again. This was a result both of the GI bill, which provided financial support for the college education of many returning soldiers (an overwhelmingly male group), and the fact that after the war, higher education became an increasingly important credential in the labor market. Over the postwar decades, the gender gap in education has nearly disappeared, with approximately equal numbers of men and women graduating from high school and college. The bar graph below shows the changing sex ratios among high school and college graduates from 1890 to 1980.

Sex Ratios of High School and College Graduates in the United States, 1890–1980

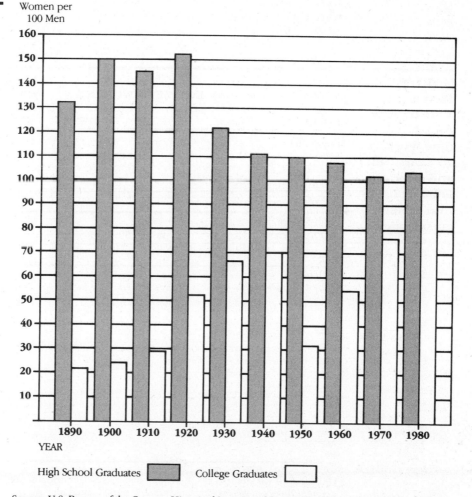

Source: U.S. Bureau of the Census, *Historical Statistics of the United States, Colonial Times to 1970* (Washington: GPO, 1975), 379, 385–86; U.S. Bureau of the Census, *Statistical Abstract of the United States: 1988* (Washington: GPO, 1987, 108th ed.), 140.

The previous graph shows the educational attainment of the entire adult population. For the smaller adult population that was in the labor force, the historical pattern of gender differences in education is fairly similar, except that the gap between women and men closed sooner. In 1940, women workers had completed a median of 11 years of education, compared to 8.6 years for men workers; by 1962, women workers had a median of 12.3 years, compared to 12.1 for their male counterparts.* However, as the following table makes clear, the experience of two decades of equality between the sexes in educational attainment was not yet reflected in the earnings of male and female workers in 1981. At all educational levels, full-time, year-round women workers had earnings of no more than two-thirds that of men with the same educational attainment in 1981. Full-time, year-round women workers who had completed high school earned less, on average, than men with less than 8 years of schooling; and full-time year-round women workers who were college graduates earned less, on average, than men with 9 to 11 years of schooling.

Median Income in 1981 of Year-round, Full-time Workers 25 Years Old and Over, by Educational Attainment and Gender

YEARS OF SCHOOL COMPLETED	MEDIAN INCOME OF WORKERS: Women	Men	WOMEN'S INCOME AS % OF MEN'S	MARGINAL VALUE OF INCREASED EDUCATION FOR: Women	Men
Elementary School					
Less than 8 years	$8,419	$12,866	65.4%	—	—
8 years	9,723	16,084	60.5	$1,304	$3,218
High School					
9–11 years	10,043	16,938	59.3	320	854
12 years	12,332	20,5998	59.9	2,289	3,660
College					
13–15 years	14,343	22,565	63.6	2,011	1,967
16 years	16,322	26,394	61.8	1,979	3,829
17 years or more	20,148	30,434	66.2	3,826	4,040

Source: U.S. Department of Labor, Women's Bureau, Bulletin 298, *Time of Change: 1983 Handbook on Women Workers* (Washington: GPO, 1983), 98.

* Figures for 1940 are from U.S. Bureau of the Census, *Historical Statistics of the United States, Colonial Times to 1957* (Washington: GPO, 1960), 214; and for 1962 from U.S. Bureau of Labor Statistics, Bulletin 2217, *Handbook of Labor Statistics* (Washington: GPO, June 1985), 164.

The gender gap in pay has been remarkably constant from 1955 to 1985, despite the dramatic increase in female labor force participation and the passage in the 1960s of national legislation prohibiting sex and race discrimination in employment. The 1985 sex ratio in earnings of year-round, full-time workers is only marginally better than the 1955 one.

Statistics were compiled on average hourly earnings, by sex, for production workers in 25 manufacturing industries between 1914 and 1948. Manufacturing jobs generally paid better than such traditionally female occupations as domestic service or clerical or sales work, but even in manufacturing, women were paid far less than men. In 1914 a woman factory worker earned 62¢ for every $1 earned by a man; in 1935 the rate was 70¢ to $1; and in 1948 it was 73¢ to $1 (U.S. Bureau of the Census, *Historical Statistics of the United States, Colonial Times to 1970* [Washington: GPO, 1975], 172).

Median Earnings of Year-round, Full-time Workers, by Sex, 1955–1985

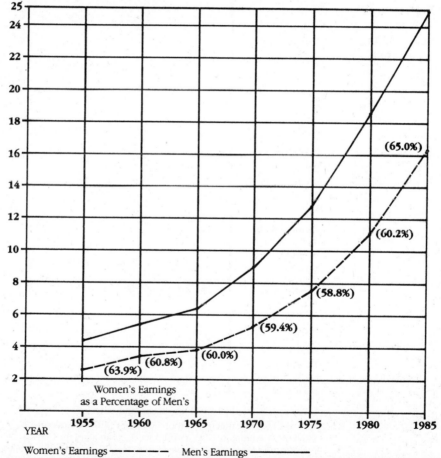

Source: U.S. Department of Labor, Women's Bureau, Bulletin 298, *Time of Change: 1983 Handbook on Women Workers* (Washington: GPO, 1983), 82; U.S. Bureau of the Census, *Money Income of Households, Families and Persons in the United States: 1986*, Current Population Reports, Series P-60, no. 159, 100–101.

The earnings gap between black and white workers has narrowed significantly over time. Black women workers continue to earn less than their white counterparts, but the race gap in earnings among men has been even more resistant to change. All the figures in the preceding graph and the following table are for full-time, year-round workers only. If part-time or part-year workers were included, the disparity in earnings by sex would be far greater, since many women work part-time.

Median Wage or Salary Income of Year-round, Full-time Workers, by Sex and Race, Selected Years, 1939–1986		YEAR				
		1939	1960	1970	1980	1986
	MEDIAN EARNINGS:					
	White Men	$1,419	$5,662	$9,373	$19,720	$26,617
	Black* Men	$639	$3,789	$6,598	$13,875	$18,766
	White Women	$863	$3,410	$5,490	$11,703	$17,101
	Black* Women	$327	$2,372	$4,674	$10,915	$14,964
	EARNINGS RATIOS:					
	White Women as % of White Men	60.8%	60.2%	58.6%	59.3%	64.2%
	Black* Men as % of White Men	45.0%	66.9%	70.4%	70.3%	70.5%
	Black* Women as % of Black* Men	51.2%	62.6%	70.8%	78.7%	79.7%
	Black* Women as % of White Women	37.9%	69.6%	85.1%	93.3%	87.8%

* Blacks only for 1980 and 1986, blacks and other minorities for earlier years.

Source: U.S. Department of Labor, Women's Bureau, Bulletin 297, *1975 Handbook on Women Workers* (Washington: GPO, 1975), 136; U.S. Bureau of the Census, *Money Income of Households, Families and Persons in the United States: 1981,* Current Population Reports, Series P-60, no. 137, 117–18; U.S. Bureau of the Census, *Money Income of Households, Families, and Persons in the United States: 1986,* Current Population Reports, Series P-60, no. 159, 100–101.

The primary reason for the large disparity between the sexes in earnings is not sex discrimination in wages for men and women doing the same jobs. Although this does occur, much more significant is the fact that women and men are segregated into distinct occupations, and those occupations that are primarily female have lower pay rates than those that are predominantly male. Even in classifications of workers by major occupational group, the concentration of women in certain types of jobs, and of men in other types, is quite apparent. An even greater degree of segregation is evident in more detailed classifications. For example, the category "professional, technical, and kindred workers" groups such predominantly female occupations as nursing, teaching, and social work with occupations that primarily employ men, such as engineering and dentistry.

The table below shows the distribution of women and men workers across major occupational categories in 1900, 1930, and 1960.

Occupational Distribution of U.S. Workers, by Sex, 1900, 1930, and 1960

| INDUSTRY GROUP | YEAR | | | | | |
| | 1900 | | 1930 | | 1960 | |
	Men	Women	Men	Women	Men	Women
Professional, Technical and Kindred Workers	3.4%	8.2%	4.8%	13.8%	10.4%	13.3%
Managers, Officials, and Proprietors	6.8	1.4	8.8	2.7	10.8	3.8
Clerical and Kindred Workers	2.8	4.0	5.5	20.9	7.2	30.9
Salesworkers	4.6	4.3	6.1	6.8	7.0	8.3
Craftsmen, Foremen, and Kindred Workers	12.6	1.4	16.2	1.0	20.6	1.3
Operatives, Laborers, and Kindred Workers	25.0	26.3	29.0	18.9	29.0	17.8
Private Household Workers	—*	28.7	—	17.8	—	8.4
Other Service Workers	2.9	6.7	4.6	9.7	6.3	14.4
Farmworkers	41.7	19.0	24.8	8.4	8.5	1.9

Note: Figures may not total 100 percent because of rounding.

*— = less than 1 percent.

Source: U.S. Bureau of the Census, *Historical Statistics of the United States, Colonial Times to 1970* (Washington: GPO, 1975), 139–40.

The pie charts show the occupational distribution for 1987. Although the categories are somewhat different in the 1987 count, the general pattern of employment by sex and the ways in which it has changed over time can be clearly seen. In 1900 nearly half of all women workers were either farmworkers or private household workers—categories which accounted for less than 3 percent of all women workers in 1987. Another fourth of the female labor force in 1900 was made up of factory workers—operatives and laborers; today only 9 percent of women workers are so employed. Conversely, the occupations employing the bulk of the female work force today—clerical, sales, and service (other than private household)—were relatively insignificant in 1900. Changes have also occurred in the distribution of men's occupations. The most striking revelation from these data is that while the particular occupations for both men and women have changed over time, occupational segregation by sex has persisted intact.

Occupational Distribution of U.S. Workers, by Sex, 1987

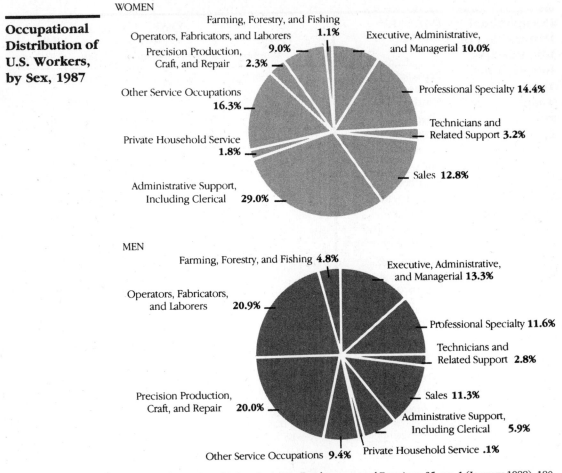

WOMEN

Farming, Forestry, and Fishing **1.1%**
Operators, Fabricators, and Laborers **9.0%**
Precision Production, Craft, and Repair **2.3%**
Other Service Occupations **16.3%**
Private Household Service **1.8%**
Administrative Support, Including Clerical **29.0%**
Executive, Administrative, and Managerial **10.0%**
Professional Specialty **14.4%**
Technicians and Related Support **3.2%**
Sales **12.8%**

MEN

Farming, Forestry, and Fishing **4.8%**
Operators, Fabricators, and Laborers **20.9%**
Precision Production, Craft, and Repair **20.0%**
Other Service Occupations **9.4%**
Private Household Service **.1%**
Executive, Administrative, and Managerial **13.3%**
Professional Specialty **11.6%**
Technicians and Related Support **2.8%**
Sales **11.3%**
Administrative Support, Including Clerical **5.9%**

Source: U.S. Bureau of Labor Statistics, *Employment and Earnings,* 35, no. 1 (January 1988), 180.

In addition to segregation by sex, segregation by race and nativity has also characterized the U.S. labor force. The table below shows the occupational distribution of women by race and nativity in 1900; the pie charts on the next page show the occupational distribution of women by race and Hispanic origin for 1987. Racial segregation was extremely pronounced in 1900, with black women virtually excluded from both factory work and the emerging white-collar occupations and confined almost entirely to agricultural labor, laundry work, and domestic service. Racial segregation has decreased throughout the twentieth century but has by no means disappeared. Black women today are overrepresented in service and factory jobs.

The segregation of foreign-born women workers was less extreme than that of black women in 1900, but virtually all immigrant white women workers were confined to domestic service and factory jobs at this time, while native-born white women were distributed over a somewhat greater

Occupational Distribution of U.S. Women Workers 15 Years and Older, by Race and Nativity, 1900		Native White	Foreign-Born White	Black
OCCUPATIONAL GROUP	*Both Parents Native-Born*	*One or Both Parents Foreign-Born*		
Agricultural Laborers *	5.0	0.6	0.6	33.5
Farmers and Other Agricultural Pursuitsᵗ	9.9	1.7	4.3	6.3
Professional Service	15.1	9.9	3.0	1.3
Manufacturing and Mechanical Pursuits	27.0	40.1	31.4	2.8
Laundresses	2.3	2.6	5.0	18.6
Servants and Waitresses	17.7	20.9	38.0	27.8
Other Domestic and Personal Service	10.4	6.5	10.6	9.4
Saleswomen	3.4	3.9	2.0	—
Clerks, Stenographers, and Typewriters	4.8	5.9	1.6	—
Other	4.3	7.8	3.6	0.2

(Figures may not total 100 percent because of rounding.)

* Wage earners performing agricultural work

ᵗ Farm owners and supervisory personnel

Source: U.S. Bureau of the Census, *Statistics of Women at Work* (Washington, GPO, 1907), 159, 161.

range of occupations. Even among native-born women, those with one foreign-born parent were much more likely to be employed in manufacturing and much less likely to be employed in professional service or farm work than their counterparts with two native-born parents.

Comparison to the present is difficult because of limitations on available data. The presence of large numbers of undocumented immigrant workers in the population today—many of whom are not counted at all in these statistics—make comparisons particularly treacherous. The pie chart presents 1987 data for "Hispanics" rather than immigrants (and many Hispanics today are not immigrants). The occupational distribution of Hispanic women is quite different than that of white women, with Hispanics overrepresented in service jobs and even more so in factory work. Of course, some Hispanics are white and others are black, so that the three categories shown are not mutually exclusive.

Occupational Distribution of U.S. Women Workers 16 Years and Older, by Race and Hispanic Origin, 1987

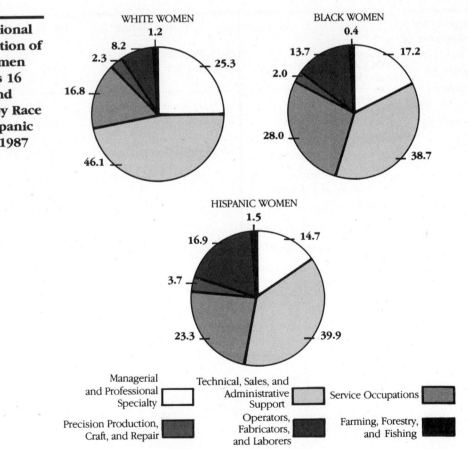

Source: U.S. Bureau of Labor Statistics, *Employment and Earnings,* 35, no. 1 (January 1988), 180; Peter Cattan, "Hispanics in the U.S. Workforce," *Monthly Labor Review,* 111, no. 8 (August 1988), 13.